ŚAṄKARA SOURCE-BOOK

VOLUME VI

ŚAṄKARA ON ENLIGHTENMENT

ŚAṄKARA ON ENLIGHTENMENT

A ŚAṄKARA SOURCE-BOOK

VOLUME VI

by

A.J. ALSTON

SHANTI SADAN
LONDON

First Edition 1989
Second Edition 2004

29 Chepstow Villas
London W11 3DR

www.shanti-sadan.org

ISBN 0-85424-060-8
(Set of six volumes: ISBN 0-85424-061-6)

Printed and bound by
J W Arrowsmith Ltd., Bristol BS3 2NT

PREFACE TO SECOND EDITION

This sixth and concluding volume of the Śaṅkara Source Book has three chapters. The first, Chapter XIV, outlines the path for release or liberation by stages achieved through the old discipline of Vedic ritual supplemented by meditation on Vedic themes. Chapter XV gives Śaṅkara's final teaching on the last and most direct part of the discipline for liberation in life, and contains material that is still of the greatest practical interest for the student today. Chapter XVI, the last of the Source Book, describes the state of the enlightened or liberated person, so far as this is possible in words.

The volume closes with two indices, the first showing the source of all the translated Extracts throughout the Source Book, the second a select general index of names and topics.

My obligations are as in previous volumes. I close, as I began, by offering the work, with all its faults, in reverent dedication to my Guru, the late Hari Prasad Shastri, founder of Shanti Sadan, London.

A. J. ALSTON
LONDON 2004

CONTENTS

		page
Preface		v
Sanskrit transliteration		ix
Chapter		
XIV.	**The Indirect Path**	
1.	Meditation in the Context of the Vedic Ritual	1
2.	Realization of Identity with Hiraṇyagarbha	21
3.	The Path of the Flame	31
4.	Supernormal Powers on the Indirect Path	66
	Notes to Chapter XIV	72
XV.	**The Direct Path**	
1.	Adhyātma Yoga	92
2.	Devotion (Bhakti)	105
3.	Communication of 'That Thou Art'	107
4.	Meditation (Dhyāna) and Repeated Affirmation (Abhyāsa)	147
5.	Meditation on OM	167
	Notes to Chapter XIV	187

CONTENTS

page

XVI. The Enlightened Man

1. Enlightenment is not a Change of State 224
2. Action during Enlightenment 236
3. The Enlightened Man Enjoys All Pleasures 262
4. The Enlightened Man as Actionless 271
5. The Enlightened Man as Bodiless: His Glory 298

Notes to Chapter XVI 327

List of General Abbreviations 343

Bibliography 346

Index to Texts Cited 365

General Index 373

Conspectus of the Śaṅkara Source Book 439

TRANSLITERATED SANSKRIT WORDS

The following table gives the most elementary indications of the value of the vowels that are variable in English (but regular in Sanskrit) and of the unfamiliar symbols and groupings of letters found in transliterated Sanskrit words. It is not intended as an accurate guide to correct pronunciation, for which see M. Coulson, *Sanskrit* (Teach Yourself Books), 4-21.

a	=	u in but
ā	=	a in father
ai	=	uy as in buy
au	=	au in audit (or French au)
c	=	ch in chant
ch	=	ch aspirated (said with extra breath)
ḍ	=	d in drake
e	=	ay in hay (better, French é elongated)
h	=	immediately after a consonant aspirates it without altering the value. (bh, ph, etc.)
ḥ	=	strong h
i	=	i in hit
ī	=	ea in eat
jñ	=	ja or gya (as in big yard)
ṃ	=	m before b, p, v, y and at the end of a word; elsewhere = n
ṅ	=	n in king
ṇ	=	n in tendril
ñ	=	n (except in jñ, q.v.)
o	=	o in note
ṛ	=	ri in rich
s	=	s in such
ś	=	sh in shut
ṣ	=	sh in shut
ṭ	=	t in try
u	=	u in put
ū	=	oo in boot

CHAPTER XIV

THE INDIRECT PATH

1. Meditation in the Context of the Vedic Ritual (Upāsana)

We have seen[1] that for Śaṅkara it was important to distinguish three main classes of Vedic texts instead of two. Beyond the texts dealing with ritual and the texts instructing the one desirous of liberation in knowledge of the nature of the Self, he recognized a third body of texts dealing with Upāsana. We have also noted[2] how Śaṅkara differentiated the performance of prescribed Vedic meditations (upāsana) from knowledge on the one hand and from ritualistic action on the other. Unlike knowledge, it involved the activity of the agent or subject, and not mere passivity before the object once the latter had been revealed through the proper instrument of valid cognition (the application of which admittedly implied action). On the other hand, it was unlike ritualistic action (karma) in that it was activity of a purely mental kind, implying no physical activity of the body on a physical object. Śaṅkara did not make a formal triple distinction between a karma-kāṇḍa, a jñāna-kāṇḍa and an upāsana-kāṇḍa. For in this context he only uses the term 'kāṇḍa' in the phrase 'first Kāṇḍa' (prathama-kāṇḍa), using it always to refer to the Pūrva Mīmāṃsā Sūtras.[3] But he recognizes Upāsana as something different either from ritualistic action (karma) or knowledge (jñāna), understood in the sense of the final knowledge of the Absolute through which nescience is destroyed.

Upāsana may be pursued for the sake of the rewards it brings on its own: but it may also be deliberately pursued as a mere auxiliary to spiritual knowledge, valuable for its power to purify the mind before the rise of the latter. This second use will be described in the section on Bhakti Yoga in the next chapter.[4] But when Upāsana is practised on its own account and in the context of Vedic ritualism, Śaṅkara assigns it three possible alternative functions, as the second Extract of the present section will show. First, meditation on the secret correspondences of things as revealed in the Veda can bring a certain kind of 'knowledge' which brings stated advantageous fruits, just as the physical performance of the ritual is rewarded with certain stated fruits. Secondly, meditation on the Absolute as associated with this or that external adjunct, according to prescribed meditations given in the Vedic texts, can either lead in this very life to a sense of unity with the Lord associated with that adjunct (which can vary in degree according to the intensity of the meditation), or it can lead to unity with or proximity to the Lord associated with that adjunct after death. When the adjunct in question is the Cosmic Vital Energy, under the name of Prāṇa, Prajāpati, Brahmā or Hiraṇyagarbha, the soul remains after death in great felicity, partaking of the consciousness of that deity until the end of the world-period, when it will dissolve in the Absolute along with that deity, never to re-emerge in individualized form. Thirdly, meditation on the ritual can simply be used to enhance the merit arising from the performance of it.

The first and third uses of meditation were not of much consequence for Śaṅkara, but they will be found to crop up occasionally in the Extracts to be cited below. The second was of considerable interest to him as it supplied the means to a certain form of release, namely krama-mukti, meaning gradual or deferred release, a form of release open to those souls who had the capacity to meditate in faith on the Absolute associated with this or that finite form, but not the capacity to discriminate the eternal from the non-eternal and attain perfect liberation in this very life. This Path of Gradual or Deferred Release, which might be called the Vedic path of salvation, is the subject of the present chapter. As we have just seen, it was available to those who meditated on the Absolute associated with finite forms. But, as we shall see at section 3 below, it was also available to those who performed life-long ritual in association with meditation, and particularly to those who performed the Meditation on the Five Fires, the Pañcāgni Vidyā.

The Extracts assembled in the present section explain how Śaṅkara regarded Upāsana. The first Extract explains very clearly how Śaṅkara differentiated meditation from knowledge. The second Extract lists the uses of meditation, Extracts 3-5 describe its basic function, that of realizing one's own fundamental identity with this or that deity or cosmic power by meditating on it. Extract 5 emphasizes the importance of adhering to one meditation exclusively till its goal is attained. The remaining four Extracts make observations about the technique of such meditations and about the interpretation of texts in which Upāsanas or meditations are prescribed. For example, when meditating on a symbol of the Self as the Self, one should remain clear that the Self is not limited to the symbol. To take the stone image of Viṣṇu *as such* for Viṣṇu is idolatry in Śaṅkara's eyes. Again, where a text prescribes meditation on two entities as identical, one must meditate on the higher as *present in* the lower. A further point made is that one should go on practising all such meditations until the aim for which the meditation was undertaken is realized. Wherever, as is most often the case, they aim at a result to occur after the death of the body, they must be performed regularly until the death of the body, especially because of the influence of regular meditation on the all-important last thought of the mind before death. Finally, one should never believe that the Absolute is *directly* accessible in its true nature through the performance of prescribed Vedic meditations. As we shall see, the most one can hope for in the present life through practising such meditations is some degree of intuitive identification with such a luminous adjunct of the Self as the Cosmic Vital Energy. After death, of course, the rewards are greater, as we may enjoy the felicity of Brahma-loka until liberation at the end of the world-period, without the need to undergo further painful experiences in an earthly body.

TEXTS ON UPĀSANA

1. But is not knowledge in fact mental action? Not so, for its essential characteristics are different. Mental action (kriyā) is something enjoined. It is not (like knowledge) determined by the nature of what already exists, but results from the free working of the human mind. We find examples of it in such texts as 'He should fix his mind on the deity to whom the oblation is being offered, saying "vaṣaṭ",'[5] and 'He should meditate on the sacred hour of twilight with his mind'.[6] Meditation is mentally dwelling on something. Though it is mental, it is to be noted that it depends on human will, and can either be done or not done or done in this or that alternative way. Knowledge, on the other hand, is what arises from the application of one of the means of knowledge (pramāṇa), and a means of knowledge bears on the true (and fixed) nature of an already existent object. Knowledge, therefore, is not anything that can be done or not done or done in this or that alternative way. It is conditioned neither by a command nor by human will but by the nature of an already existent reality. Thus, although knowledge is mental, there is a very great difference between it and a mental action such as meditation.

In the text, 'Man, O Gautama, is verily the sacrificial fire!'[7] the conception of man and woman as the sacrificial fire is purely mental. As it comes into being by the mere force of (obedience to) an injunction, it is 'mental action' and subject to human will. But the notion of fire in relation to that well-known object so named is not subject to injunction nor to the vagaries of human will. On the contrary, it is conditioned by reality in the form of an object of sense-perception. It is knowledge and not a piece of mental activity. The same holds true of *any* entity apprehended through direct perception.[8]

❖

2. (Thus) thousands of texts show how the Absolute has two different forms according to whether it is viewed from the standpoint of knowledge or that of nescience. The notion that the Absolute is the object of an act of meditation by a meditator is something that falls within the realm of empirical experience, and all empirical experience takes place in the state of nescience. Some meditations on the Absolute are performed for the sake of worldly prosperity, some for the sake of gradual release (krama-mukti), some to enhance ritualistic merit.[9] They differ from one another according to the quality of what is attributed to the Absolute. Though it is ever the same one supreme Self, the Lord, who is meditated on as invested with this or that different quality, the results of the various meditations vary according to the qualities superimposed. For we have such Vedic texts as, 'Under whatever form one meditates on Him, that one oneself becomes',[10] 'What a man wills in this world, that he becomes after death'.[11] And there is the text from the derivative literature, 'And whatever being he is thinking of when he dies, to that he

goes after death, O son of Kuntī, ever impregnated with the thought of that'.[12]

It is true that it is the same one Self hidden in all animate and inanimate beings. But the Self is eternal and unchanging and has only one nature. There are texts attributing divine powers to it of ascending degree as it manifests in ascending forms according to the different qualities of the human mind, as is shown by the text, 'He who knows the higher manifestations of the Self in him'.[13] And the derivative literature also says, 'Know that whatever special being of peculiar beauty or power exists proceeds from a ray of My light',[14] whereby it implies that wherever there is such a special manifestation, there we have the Lord in a form in which He can be worshipped.

And here in the Brahma Sūtras, too,[15] the author will refer to the golden man (puruṣa) in the sun and say that the phrase[16] must stand for the supreme Self, because it mentions the characteristic of being beyond all sin. (Thus the Chāndogya Upanishad attributes the form of a golden man to the formless Self for purposes of meditation.) And we find the same process in such Sūtras as, 'The ether (must stand for the Absolute at this point) because of its (similar) characteristics'.[17]

And thus knowledge of the Self, the means to immediate release, can sometimes be taught indirectly through various external adjuncts. And as the object of such passages will never be to affirm any real relation of the Self with any external adjunct, the doubt may always arise (in the case of texts attributing finite forms to the Absolute) as to whether it is the supreme form of the Absolute that is being taught (through the mere attribution of an external adjunct) or a lower form.[18] And this doubt has to be resolved by an examination of the context[19]

❖

3. And in this section[20] devoted to knowledge within the sphere of duality, some meditations leading to a higher worldly station are taught. The ones included here, however, lead on ultimately to high results, approximate to liberation. They have for their subject-matter the Absolute in a form only mildly distorted from its true non-dual nature, as in such texts as, 'Made up of mind, with the Vital Energy as its body'.[21] They are concerned with enhancing the effect of merit derived from performance of the Vedic ritual and are specially related to parts of that ritual. (They are, however, placed here in the Chāndogya Upanishad and away from the ritualistic section of Veda proper) because they have two points in common (with the upanishadic teaching conveying knowledge of the Self as opposed to ritual). In the first place, they are esoteric (secret) in character.[22] And in the second place, they consist in mere manipulations of the mind.[23] All the various Vedic meditations have this one point in common with knowledge of non-duality, namely that they imply (no ritual and) only a manipulation of the mind.

What, then, is the difference between knowledge of non-duality and these meditations? The answer is that knowledge of non-duality puts an end once and for all to that notion of a distinction between agent, action, factors of action and results of action which we have the natural tendency erroneously to superimpose onto the actionless Self. It is similar to the dissolution of the superimposed snake or the like which occurs through right knowledge of the true nature of the rope. Meditation, however, is different. Here one takes some conception laid down by the Vedic texts and makes the stream of ideas in one's mind conform to it continuously over a period, without admitting the intrusion of ideas of anything different.

Such meditations (upāsanas) contribute to the final understanding of the metaphysical truth by purifying the mind, and are in this sense auxiliaries to knowledge of non-duality; and because they offer a definite conception for the mind to hold on to, they are easy to practise, and are hence placed here at the beginning of the Upanishad before the transition to the metaphysical teaching proper.[24] To begin with, however, they are presented as parts of the ritual, because people are habituated to ritual and might think that meditation alone without ritual would be a mere useless burden on the mind.[25]

❖

4. Performance of prescribed Vedic meditation (upāsana) means approaching the deity mentally in the form in which it is described in the texts presenting deities as objects of meditation[26] in various guises by way of eulogy, and meditating on it (in that form) to the exclusion of all worldly thoughts, until there arises a conviction of one's identity with the true form of that deity as powerful as one's (previous) conviction of identity with one's individual personality. And we say this on the evidence of such Vedic texts as, 'Having become a god, he joins the gods'[27] and 'What deity of the East are you?'[28]

❖

5. Admitting that the various meditations taught in the Veda[29] constitute a separate item of discipline, we now discuss whether one may either combine them or choose one and keep to it, or whether one can only choose one and keep to it. And one might initially suppose that, when the difference of the meditations is an admitted fact, there would be no grounds for any rules as to combining them. Nor would the example of the rules about combining the Agnihotra and the New and Full Moon Sacrifices carry any weight. For there is there the special reason that the Veda teaches that the Agnihotra must be performed every day, whereas there are no injunctions saying that the meditations must be performed daily. So we might initially deny that there were any rules for their combination, and deny equally that there is any rule about choosing one meditation and keeping to it. For there is nothing to prevent a man who is able to perform one meditation from performing another as well. On this basis we should conclude, as the only remaining alternative, that there are no rules in this matter whatever.

But should we not conclude from the presence of several different meditations for which the same reward is promised that one must choose one and keep to it? For example, such different meditations as, 'Made up of mind, with the Cosmic Vital Energy for body',[30] 'The Absolute is joy, the Absolute is the ether',[31] 'Whose desires are true, whose purposes are true'[32] all carry the same reward of God-realization (īśvara-prāpti). According to our initial theory, however, there need not necessarily be choice of and adherence to one alternative only. For in the case of the wide range of optional rituals all leading to heaven, there is complete freedom of choice to do what one likes.[33]

Against this initial view, the author of the Sūtras, while agreeing that there cannot be simultaneous combination, affirms that there must be a choice of one alternative and adherence to that. Why is this so? For the very reason that the result of the meditations is the same, being awareness of one's identity with the object of the meditation. If realization of God had been obtained through one meditation, it would be purposeless to start another. As for the theory of a combination of different meditations, this would render God-realization impossible by throwing the mind into confusion. And the texts are clear on the point that meditations should culminate in realization of one's identity with the being on whom meditation is being performed, as, for example, 'Whoso has direct vision of this does not fall into doubt',[34] and 'Having become a god, he joins the gods'.[35] And there are also texts from the derivative literature teaching the same point, such as 'And whatever being he is thinking of when he dies, to that he goes after death, O son of Kuntī, ever impregnated with the thought of that'.[36] Therefore one should choose only one of the various meditations which bring the same reward and adhere to that until the reward is attained in the form of realization of one's identity with the object of meditation.[37]

❖

6. We have the Vedic texts, 'On the microcosmic plane (adhyātma) one should meditate on the mind (manas) as the Absolute, and on the macrocosmic plane (adhidaivata) one should meditate on the ether as the Absolute', and 'The teaching is, "The sun is the Absolute",' and 'He who meditates on Name as the Absolute'.[38] These are texts enjoining symbolic meditations (pratīka), and in their case and

the case of others of their kind there arises the doubt whether or not one should see one's Self in the symbol. And one might initially suppose that one should. For it is well known that in the Upanishads the Absolute is identified with the Self, and since the symbols are but modifications of the Absolute, they must also be the Self.

To this we reply, in the words of the author of the Sūtras, 'No: one should not meditate upon the symbols as one's Self'. For the meditator cannot conceive all the diverse symbols as his own Self. As for the view that because the symbols are modifications of the Absolute they must be the Absolute and also be the Self — that is wrong, as it would imply the non-existence of all symbols. For 'Name' and the rest of the objects to be meditated upon as the Absolute can only 'become' the Absolute insofar as they give up their nature as modification. And if they have given up their own nature, how could they be symbols and how could one see one's Self in them? Nor have we any right to suppose that, because the Absolute is identified with the Self, one may see one's own Self where one is instructed to see the Absolute. For agency and other characteristics will not have been negated.[39] The Absolute is only taught to be the Self when agency and all empirical qualities of the Self have been negated. And meditations can only be enjoined where these qualities have not been negated. It cannot be claimed that the symbols communicate the Self through being themselves fundamentally identical with the meditator. A necklace and a swastika (made of gold) are not mutually identical. And if (it be said that) they are identical as gold, then we have already explained how, if the meditator and the symbol are identical through the

Absolute and the Self being identical, no symbol could exist. So one should not see one's own Self in the symbols (taught in the Veda as media for meditating on the Absolute).[40]

❖

7. Another doubt arises in regard to these symbolic meditations. The doubt is: 'Is one to impose the notion of the sun and the like onto the Absolute or is one to impose the notion of the Absolute onto them?' The doubt arises because when you only have the Absolute in apposition with another word, as in such phrases as 'Sun the Absolute', 'Vital Energy the Absolute', 'Lightning the Absolute',[41] where each word is in the same grammatical case, there is nothing to show which entity is to be imposed on which. At the same time, being in the same gramatical case does not here imply identity, as words like 'the Absolute' and 'the sun' have different meanings. The words 'ox' and 'horse' do not mean the same when they happen to occur together in the same grammatical case.

Perhaps you will say that grammatical agreement between the words for the Absolute and the sun and the rest is explicable because they have the relation of substance and modification. But this is wrong, because, as we have already explained in the section on the symbol,[42] where a modification is identified with the substance of which it is a modification this implies the dissolution of the modification.[43] To take these texts in this way would convert them into statements of the nature of the supreme Self, and then they could no longer be themes for symbolic meditation, while to make factual statements about minor modifications would be useless from the Vedic standpoint. Hence symbolic meditations involve the deliberate superimposition of the idea of one thing onto a completely different thing, as in the case of such texts as, 'The Brahmin is Fire (agni) in its universal form (vaiśvānara)',[44] and the doubt still remains which has to be superimposed on which.

And one might initially suppose that this doubt was not capable of resolution, there being no text to resolve it. Or else one might suppose that the notions of the sun and the rest had to be superimposed on the Absolute and not *vice versa*. For, after all, the Absolute would then be being meditated on as the sun and the like, and the Vedic rule is that it is meditations on the Absolute which bring fruit. Hence one should *not* meditate on the sun and the like as the Absolute (but should meditate on the Absolute as the sun and the like).

To this the author of the Sūtras replies, 'There should be meditation on the sun and the like as the Absolute'. Why? 'Because of the resultant elevation'. The sun and the like are elevated when the idea of something elevated is superimposed on them.[45] And this follows the worldly rule, which says that the notion of something superior should be attached to something inferior (and not *vice versa*): for example, the charioteer may on certain occasions be treated like the king. And this rule should be adhered to, as the opposite procedure can lead to trouble. No good end would be served by treating the king like the charioteer and thereby demeaning him.

Against this you might object that no trouble is to be apprehended here as we are following the authority of the Veda, and it is not right to interpret the Vedic view on the basis of secular maxims. We reply that this would be true where the meaning of the Vedic text had been definitively settled. But if the meaning of a Vedic text remains doubtful, there is nothing reprehensible in resorting to a secular maxim to settle it. Therefore, when it has been settled that the meaning of such texts implies the superimposition of the more elevated entity onto the less elevated, it follows that whoever superimposes the less elevated onto the more elevated commits a fault. And because the words 'sun', etc., precede the word for the Absolute in these texts, and are intelligible as they stand, they should initially be interpreted in their primary sense. And when these words have already penetrated into the mind in their primary meanings first, they cannot afterwards be brought into agreement with the primary meaning of the word for the Absolute (brahman) when it follows later.[46] This leaves us with only one possible meaning for such texts. They must be injunctions to meditate on the sun, etc., *as* the Absolute (addressed to one who is clear that the Absolute is not identical with anything finite).

That texts of this kind involving the Absolute must have this meaning is confirmed by the presence of the word 'as' (iti) in each case.[47] Everywhere in this context the Veda enunciates the word for the Absolute ('brahman') in association with the word 'as', ...whereas the other words like 'sun' are left without an 'as'. Similarly, in the sentence 'He sees nacre *as* silver', the word 'nacre' means real nacre, whereas the word 'silver' (because it is accompanied by the word 'as') means the imaginary idea of silver. One merely imagines silver, and the nacre is not really silver. In the same way, one should conclude that the texts now under consideration mean 'One should imagine the sun and the like *as* the Absolute'.

The sequel, too, shows that it is the sun and other objects expressed by nouns in the accusative that have to be meditated on in each case. Thus we find, 'That man of enlightenment who meditates on the sun *as* the Absolute', 'He who meditates on Speech *as* the Absolute', and 'He who meditates on Will *as* the Absolute'.[48]

The statement made earlier that one should invariably meditate on the Absolute in these cases, as that alone brought a reward, was wrong. For it is clear from the principle we have stated that it can only be the sun and the rest that have to be meditated on. The Absolute (brahman) will distribute the rewards of meditation on the sun and the like, just as it distributes rewards for action as explained above at Sūtra III.ii.38.[49] For the Absolute ordains everything. And in any case the Absolute is itself the object of meditation in these cases, to the extent that the idea of the Absolute has to be projected onto a symbol, as one projects the idea of Viṣṇu onto a stone image and the like.

There is, however, another series of meditations which assume the following sort of form: 'One should meditate on that (sun) that shines as the Udgītha',[50] 'One should meditate on earth, fire, atmosphere, sun and sky and the five parts of the Sāma Veda',[51] 'One should meditate on Speech and the seven parts of the Sāma Veda',[52] 'This earth is the Ṛg Veda, fire is the Sāma Veda'.[53] These meditations are divided into parts, and the doubt arises whether the texts intend to enjoin meditation on the sun and the like as the Udgītha or meditation on the Udgītha as the sun and the like.

And one might initially suppose that there is no solution to the doubt, as there is nothing that could solve it. For there is no elevation in question here as there was in the case of meditations connected with the Absolute. The Absolute, indeed, is the cause of the whole world, and has qualities such as freedom from all defect[54] that transcend the whole empirical order, which show the Absolute to be 'elevated' in comparison to the sun and the like. But in the case of the sun and Udgītha and the like, there is nothing to make any of them 'elevated' in this way, as all alike are modifications of the Absolute.

Or, alternatively, if there were a maxim to apply here, it would show that the sun and the like had to be meditated on as the Udgītha and the like. For the Udgītha and the like constitute ritualistic activity, and it is agreed that it is from ritualistic activity that results flow. When the sun and the like are meditated on as the Udgītha and the like it will convert them (i.e. will convert the sun, etc.) into the nature of ritualistic activity and they will yield fruit. Take the passage, 'This earth is the Ṛg Veda, fire is the Sāma Veda'.[55] Here the text refers to the element earth with the word 'Ṛk' and the element fire with the word 'Sāman'. And this suggests that its aim is to inculcate meditation on earth and fire as Ṛk and Sāman respectively, and not meditation on the Ṛg Veda and the Sāma Veda as earth and fire. For when one wants to inculcate treatment of the chamberlain as the king, one speaks of him figuratively as the king, and not of the king as the chamberlain....

To this opinion the author of the Sūtras replies that, on the contrary, it is the parts of the ritual, such as the Udgītha and the like, which have to be meditated on as the various other entities, including the sun, which are not part of the ritual.

And this is so, he says, on account of intelligibility. For it is quite intelligible to suppose that the merit arising from the Udgītha and other parts of the ritual should be increased when the Udgītha and the rest are being enhanced by being meditated on as the sun and the like. For the Udgītha and the rest are connected with the special merit that flows from ritual.[56] And the text 'Whatever (ritual) is done with meditation, faith and awareness of the secret correspondences[57] becomes more powerful'[58] shows that meditation increases the merit arising from ritual.

One might concede that this would be the case where the effect of meditation was to increase the merit arising from the performance of some ritual. But what about the cases where the merit arises independently from the meditation itself? For example, there is the meditation implied in the text 'whoso thus meditates on earth, fire, atmosphere, sun and sky as the five parts of the Sāma Veda'.[59] We reply that in their case, too, the right view is that their results only arise through connection with the special merit that flows from ritual, as in the case of the subordinate injunction about the milk-pail.[60] For only he has a right to perform them who is engaged in some Vedic sacrifice for which he is duly qualified. And it is moreover intelligible that the sun and the like should be superior to the Udgītha and the like, since they are the goals of ritualistic activity, while the Udgītha and the like are only parts of ritualistic activity. For there are Vedic texts declaring that the results of ritualistic activity are attainment of the sun and the like. And the passage beginning, 'OM: One should meditate on the Udgītha as this syllable' and ending 'Such is the further explanation of this same syllable'[61] also prescribes meditation on the Udgītha first, and it is only afterwards that it is specified that one may meditate on the Udgītha as the sun and other entities.[62]

As for the statement made earlier that if the sun and the like were meditated on as the Udgītha, they would be brought into the ritual and would bring merit, this statement was simply wrong. For meditation performed in conjunction with ritual is itself already ritual and so capable of bringing merit, and the Udgītha and the like do not lose their nature as ritual merely because they are meditated on as the sun and the like.

And in the passage, 'This earth is the Ṛg Veda, fire is the Sāma Veda'[63] referred to earlier, the later phrase 'This Sāman rests in this Ṛk' shows that the words 'Ṛk' and 'Sāman' are here used figuratively for the elements earth and fire, and the figurative meaning of a word can depart to a greater or less degree from the primary meaning according to the occasion.[64] True, the passage beginning 'This (earth), verily, is the Ṛk' teaches meditation on the Ṛk and Sāman as earth and fire respectively. But because (in the phrase 'This Sāman rests in this Ṛk') there is a second separate mention of the Ṛk and the Sāman after they have already been introduced, we must assume that (in this second phrase) the words Ṛk and Sāman are used figuratively to mean earth and fire respectively, (the primary meaning of the words Ṛk and Sāman being ruled out here on the ground that it would lead to useless tautology). This figurative usage is possible because the meanings 'earth' and 'fire' have already been brought into proximity with the words Ṛk and Sāman (through the meditation on the Ṛk and Sāman as earth and fire respectively just prescribed). There are occasions when even the word 'charioteer' can be used to denote the king (if the king is somehow brought into proximity with the idea of charioteer, for instance while he is driving his chariot).

The phrase 'This (earth), verily, is the Ṛk' showed by its very construction that (it is prescribing a meditation in which) the Ṛk has to be viewed as the earth (and not *vice versa*). For if it had been intended that the earth should be viewed as the Ṛk, the phrase would have been cast as 'This (earth) is verily the Ṛk'.[65] And the text, moreover, concludes 'Whoso knowing thus sings the Sāman',[66] which refers to knowledge of parts of the ritualistic text and not to knowledge of the earth and the like, (thereby showing that the meditation ought to have been on the Ṛk and the Sāman imagined as earth and fire)....

So it stands established that it is the idea of the sun and the like that has to be superimposed on elements of the ritual like the Udgītha, and not *vice versa*.[67]

❖

8. It has already been established in the first topic of the present Book[68] that all meditations (upāsana) imply repeated activity. Amongst meditations in general, those which aim at leading to right intuitive knowledge have to be performed until the end is achieved, like pounding the paddy to extract the rice. In their case, therefore, the extent of the repetition is clear. For after their final goal of right intuitive knowledge has been achieved, no further action could be prescribed. The Absolute is not within the realm of injunction. And the knowledge that one is oneself the Absolute takes one beyond the realm of the Veda.

But in regard to those meditations which are for the sake of personal advantages, the question might arise whether they had to be performed for a certain time only or for the whole of one's life. And one might initially suppose that they had to be performed for a certain time and then given up, for this would satisfy the demands of the texts that merely called for 'some repetition'.

To this the author of the Sūtras replies that the idea has to be affirmed one's whole life up to death. For (in meditations connected with the sacred ritual), it is one's last cognition before death that is decisive as regards gaining rewards arising from the mysterious potency of the ritual (adṛṣṭa). For even the mere ritualistic actions themselves which have initiated merit to be enjoyed in a future birth give rise at the time of death to a creative cognition corresponding to the future enjoyment, as is known from such texts as, 'He acquires a certain form of consciousness (vijñāna), he departs in the company of that consciousness',[69] 'Whatever one is thinking of, one joins one's life-breath accompanied by that. One's life-breath combined with fire (tejas) proceeds with the soul to the world that has been imagined'.[70] The image of the leech passing from one blade of grass to another implies the same principle.[71]

But what could the ideas affirmed in meditation need in order to produce a creative cognition bearing on enjoyments in a future birth except a final repetition? Such meditations are by their very nature creative projections of experiences to come, and should be repeated regularly till death. The Vedic texts themselves show that the affirmations should be repeated even at the time of death when they say, 'With whatever idea he leaves this world'.[72] And there are such texts from the derivative literature as, 'O son of Kuntī, a person goes to whatever being he is thinking of at the time he leaves the body, his mind being always impregnated with that vision' and 'At the time of death with mind fixed and motionless'.[73] And the text, 'He should resort to these three at the time of death' also shows that there is still something to be done at the time of death.[74]

2. Realisation of Identity with Hiraṇyagarbha

In Advaita teaching there is ultimately no duality. All deities, therefore, are reducible in the end to the non-dual Self. In their own true nature, as distinct from their form as manifest or conceived, they are identical with the true nature of the person meditating on them. It is therefore possible for a meditator to reach through meditation an intuitive awareness of his identity with the deity on whom he is meditating, and that awareness may have different degrees of intensity, ranging from a full sense of identity to a mere sense of proximity, according to the degree of intensity with which the meditative path is pursued. The first and second Extracts below expound the possibility of attaining partial or full awareness of one's identity with the Cosmic Vital Energy, the external adjunct of the Self which embraces all lesser adjuncts and of which the various deities and all the human powers of activity and knowledge are so many modifications.[75]

The third Extract stresses that realization of a sense of one's identity with the object of meditation is already possible in the present life. The fourth deals with meditation on Hiraṇyagarbha as present in the heart. The fifth and last Extract explains how meditation on particular deities, which are in fact meditations on aspects of the Self, may lead to the emergence of the soul at death through a subtle canal (nāḍī) in the body that is in contact with that deity and enables it to reach the 'world' of that deity, and how only those who pass along the subtle canal called the suṣumnā pass to the world of Brahmā and escape further transmigration, while those who go to other deities have to return eventually to the evils of worldly life.[76] The subtle canal called the suṣumnā was for Śaṅkara the subtle canal of that name proceeding from the heart-centre as taught in the Upanishads, which cannot be identified with the suṣumnā of the Hatha Yoga treatises, which rises up from the base of the spine.

TEXTS ON IDENTITY WITH HIRAṆYAGARBHA

1. Though it has been established in the sixth and seventh chapters (of the Chāndogya Upanishad) that the Absolute is void of all distinctions of direction, place or time, etc., and is Being only, one without a second, and that 'all this' is the Self alone,[77] yet the minds of less gifted souls, which have long been accustomed to thinking of reality as containing distinctions of direction, time and place, etc., cannot easily be fixed on the supreme transcendent principle. And without knowledge of the Absolute man's highest ends are not realized. So the text proceeds now, with a view to conveying some sort of knowledge of the Absolute, to teach that it is located in the heart-lotus.

Although the Self as a metaphysical principle is without qualities, and can only be represented by the pure notion of Being, yet it is supposed by less gifted souls to have qualities, and hence will be described (for their sake) as having qualities such as the power to realize immediately all its desires.

In the case of knowers of the Absolute, withdrawal from all objects of sensual enjoyment, such as women, occurs spontaneously. But because thirst for objects as generated by indulgence in them for many births cannot be brought to an end immediately, certain ways and means such as the discipline of celibacy have to be laid down (for the benefit of the less gifted souls). Again, for those who know their own identity with the Self, there exist no such distinctions as goer, going and destination. When the remnants of nescience, etc.,[78] which occasion the continuation of empirical existence are exhausted, then empirical existence just disappears, swallowed up in the Self, like the squall of wind accompanying a stroke of lightning that vanishes into the sky, or the fire that sinks down into the burnt-out fuel. Nevertheless, for the sake of those whose minds are conditioned by the ideas of goer and going, etc., and who meditate on the Absolute as occupying a place in the heart and as associated with distinct qualities, the eighth chapter of the Chāndogya Upanishad is begun to expound the theme of 'going' — by the subtle canal (nāḍī) at the crown of the head. For the Absolute, which is Being in the full sense, and which is void of distinctions pertaining to direction, place, quality, going and result, seems to less gifted souls (when taught in its true nature) as if it were non-being. The attitude of the Vedic text in this situation is, 'First let me put them on the right path, and then I will gradually be able to bring them round to the final truth afterwards'.[79]

❖

2. He who has the vision just mentioned of the three kinds of food as identical with himself becomes the Self of all beings,[80] the Vital Energy of all beings, the mind of all beings, the voice of all beings, and, being thus the Self of all beings, becomes omniscient. He also becomes the doer of everything.

He becomes, says the text, like this deity, like Hiraṇyagarbha, whose existence has already been proved. Nothing, therefore, can obstruct his omniscience and omnipotence.... Moreover, just as all beings cherish, nourish and worship the god Hiraṇyagarbha with sacrifices and in other ways, so do they also continuously worship him (the one who has 'become' identical with Hiraṇyagarbha) with sacrifices and the like.

Here a doubt arises. It has been said that he becomes the Self of all beings. In that case he will become the Self of all their bodies and organs. Does that mean that he will partake of all their pains and pleasures? No! For he feels himself to be infinite. Those who identify themselves with anything limited are subject to pain, as might arise, for instance, on the occasion of an insult when they feel 'So and so insulted me'. But he whom we are now considering is different. As the Self of all, he feels himself equally to be the Self of the one who offers and of the one who receives the insult, and hence feels no pain on account of it. Nor is there any occasion for grief at personal loss. Amongst those who identify themselves with limited personalities, one will feel grief when another dies, thinking 'He was my son' or 'He was my brother', and the occasion of such grief will be the fact of the dead person being a relative. But when this occasion is not present (i.e. when they do not feel themselves to be relatives) even the bystanders who are actually present look on unmoved. Such is the case with this exalted being also, who, being infinite in nature, is without any defects like false knowledge which could occasion grief through possessive feelings and the like.

And this is just what the text goes on to say. Whatever grief these people feel, the pain of the grief is theirs alone, because it springs from their sense of personal bereavement. But how can he who is the Self of all be either connected with or disjoined from anything?

To him who has attained the state of Prajāpati (Hiraṇya-garbha) there come only the results of merit. For he must have performed deeds of quite exceptional merit, so that he experiences their results only. The gods, says the text, are not visited by the results of sinful deeds, there being in their case no occasion for it. That is, they do not experience pain, the result of sin.[81]

❖

3. Speech and the other deities in man, and fire and the other deities on the cosmic plane, never depart from this one 'vow' consisting in the constant oscillation of the Vital Energy, as breath in man and as wind in the cosmos. Since none of the gods deviate from this vow, an ordinary mortal, too, must follow it.

What is this vow? He has to breathe in and out. Breathing in and out is a process which cannot stop. This 'vow' must be performed even when the other organs are at rest (in sleep), lest death-through-exhaustion overtake one. 'Lest' in the text implies dread. It means he has to observe the 'vow' of breathing possessed by the feeling of dread, 'If I depart from this vow, I shall be swallowed by death'.

If a person once starts this vow, he must aim to complete it. To desist from it amounts to an insult to the Vital Energy and to the gods. Through this 'vow', if one meditates on oneself as identical with the Vital Energy and thinks of the physical faculties in all individuals and the elemental powers in the cosmos as identical with oneself, if one meditates on 'I am the Vital Energy, the Self, the source of all movement', then through the observance of this 'vow' one attains either to identity or to proximity with this deity of the Vital Energy. Proximity ensues when the meditation is weaker.[82]

❖

4. It has been declared that 'Bhūr', 'Bhuvaḥ' and 'Svaḥ' are other worlds of divine experience forming limbs of Hiraṇyagarbha, the 'vyāhṛti' called Mahar.[83] The ether of the heart is said to be the locus for meditation on that Hiraṇyagarbha of which these are the limbs, as the Śālagrāma stone[84] is the locus (i.e. the symbol) for meditation on Viṣṇu. Such meditation culminates in a sense of identity with that deity. For it is when meditated upon in the ether of the heart that the Absolute as associated with such qualities as 'composed of mind', etc.,[85] becomes immediately evident[86] like a plum held in the hand. And here a new section is begun, because the path for realizing one's nature as the Self of all has to be taught.

The text says, 'This well-known ether within the heart'. The heart means the lotus-formed fleshly organ, the abode of the Vital Energy (prāṇa), with many apertures for subtle canals (nāḍī), with a cavity at the bottom and a tube at the top, the same that is clearly seen when animals are dissected. Within the heart stands 'this well-known ether', like the ether apparently enclosed in a vessel. Within that ether is this Spirit (puruṣa) so-called because it lies (śayana) within the city (puri) of the heart (puri-śayana = puruṣa). For it pervades all the worlds, beginning with Bhūr.

The Spirit is 'composed of mind'. Here 'mind' means knowledge. The Spirit is said to be 'composed of knowledge' in the sense of being attainable through knowledge. Or else 'mind' may here mean the internal organ (antaḥ-karaṇa), on the principle that the mind is what thinks of anything. In that case the phrase 'composed of mind' would mean either 'that which adopts mind' or 'that which has mind for its sign'. 'Immortal' means not subject to death, 'golden' means self-luminous.

This 'Indra'[87] subject to direct experience through self-identification in the ether of the heart, is the Self of the enlightened man. And now the path to its realization is being declared. It is known from the classical treatises on Yoga that there is a subtle canal proceeding upwards from the heart called the 'suṣumnā'.[88] It passes between a cleft in the palate and through a little nodule of flesh like a nipple that hangs down at this point. Then it proceeds upwards to (the crown of the head which is) the place from which the roots of the hair spiral outwards.[89] Splitting the skull into two halves, this path to the Absolute proceeds forth as the route to the 'attainment' of one's own true nature.

By this, the one who 'has knowledge' in the sense of identifying himself with the 'Self composed of mind' proceeds forth from the organ of the head and goes to pervade this world as Agni (fire). That is to say, he becomes established in Agni, which, under the sacred name of Bhūr, is the deity presiding over the world, and who is a limb of Hiraṇya-garbha.[90]

Then he becomes established in Vāyu (the wind), which is Bhuvaḥ, the second sacred name, and then the sun, which has the sacred name of Suvaḥ.[91] The word 'mahaḥ' means that he is established in Hiraṇyagarbha, the fourth sacred name, and the whole of which the others are parts.

Identified with these, he becomes Hiraṇyagarbha[92] and attains to sovereignty (svārājya).[93] Like Hiraṇyagarbha, he becomes the master of the other gods, who are his limbs. As he is the whole, all the other gods, who are but his limbs, bring him their various offerings. He becomes the lord of all minds, as Hiraṇyagarbha is the all, and thinks through all minds. He is the lord of all organs of speech, all eyes, all ears, all understandings, and assumes the organs of all living beings.

But there is more. He is the 'ether-body'. Or else this could mean mean that his body is subtle like the ether. Who is such? The Hiraṇyagarbha who is the topic of this section. He is that which has the whole empirical reality or the tangible and the intangible[94] for his nature. The play of the Cosmic Vital Energy (prāṇa) is his sport; or else the phrase may mean 'The play of the Cosmic Vital Energy takes place in him'. His mind knows only joy. 'Whose wealth is peace'. Here 'peace' means withdrawal. Or the phrase may mean 'Who is that abundant wealth known (only) through withdrawal'.[95] Immortal in the sense of deathless (until the final dissolution at the end of the world-period). These are those 'other qualities' that had to be added beyond 'composed of mind'.[96] 'O Prācīnayogya, meditate on Hiraṇyagarbha as associated with these qualities!' The text quotes the words of the Teacher to impress the listener with the seriousness of the subject....

It has now been declared that this Hiraṇyagarbha, the being designated by the name 'Mahaḥ' (or Mahar), has to be meditated on. It is now explained how it should be meditated on as identical with the group of five (elements) beginning with the earth, and also with the metre 'Paṅkti',[97] where all are five-fold. Sacrifice is also five-fold (pāṅkta):[98] and the Paṅkti metre is so called on account of its five feet. It is from the Veda itself that we know that 'sacrifice is five-fold'.[99] Whatever, from the world up to the 'Self',[100] a person represents as five-fold, he represents by that very fact, as sacrifice. Through such a representation of Prajāpati (Hiraṇyagarbha) as sacrifice, one attains Prajāpati. But in exactly what way are we to meditate on all this as five-fold?

The world is five-fold as earth, sky, heaven, the cardinal points, the half points. Deity is five-fold as Agni (fire), Vāyu (wind), Āditya (sun), Candramas (moon), and Nakṣatrāṇi (the astrological houses). The elements are five-fold as water, plants, trees, ether and 'self', where 'self' means the totality of matter (virāṭ), since we are dealing with matter....

Then three five-fold groups on the microcosmic plane (adhyātma) are mentioned. The five-fold drives of the Vital Energy in the body; the five-fold group of senses such as sight; and the five constituents of the body such as skin.[101] To this extent, all the microcosm and all the macrocosm is five-fold. Seeing all this, says the Upanishad, or imbued with this vision, a certain seer declared, 'All this is five-fold'. Because of this identity of number, one transfigures, strengthens, perfects the macrocosmic five-fold through the microcosmic five-fold. It means that he perceives[102] the macrocosm as forming one Self. Whoso knows all this as five-fold acquires the nature of Prajāpati.[103]

5. It has been explained how there is no 'departure' after death in the case of the man of enlightenment who has become the Absolute while yet alive, the knots of whose heart have been entirely cut by the knowledge that he is himself none other than the all-pervading Absolute, void of all distinctions. The decisive text here was, 'He attains the Absolute here'[104] and we have another similar passage from another Upanishad, 'His Vital Energy does not ascend (at death). He "attains" the Absolute in the sense that he already *is* the Absolute (and now becomes aware of the fact)'.[105]

But the case is different with those whose knowledge of the Absolute is yet incomplete and who follow other indirect paths of symbolic meditation and go to the 'world of Brahmā', and with those others who remain in the cycle of rebirth. The text states that they have their own particular mode of departure, in order to eulogize (by comparison) the supreme results of knowledge of the Absolute, which is the present topic of discussion. Moreover, there has already been a question and answer about 'knowledge of Agni',[106] and there is occasion to explain how the fruit of this is attained.

There are a hundred[107] subtle canals (nāḍī) issuing from the heart of man, and one extra one, called the suṣumnā.[108] Of these, the suṣumnā pierces the skull and runs out. A man may establish connection with this canal in the heart at the time of death, through concentration on the mind,[109] and may pass upwards through it to *conditioned* immortality through the gateway of the sun, as the derivative literature says, 'Remaining in the same place until the dissolution of the elements is referred to as "immortality".'[110] Or else it may attain to real immortality in company with Brahmā at a later time,[111] having enjoyed incomparable pleasures in the world of Brahmā.[112]

There are other canals leading out by different ways.[113] They, too, lead upwards, but only into further transmigratory experience.[114]

3. The Path of the Flame

Reference has already been made in an earlier Extract[115] to the practice of 'Meditation on the Five Fires', the Pañcāgni Vidyā, which has been described as 'the means to the attainment of the Northern Path'. Another name used by Śaṅkara for the 'Northern Path' is the 'Path of the Flame'. It is also known as the 'Path of Fire' in contradistinction to the 'Path of Smoke' and as the 'Path of the Gods (deva-yāna)' in contradistinction to the 'Path of the Ancestors (pitṛ-yāna)'.[116] Extracts in which Śaṅkara deals with this topic have been gathered together in this section. But a few preliminary paragraphs of explanation seem needed.

It is well known that the doctrine of transmigration was only introduced into the Vedic corpus gradually. It first appears in complete form in the Śatapatha Brāhmaṇa, and the doctrine is repeated with only minor variations at Bṛhadāraṇyaka Upanishad VI.ii and Chāndogya Upanishad V.iii. We have already heard detailed accounts of the process above, Volume V, 21ff. The soul that performs ritual, in particular the Agnihotra, constructs for itself a watery body in which it sojourns on the moon, eventually re-descending for further earthly life by falling from the sky in rain, entering crops, being eaten by the future father, emerging as his seed and entering the womb of the mother. There is, however, a hidden truth about the process, the fact, namely, that the five stages of the descent constitute five sacrificial fires.[117] The starting-point, the world of the gods, is a sacrificial fire, with the sun for fuel and the stars for sparks. Rain is a sacrificial fire, with air for fuel, lightning for the flame and thunder for sparks. The earth, which receives the rain, is a sacrificial fire, with the various divisions of time and space for fuel, flame and sparks. Man, who eats the crops of the earth into which the rain has entered, is a sacrificial fire, his tongue being the flame, his eyes the coals, his breath the smoke. And finally woman is a sacrificial fire, the elements of the sacrifice being in her case various aspects of the sexual act.

Possession of this 'knowledge' of the Five Fires is associated at Chāndogya Upanishad V.x.l with retirement to the forest and a life of austerity and meditation. The Āraṇyakas and Upanishads, as is well known, are texts handed down by the priests primarily for the benefit of those who retire from household life to the forests. Here they may live in huts and continue to perform the simpler rituals, but the main preoccupation is meditation on the ritual, particularly on the hidden facts about certain elements in it that have been discovered by the sages and taught by them to suitable pupils. For Śaṅkara, this life sufficed for 'deferred' or 'gradual' release (krama-mukti), but there existed a higher discipline, described in the following chapter, which led to immediate release (sadyo-mukti), in which the released soul became aware of his true nature as the Self in this very life. The seeker on this latter path (mumukṣu) would normally give up all connection with ritual whatever and any form of permanent residence along with it, wandering the earth as an ascetic with a single staff (eka-daṇḍin), a monk of the 'paramahaṃsa' order. The person who merely practised meditation on the hidden significance of the ritual, on the other hand, could be either a householder or a dweller in a forest hut or else a monk carrying a staff of three staves bound together (tridaṇḍin), and retaining the sacred cord which would entitle him to perform ritual.

The body of a person practising this latter form of discipline was normally cremated at death, and it was thought in early times that the soul of such a person ascended, not with the smoke of the funeral pyre to the moon and the realm of the ancestors, but with the fire to the sun and the realm of the gods. It is the deities presiding over the various 'realms' traversed that conduct the soul along the Path of Fire, which is the path leading to deferred release. Like the soul on the Path of Smoke, it also proceeds to the moon, but here it is met by a Being 'not belonging to the race of men' who conducts it to the 'World of Brahmā'. Once it has gained this refuge, the soul is not required to descend again for rebirth, but remains aloft in great felicity until the end of the world-period, when the temporary dissolution of Brahmā and his 'world' in the Absolute entrains the final dissolution into the Absolute of all the souls inhabiting his 'world'. Śaṅkara conceived the 'world' of Brahmā as in some sense located in space, as he contrasts it with the Absolute as somewhere you 'go to' with the services of a guide. In the Extracts to follow, the path being described will usually be referred to as the 'Path of the Flame'.

TEXTS ON THE PATH OF THE FLAME

1. Those who meditate on the bliss-ether in the eye as 'that to which all desirable things go', as 'that which brings all desirable things' and as 'the shining one', and who meditate on the Five Fires as associated with the Vital Energy — such people attain to the deity adopting the Flame, whether they perform any other ritualistic activity or not. From the Deity of the Flame they pass to the Deity adopting the Day, from the Deity of the Day to the Deity of the Fortnight of the Waning Moon, from him to the Deity of the Fortnight of the Waxing Moon, from him to the Deities of the Six Months, where the 'Six Months' are understood as the six months of the northern passage of the sun; from the Deities of the Six Months they proceed to the Deity of the Year, from the Deity of the Year

to the Deity of the Sun (āditya), from him to the Deity of the Moon (candramas), from the Deity of the Moon to the Deity of Lightning. And when they are in the realm of the Deity of Lightning, a certain superhuman Being, not belonging to the race of men, comes from the world of Brahmā and takes them over to the world of Brahmā, understood as the world of 'satya' (and not as the Absolute in its supreme form), because of the mention in connection with it of going, guide and goal. If it had meant attainment of the Absolute in the sense of 'pure Being' (san-mātra) this would have been out of place, for in this context we should expect to find expressions like, 'Being himself already the Absolute, he dissolves in the Absolute'.[118] And the texts will later (in the sixth chapter of the Chāndogya Upanishad) explain how attainment of pure Being arises through the negation of all distinctions. And if a path is invisible, no one can (be said to) 'go' on it,[119] for we have the text, 'If he does not know it, it does not protect him'.[120]

This path is also called the Path of the Gods, because it is presided over by the gods, adopting the flame and the rest and functioning as guides. Because it leads (eventually) to the Absolute it is called the (indirect) Path to the Absolute (brahma-patha). Those who go to the Absolute (even) by this (indirect) path do not return to the whirlpool of human life again and do not remain bound to the wheel of birth and death like buckets on a revolving wheel at a well. The phrase 'do not return' is repeated twice and thus indicates the end of a section dealing with a meditation that leads to a particular result.[121]

❖

2. The question that has to be faced is, 'Do you know where men go to after death?' Amongst householders actively engaged in the performance of their rituals and who are about to depart for another world, those who have performed meditation on the Five Fires and know that they were born from the Five Sacrificial Fires beginning with that of the heavenly world of the gods (dyu-loka) and afterwards from the others in due order, and that they are themselves of the very nature of Fire (agni), they go to the Flame.

But how do we know that this going to the Flame is restricted to householders who know about the Five Fires? Because the text is going to say later that those householders who do not have this knowledge and who have aspired no further than public and private charities will go to the moon by the Path of Smoke. The text will also refer, by using the word 'forest', to the Vaikhānasas (retired forest-dwellers) and wandering ascetics who practise faith[122] and austerity, and will say that they go to the Path of the Flame (at death) together with those who have the knowledge of the Five Fires. From this we conclude, on the principle of 'the only remaining alternative', that the phrase 'those who have this knowledge of the Five Fires' must refer to householders actively engaged in performing their rituals, especially as there is also the reference to the oblations of the Agnihotra.[123]

Perhaps you will say that our 'principle of the only remaining alternative' does not apply, as the religious students (brahmacārin) have not been mentioned, nor have they been implicitly referred to by the texts speaking of villages or of forests. But there is nothing wrong here. As regards the celibate students of life-long vows, it is well known on the authority of the Purāṇas[125] and the Epics that they proceed at death by the Path of the Sun, and they will therefore go with the forest-dwellers.[126] As for the religious students who are still under instruction from a Teacher, they are intent only on learning their texts (and have not yet selected a mode of life), so there was no need to mention them specially.

Perhaps you will now suggest that if we have the authority of the Purāṇas and Epics for knowing that life-long celibacy is the means to attain the Northern Path,[127] acquisition of the knowledge of the Five Fires must be useless. But this is wrong, as it is useful precisely in the case of the householder. It is well known that householders who do not possess this knowledge proceed naturally at death by way of the Southern Path and by way of the Path of Smoke. But those who have acquired spiritual knowledge through the performance of prescribed symbolic meditations, whether on the Absolute as associated with empirical qualities or on the Absolute in some other form, go at death by the Northern Path indicated by the Flame, whether they undergo cremation or not.[128]

Perhaps you will argue that life-long celibates (who do not marry but do not retire completely from the world and cast away their sacred threads either) belong to the same station of life (āśrama) as householders, and that it is wrong to say that lifelong celibates *automatically* go by the Northern Path, whereas householders do not (unless they acquire a knowledge of the Five Fires), even though they have an immense superiority over the life-long celibate in respect of performance of the Agnihotra and other household Vedic ritual. But this is not right. For there is a basic impurity in householders. They are constantly in touch with enemies and friends, which engenders attachment and aversion, and which leads them to heap up merit and demerit through acts of kindness and aggression. It is impossible for them to avoid many causes of impurity such as causing harm to others, lying, lapses from continence and so on. All this renders them impure, and, being impure, they cannot (without the performance of special practices) go by the Northern Path. But the case with the life-long celibates is otherwise. Their souls are pure through avoidance of harming others, deceit and lapses from continence. And they acquire detachment from the things of this world because they are able to avoid attachment and aversion for friends and enemies. Hence it is but right that they should go by the Northern Path after death. And the authors of the Purāṇas confirm the point, in the words, 'Those unwise ones who desired progeny ended up in the charnel house: those wise ones who avoided the desire for progeny (automatically) obtained immortality'.[129]

To this you might object that if the householders who possessed the knowledge of the Five Fires and forest-dwellers both went by the same path after death and both attained immortality, there would be no point in forest-dwellers ever acquiring knowledge. But this would contradict the Veda, for instance the text, 'The southerners (those who go by the Southern Path) do not go there, nor do the ascetics who have not acquired knowledge'[130] and also the text, 'If he does not know it, it is of no service to him'.[131]

But this objection is not right, for in the quotation from the Purāṇas about automatically obtaining immortality, 'immortality' does not mean complete immortality, but only remaining in the same place until the dissolution of the elements at the end of the world-period. The authors of the Purāṇas themselves say on this head, 'Remaining in the same place until the dissolution of the elements is referred to as "immortality".'[132] And the Vedic passages such as 'The southerners do not go there' and 'If he does not know it, it is of no service to him' refer to immortality in the full sense. So there is no contradiction.[133] Nor can you say that there is contradiction with such Vedic texts as, 'And they do not return' and 'They do not return to this whirlpool of human life'.[134] For the specification 'to this... human life here' shows that it was only meant that they did not return here. If it had been meant that they did not return anywhere at all, the specification 'to this... human life here' would have been unnecessary.[135] Nor can you say that 'this' and 'here' are just meaningless generalities.[136] For as the mere phrase 'no return' would have meant complete immortality, the fact that the words 'here' and 'this' were added at all shows that the theory that they are mere empty generalities is groundless. Therefore, to give the meaning of the words 'here' and 'this' their due measure of particularity, we have to assume that the celibates without knowledge, who are said in the text to gain 'immortality', do in fact return to some other place apart from 'this human whirlpool here'.[137]

But those who have the firm conviction 'Being is one only without a second' do not go by means of the subtle canal at the crown of the head on the Path beginning with the Flame. We know this from hundreds of texts, such as 'Being himself already the Absolute, he dissolves in the Absolute', 'Therefore he became all that', 'His Vital Energy does not rise up', 'They actually dissolve here'.[138] Nor can it be claimed that the meaning is that when that soul is itself about to rise up, the

Vital Energy does not rise up *from* it but rises up *with* it. For this would render void the qualifying phrase of the text 'dissolve *here*', and moreover the text explicitly contradicts the notion that the soul departs with the Vital Energy by replying 'No' to the question 'Does the Vital Energy rise up?'[139] So there is no question of the Vital Energy of the man of enlightenment departing upwards at the death of the body.

Even if the statement that the Vital Energy does not depart upwards was interpreted to mean that at liberation the soul left this world, but that the Vital Energy did not accompany it on account of the profound difference between liberation and the 'going' of ordinary empirical experience, this would also render void the qualifying phrase, 'dissolve *here*'.[140] Nor can there be either 'going' or 'individual soulhood' without the Vital Energy.[141] This is certainly the case if one accepts the Veda as an authority. For the Self is omnipresent and partless. And it is the Vital Energy alone that introduces distinctions into it which seem like sparks in a fire. Without the Vital Energy, 'soulhood' and 'going' are both inconceivable. (Nor can one dispense with the theory of the soul's being dependent on the Vital Energy, for) it could not be right to hold that some atomic fragment broken off from the whole, and, under the name of the 'individual soul', could have the power to pierce pure Being and make its exit. Therefore the text, 'Going up by that (subtle canal that leads to the crown of the head) one attains immortality'[142] does not refer to liberation in its direct and immediate form. It refers, rather, to the departure from the body of one who had meditated on the Absolute as associated with empirical qualities, such departure being effected through a subtle canal and in the company of the

Vital Energy. The 'immortality' spoken of is conditional immortality. For after speaking of the city Aparājitā and the Airammadīya lake and other features, a text speaks of those who find them as 'possessing the world of Brahmā'.[143]

So we conclude that householders who have knowledge of the Five Fires and the retired folk and the wandering ascetics living in the forests, together with the life-long celibates, all attain to the guiding Deity who has adopted the Flame, so long as they are possessed of faith (śraddhā) and given to asceticism (tapas).... This is called the Path of the Gods which ends in Satya Loka and does not pass beyond the (Cosmic) Egg. It is as in the text, '(I have heard of two paths for men, the one that leads to the fathers and the one that leads to the gods. By these two, all that lives moves on,) whatever there is between father (heaven) and mother (earth)'.[144]

❖

3. But those others, forming quite an opposite class, householders possessed of the merit arising from the performance of meditations prescribed in the Veda, along with forest-dwellers and renunciates[145] carrying out 'austerity' in the form of the ritualistic and other observances assigned to their caste and station, and pursuing 'faith' in the form of meditations on Hiraṇyagarbha and other deities,[146] and who are 'peaceful' in the sense that their senses have (practically) ceased from their functions, go to the forest to live on alms, and, being cleansed of their merits and demerits alike, proceed after death by the Northern Path, here called 'The Gate of the Sun' because it involves the sun,[147] accompanied by those householders who have performed meditation on the Five

Fires[148] and other Vedic themes. They go in glory to the world of Brahmā (satya-loka), where dwells the first-born[149] spirit called Hiraṇyagarbha, who is called indestructible in the sense of being coeval with the world of transmigratory experience. This is the culminating point of experience in the transmigratory world resulting from the lower meditations.

Some, indeed, say that this result is itself liberation. But this is not correct. For we have the texts (which teach of immediate liberation here on earth) such as 'All desires dissolve here in this very world'[150] and 'these wise ones of concentrated mind reach the omnipresent Spirit on all sides and enter the great Whole'.[151] Nor is liberation the present topic. When the lower meditations are under discussion, there is no question of introducing the topic of immediate liberation.[152] And the cleansing of merit and demerit spoken of must be taken as relative and not absolute. Attainment of Hiraṇyagarbha is the culminating point of experience in the realm of ends to be gained through the lower meditations, that realm constituted by the world of duality characterized by ends and means and the distinction between action and its factors and fruits. And Manu, in enumerating the various states attainable in the course of transmigration, from that of stocks and stones upwards, says 'The wise declare that the highest, most luminous (sāttvika) states are those of Brahmā, the ṛṣis like Marīci who make cosmic projections, Yama, the Cosmic Intellect (mahat) and the Unmanifest Principle (avyakta)'.[153]

❖

4. As the teaching about knowledge of the Self and its beneficial results which is given in the sixth, seventh and

eighth chapters of the Chāndogya Upanishad is quite intelligible as it stands, it might be thought that the teachings (in the earlier chapters of the Upanishad) about ritual were useless. To rebut this charge, the text explains the special beneficial result that accrues from practice of ritual even in the case of the man of knowledge.

The text refers to one who learns the text of the Veda by repeating it and also acquires knowledge of its meaning by living with the Teacher in his house like a family-member. He learns it 'according to rule', which means according to the rules laid down in the derivative literature, and which, in the case of the celibate student learning the Veda and proposing later to marry, are mentioned mainly to emphasize the paramount importance of service of the Teacher. Learning the Veda 'according to rule' means learning it in the intervals of the day whenever the immediate work for the Teacher has been done. The Veda is an instrument for acquiring knowledge of rituals and their fruits only when it is learned in this way, and not otherwise.

When such a student has completed his enquiry into the ritualistic teaching of the Veda and has returned home from the house of the Teacher, he takes a wife according to rule, establishes a family and engages in the enjoined ritual. If the ritualistic duties of the householder are mentioned, it is in order to emphasize implicitly that the chief one is repetition of the Veda. Seated properly in a clean and secluded spot, he goes through at least a daily regular portion, and if possible more, of the Ṛk or other Vedas. He has sons and pupils who follow the spiritual law (are 'dhārmika'), training them himself in the law. He restrains all his senses from flowing out in sense-perception, and concentrates their attention within on the Absolute in the heart-centre. He gives up action.[154] He refrains from causing harm to any being, whether moving or fixed, except in the form of begging at holy places.[155] If he spends his whole life with his family in this way, he attains to the world of Brahmā at death and does not return to earth for further embodied existence, as there are texts which deny that such a thing is possible.[156] When one has attained the world of Brahmā by the Path beginning with the Flame, one stays in that world as long as it lasts before the final cosmic dissolution. The last phrase is repeated to mark the end of the Upanishad and its teaching.[157]

❖

5. Next the Lord considers it necessary to declare the nature of the 'Northern Path' for the attainment of the Absolute, that followed by Yogins of the type we are here discussing, who have been raised to a consciousness of the Absolute through meditation on the syllable OM, and who are to acquire liberation at some future time. He also mentions the other (Southern) Path, on which men return for further experiences on earth, in order to eulogize the Northern Path....

By 'Yogins' the Lord means both Yogins proper[158] and persons on the path of works, since the latter are 'Yogins' in a secondary sense, inasmuch as they are men of application. And the Lord continues, 'I will tell you the times when, if a Yogin dies, he does not return for further transmigration, and also the times when, if he dies, he does return'.

Where the text says Agni and Jyotiḥ (fire and light), the expressions 'Agni' and 'Jyotiḥ' both stand for the deity presiding over time. Or it may mean fire and light literally, but taken in their aspect as deities. It would then follow that the Lord had mentioned the word 'time' twice to indicate the importance of time in the way these deities function in the present context. The word 'time' would be being used here like the word 'mango' in the phrase 'a mango grove' (where mango trees predominate but are not the only trees present).[159]

The words of the text 'Day', 'Light Fortnight' and 'Six Months of the Northern Passage of the Sun' refer to deities forming a path, as has been shown elsewhere.[160] Where the text here says 'Those who know the Absolute', it only means 'Those who perform meditation on the Absolute'. And when it says that those on the present path engaged in meditation on the Absolute 'reach the Absolute', we have to understand the extra phrase 'gradually and in the course of time'. For those who are established in right knowledge and have attained immediate liberation (sadyo-mukti)[161] are beyond either 'reaching' or 'not reaching', as the text 'His Vital Energy does not rise up'[162] shows. Their life-breaths are dissolved in the Absolute and they have themselves verily become the Absolute.

'Smoke' and 'Night' (in the following verse of the text under comment) mean the deities which identify themselves with smoke and night, the same being the case with the 'Dark Fortnight', as also with the 'Six Months of the Southern Passage of the Sun'. The text says, 'A Yogin who dies at these times reaches the light of the moon and from thence turns back'. 'Yogin' means 'man of action' (karmin). 'Light of the moon' means 'existence on the moon'. And when he has enjoyed and exhausted his earned and allotted existence on the moon, he returns back to earth.

The next verse speaks of these two paths as 'white' and 'black'. One is white because illumined by knowledge, and the other black because of the absence of knowledge. They pertain, not to the whole world, but only to those who are qualified for spiritual knowledge or ritualistic action respectively. They are admitted to be eternal because transmigratory life is itself admitted to be eternal. If one leaves the world by the white path one does not return for further transmigration; if one leaves by the black path one does.[163]

❖

6. But who is to have this knowledge (of the Five Fires)? Evidently householders. But is it not the purpose of the Veda that householders should be enjoined to reach the (Southern) Path beginning with Smoke through the practice of the sacrificial ritual? This objection does not affect our position, as there will also be householders who do not have this knowledge (of the Five Fires), and the practice of the sacrificial ritual will be appropriate for them. Moreover, monks living on alms and retired persons living in the forest have been excluded (from the knowledge of the Five Fires) by the reference to the forest, the meditation on the Five Fires being specifically connected with the householder's ritual. From this we should conclude that lifelong celibates (brahmacārin) do not acquire knowledge of the Five Fires either. We know from the derivative literature that they proceed by the Northern Path, the text being, 'Eighty-eight-thousand celibate seers proceeded on the Northern Path by the Path of the Sun and attained immortality'.[164] Therefore, those householders who know themselves to be born of fire, to have been born from the various sacrificial fires in order, go by the Path beginning

with the Flame, as also do those retired persons living in the forests as well as the renunciates who live their whole lives in the forest, provided they meditate upon the Satya-Brahman or Hiraṇyagarbha. The text does not mean that they have to meditate *on* faith but only *with* faith.

As long as householders do not know either the knowledge of the Five Fires or Satya Brahman they continue to be born of the fire of woman, when the fifth oblation has been made in the series beginning with 'faith', and, coming back into the world again, they continue to apply themselves to the Agni-hotra and other rituals. Through this ritual.[165] they again pass at death on the Path beginning with Smoke to the World of the Ancestors (pitṛ-loka) and later return back to earth downwards through rain. Again they are born of fire (i.e. through the natural process of reproduction, symbolized by the five sacrificial fires on which one meditates) and again they perform ritual and in this way continue to come and go in a cycle like a bucket mounted on a machine at a well. But when they know the Five Fires, they are released from this revolving on the machine for buckets in a well, and they proceed at death to the flame.

The Flame is not a mere tongue of fire but is the Deity of the Northern Path, who adopts a flame of fire and is called 'the Flame'. It is said that they 'reach' it because monks (at death) are not directly connected with a flame,[166] and this shows that the word 'Flame' refers here to a deity only.

The text says that the Deity of the Day is the next reached. The word 'Day' also refers to a deity, as there cannot be any rule about what time in the day a person dies. He just dies when the life-force is exhausted. One cannot introduce a restriction and say that one who has knowledge of the Five Fires invariably dies by day-time. Nor can it be said that those who (have knowledge of the Five Fires and) die during the night wait for the day (to leave the body), as there is another Vedic text which says, 'He goes to the sun as quick as thought'.[167]

Conducted by the Deity of the Day, they proceed to the Fortnight of the Waxing Moon. Conducted by the latter, they proceed to the Six Months of the Northern Passage of the Sun. The fact that the word 'months' is in the plural shows that there are six Deities of the Northern Passage of the Sun, forming a group. These six Deities conduct them from the Six Months to the Deity of the World of the Gods. From the World of the Gods, they reach the Sun (āditya), and from the Sun they reach Lightning, that is to say the Deity that adopts lightning. When they have reached the Deity of Lightning, a Being who dwells in the Worlds of Brahmā, a 'mental Being', created by Brahmā through his mind, comes up to them and conducts them to the world of Brahmā. The mention of 'Worlds' in the plural shows that there are higher and lower planes, in keeping with the fact that meditations vary in quality. Conducted by that Being, they dwell there in glory many years, that is, for many aeons or 'ages of Brahmā'. Having gone to the world of Brahmā, they do not again return to the world of transmigratory life.[168]

❖

7. It has been shown that the exit (from the body) up to the point of departure is the same (in the case of all pious souls

proceeding to the Absolute indirectly by the 'Path of the Gods'). But the actual journey is described differently in different Vedic passages. For example, one passage which teaches that the subtle canals (nāḍī) in the body are connected with the rays of the sun, says that the soul 'mounts upwards on these self-same rays'.[169] Another passage makes 'the flame' the starting-point and says 'They first reach the Flame and from thence the Day'.[170] Another passage says, 'Reaching this Path which is the passage of the gods, he goes to the World of Fire (agni)'.[171] Another says, 'When the soul leaves this world at death, it proceeds, verily, to Wind (vāyu)'.[172] Yet another says, 'Stainless, they proceed through the gate of the sun'.[173]

Here the doubt might arise as to whether all these paths were quite different, or whether they constituted one path with different phases. And one might begin by supposing that all these paths were different, first because they are taught in passages containing different subject-matter, and secondly because the meditations from which they are said to result are different. Again, the words 'on these self-same rays'[174] would be contradicted if the path depended on first reaching the Flame, as would the statement about the speed with which the pious soul goes, namely, 'he goes to the sun as quickly as one could project the mind to the sun'.[175] So all these paths must be regarded as quite different.

To this the author of the Sūtras replies, 'On the Path that begins with the Flame'. Our position is that everyone who wishes to reach the Absolute (i.e. to attain to it indirectly through going a journey after the death of the body) must go by the Path that begins with the Flame. For the existence of this Path is familiar to all who are versed in these subjects. In the section on the Knowledge of the Five Fires (pañcāgni-vidyā) a Path beginning with the Flame is mentioned as being the lot of those who practise this quite different form of meditation, as witness the text, 'Those who meditate with faith on Hiraṇyagarbha'.[176]

To this you might object that our account of the matter might be allowed to stand in those courses of prescribed Vedic meditations which were not explicitly taught to result in the traversing of any particular path after death. In their case, this Path beginning with the Flame might be possible. But how could this Path apply to those whom the Veda describes as traversing quite a different path after death? We reply that the objection might hold if the other paths traversed after death that are mentioned in the Veda were *altogether* different from the Path beginning with the Flame. But our own view is that we always have one self-same path mentioned, which leads to the world of Brahmā, but which has many stages and which is referred to sometimes by one and sometimes by another of those stages. As we always recognize them as stages on one path, they can all be used to refer to each other mutually.[177] Wherever the passages and contexts in which a particular meditation is taught are quite separate, the complete meditation in all its details as gathered from all the separate texts has to be understood each time any part of it is mentioned. And the same holds true of the Path as traversed by the soul after death.[178] Even if the meditations separately mentioned are taken as distinct and different, the Path is always the same, as one can always recognize one or the other stage of it, and the ultimate goal towards which it is proceeding is always the same. The same final result of attainment of the World of

Brahmā is found in all the various texts such as, 'They live for extremely long periods in the Worlds of Brahmā',[179] 'They live there for eternal ages', 'Such an one conquers and expands wherever Brahmā had conquered and expanded', and 'Whoso find this World of Brahmā through the practice of the celibate spiritual life (brahmacarya)'.[180]

As for the opponent's earlier contention that the text, '(The soul) mounts upwards on these self-same rays'[181] would exclude the possibility of the soul attaining to the Flame and other stages on account of its specifying *these self-same* rays, we reply that this does not affect our position at all, as the phrase as a whole is concerned with affirming that the soul attains the rays, and the word 'self-same' cannot have the double function both of affirming that the soul attains the rays and also of denying that it attains the Flame and other stages on the Path. Hence the element of extra emphasis in the phrase should be taken only as affirming heartily attainment of the rays (and not as excluding the attainment of anything else). The mention of speed,[182] too, forms no obstacle, as it is only meant to show that one attains to the Flame and the other stages quicker than one attains to other things, as one might say 'one gets there in the twinkling of an eye'.

Even the text 'By neither of these two paths',[183] which refers to the third and evil state attained by those who fail to traverse either the path of the Ancestors or the Path of the Gods, shows (by its use of the dual number) that there is only one other path apart from the Path of the Ancestors, namely the Path of the Gods with its various stages beginning with that of the Flame. Sometimes this Path is mentioned in its full form containing all the stages beginning with the Flame, sometimes it is referred to in curtailed form. And in such a case, the right method of interpretation is to fill out the curtailed references to bring them into line with the complete references. And this is another reason why the Sūtra here says, 'By the Path beginning with the Flame, because this is recognized and familiar'.

But what is the exact order in which the various stages of the path condition one another mutually? The Teacher compassionately enlightens us on the point. In the Kauṣītaki Upanishad the Path of the Gods is described as follows: 'Having attained to this Path of the Gods, he proceeds to the World of Fire (agni), to the World of Wind (vāyu), to the World of Water (varuṇa), to the World of Indra, to the World of Brahmā'.[184] Since the words 'Fire (agni) and 'the Flame' both mean burning, there is no problem here about where the Flame comes in the order. But Wind (vāyu) is not mentioned at all on the Path when it is described as beginning with the Flame, so the question does arise where Wind ought to be placed. To understand the answer to this question, we must turn to the text, 'They go to the Flame and from this to the Day and from the Day to the Waxing Lunar Fortnight and from this to the Six Months of the Northern Passage of the Sun and from these to the Year and from this to the Sun (āditya)'.[185] From this text it is clear that they reach the Wind after the Year and before the Sun.

Why so? The author of the Sūtras explains, in the words 'Such an one attains to the Wind (vāyu) after attaining to the Year and before attaining to the Sun (āditya) because of the absence of specification at one place and the presence of specification at the other'. For the 'World of the Wind' is mentioned (at Kauṣītaki Upanishad I.3) without specification, whereas in another text there is specification as follows, 'When the soul (puruṣa) leaves this world at death it comes to the Wind and the Wind makes a hollow in itself like the hollow in the hub of a chariot-wheel and the soul passes upwards through this and reaches the Sun (āditya)'.[186] On account of this specification showing that the Wind comes immediately before the Sun, the Wind has to be inserted in the series between the Year and the Sun.

But, you will ask, why is the Wind not inserted immediately after the Flame, seeing that in one passage[187] it is specified as coming directly after Fire (agni)? True, the text 'Having attained to this Path of the Gods he proceeds to the World of Fire, to the World of the Wind, to the World of Water' has already been quoted. But we maintain that the various stages are merely enumerated one after the other pell-mell here, and that there is not a word to say that the order of enumeration corresponds to the actual order in which the soul proceeds from one stage to the next. The text is just enumerating the various stages to which the soul attains (as one might enumerate them in the order they occur to the memory rather than in the order in which they occur in actual fact). In the Bṛhadāraṇyaka text, on the other hand, a definite order and succession is implied when there is mention of the Wind offering a hollow the size of the hollow in the hub of a chariot-wheel through which the soul passes upwards and emerges into the World of the Sun (āditya). Hence the author of the Sūtras was quite justified in saying (that the soul attained to the Wind after attaining to the Sun) 'because of absence of specification at one place and the presence of specification at the other'.

The Bṛhadāraṇyaka Upanishad, too, says 'From the (Six) Months (of the Northern Passage of the Sun) to the World of the Gods (deva-loka), from the World of the Gods to the Sun (āditya)'.[188] Here we must assume that the soul passes from the World of the Gods to the Wind, so that it passes directly from the Wind to the Sun. But when the author of the Sūtras now says 'Such an one attains to the Wind after attaining to the Year and before attaining to the Sun' he has the text from the Chāndogya in mind.[189] In this context, the Chāndogya omits the World of the Gods and the Bṛhadāraṇyaka omits the Year from the series. Because both texts are authoritative pieces of revelation, both the World of the Gods and the Year have to be interpolated where they have been omitted. And the year has to be taken as coming before the World of the Gods on account of its direct connection with the Six Months.

In the text 'He goes from the Sun to the Moon, from the Moon to the Lightning', Water (varuṇa) is to be inserted after this 'Lightning', on account of the text 'He goes to the world of Varuṇa'.[190] The World of Water belongs here as there is a connection between it and Lightning. For it is when great flashes of lightning are issuing from the entrails of the clouds and dancing to the deep music of the thunder that the rain begins to fall. And there is the text, 'People say "There is lightning and thunder, it will certainly rain",'[191] while the fact that the deity Varuṇa presides over water (and rain) is well attested by the Veda and derivative literature alike. Indra and Prajāpati must be placed after Lightning in the series, both on the strength of the order in which they are mentioned in the Kauṣītaki text and also because there is nowhere else they could go anyway. Varuṇa, Indra and Prajāpati must also be placed last because they are additions: no special place is allotted to them on the Path beginning with the Flame, which ends with Lightning.

In regard to the Flame and other stages of the Path, there arises the question whether they are 'Landmarks on the Path' or 'Places for Experiences' or 'Guides'. And one might *prima facie* suppose that they were Landmarks on the Path. One might suppose, that is, that one goes to the Flame and the rest in the same way as a person setting out to some town or village might be told. 'You go from here to that mountain and from there to a certain banyan tree and from there to the river, where you will find your town or village'. When the text says, 'From the Flame to the Day, from the Day to the Bright Lunar Fortnight (or Fortnight of the Waxing Moon)',[192] it means, you will say, something of this kind.

Or else you might take the line that the various stages on the Path were Places of Experience. For Fire (agni) and other stages are found connected in this context with the word 'world (loka)' (meaning 'realm of experience') as at 'He comes to the World of Fire (agni)'.[193] And the word 'world' (loka) is used to mean the 'realm of experience' of particular classes of living beings, as in such a text as, 'The World of Men, the World of the Ancestors and the World of the Gods'.[194] And there is also the Brāhmaṇa text, 'They (who perform rituals and prescribed symbolic meditations) become enmeshed in the Worlds of Day and Night'.[195] It follows (on the *prima facie* view) that the various stages cannot be Guides, which is confirmed by the fact that they are not conscious beings. For in the world guides are men possessed of consciousness and intelligence appointed by the king to take people over difficult routes.

To all this we reply that the various stages are Guides, for there is an indication that this is so. For we have the text, 'From the Moon they go to Lightning. There is there a superhuman Being who conducts them on to the Absolute (in its lower form)'.[196] This text assumes it to be well-known that they are Guides. Nor can you retort that this reference to a superhuman Being who acts as guide is debarred (by the reference to 'superhuman') from referring to anything else (so that only the superhuman Being would be a guide), for the word 'superhuman' is only intended to negate any wrong impression that the Being was human. It could therefore quite well be meant to negate any wrong impression that the Beings (puruṣa) in the Flame and the rest, which acted as guides, were human.

But a mere indication, you will say, proves nothing without a logical reason. For those on the Path beginning with the Flame have lost their physical bodies and, consequently, their senses and faculties are all closely confined and unable to act independently. Similarly the Flame and the rest, being non-conscious, are likewise incapable of independent action (i.e. can only act as instruments of some conscious agent who 'wields' them). Hence we reason logically that there must be certain deities who are appointed to descend into the Flame and the rest and enable the journey to proceed. Even in the world, drunkards and epileptics and the like find their senses and faculties blocked and are taken on their journey by others (by other conscious agents).

A reason why the Flame and the rest cannot be landmarks on the Path is that they are not all regularly present. One who dies at night cannot pass immediately to the Day. And we have already seen that there is no question of waiting.[197] But if by 'the Flame' and the rest we understand deities, these are ever-present and the difficulty does not arise. And the fact that the deities are referred to *as* the Flame and the rest is explicable if the deities have appropriated those entities. Nor do such expressions as 'He goes from the Flame to the Day' militate against the various stages of the journey being taken as themselves guides and conductors. For the expression could mean 'He reaches the Day through the instrumentality of the Flame',[198] and this would mean that he later reached the Bright Lunar Fortnight through the instrumentality of the Day. Even in ordinary worldly experience, one receives directions of a similar kind about guides whom one knows. People may go first to Balavarman and from him (i.e. through his guidance) to Jayasiṃha and from him (i.e. through his guidance) to Kṛṣṇagupta. Further, the beginning of the teaching speaks only of some relationship between the various stages of the journey, without specifying the nature of the relation — as when it says, 'They (who meditate) pass into the Flame (at death)'.[199] But at the conclusion it is said, 'He takes them to the world of Brahmā',[200] showing that the relation between the stages was one in which each was a Guide leading to the succeeding one. And (since no specification of the nature of the relation is offered at the beginning) one must assume that this was the idea meant at the beginning of the teaching too. And the voyagers could not have any enjoyments on the way, from the very fact of their senses being blocked. But the stages may be called 'worlds' even in reference to voyagers through them who cannot enjoy any experience in them, because they are places of experience for others who dwell there permanently. So one has to understand the meaning to be that, on this Path, after one has attained to the World over which Fire (agni) presides one is conveyed further by Fire, and that after one has attained the World over which the Wind (vāyu) presides one is led further by the Wind.

But, you might ask, on the view that the various stages are really deities conveying those on this Path further on, how could Varuṇa, Indra and Prajāpati form part of the series? For they are interpolated as coming after Lightning, and yet there is a text which says that it is the same one superhuman Being who conveys the souls all the way from Lightning to the World of Brahmā. To this the author of the Sūtras replies that we have to understand that they attained to the World of Brahmā through the superhuman Being who appears next after Lightning and operates in the Worlds of Varuṇa, Indra and Prajāpati alike. For there is a text which shows that he alone is the one who conducts them, namely 'That superhuman Being goes up to them in the realm of Lightning and conducts them to the World of Brahmā'.[201] As for Varuṇa, Indra and Prajāpati, it has to be understood that they help in some way, either by removing obstacles or by giving positive assistance. So it was but right to say that the Flame and the rest are deities who convey the soul on its course.

Next we examine the text, 'He leads them to the Absolute (brahman)'.[202] Does it mean the Absolute in its form as effect, or does it mean the Absolute in its supreme or true form, not subject to modification? The doubt arises because on the one hand the word 'Absolute' is used, whereas the text on the other hand mentions 'reaching' it.[203] The Teacher Bādari holds that the superhuman Being conveys his charges to the Absolute in its lower (apara) form, associated with finite qualities (saguṇa). This is because the Absolute in its form as effect has a particular position and so can be 'reached'. But one cannot conceive 'goerhood' or 'being-gone-to' or 'the-act-of-going' in relation to the Absolute in its highest form, for the Absolute in this form is all-pervasive and is also the inmost Self of the goer.[204]

There is another text, 'They live for extremely long periods in the Worlds of Brahmā',[205] which must refer to the Absolute in its form as effect, because, as the author of the Sūtras says, it is presented as something distinct. The Absolute in its supreme form cannot be made to undergo differentiation through application of the plural number,[206] while the Absolute in its form as effect can accept the plural, as it is subject to modification. The word 'world', too, can only apply within the realm of modification. It may be applied directly to a realm of experience which is subject to being 'entered'. When it is applied to the Absolute in its supreme form, as in the text 'This is the world of the Absolute, O Emperor',[207] that implies metaphorical speech usage. The distinction between souls living somewhere and the place where they live (in the above-quoted text 'they live for extremely long periods in the Worlds of Brahmā') cannot involve the Absolute in its supreme form. Hence it is to the Absolute in its form as effect that this 'leading' takes place.

Now it might be thought that the term 'the Absolute' (brahman) could not apply to anything that was an effect. For it has already been shown in the opening Sūtra of the Brahma Sūtras that the Absolute is the cause of the rise, maintenance and withdrawal of the entire universe. This doubt the author of the Sūtras rejects with the word 'But'. One may use the word 'Absolute' to designate the Absolute in its lower form without contradiction, because the latter is *similar* to the Absolute in its supreme form. For the orthodox doctrine is that it is the Absolute in its supreme form itself which is really being taught (i.e. when the Absolute in its form as effect is overtly being taught), in a few places only, and on the basis of association with apparent adjuncts (upādhi), and for the sake of meditation. It then has characteristics such as 'being composed of mind'[208] and others. As such, it becomes known as the Absolute in its 'lower form'.[209]

Here you might object that if it were only the Absolute in its form as effect that were attained, the text saying that there is no return from it would become indefensible. For eternal and changeless existence is not possible outside the Absolute. And the Veda does declare that those who go forth on the Path of the Gods do not return to the whirlpool of human life.[210] They do not have to return here, as is also the case in the text, 'Going up by that, he attains immortality'.[211]

Against this we reply as follows. When (towards the end of the world-period) the dissolution of the Absolute in its form as effect is at hand, they (the souls who have attained to it), having attained to right knowledge in the World of Brahmā, proceed, together with Hiraṇyagarbha,[212] the overseer of that world, to (as the author of the Sūtras puts it) 'something higher'. And that 'something higher' is the supremely pure 'Highest Abode of Viṣṇu'. Thus a liberation by stages (krama-mukti) has to be assumed, on account of the mention of non-return and other circumstances in certain Vedic texts.[213] For we have already explained how attainment of the Absolute in its supreme form is not strictly possible by a method that involves a journey.

The derivative literature also supports this view: 'When Cosmic Dissolution has come and Hiraṇyagarbha's days are at an end, then they all enter the supreme state along with Brahmā, having realized the Self'.[214]

This, then, is the settled conclusion. But what is the *prima facie* view against which it is being established, given in the Sūtras which follow the Sūtra that has given the final view in the words 'Bādari avers that it is the Absolute as effect that is meant, as in this context the mention of going is appropriate'?[215] The Sūtras themselves now give the answer to this question. They say, 'Jaimini (taught that it was) the Supreme, for that is the literal meaning'. By this they mean that Jaimini thought that the text 'He (the superhuman Being) conducts them on to the Absolute'[216] referred to the Absolute in its supreme form. And they add that the reason is that the term 'Brahman' refers primarily to the Absolute in its supreme form, and only metaphorically to the Absolute in its lower form (as effect), while the primary meaning is always to be preferred to the metaphorical one (in interpreting a term in the Veda, unless there is some reason to show that the primary meaning is impossible).

The supporters of this (Jaimini's) view claim that the Veda itself shows that immortality can result from 'going', in the text 'Going up through that one becomes immortal'.[217] And immortality is possible only in the case of the Absolute in its supreme form and not in its form as effect, the latter being subject to inevitable destruction, as we know from the text,

'But where one sees anything else, that is limited, that is mortal'.[218] And we find this same 'going' mentioned in the Kaṭha Upanishad with reference to the Absolute in its supreme form, as we know from the fact of the topic (of the Absolute in its supreme form) having been introduced in the words 'Other than good, other than evil'[219] and no other topic of meditation (such as would change the topic of the Absolute in its lower form) is introduced afterwards....

This view, however, is wrong. For the Absolute is not susceptible of being 'gone to', as there are texts like 'All-pervading, within all, the Self of all'[220] which specify all-pervasiveness and so render it impossible that anyone should 'go' to it. For it is recognized in the world that when there is 'going', that which goes must be different from that which it goes to.

You might object that in worldly experience one who has already gone to some place may still have going to do if he is to reach another part of it. A person already on the earth, for instance, may 'go to' the earth if he goes to a different part of it. It is also seen that a child has to 'attain' to his own nature as a grown-up at a later time, even though he is never different from his own nature. Why should it not be possible to 'attain' the Absolute in some such sense as this, seeing that it is 'possessed of all powers'?

But this objection is wrong, as all distinctions are denied of the Absolute in such texts as 'partless, actionless, at rest, faultless, stainless'.[221] Such texts of the Veda[222] and derivative literature preclude any possibility of attributing particularities of space or time to the highest Self, so that there can be no 'going' or 'attaining' to it in the way that one goes to a different part of the place one is in or attains to another age of life. Such a possibility is open in the case of places and stages of life, as places have particular parts, and stages of life particular different states....

But if the texts speaking of 'going' do not refer to any journey to the Absolute in its highest form, what do they refer to? We reply that they refer to the Path of Meditation on the Absolute as associated with qualities. A journey, for instance, is referred to in the context of the Meditation on the Five Fires,[223] in the Meditation on the Couch (Amitaujas),[224] in the Meditation on Vaiśvānara.[225] There are, of course, some passages in which a journey is mentioned in relation to the Absolute such as those beginning 'The Vital Energy is the Absolute, joy is the Absolute, the ether is the Absolute'[226] and 'Here in this city of the Absolute (i.e. in this body) is a house in the form of a small lotus'.[227] But here 'going' is possible because the subject-matter is meditation on the Absolute as associated with qualities, as the reference to such qualities as 'bountifulness' and 'possession of true desires'[228] shows. On the other hand, no Vedic text speaks of 'going' when the context is that of teaching the Absolute in its supreme form. In fact all possibility of 'going' is denied in this context in the text 'His Vital Energy does not depart upwards'.[229]

What then are we to make of such texts as 'The knower of the Absolute reaches the supreme'?[230] Here it is true that a word like 'reaching' implies going. But, as has already heen explained, there is here no question of attaining a new spatial position. The reference is therefore only to right apprehension of one's own true nature, and it is called 'reaching' because it implies the destruction of name and form set up by nescience. One has to understand this text in the light of such other texts as 'Being already the Absolute, he yet (in some sense) attains the Absolute'.[231]

(And these texts refer to one who already knows the Absolute), so what possible purpose could there be in speaking of a 'going' to the Absolute in its supreme form? Could it be to promote delight or to promote recollection? He who knows the Absolute would not find that his delight in the Absolute was in any way promoted by a statement about 'going there', as he is already familiar with the Absolute through self-luminous direct knowledge. Nor can knowledge which bears on the eternally present supreme good and has no further goal to aim at be in anyway connected with recollection of any act of going. Hence 'going' refers to the Absolute in its lower form. It is because people do not always distinguish between the higher and lower form of the Absolute that they incorrectly attribute the texts about 'going', which really refer to the lower Absolute, as if they were texts about the Absolute in its supreme form.

Are there then (in some sense) two Absolutes, a supreme (para) and a lower (apara)? Yes, certainly there are, as is shown by such texts as 'O Satyakāma, OM is verily both the supreme and the lower Absolute'.[232] What, then, is the supreme Absolute, and what the lower? We reply: wherever all particularities arising from name and form and the rest set up by nescience are negated, and negative terms like 'not gross' etc., are used, there the Absolute in its supreme form is being taught. When that same Absolute is declared, for purposes of meditation, to be characterized by some particular attribute of name and form and the rest, as in such words as 'made up of mind, having the Vital Energy for its body, of the nature of effulgent light',[233] there we have the lower Absolute.

But will not this contradict the texts which say that the Absolute is 'without a second'? No. Any such contention fails because the distinction depends on mere adjuncts of name and form set up by nescience. And the text near the instructions about meditation on the lower Absolute, beginning 'If he is desirous of the World of the Ancestors'[234] states a fruit for the meditation that lies within the realm of transmigratory life — namely, overseership of the universe. For the nescience of such an one will not have been brought to an end. Since he is bound to a particular spatial position, there is nothing contradictory in supposing him to 'go' to attain this fruit. We have already explained this in commenting on the Sūtra 'The soul is spoken of in this way because it is considered predominantly under the qualities of the intellect'.[235]

Hence we conclude that the only view that stands is that conveyed in the Sūtra 'Bādari holds that the superhuman Being conveys his charges to the Absolute in its lower form as effect'.[236] The Sūtra 'Jaimini thinks that it is the Absolute in its supreme form that is meant, since that is the primary meaning of the word "Brahman"'[237] should be seen to present a mere semblance of an alternative view to help deepen the student's understanding of the questions involved.

It is established, therefore, that 'going' implies going to the Absolute in its form as effect, not in its supreme form. Now the question is raised: Does the superhuman Being take without qualifications *all* those who take their stand on the

Absolute in its form as effect, or does he only take a few of them? And one might initially suppose that all persons (who had spiritual knowledge gained through prescribed meditations on the ritual), apart from those who knew the Absolute in its supreme form, might go to the World of Brahmā. For this is suggested by the Sūtra 'All meditations without restriction (lead to the Path of the Gods)'.[238] It is to oppose this idea that the present Sūtra gives the specification 'Those who do not use images and symbols'.[239] It begins, 'The Teacher Bādarāyaṇa[240] holds that the superhuman Being conducts all others who meditate on the Absolute in its form as effect to the World of Brahmā, excepting only those who depend on images and symbols'. Nor is there anything wrong in accepting such a distinction, the Sūtra argues, as the rule about 'All meditations without restriction (lead to the Path of the Gods)' properly refers to those meditations only which are not directed to images and symbols. (And, argues the Sūtra), the principle 'Whoso wills the Absolute attains the Absolute' supports the distinction. For it is quite comprehensible that he who wills the Absolute should acquire the glorious condition of the Absolute, as we have the Vedic text, 'In whatever way one meditates on Him, one becomes that'.[241] But in meditation on images and symbols this will to attain the Absolute is not present, as here it is the image or symbol that is the primary object of meditation.

But does the Veda teach that even he who has no will to attain the Absolute attains the Absolute? For we find in the passages on Meditation on the Five Fires such a text as 'He conducts them to the Absolute'.[242] We can admit that this is so in cases where the text goes out of its way to emphasize it.

But where no such special direction is forthcoming, the general rule, based on the principle of the will to attain the Absolute, holds — namely, that only those who will to attain the Absolute do attain it, and no one else.[243]

4. Supernormal Powers on the Indirect Path

The last chapter of the last Book of the Brahma Sūtras includes some accounts of supernormal powers that come to men practising the upanishadic meditations. As Śaṅkara classes these phenomena as occurrences pertaining to the gradual or deferred path to release, his account of them is placed here. The second Extract is in fact the closing passage of Śaṅkara's Brahma Sūtra Commentary.

TEXTS ON SUPERNORMAL POWERS ON THE INDIRECT PATH

1. It has been declared that the liberated man has a physical body in the words, 'Jaimini taught that the liberated man had a body and organs, because of the mention of choice'.[244] In this connection, do we have mention of the projection of soulless automatons like wooden puppets? Or are they ensouled bodies like ours? And one might initially suppose that, since neither the mind nor the soul can be divided up, they would be joined to one body only, while the other bodies would be soulless.

Against this, the author of the Sūtras says, 'Their entry (into their multiple bodies) is like that of a light'. That is, it is like the case of a single light which becomes many lights through its power of self-multiplication. In the same way, the one man of knowledge is possessed of supernormal powers and becomes many, entering all the bodies that he projects. We know this because the Veda tells us he becomes many in such passages as 'He becomes unitary, he becomes three-fold, he becomes five-fold, he becomes seven-fold, he becomes nine-fold'.[245] This text is inexplicable on the assumption that the bodies are inanimate puppets or on the assumption that they are animated by souls other than that of the man of knowledge himself. Nor can inanimate bodies engage in activity of any kind.

As for the objection that because the mind and the soul are not capable of division they cannot be joined to more than one body at the same time — this presents no difficulty. For the man of knowledge projects bodies with minds that follow his own mind through his power of being able to bring his mere wishes to fruition. And once he has projected them he can unite them with an animating soul through dividing his own soul on the basis of external adjuncts. And this is exactly the same procedure as that which is mentioned in the treatises on Yoga, which say that the Yogins can unite themselves with more than one body.[246]

But how can one accept that the liberated person could have supernormal powers enabling him to enter various bodies when there are passages in the Veda which deny that he has any particular knowledge, such as 'What then, should he know, and with what?', 'But no other thing apart from that exists that he should know anything as separate from that' and 'He becomes (transparent like) water, the One, the Seer, without a second'?[247]

To this the author of the Sūtra replies as follows. In his reply, the word 'svāpyayaḥ' refers to dreamless sleep. This is on the basis of the Vedic text 'He goes to his own Self (svam apīto) and therefore they say "he sleeps" (svapiti)'.[248] And by the word 'sampattiḥ' the author of the Sūtras means realization of one's true transcendent state (kaivalya), in consonance with the Vedic text 'Being already the Absolute, he "attains to" the Absolute'.[249] And the Sūtra says that absence of all particularized consciousness is predicated of both these two states (avasthā).

How do we know this? Because the Upanishad makes clear statements in this regard, as we see from such texts as 'He arose from these elements and is destroyed with them. There is no consciousness after death', 'But when all this has become his Self (then what should he see and with what?)', 'When he is asleep and has no desire and dreams no dream'.[250] But the present passage in the Sūtras is not treating of this. It is treating of the state that results like heaven and realization of one's identity with deities, from maturation of one's meditation on the Absolute as associated with limited form. And it is to *this* state (of maturation of meditation on the Absolute as associated with limited form and *not* to the state of direct and immediate liberation) that this supreme power (of projecting bodies and entering into them) is attributed. So there are no difficulties.

What then is the case with those who, together with their minds, attain proximity to the Lord through meditation on the Absolute as associated with limited forms? Does their sovereign power admit of limits or does it not? And one might initially suppose that it was limitless. For we have such texts as 'He attains spiritual sovereignty', 'All the gods bring him tribute' and 'They become able to move at will in all the worlds'.[251]

Against this the Sūtra runs, 'Except the government of the universe'. The liberated ones[252] have every supernormal power from that of voluntarily assuming a very small form onwards,[253] except that of governing the universe. The power of governing the universe belongs to the ever-perfect Lord alone. For He is, as the author of the Sūtra puts it, 'The one under discussion in the texts where the government of the universe crops up',[254] whereas other beings are not the main topic in these passages. Only the supreme Lord has the right to govern the universe, for creation, maintenance and dissolution of the universe are only taught when He is the chief topic under discussion. Also because He is associated with the word 'eternal', whereas the supernormal powers of others, such as that of making their bodies minute and the like, are taught as having to be preceded by enquiry and search.[255] In this sense, too, the others are remote from government of the universe. Moreover, because they each have a mind, they could each be of a different mind. There could be a conflict, where one wanted to keep the universe in being while another wanted to withdraw it. Since this conflict could be removed only if other wills conform to one will, it follows that all others must obey the will of the supreme Lord.

The next opinion which the author of the Sūtras has to refute is that which says that the sovereign power of those who have acquired knowledge is limitless, because there are texts such as 'He attains spiritual sovereignty'[256] which directly proclaim this to be the fact. This opinion, however, constitutes no serious objection, for the reference is to the one who controls all, abiding in the disc of the sun. The supreme Lord abides in the disc of the sun and other special abodes and controls all. This 'attaining to spiritual sovereignty' occurs under his control, which is why the text says immediately afterwards, 'He attains to the Lord of Mind'.[257] What this amounts to is that the lord of all minds is He who was ordained before them, the Lord; and the soul (eventually) attains to Him. It is in this sense that it is said immediately afterwards that the soul becomes the lord of speech, lord of hearing, lord of understanding.[258] In the same way, the passages mentioning other superhuman powers of the Lord must somehow or other be construed so that they are seen to arise under the control of the eternally perfect Lord.[259]

❖

2. Well, you might think that if this were so, the supernormal powers (of the man of knowledge) will be a matter of degree and hence non-eternal, so that the man who acquired them would have to return to earth. To this the holy Teacher Bādarāyaṇa[260] makes the following reply.

There are those who go to the world of Brahmā as described in the Veda by the Path of the Gods, which has its stages beginning with that of the Flame, and is associated with the subtle bodily canals and the rays of the sun.[261] Of the World of Brahmā it is said, 'Ara and Ṇya are two oceans in the World of Brahmā, the third heaven from here. And there is the lake Airammadīya and the Fig Tree showering Soma and the fortress of Brahmā called Aparājitā and a golden palace made by Brahmā himself'.[262] And it has been described in different ways in various places in the verse and prose of the Veda. Those who attain to that world do not return to this world after enjoying the experiences allotted to them, while those who proceed to the World of the Moon do return.

How do we know this? On account of such texts as, 'Passing upwards by means of that, he attains immortality', 'They do not return', 'Those who proceed by this Path do not return to the human whirlpool', 'He reaches the Worlds of Brahmā, he does not return'.[263] Although their supernormal powers come to an end, yet it is stated in the text that they do not return to earth, as has been shown in the Sūtra, 'When the universe dissolves (at the end of the world-period) he proceeds higher, in company with the Lord of that World (i.e. Brahmā)'.[264] They do not return because their ignorance becomes destroyed by right knowledge and they become established in that dissolution of the individual personality (nirvāṇa) which is the eternally true fact (nitya-siddha). It is through conversion to this ideal that even those who resort to the Absolute as associated with finite forms can avoid returning to the earth.

The Sūtra repeats twice the words 'They do not return, because this is what the Veda teaches' to show that this is the end of the Brahma Sūtras.[265]

NOTES TO CHAPTER XIV

References to Extracts are in bold type

1 Above, Vol.V, 312f.

2 *Ibid.*

3 B.S.Bh. III.iii.1 (*ad fin.*), III.iii.33 (*ad fin.*), III.iii.44 (*ad fin.*), III.iii.50 (*ad fin.*).

4 Chapter XV, section 2.

5 Aitareya Brāhmaṇa III.viii.1.

6 *Ibid.*

7 Chānd. V.vii.1, see also V.viii.1.

8 B.S.Bh. I.i.4.

9 Govindānanda instances: 'Name is the Absolute' (Chānd. VII. i.5) as an example of symbolic meditation (pratīka-upāsana) leading to the explicitly stated worldly reward of acquiring the power to go wherever one wills; meditations like that on the Absolute present in the ether of the cave of the heart (B.S. I.iii.14-21, Chānd. VIII.i.1ff.) which lead to gradual release, krama-mukti; meditations (dhyāna) on the Udgītha and other texts in the ritual which lead to the enhancement of merit arising from the performance of the ritual.

10 Untraced.

11 Chānd. III.xiv.1.

12 Bh.G. VIII.6.

13 Aitareya Āraṇyaka II.iii.2.1.

14 Bh.G. X.41.

15 B.S. I.i.20-21.

16 Occurring at Chānd. I.vi.6.

17 B.S. I.i.22, cp. B.S.Bh. I.i.22 *ad fin*. The phrase 'kham brahma' (Bṛhad. V.i.1), literally 'Brahman is the ether', is widely interpreted today as 'All is Brahman', and is used as a theme of affirmation and meditation. Śaṅkara's interpretation is not fundamentally at variance with this, but is more complex. See Bṛhad.Bh. V.i.1, trans. Mādhavānanda, 562f.

18 That is, whether the text is not simply stating the nature of a conditioned form of the Absolute as such.

19 B.S.Bh. I.i.11.

20 I.e. in the early parts of Chānd. from the beginning up to the end of the fifth chapter.

21 Chānd. III.xiv.2.

22 That is, they have to be given in private, preferably away from human settlements and in the open forest, and only to qualified and disciplined students.

23 That is, as opposed to the physically performed ritual.

24 Which might be said to begin with the teachings of Uddālaka to his son Śvetaketu at the beginning of the sixth chapter.

25 Chānd. Bh. I.i.1 (introduction).

26 What would in later times have been called the Upāsana Kāṇḍa.

27 Bṛhad. IV.i.2.

28 Bṛhad. III.ix.20. **Bṛhad. Bh. I.iii.9.**

29 *Viz.* the Upāsana Kāṇḍa.

30 Chānd. III.xiv.2.

31 Chānd. IV.x.4.

32 Chānd. VIII.i.5.

33 I.e. without necessarily adhering to one ritual, also applicable in the case of the meditations.

34 Chānd. III.xiv.4.

35 Bṛhad. IV.i.3.

36 Bh.G. VIII.6.

37 B.S.Bh. III.iii.59.

38 Chānd. III.xviii.1, III.xix.1, VII.i.5.

39 As long as one is obeying instructions one is an agent. It is contradictory to identify oneself with the Absolute through a symbol while one is still affirming in practice that one is an agent.

40 B.S.Bh. IV.i.4.

41 Chānd. III.xix.1, Kauṣītaki II.2, Bṛhad. V.vii.1.

42 The immediately preceding Extract.

43 'The pot is (now) clay' would mean the pot was destroyed.

44 Cp. Kaṭha I.i.7.

45 Reading utkṛṣṭa-dṛṣṭes teṣv adhyāsāt.

46 I.e. they cannot be statements of the form 'The sun is the Absolute' as the sun and the Absolute, as such, are clearly different.

47 The word 'iti' (as) is also present at Chānd. III.xix.1, Kauṣītaki II.2 and Bṛhad. V.vii.1, the three places mentioned above.

48 Chānd. III.xix.4, VII.ii.2, VII.iv.3.

49 See above, Vol.II, 49ff.

50 Chānd. I.iii.1. Certain parts of the ritual in its more elaborate form, especially the pressing of the soma plant, were accompanied by hymns (stotra) sung by the Udgātṛ priests of the

Sāma Veda tradition, and the Chāndogya Upanishad is amongst the texts handed down by these priests. Each hymn was divided into five sections, of which the Udgītha was the third. Sometimes the syllable OM was inserted before the Udgītha, and at Chand. I.i.1, OM is identified with the Udgītha on this ground. See Deussen, *Sechzig Upanishad's,* 66ff.

51 Chānd. II.ii.1. Five parts of the cosmos and five parts of the Sāma Veda are mentioned. The question is being raised whether it is the parts of the Sāma Veda that have to be meditated on as the parts of the cosmos or *vice versa.*

52 Chānd. II.viii.1. On the 'five parts' and the 'seven parts' of the Sāma Veda, cp. Deussen *loc. cit.*

53 Chānd. I.vi.1.

54 Chānd. VIII.i.5, VIII. vii.1, Bṛhad. IV.iii.21.

55 Chānd. I.vi.1.

56 Whereas no advantage could be expected from meditating on the sun as the Udgītha, because the sun is not a part of the sacrificial ritual leading to merit.

57 In this case, of the identity of the Udgītha with OM. Deussen, *op. cit.* p.67. The word used for 'secret correspondences' here is 'upanishad'. Proof of the early use of the word in this sense is given at Silburn, 62.

58 Chānd. I.i.10.

59 Chānd. II.ii.1. Cp. the previous reference earlier in the present Extract.

60 In the course of a certain sacrifice, the sacrificer is enjoined to fetch a milk-pail if he wants cattle. It seems as if the milk-pail would directly serve the sacrificer by being the occasion for his receiving cattle. But the P.M. decides that it is the fetching and not the pail that contributes to the sacrificer's future welfare,

and that it does so as a ritualistic act forming a subordinate part of the larger sacrifice in which he is engaged. Cp. Āpa Deva, trans. Edgerton, 141. Here, the meditations would seem at first sight to bear their own fruit. But on the analogy of the milk-pail injunction, it turns out that they can only be performed by a qualified agent performing some Vedic sacrifice, and that their good results arise not directly and independently from themselves but through their enhancing the merit arising from the ritualistic sacrifice.

61 Chānd. I.i.1 and I.i.10.

62 Chānd. I.iii.1ff.

63 Chānd. I.vi.1.

64 Ānandagiri instances 'the chestnut is trotting' (for 'the chestnut horse is trotting') as close, and 'fire is reciting the texts' (for 'the fiery student is reciting the texts') as remote.

65 Where a meditation is expressed in the words 'This (earth) is the Ṛk', one might either meditate on the earth as the Ṛk or on the Ṛk as the earth. Śaṅkara says that the insertion of the word 'eva' (verily) immediately after the word 'this' (earth) shows that it is the Ṛk that has to be meditated on as the earth. Had the word 'eva' been placed immediately after the word 'Ṛk' it would have meant that the earth had to be meditated on as the Ṛk.

66 Chānd. I.vii.9.

67 B.S.Bh. IV.i.5-6.

68 At B.S.Bh. IV.i.1.

69 Bṛhad. IV.iv.2.

70 Praśna III.10.

71 See Bṛhad. IV.iv.3, discussed above, Vol.V, 37f.

72 Ś.B. X.vi.3.1.

73 Bh.G. VIII.6 and 10.

74 Chānd. III.xvii.6. **B.S.Bh. IV.i.12.**

75 Cp. above, Vol.II, 184f.

76 The subtle canal whereby the soul passes out through the crown of the head at death. Cp. above, Vol.V, 59.

77 Chānd. VI.ii.1 and VII.xxv.2: i.e. 'all this' (the world) is not self-existent and is in fact nothing but an appearance of the transcendent, immutable principle of reality, the Self.

78 The translation follows the avidyādi-śeṣa of the Ā.Ś.S. text, although Ānandagiri's Commentary printed below it reads avidyā-viśeṣa. The 'remnant of nescience' (avidyā-śeṣa, avidyā-leśa, avidyā-saṃskāra), which accompanies the man of enlightenment and provides for his empirical experiences until the death of the body, is referred to by Śaṅkara at B.S.Bh. IV.i.15 (Gambhīrānanda, 840), though at Bh.G.Bh. XVIII.48 he refutes the doctrine, using the same example to refute it as he uses to establish it at B.S.Bh. IV.i.15 — that of a person cured of a disease causing him to see the one moon as many. In the one case the impressions of his former erroneous experience are taken as abolished once and for all (like the illusions of a man cured of squinting), in the other as persisting for a time (equally 'like the illusions of a man cured of squinting'). Somehow the former erroneous impressions linger on, though weakly, in the memory. Here in the present Extract, the 'etc.' of 'nescience, etc.' probably refers to egoism, attachment, aversion and clinging to life as mentioned along with nescience at Yoga Sūtra II.3. This is how the phrase avidyādi-doṣa (defects such as nescience, etc.) is explained by Ānandagiri at Chānd. Bh. III.xiv.2.

79 Chānd. Bh. VIII.i.1.

80 Sureśvara explains that this state is not equivalent to liberation, being a *result* obtained from meditation and rituals, and hence impermanent, B.B.V. I.v.341.

81 Bṛhad. Bh. I.v.20.

82 Bṛhad. Bh. I.v.23.

83 Mahar, here identified with Hiraṇyagarbha, is one of the seven 'worlds' or planes of divine consciousness which begin with 'Bhūr'. The names of these worlds, considered mystically as invocations of the deities presiding over them, are called 'vyāhṛtis', a word that could here be translated 'invocations' or 'invocatory words'. From the physical standpoint, Bhūr is the earth on which we stand, Bhuvaḥ is the space between the earth and the 'roof' of the sky, the space where the gods and heavenly beings move about, while Svaḥ is the immobile, infinite sea of light beyond the roof of the sky. In this particular text, 'Bhūr' is presided over by the fire-deity, Agni, Bhuvaḥ by the wind deity, Vāyu, and Svaḥ by the deity of the sun. Cp. below, Notes 90 and 91.

84 The Śālagrāma is a black ammonite stone found by the Gaṇḍakī river north of Patna. It is worshipped in its natural state as a symbol of Viṣṇu.

85 See below.

86 Through a feeling of identification — an intuitive, self-identifying kind of knowledge, not a rational subject-object kind of knowledge.

87 The name of the great Vedic deity is used here to indicate the Self.

88 Sac remarks that this nāḍī is also referred to at Kaṭha II.iii.16, Praśna III.7 and Chānd. VIII.vi.6. The reference is not to Haṭha Yoga treatises as we know them, for they trace the suṣumnā, not (in the upanishadic manner) as running up from the heart. but from the base of the spine.

89 The word for 'spiral out' is 'vivartate', which Śaṅkara takes over from the upanishadic text under comment. 'Vivartate' and 'Vivarta' did not originally have any connotation of illusion. We do not find either of them used to mean illusory change as contrasted with 'empirically real' change, or with change in which the effect is of the same reality-grade as its cause, in the writings of Śaṅkara and Sureśvara. Cp. above, Vol.II, Chapter V, Note 86.

90 There is a distinction between three worlds with Agni presiding over this world here below at Ś.B. XI.ii.3.1, cp. Oldenberg, 56f.

91 'Suvaḥ' is an alternative form of 'svaḥ'. The same three deities are assigned to the same three worlds at Ś.B. XI.ii.3.1. The reference here is to successive courses of meditation (upāsana).

92 The text says 'brahman' throughout, meaning the 'lower Brahman', Hiraṇyagarbha.

93 Not absolute sovereignty, but the sovereignty of the god in the disk of the sun. Here he enjoys all powers except those of projecting, maintaining and withdrawing the universe. Cp. B.S.Bh. IV.iv.17, 18. Sac.

94 mūrtāmūrta, cp. Bṛhad. II.iii.1ff.

95 Sac connects this with a passage of Bṛhad. Bh. I.iv.2 (trans. Mādhavānanda, 67f.)

96 Cp. above, towards the beginning of the Extract.

97 A metre of 5 feet having 8 syllables each.

98 It has five necessary factors — the sacrificer, his wife, his son, divine wealth (merit arising from meditation on the symbolic significance of the ritual) and worldly wealth (needed to assemble the materials required for the physical performance of the sacrifice).

99 Bṛhad. I.iv.17.

100 Taken as 'Virāṭ', or the totality of matter.

101 Skin, flesh, muscle, bone and marrow.

102 Reading upalabhate with Sac.

103 Taitt. Bh. I.6 and 7.

104 Kaṭha II.iii.14.

105 Bṛhad. IV.iv.6.

106 Kaṭha I.i.13ff.

107 Generic for a very large number, cp. Chānd. Bh. VIII.vi.6. Sac.

108 Cp. Note 88 above.

109 The process is described in more detail at Bh.G.Bh. VIII.10.

110 V.P. II.viii.97, quoted also below, cp. Notes 125, 132 and 164.

111 I.e. at the time of the dissolution of the world of Brahmā at the end of the world-period.

112 As described in Chānd. VIII.v.3 and 4. Sac.

113 The subtle canal called the Suṣumnā, as understood in the upanishadic manner by Śaṅkara, leads up from the heart centre out through the crown of the head and on to Satya Loka or the World of Brahmā, with which it is connected. There are other subtle canals which lead out of the body to the other 'worlds'. Cp. Bṛhad. Bh. IV.iv.9.

114 Kaṭha Bh. II.iii.16.

115 Above, Vol.V, 40f.

116 Cp. above, Vol.V, 21. The Path of the Ancestors is described there at length, 22ff. The soul is in company with the ancestors on the moon. The Path of the Gods is about to be described now. According to the original conception, the soul on the

funeral pyre either ascended in the smoke from the pyre to the realm of the ancestors on the moon, or else ascended on the flame rising up from the pyre to the realm of the gods beyond the sun.

117 Chānd. V.iv.1 - viii.2.

118 Bṛhad. IV.iv.6. This argumentation is needed because the expression 'World of Brahman' (indistinguishable in Sanskrit orthography from 'World of Brahmā') can mean the Absolute in its supreme form, cp. Bṛhad. IV.iii.32.

119 Adopting the reading gamanāya for agamanāya from Ānandagiri's second explanation.

120 Bṛhad. I.iv.15.

121 Chānd. Bh. IV.xv.5.

122 Professor Hacker has argued that faith (śraddhā) could be regarded as a sort of tapas or ascetic practice because it is a 'mental effort'. *Kleine Schriften*, 475. But see also Note 146 below in the present work.

123 Cp. Chānd. V.xxiv.2.

124 Living in villages one has a wife, and the religious student has no wife. Nor does he live in the forest, as he lives in the house of his Teacher. Ānandagiri.

125 See V.P. II.viii.92 and 94.

126 They have no need to have a knowledge of the Five Fires as they will go on the Path of the Sun (or Flame) anyway. Ānandagiri.

127 The same as the Path of the Flame.

128 A wandering ascetic would not normally be cremated.

129 Quotation untraced.

130 Untraced.

131 Bṛhad. I.iv.15.

132 V.P. II.viii.97. The phrase translated here 'authors of the Purāṇas' may really intend to attribute them to one author, Vyāsa, using an honorific plural.

133 I.e, because the forest-dwellers do have to obtain knowledge if they are to have immortality in the full sense.

134 Chānd. VIII.xv.1, IV.xv.5. The objector quotes texts which he thinks imply complete immortality for the celibate even without knowledge.

135 According to Ānandagiri, Śaṅkara is arguing that they might return in the next world-period.

136 That is, the opponent cannot return to his theme that the texts say that the celibate ones go to immortality in the full sense on the ground that in the phrase 'do not return to this whirlpool here' (Chānd. IV.xv.5) the 'this' and the 'here' are so general in meaning as to be meaningless, so that the phrase would mean 'do not return anywhere at all'.

137 I.e. to Brahma Loka.

138 Bṛhad. IV.iv.6, I.iv.10, IV.iv.6, III.ii.11. Read samavalīyante (are dissolved in).

139 At Bṛhad. III.ii.11.

140 Śaṅkara is trying to show that 'going' on the Northern Path after death does not apply to the man of enlightenment, but does apply to the celibate or wandering ascetic who has not acquired enlightenment, and also to householders of a certain class.

141 So that, as in the context of liberation the Veda speaks of the dissolution of the Vital Energies, it follows that liberation and the departure of the soul at death by the Northern Path must be two different things.

142 Kaṭha II.iii.16.

143 Chānd. VIII.v.3 and 4.

144 Bṛhad. VI.ii.2. **Chānd. Bh. V.x.1 and 2.**

145 Renunciates here means those observing the formal rules of 'saṃnyāsa' as a 'stage of life' (āśrama) as laid down in the Law Books.

146 Faith (śraddhā) is interpreted in the same way at Chānd. Bh. V.x.2 and Bṛhad. Bh. VI.ii.15.

147 Śaṅkara's most detailed account of this path appears below, Extract 7.

148 Cp. above, 31.

149 Bṛhad. V.iv.1.

150 Muṇḍ. III.ii.2.

151 Muṇḍ. III.ii.5.

152 Because the lower meditations lead to the attainment of the 'worlds' of deities, and Muṇḍ. I.ii.12 will show that the enquiry into immediate liberation cannot begin until desire for these worlds has been given up. Sac.

153 Manu Smṛti XII.50. From Śaṅkara's standpoint, the 'worlds' of Marīci and Yama would be within the realm of transmigration, while that of Brahmā would not. Cp. above, 30. For Śaṅkara, Brahmā, Cosmic Intellect (mahat), Cosmic Vital Energy (prāṇa) and the Unmanifest Principle (avyakta) were all closely related terms. At Bṛhad. Bh. I.vi.1 he says that this universe of ends and means has realization of one's identity with the Cosmic Vital Energy as its highest end (liberation being a goal falling outside the universe) and the Unmanifest Principle as its seed or origin. **Muṇḍ. Bh. I.ii.11.**

154 According to Sac, B.R.V., 104, this should not be taken literally. It means that even while living with his family, the spiritual seeker practises as much as he can of the life and duties of a retired forest-dweller and a wandering ascetic.

155 This appears to be a forced interpretation of the text, as the latter is speaking of harmlessness except at the sacrificial altar, where beasts may be sacrificed. Śaṅkara himself quotes it in the correct sense at B.S.Bh. II.iii.44.

156 E.g. Chānd. IV.xv.5, Bṛhad. VI.ii.15.

157 Chānd.Bh. VIII.xv.1.

158 Those engaged in a life of meditation in caves and distant solitary places as taught in the sixth chapter of the Gītā.

159 I.e. the deities in question have other functions apart from determining time, but their importance in the present context lies in their determining time.

160 B.S. IV.iii.4ff. Cp. present section, 58. There is a hint here that Śaṅkara had written his B.S.Bh. before his Gītā Commentary, seeing that the present Extract is from the latter.

161 The term 'liberated while alive', jīvan-mukta, common among Śaṅkara's followers and used by his contemporary, Maṇḍana Miśra, seems to be found only once in Śaṅkara's probably authentic works, *viz.* at Bh.G.Bh. VI.27. But Sac explains that 'immediate liberation' (sadyo-mukti) in Śaṅkara is the same as the 'liberation while yet alive' (jīvan-mukti) of the later writers. See his Kleśāpahāriṇī Commentary on Sureśvara's N.Sid. IV.60. An important text for this terminological question is B.S.Bh. IV.i.15.

162 Bṛhad. IV.iv.6.

163 Bh.G.Bh. VIII.23-26.

164 Mādhavānanda Svāmin points out the connection with V.P. II.viii.92 and 94.

165 Cp. above, Vol.V, 22ff.

166 Their bodies are not burnt on a pyre, for instance, as those of householders are.

167 Chānd. VIII.vi.5.

168 Bṛhad.Bh. VI.ii.15.

169 Chānd. VIII.vi.5.

170 Bṛhad. VI.ii.15, Chānd. V.x.1.

171 Kauṣītaki I.3.

172 Bṛhad. V.x.1.

173 Muṇḍ. I.ii.11.

174 Chānd. VIII.vi.5.

175 *Ibid.*

176 Bṛhad. VI.ii.15. Cp. previous Extract.

177 That is, there is no logical impropriety if the phrase 'the Flame' is used to indicate the Wind and Fire, while Fire and the Wind are elsewhere used to indicate the Flame. This is because the various stages of the Path are used at different parts of the Veda to indicate the whole Path, including the other stages. Thus if the Path begins with the Flame, there is no contradiction if Bṛhad. V.x.1 says that the soul at death proceeds to the Wind, as the term 'the Wind' here means the whole Path beginning with the Flame.

178 I.e. each time in any separate passage any part of the Path is mentioned, the whole Path as gathered from all the relevant texts is being referred to.

179 Bṛhad. VI.ii.15. Deussen claims that the phrase parāḥ parāvataḥ originally meant not 'extremely long periods' but '(inhabit) extremely wide spaces'. He quotes R.V. X.58.11, *Sechzig Upanishad's*, 508.

180 Bṛhad. V.x.1, Kauṣītaki I.7, Chānd. VIII.iv.3.

181 Chānd. VIII.vi.5. Cp. opening of the present Extract.

182 By the objector earlier in the Extract, quoting the same Chānd. passage.

183 Chānd. V.x.8.

184 Kauṣītaki I.3.

185 Chānd. V.x.1 and 2.

186 Bṛhad. V.x.1.

187 Kauṣītaki I.3.

188 Bṛhad. VI.ii.15.

189 I.e. Chānd. V.x.1.

190 Chānd. IV.xv.5.

191 Chānd. VII.xi.1.

192 Chānd. V.x.1.

193 Kauṣītaki I.3.

194 Bṛhad. I.v.16.

195 Ś.B. X.ii.6.8.

196 Chānd. IV.xv.5.

197 B.S.Bh. IV.ii.19.

198 Chānd. V.x.1.

199 *Ibid.*

200 Chānd. V.x.2.

201 Bṛhad. VI.ii.15.

202 Chānd. IV.xv.5.

203 The Absolute in its pure form exists everywhere and so is obviously not capable of being 'reached'.

204 As such, it is not capable of being 'gone to', for nothing can be agent and object of the same act.

205 Bṛhad. VI.ii.15.

206 As in the phrase translated here 'the Worlds of Brahmā'. When forming part of a grammatical compound, the words of Brahmā and Brahman are identical in classical Sanskrit. So Śaṅkara is here saying that the words 'brahma-loka' in the present context cannot mean 'Worlds of the Absolute', as the Absolute in its supreme form cannot be associated with plurality. It can only refer to the Absolute 'in its form as effect', which is personified as Brahmā.

207 Bṛhad. IV.iv.23, cp. B.S.Bh. I.iii.15.

208 Chānd. III.xiv.2.

209 In other words, the Absolute in its lower or 'effect' form (apara-brahman) *is* the Absolute in its supreme form, only viewed under external adjuncts which give it the appearance of a limited form without touching its real nature. The Absolute in its supreme form (para-brahman) and the Absolute in its lower form (apara-brahman) are not two separate entities, respectively cause and effect. They are the same entity viewed respectively as free from and encased in adjuncts.

210 Chānd. IV.xv.5.

211 Chānd. VIII.vi.6. 'That is the subtle canal leading upwards from the heart, the Suṣumnā'. Ānandagiri says that these texts are quoted to show that even texts speaking of 'no-return' still imply only passage to the Absolute in its form as effect, not its supreme form.

212 Taken as identical with Brahmā.

213 That is, because some texts combine 'attaining' the Absolute with non-return from the Absolute, we have to assume that they mean attaining to the Absolute in its lower form, from which there is a 'proceeding' to the Absolute in its supreme form. The Absolute in its supreme form is also involved because from going anywhere else there must be some form of return. Because these texts refer by implication to the Absolute both in its form as effect and in its supreme form, they refer to a form of liberation that takes place by stages (krama-mukti).

214 Swami Gambhīrānanda cites Kūrma Purāṇa, Pūrva Bhāga XII.269.

215 Bhāskara, Rāmānuja, Vallabha and Nimbārka all take Bādari's doctrine as the *prima facie* view. It is indeed against usual precedent to state the settled conclusion (siddhānta) before the statement of any *prima facie* view, and Śaṅkara's handling of this topic does give the impression that his own view leaned towards that of Bādari and differed from that of the last redactor of the Sūtras.

216 Chānd. IV.xv.5.

217 Chānd. VIII.vi.6.

218 Chānd. VII.xxiv.1.

219 Kaṭha I.ii.14.

220 Bṛhad. III.iv.1. Śaṅkara quotes more of this text here, and also from Chānd. VII.xxv.2 and Muṇḍ. II.ii.11.

221 Śvet. VI.19.

222 Śaṅkara also quotes here from Bṛhad. III.viii.8, Muṇḍ. II.i.2, Bṛhad. IV.iv.25 and III.ix.26.

223 Chānd. V.iii-x and Bṛhad. VI.ii.

224 Kauṣītaki I. 3 and 5.

225 Chānd. V.xi.1 - V.xxiv.5.

226 Chānd. IV.x.4.

227 Chānd. VIII.i.1.

228 Chānd. IV.xv.3, VIII.i.5.

229 Bṛhad. IV.iv.6.

230 Taitt. II.1.

231 Bṛhad. IV.iv.6.

232 Praśna V.2.

233 Chānd. III.xiv.2.

234 Chānd. VIII.ii.1.

235 B.S. II.iii.29. On this much-discussed Sūtra, cp. above, Vol.III, 2 and 24ff.

236 B.S. IV.iii.7.

237 B.S. IV.iii.12.

238 B.S. III.iii.31.

239 B.S. IV.iii.15.

240 It is clear that this Sūtra, at least, was not composed by Bādarāyaṇa.

241 This text is not traceable amongst the extant Upanishads, but Śaṅkara quotes it also at B.S.Bh. I.i.11, there in conjunction with Chānd. III.xiv.1.

242 Chānd. IV.xv.5, V.x.2.

243 B.S.Bh. IV.iii.1-15.

244 B.S. IV.iv.11.

245 Chānd. VII.xxvi.2.

246 Y.S. III.38, cp. B.S.Bh. I.iii.27.

247 Brhad. IV.v.15, IV.iii.30, IV.iii.32.

248 Chānd. VI.viii.1.

249 Bṛhad. IV.iv.6.

250 Bṛhad. II.iv.12-4, IV.iii.19.

251 Taitt. I.vi.2, T.S. I.v.3, Chānd. VII.xxv.2, VIII.i.6.

252 I.e. liberated in stages through krama-mukti, not liberated in life.

253 Y.S. III.45 (in some editions 44).

254 Rāmānuja quotes creation-texts in his commentary to this passage: Taitt. III.i.1, Chānd. VI.ii.1, Bṛhad. I.iv.11, III.vii.3, etc.

255 Being preceded by enquiry and search they cannot be eternal, and not being eternal they cannot be natural.

256 Taitt. I.vi.2.

257 *Ibid.*

258 *Ibid.*

259 B.S.Bh. IV.iv.15-18.

260 Elsewhere in the B.S., Bādarāyaṇa is referred to as one of a group of rival earlier authorities. But Śaṅkara's naming of him here, in his commentary to the very end of the work and at a place where he is not named in the Sūtra itself, seems to show that Śaṅkara regarded him as the author of the Sūtras.

261 Cp. Chānd. VIII.vi.2.

262 Chānd. VIII.v.3.

263 Chānd. VIII.vi.6, Bṛhad. VI.ii.15, Chānd. IV.xv.5, VIII.xv.1.

264 B.S. IV.iii.10.

265 B.S.Bh. IV.iv.22.

CHAPTER XV

THE DIRECT PATH

1. ADHYĀTMA YOGA

In the present chapter we reach the heart of Śaṅkara's mystical teaching. The purpose of all that has preceded the Extracts in the present chapter has been to clear the way for them. The upward path to the temple gates has now been completed, and we have now to open them and make our way through the corridors into the silence of the innermost shrine. The various sections of the present chapter each have both a doctrinal and a spiritual content. They describe the final steps that have to be taken to intensify the spiritual life to the point where the student becomes capable of receiving the highest upanishadic texts from the Teacher. They describe the communication of the supreme text 'That thou art'. And they also describe the highest phases of reflection and meditation which enable the student to assimilate the final upanishadic wisdom and pass beyond the realm of dogma and doctrine to that of immediate certitude and direct intuition.

There seems to be no definite authority in Śaṅkara's texts for arranging the various final items in a series of stages forming an ascending path. On the one hand 'hearing, cogitation and sustained meditation' appear to form such an ascending series. On the other hand intuitive knowledge is by definition immediate and must either spring up or not spring up immediately on hearing the supreme text, according to whether the hearer is or is not sufficiently prepared to be capable of it. And then again, Brahma Sūtra IV.i.1 recommends 'repetition of the discipline'. Śaṅkara's solution of this apparent *impasse* is to prescribe repetition of the whole discipline of hearing, reflection and sustained meditation until, through the gradual shedding of all misconceptions, there comes a time when the hearer attains to immediate intuition on hearing the text for the last time. As there is from then on nothing further to be said, the sections of the present chapter will be arranged in the order in which they concern the one still striving for knowledge (jijñāsu). The first two sections will deal with the preparatory intensification of the spiritual life in the realm of mental concentration (adhyātma-yoga) and self-dedication to the Lord (bhakti-yoga). The third section will treat of hearing the supreme text 'That thou art', the fourth will deal with the 'assimilative' disciplines of reflection (vicāra) and meditative affirmation (abhyāsa, dhyāna, nididhyāsana), and the fifth with the concomitant discipline, much stressed by Śaṅkara, of meditation on the sacred syllable OM.

The opening section deals with the topic of 'yoga' as Śaṅkara conceived it. This is not the 'Rāja-yoga' taught in the classical Yoga Sūtras of Patañjali, where the goal may either be supernormal perception or supernormal powers — but only *within* the phenomenal world — or the complete *suppression* of all the activities of the mind. Such achievements, even if attainable, would be no substitute for the enlightenment taught on the upanishadic path.[1] Śaṅkara's conception of yoga comes directly from the 'middle' Upanishads, where it is named 'adhyātma-yoga'.[2] The gist of the Extracts on this topic is as follows. Practical realization of one's identity with the supreme Self does not normally arise without the three-fold discipline of hearing, cogitating over and meditating on the highest texts of the Upanishads. The Self is already self-evident and is reflected in the mind, but it is overlaid and hidden by the deposits (saṃskāra) arising from our self-interested thoughts and actions. Hence the Kaṭha Upanishad says it is 'hard to perceive', 'hidden in the cave'.[3] The discipline recommended by this Upanishad is 'adhyātma-yoga', that 'spiritual discipline' whereby one withdraws the mind from sense-objects and concentrates it on the Self. The lower faculties of the mind must be restrained until gradually a concrete sense of one's identity with the supreme Self is attained.

Śaṅkara explains the stages of adhyātma-yoga at the end of his commentary to Brahma Sūtra I.iv.1.[4] In the first stage, the active functions of the body such as speech are 'merged in mind'. That is to say, the yogi has to give up all external sense-activity and remain identified with the mind. The mind, however, may revolve round objects. This activity also should be given up, and one should remain identified with the spirit of discrimination latent in the mind. Then one should abandon the sense of identity with an individual mind altogether and rest in a sense of identity with the collective mind from which all comes forth, Hiraṇyagarbha. Finally one should pass beyond identification with Hiraṇyagarbha to the Self in its form as pure inactivity and peace.

When the mind is at rest and has no false fantasies, it in some sense 'knows' the Self. The one liberated in life is aware of the presence of the Self 'in the heart-centre' and *through the mind.* It is not that the mind knows the Self as an object. But when the mind is freed from all passions and impurities, the Self stands self-illuminated. When the mind is absolutely still and 'no longer manifests the form of any illusory object...' it has assumed the nature of the Absolute (brahman). One who is 'established in yoga' in this sense gives up all individual desires and purposes and consequently cannot properly be said to act.

TEXTS ON ADHYĀTMA YOGA

1. Therefore the Self is to be seen, to be made an object of direct vision. First it has been heard — heard from the Teacher and from the Vedic texts as interpreted by the Teacher. Then it has to be reflected on rationally. Then it has to be meditated on. For this is how the Self comes to be seen. It comes to be seen by those who apply themselves to hearing, reflection and meditation. True realization of the Absolute as the sole reality only dawns when the three disciplines of hearing, reflection and meditation are fused into one. It does not (normally) dawn otherwise, for instance on the basis of mere hearing.[5]

❖

2. The wise man takes cognizance of the Self, which is hard to perceive on account of its extreme subtlety, and hidden by our cognitions of the changing objects of Nature. It lies in the cave of the intellect, as that is where it is experienced,[6] but is hidden beneath a host of evils and is hence said to be 'dwelling in the deep'. Because it is thus hidden, and lies 'in a cave', and 'dwells in the deep', it is said to be 'hard to perceive'.

This primeval reality, the Self, is known through success in spiritual discipline (adhyātma-yoga).[7] Spiritual discipline (adhyātma-yoga) means the withdrawal of the mind from the sense-objects and its concentration on the Self. Through attaining success in this, the wise man comes to know the Self and 'abandons joy and sorrow' in the sense that, because the Self is subject neither to increase nor diminution, joy and sorrow for him no longer exist....

The wise man, the man of discrimination, should dissolve[8] speech in mind, where 'speech' stands for all the activities of the senses. And he should dissolve mind into the luminous principle, the higher mind (buddhi). The higher mind may be viewed as the inner self of the lower mind (manas), and of the other organs, because it operates with them as its instruments. He should dissolve the higher mind into 'the great Self', by which the Upanishad means the First-born (Hiraṇyagarbha). And this 'great Self' he should dissolve into the true Self that is pure peace (śānta), void of all distinctions, without modifications, existent within all, the Witness of all the ideas of the higher mind.[9]

❖

3. Afterwards the text points out that the highest state of Viṣṇu is difficult to attain, in the words: 'He is present in all beings but hidden and not manifest. He is seen by those of subtle intellect through their sharp and subtle faculties'.[10] And then it goes on to teach yoga (i.e. adhyātma-yoga, cp. preceding Extract) as the means to attain it, in the words: 'The wise man should dissolve the senses in the mind and should dissolve the mind in the higher mind.[11] The higher mind he should dissolve in the great Self,[12] and he should dissolve that in the Self that is pure peace'.[13]

That is, he should give up the use of speech and the other powers of action and sense-perception and should remain identified with the mind alone. He should then note that the mind, too, has defects such as inclination towards the sense-objects and unsteadiness in its decisions, and he should dissolve it into that higher aspect of mind (buddhi) which is sometimes known by the technical term 'knowledge' (vijñāna). He should then refine the higher aspect of the mind (buddhi) and dissolve it into 'the great Self', a term which may stand for the mind as the ultimate experiencer (in the individual) or for the higher aspect of the mind in its most subtle state. 'The great Self', however, must be dissolved in 'the Self that is pure peace', the supreme Spirit that is the subject of the section, the highest possible summit of human experience.[14]

❖

4. But how can that which has no mark be seen? This form of the inmost Self (says the upanishadic text) does not fall within the realm of vision. No one can see this Self through sight, which is taken here as emblematic of all the sense-powers.

How, then, can it be seen? Through the intellect, which is seated in the heart and which rules, as controller, the mind consisting of intentions and the like. The text means that the Self can be known. 'Known' here means illumined through thought in the form of right-knowledge by the intellect in the heart, when it ceases to have false fantasies. Those who thus know that the Self is the Absolute, says the text, are immortal.

But how does one attain to an intellect of this quality? The text next goes on to outline the discipline (yoga) that leads to it.[15] The highest state is said to be achieved when the five senses are turned back from their objects and concentrated on the Self within, along with the mind (manas), turned back from forming intentions and the like, and along with the intellect (buddhi), now inactive and not exercising its natural function of making decisions.[16]

This state is called a state of connection (yoga) though it is really a state of disconnection (viyoga).[17] For it is the state of the yogin who is disconnected from all evils. In this state the Self stands out free from all the superimpositions on it made through nescience. It is a state, says the text, in which all the organs, both the sense-organs and the internal organ (mind), are held fixed and motionless. In such a state, the yogin is never careless about keeping his mind in concentration. The text means, by implication, that the yogin is never careless about concentration from the time when the yoga begins, for there cannot be negligence when the intellect and the rest are motionless (since negligence is a quality of the intellect). Hence avoidance of negligence and like qualities are enjoined for the time before the intellect has reached quiescence.[18]

Or else the reasoning starts from the assumption that only when the organs are held perfectly still can there be perfect absence of negligence, and concludes that when this state is reached there *is* absence of negligence.

Why?[19] Because yoga is a thing that comes and goes.[20] So there must be absence of negligence to ensure that, once come, it does not go.[21]

❖

5. Again a special means for realizing the Self is being taught. No one can perceive the Self through the power of sight, as it is without form or colour. Nor can speech attain to it, as it is 'unspeakable'. Nor can it be comprehended by any of the other senses. Though austerity is the means for attaining everything, yet the Self cannot be attained through

austerity. Nor can it be attained through ritual (karma), which means the Vedic ritual such as the Agnihotra, even though this is well known to have extraordinary powers.

Well then, if all these are not the means to realizing the Self, what is the means? It can be realized through the purification of the instruments of knowledge. The knowledge of all living beings is naturally obscured by desire for external objects and other such defects. Hence it cannot reflect the Self, the ultimate reality, even though the Self is ever in proximity, any more than a mirror encrusted with filth or a broken surface of water (can reflect a face). First the filth arising from attachment to commerce with sense-objects has to be removed.[22] Through this the instruments of knowledge become clear, peaceful and pure, like a clean mirror or a calm surface of water. Then knowledge becomes clear.

When this clear knowledge arises, the pure intellect becomes capable of apprehending the Absolute. The meditator then perceives the Self in contemplation, devoid of all distinction, being himself possessed of truthfulness and other helpful virtues, with mind one-pointed and senses withdrawn from objects.

He (the Self) is subtle and only to be known when the instruments of knowledge have been purified. He is to be known in the body, through consciousness, in the heart-centre — in this body into which the Vital Energy has entered under five forms.[23]

But what exactly is meant here by, 'through consciousness'? The reference is to 'citta', here meaning the mind (antaḥ-karaṇa) of living creatures, in all its aspects, plus the senses. And the particular 'consciousness' (cetas) is that consciousness which pervades these organs intimately, like butter-milk in milk or fire in wood.[24] That consciousness abides in the minds of all living creatures is generally accepted in the world. The meaning is that the Self will manifest, will stand self-illumined, in that mind which has been freed from passions (kleśa) and other impurities.[25]

❖

6. So the text proceeds, '(He should apply himself) to the spiritual forms of yoga (adhyātma-yoga)'. They are so called (adhyātma = adhi + ātma) because they envisage (awareness of) the Self. The initial 'ā' (of 'ādhyātmikān') is shortened to 'a' by a deliberately assumed licence.

What are these spiritual forms of yoga? Those to be taught later, such as 'avoidance of anger', etc.[26] They are 'yogas' in the sense of being means to the concentration of the mind. They are spiritual (ādhyātmika) in the sense of not being dependent on any external equipment. They are 'rational' in the sense that one might rationally expect them to be efficacious in extirpating anger and the rest. They are 'introvertive' in the sense that while anger and the other passions turn the mind, by nature internal, outwards towards the sense-objects, these yogas inhibit this tendency. For when they are established the mind remains in its natural state, not extraverted, clear and contented and directed to the Self. So one should apply oneself to these yogas, should practise concentration of mind in the form of avoidance of anger, etc. For this is the means whereby one's own Self, the supreme, is 'attained'. For although one's own Self is the supreme, it remains for everyone initially unknown and as if 'unattained' because the mind is forcibly swept away from it by anger and the other passions. Hence one must practise yoga (in the sense here understood) to 'attain' it.[27]

❖

7. The Yoga called the Yoga of Non-Contact (asparśa-yoga)[28] is well-known to be traditionally so called in the Upanishads[29] because it implies breaking free from all contact or relation with everything. When it is said that it is hard to comprehend for any yogin, it means for any yogin who does not possess the knowledge given in the Upanishads. The idea is that it requires that degree of effort which is always required to become awake to the reality of the true Self.

Although there is no danger in this yoga, yet yogins in general feel afraid of it. They think it will spell self-destruction, but in this they show lack of metaphysical discrimination.

There are some persons who take the mind and the senses and all else other than the Absolute in its true form as non-existent from the highest standpoint. They have 'become' the Absolute and feel no fear and have perfect natural certitude as to the indestructible peace called liberation which depends on nothing external. As we have already explained,[30] there is nothing for such a person to do.[31] But there are other yogins on the spiritual path who are of weak or middling powers of vision. They regard the mind as something other than the Self but related to the Self, and are not awake to the sole reality of the transcendent Self. In their case, passing beyond fear depends on rigid control of the mind (mano-nigraha). So also does eradication of misery; for those who lack discrimination and regard the Self as related to the mind cannot escape misery as long as the mind is in motion. In their case, awakening to the Self also depends on rigid control of the mind, as also does that indestructible peace which is called liberation.

Only those who possess the kind of buoyant will that would be capable of draining the ocean with the tip of a piece of grass can acquire rigid control of the mind. But is a buoyant will the only means for acquiring a rigid control of the mind? The man of buoyant will must take a grip of the mind when it becomes distracted by worldly objects of pleasure, and should pull it back and turn it in onto his own Self. And when it tends to dissolve in sleep he should also restrain it, even though sleep is a happy and effortless state. It should be restrained from this state, even though it is a happy one, because dissolution in deep sleep is as harmful as distraction amid desires.[32] So the mind has to be restrained from sleep as well as from the objects of desire.

What is the means to this? This will now be explained. One should remember that all duality is set up by nescience and is misery. When the mind runs after objects of desire and their enjoyment, one should restrain it by dwelling on the merits of passionlessness. One should remember the teaching of the Veda and the Teacher that all is the Absolute, the Unborn, and should not so much as behold the world of duality, because it does not exist.

By these two means, affirmation of the spiritual truth and passionlessness, one may dissolve the mind in sleep. Should this begin to occur, one should awaken it by making attempts at the discriminative vision of the Self. The author Gauḍapāda uses the word 'citta' to designate the mind, but it only means 'manas'.[33] And when it is distracted in enjoyment of desires he should again quell its movements. In this way he must engage in spiritual efforts repeatedly and arouse the mind from slumber and pull it back from the sense-objects. But one must know that as long as the mind is in this condition of oscillating between distraction in desires and dissolution in sleep it is yet impregnated with the seeds of future experience, and one must redouble one's efforts accordingly in working for stability. And when a good approximation to stability has been achieved, one should not then permit the mind to wander any more towards objects.

When the yogin is on the point of acquiring concentration (samādhi) great joy comes to him, but he should not pause to savour it, he should not develop attachment for it. He should practise intellectual discrimination and avoid all desires and constantly revolve in his mind the idea that whatever joy comes to him is a fantasy of nescience and quite unreal. That is to say, he should restrain the mind even from such joy as this. And if the mind, after first being held back from attachment and rendered motionless, should again move out towards the things of the external world, he should expend great efforts and patience in restraining it and turning it back onto his own Self within in the manner already described. That is, he should reduce all to pure Being, to Consciousness in its true form.[34]

When the mind has been restrained in this way and is no longer inclined either to fall asleep or into distraction amid objects, when it is motionless like the flame of a lamp shaded from the wind, when it no longer manifests under the form of any illusory object, then the mind has assumed the nature of the Absolute (brahman).[35]

❖

8. The text now explains when it is that a person is established in yoga (yogārūḍha). When the yogin's mind is submitting to concentration; when he has no attachment or desire for the objects of the senses consisting of the gross elements, or for acts, obligatory, occasional, optional or forbidden[36] as he sees no point in them; and when he has given up all purposes connected with desires for personal ends in this world and the next — then he is said to be 'established in yoga'. When the text says 'giving up all purposes', it implies that all desires and all acts are given up. For all desires rest on purposes. Manu says, 'Desire rests on purpose: sacrifice results from purposes'.[37] And a passage from the derivative literature says, 'O Desire: I know thy origin, thou art born from Purpose. I will never cherish any purpose and will thus get rid of thee'.[38]

When all desire is lost, renunciation of all action is achieved. This is shown by such Vedic passages as 'Whatever a man's desire, his resolve follows that and his action follows his resolve'[39] and also by such passages from the derivative literature as 'Whatever a man does is all the prompting of desire'.[40]

Reason also leads to the same conclusion. For if all purposes are given up, one cannot so much as twitch.[41]

2. Devotion (Bhakti)

The topic of devotion (bhakti) has already come up for discussion earlier at several places in the present work.[42] Broadly speaking, Śaṅkara was capable of taking two different lines of interpretation where the term 'devotion' (bhakti) occurred in the texts on which he was commenting. If the text considered devotion in isolation from knowledge — for instance if it spoke of the path of devotion or 'bhakti yoga' — he made it a preparatory and subordinate phase of the path leading to knowledge, or at best one which would lead to union with the Lord in the 'indirect' manner, after death. But his more typical course was to appropriate texts on devotion to the Lord and *identify* them with the path of knowledge. In fact he frequently refused to acknowledge any difference between devotion and spiritual knowledge at all.[43]

Saccidānandendra Svāmin argued that Śaṅkara is justified in taking the latter course both by the ancient texts and by the facts of the spiritual path.[44] Knowledge and devotion, he claims, are not two separate things, but one thing viewed under different 'aspects', as the power of the sun is one thing, though it may artificially be viewed as two separate things, heat and light. But knowledge and devotion are entirely inter-dependent. There cannot be knowledge of the true nature of the Lord through mere reasoning without the spirit of devotion. This is because the Lord is 'the Self seated in the heart of all creatures'[45] and the Self is that which is dearer than a son, dearer than wealth, closer than anything else.[46] And on the other side there cannot be devotion without knowledge. Of the four kinds of devotee mentioned in the Gītā, the man of knowledge is the highest,[47] as devotion is spiritual sensibility and not mere blind application of the will. When either knowledge or devotion are brought to their highest pitch they transcend themselves: the knower becomes one with the known, the lover one with the beloved.

Passages illustrating both of Śaṅkara's two typical attitudes to

Bhakti just mentioned are to be found in Extracts quoted in the last two sections of Chapter XII in Volume V above. It is proposed to conclude the present section with further Extracts which illustrate the two attitudes in turn. In the first Śaṅkara speaks of 'Bhakti Yoga' as a species of *indirect* path to the Absolute. In the second he fuses devotion with realization of the Absolute in the highest sense — that is to say he *reduces* it to knowledge. The highest form of devotion is that 'whereby nothing other than Vāsudeva is perceived'.

TEXTS ON DEVOTION

1. Those who pursue action receive the fruits of action from Me, and those who pursue knowledge receive the fruits of knowledge from Me. Hence even those who serve Me through the Yoga of Devotion (bhakti yoga) pass through stages to acquire spiritual knowledge and are eventually liberated through My grace. If liberation comes to those who perform the Yoga of Devotion, how much more certainly does it come to those who acquire a correct intuitive knowledge of the nature of the Self in this very life.[48]

❖

2. How, then, can the Lord be seen? Through devotion (bhakti). But through devotion to what? Devotion to nothing else. The phrase refers to that devotion which never swerves from the Lord. Devotion-to-none-other is that devotion whereby nothing other than Vāsudeva is perceived by the senses or any organ of cognition. Through such devotion, O Arjuna, can I be known in this form — that is, in the form of

the universe. I can be known from the traditional texts (śāstra), and not only known from the texts but directly known in My true nature and can be 'entered' — that is, there can be liberation.

And now the whole teaching of the Gītā-Śāstra is epitomized and summed up and stated for the sake of man's highest good. 'O Son of Pāṇḍu, whoever acts for My sake, has Me for his supreme goal, who is devoted to Me, free from all attachment, and who lives without enmity for any creature, he comes to Me'.... A servant works for his master's sake, but he does not think of his master as his supreme goal which he will attain to after death.... 'Devoted to Me' means that he worships Me in every way with his whole being and with all zeal. 'Without attachment' means without servile love or affection for wealth, sons, friends, wife or relatives. 'Without enmity for any creature' means without any feeling of enmity even for those intent on inflicting grievous harm on him.[49]

3. Communication of 'That Thou Art'

Śaṅkara's pupil, Troṭaka, who adhered closely to the letter and spirit of his master's teaching, declares[50] that the text 'That thou art' negates the feelings 'I am this body' and 'This body is mine' and supplies the pattern on which all upanishadic texts which identify the individual soul with the Absolute must be interpreted. Though cast in affirmative form, they are essentially negations of the not-self, even as Draviḍa had said.[51] And we have already heard Śaṅkara say, 'The function of the teachings like "that thou art", associated with reasoning on their content, is merely to negate the not-self element from this Self, the latter being already existent and evident as "I".'[52]

Indeed, if the Absolute is not to be limited and reduced to an object among objects, the final truth can only be communicated by a negation. And Śaṅkara remarks, 'Is it then impossible that the Absolute should be communicated by the Veda, since the Absolute is not an object of knowledge? No. For the function of the Veda is to put an end to the distinctions imagined through nescience'.[53] In another passage not quoted in the present work Śaṅkara expressed himself as follows: 'It is the supreme Self as apparently delimited by the adjuncts of body, senses, lower mind (manas), intellect (buddhi) and so on which is falsely referred to by the ignorant as "the embodied"... And the empirical distinctions such as "I am the agent and this is the object of my act", which depend on this false notion, are not contradicted until the truth declared in the text "That thou art" that only the Self exists has been directly apprehended. But when there has once been a direct apprehension of the fact that only the Self exists, all empirical notions, such as those of bondage and liberation, cease'.[54]

The knowledge promoted by the text 'That thou art', when consummated, is an immediate intuition. Although it is communicated through speech, yet it is still what Bertrand Russell would call 'knowledge by acquaintance'. For, as the Advaitins of Śaṅkara's school were later to affirm, whereas most knowledge gained from speech is indirect, such knowledge is direct if it concerns the Self of the hearer.[55] The fundamental function of the text 'That thou art' is summed up by Śaṅkara's pupil, Sureśvara, as follows: 'The Absolute is nothing other than man's Self; man's Self is nothing other than the Absolute. But as long as their identity is not known, their relation is wrongly conceived. The Absolute is identical with man's immediately evident Self, but is not known, and is conceived as "other" (parokṣa); similarly, man's Self is the Absolute, but it is conceived as having a second reality over against it. But in the case of the ascetic whose ignorance has been destroyed by the true knowledge conveyed by the text ("That thou art"), all causes of distinction are eradicated and only the conviction "All is the Self alone" remains.'[56]

Eight Extracts will be offered below, to illustrate thoroughly

Śaṅkara's evaluation of the supreme text 'That thou art'. The first Extract clears away preliminary difficulties raised by the Mīmāṃsakas, who did not want the great metaphysical statements of the Upanishads to be taken seriously. Against them, Śaṅkara shows that the text 'That thou art' is not a mere fanciful meditation, as it is not followed by the word 'iti' (the Sanskrit equivalent of inverted commas). It cannot be dismissed as a mere figurative statement either, for the Chāndogya Upanishad in which it occurs makes it clear on metaphysical grounds that in his true nature the pupil cannot be anything other than pure Being, any more than a clay-pot can be anything other than clay. The statement cannot be a mere eulogy of the pupil, as this would only be possible, according to the Mīmāṃsaka's canons, if the pupil were an object of worship, which he is not. Still less can the text 'That thou art' be interpreted as an eulogy of pure Being, as to circumscribe pure Being by limiting it to the pupil is not to eulogize it. Nor is the text put forward as a mere 'helpful idea' to be dwelt on in meditation, as the upanishadic passage in which it occurs goes on to speak of knowledge. Since it is that through which one hears what was previously unheard, it qualifies through its 'novelty' or 'originality' (apūrvatā) as a genuine means of knowledge (pramāṇa) in the sense accepted by the Mīmāṃsakas. That an intuitive awareness 'I am pure Being' arises from the text 'That thou art' cannot be gainsaid, as it is corroborated by many other upanishadic texts carrying the authority of Vedic revelation, and these in turn are subject to confirmation in immediate experience. The view that the pupil cannot be the Self, or he would already know it and so not require to be informed about it, is one that cannot be maintained by the Mīmāṃsaka, for he himself admits that the average pupil does not even realize that he is an eternal soul separate from the body and that he requires to be instructed about it.

The second Extract, from the Brahma Sūtra Commentary, is the only detailed and important account of 'That thou art' in the Commentaries, and the remaining Extracts are all taken from the Eighteenth Chapter of the Upadeśa Sāhasrī, which explains the metaphysical implications of this text as Śaṅkara saw them.

The second Extract begins by making the point that 'realization of the Absolute' is a goal which can be attained in this very life, and consequently that 'repetition' of the discipline that leads to it — hearing the supreme texts, cogitating over them and subjecting them to sustained meditation — does not have to be performed all one's life as a kind of enjoined duty that it would be a sin to omit, but only has to be continued until the desired goal is reached. Nor need it be performed at all, if there are no psychological obstructions to prevent the instant rise of a direct intuition of the final truth the moment the text 'That thou art' is first heard. One may argue *logically* that if the text is not understood at the first hearing it will never be understood by any amount of pondering and meditation, but this logical argument has no weight against the fact that it has been the actual *experience* of many people that they have arrived at a direct awareness of the truth through repeated application to the discipline. Though the knowledge must arise from the text either immediately or not at all, people shed the misconceptions which prevent them from understanding the text one by one, gradually and as a kind of process. This Extract incidentally confirms that Śaṅkara understood knowledge of truth essentially as the shedding of misconceptions, and set small store by system-building. As a theologian, he made use of syntheses to demonstrate the unity and harmony of the Vedic texts. But when it comes to philosophical or purely rational enquiry, he is not interested in the construction of syntheses or frames of reference but simply in the elimination of the error of supposing that one is an individual experiencer.

In the sequel this second Extract discusses the interpretation of the words of the text 'That thou art'. The meaning of 'Thou' is partially evident to the ignorant hearer as referring to his own Self, but his notion of the Self has to be discriminated from the body, senses and mind with which in ordinary experience it is inextricably mixed. This correction is effected by the negation of the not-self implicit in the affirmation 'That thou art'. But the meaning of the word 'that' is not immediately evident to the ignorant hearer. It has to be gathered by pondering over the significance of other upanishadic texts. Positively it is to be viewed as that from which the origin, maintenance and dissolution of the world proceed. But this positive notion of 'that' or 'the Absolute' as the source of the world has to be corrected in the light of other texts which refer to it through the negation of all empirical characteristics. The themes already rehearsed in Chapters III, IV and VII above are relevant here. Chapter IV has outlined positive teaching about the Absolute that is useful and necessary to the pupil treading the path, while Chapters III and VII offer texts which state the final truth in terms of negation. The Extract of the present chapter now under discussion treats these themes in logical order. It begins with a positive statement of the meaning of the word 'that' as the first cause of the world, and then adds subsequent negations to purify and correct this initial notion.

The remaining six Extracts, the group beginning with the third and ending with the eighth, are taken from the Eighteenth Chapter of the Upadeśa Sāhasrī, the place where Śaṅkara examines 'That thou art' in greatest detail. Extract 3 establishes that the ego of the hearer is a complex of Self and not-self. The words in the supreme metaphysical texts of the Veda are not capable of 'designating' the true Self of the hearer, as the latter is beyond the scope or the direct designation of words, since the meaning of words is confined, according to the grammarians, to universal nouns (the meaning of which may be restricted to particulars through the qualifying force of other words co-present in the same sentence), attributes, acts and relations. The true Self has none of these characteristics. But the 'ego' or 'empirical self' of the hearer has. It is consequently subject to direct designation by pronouns, and the true Self may be indirectly indicated through it. What words, strictly regarded, 'say' is not always the same as what they are used to mean. We say 'The torch burns', which is a loose way of speaking to mean 'The fire in the torch burns'. In the same way, the true Self of the hearer is not, in strict usage, 'speakable' by the pronouns in the supreme texts, yet they can be used to 'mean' it loosely, and this because they refer in their direct meaning to the ego of the hearer, with which he is already acquainted.

The fourth Extract is long and argumentative. The ordinary empirical notion 'he knows' is the product of a false superimposition. (Cp. above, Vol. I, 92ff.) The Self is the light in all knowledge. But it is changeless. The empirical consciousness that conforms to the states of the mind is the mere reflection of consciousness in the mind, the mind being conceived as composed of subtle matter. (Cp. above, Vol.III, 59ff.) The 'theory of a reflection' is no luxury. It is required if the text 'That thou art' is to be made intelligible. The Buddhists say that every individual cognition is active, momentary and self-luminous. Such a theory would undermine the chief glory of the upanishadic teaching, its affirmation of a non-dual ground, eternal, changeless and of the nature of consciousness and bliss. The Sāṅkhyas take the first step towards the correction of the Buddhist doctrine in affirming the existence of a changeless Witness over against the changing flux of mental presentations. But they do not, and cannot, bridge the gap between the Witness and the flux because they believe that the Witness illumines the flux by its mere proximity and not through the instrumentality of a reflection. 'That thou art' cannot be explained on the principles of Sāṅkhya dualism. For the Sāṅkhya, only the intellect, and not the pure Witness (sākṣin, puruṣa), could be the ignorant sufferer asking the question 'Who am I?' And if the question were raised under the conditions that he conceives, the reply 'That thou art' simply would not be true. The changing intellect could not be the upanishadic Absolute, beyond all change. The text 'That thou art' is intelligible only if conceived as addressed to the soul as empirical knower, before it has effected spiritual discrimination. And it informs him that he is the pure Self, free from association with anything external such as mind or body. The term 'Thou' indicates the Self in its true nature indirectly through the ego-sense of the enquirer, to which it refers directly. As the Sāṅkhya can affirm no genuine relation of the pure Self with the ego-sense (for example, that of being reflected in it), he cannot claim, on his own principles, that the term 'thou' can serve as an indirect indication of that pure Self. An indicated meaning must have some intelligible relation with a direct meaning, or any word could be used to mean anything.

The meaning of the term 'Thou' in 'That thou art' undergoes a partial negation through the presence of the word 'That' in the same sentence. It loses its reference to all external components of the ego, and thus refers to the pure Self as Witness. But the Witness itself cannot be negated. Its presence throughout waking, dream and dreamless sleep makes it the limit (sīman) beyond which negation cannot go. And all that (from the empirical standpoint) the Witness appears to illumine is a mere qualification of the Witness, depending on the latter for its existence. Only the Witness stands self-existent. In the end, only the Witness exists.

The meaning of the pronouns 'I' and 'thou' in the texts 'I am the Absolute' (aham brahmāsmi) and 'That thou art' (tat tvam asi) has to be determined by a consideration of what they could rationally be supposed to mean in the present context in the light of what they are known to be used to mean elsewhere. But one cannot limit one's consideration of their use elsewhere to worldly life. One has also to examine how these pronouns are used in other upanishadic texts and also the use of terms found there in apposition with them, such as Consciousness (vijñāna), the Absolute (brahman), Being (sat), etc. They are found to be used, like the term 'Witness', of that which has independent existence. On the other hand terms like 'agent' and 'enjoyer' are invariably applied in the world to beings dependent on some external factor such as a physical body and sense-organs for their existence as agent or enjoyer. Such considerations force us to interpret 'That thou art' and kindred texts according to the Advaitic analysis given above. When the meanings of the words 'that' and 'thou' in the sentence 'That thou art' have been arrived at by such means, the student is at last in a position to understand the text immediately the next time he hears it spoken, as Rāma immediately comprehended the words of Brahmā reminding Him He was Viṣṇu.

The function of the affirmative text 'I am the Absolute' is not much different from that of 'That thou art'. The Prasaṅkhyāna Vādins (cp. above, Vol.V, 294ff.) are wrong to say that the knowledge communicated by the supreme texts is false as it stands, since it is conveyed by words and hence has an element of plurality, but that it can be *converted* into knowledge of the non-dual truth through pondering and meditation. For this would mean that the Vedic texts proclaimed what was not true, and would undermine faith in the Veda as an authoritative means of knowledge. Nor is it correct to say that Advaita undermines the authority of the supreme Vedic texts because no 'fruit' of liberation can accrue to the Self, so that the texts are useless. It is legitimate to speak of the 'fruit of liberation' accruing to the Self, just as it is legitimate to speak of the king winning a victory, though he may have had no hand personally in the campaign. Alternatively, one may say that the 'fruit of liberation' accrues to the reflection of consciousness in the mind of the liberated soul, and so accrues in a sense to the Self, as the reflection is non-different from the Self.

The fifth Extract explains the mechanism by which the words 'that' and 'thou' exclude part of each other's meaning in the sentence 'That thou art'. In this sentence, 'thou' must be the subject and 'that' the predicate, since only the 'thou' is in any sense known to the hearer initially, so that the sentence can only make sense for him if taken this way round. Further, if 'thou' is taken as standing in apposition to the earlier word 'the real' (sat), which lays down the topic in the section of the Chāndogya Upanishad in which 'That thou art' occurs, it eliminates that part of the meaning of the word 'thou' which refers to 'the sufferer', leaving the pure Self, untouched by external adjuncts. The conviction produced by the supreme texts, when once firmly established, is no more open to contradiction by perception than a man who has awoken from a dream that his finger was cut can be persuaded that it is still cut when he is awake. The final meaning of the text 'That thou art' is not different from that of 'not this, not this'.

The sixth Extract makes the point that while speech in general yields only abstract knowledge, it yields concrete knowledge about the Self of the hearer. It is therefore worth analysing such a text grammatically in order to understand it because, though the analysis takes you into ever more abstract realms, the end-product is a clear understanding first of the meaning of the words and then of the sentence, and this may result eventually in a concrete experience, if purity and other necessary conditions are attained.

The seventh Extract quotes the Dharma Śāstra to show that one can only come to a knowledge of the meaning of the word 'thou' through adoption of total renunciation of all action, not through the compromise discipline of Prasaṅkhyāna Vāda, which could include continual performance of the ritual. First the student must learn to find his own inmost Self as the meaning of the word 'thou'. Then he must come to understand the meaning of the text 'That thou art' as a whole by seeing that all is his own Self alone. When the meaning of this text has been properly apprehended, no other means of knowledge can remain, since the means of knowledge all depend on false identification of the Self with an external adjunct. Nor can there be any action, as the two ideas 'I am the Absolute' and 'I am the agent' are contradictory.

Extract 8 enquires into the function and justification of the text 'That thou art'. It reveals the Witness, by negating the not-self. But is not the Witness self-revealed? Yes, but through nescience we become ignorant of it as it is in its pure state, and therefore require a means of knowledge, the text 'That thou art', to know it. Even if, for argument's sake, we accept the opponent's view that 'establishment' (proof) of anything implies a mental act with an agent and an object, nevertheless the existence of a Witness beyond act, agent and object is implied by this very assumption. And the purpose of the 'That thou art' is to reveal this Witness in its true nature.

TEXTS ON THE COMMUNICATION OF 'THAT THOU ART'

1. Now, in the matter of the Self which is here under consideration, what is the advantageous end-product resulting from the authoritative teaching of the sixth chapter of the Chāndogya Upanishad (now drawing to a close)? We have already explained that the advantageous end-product is the final cessation of the notion that in one's true Self one is capable of being an agent and experiencer. Competence to hear and reflect on the meaning of the word 'thou' in 'That thou art' is granted to enable one to have the advantage of knowing something that cannot be known in any other way. And before that knowledge, one has the competence to perform the Agnihotra and other ritual on the basis of the conviction 'I will do such and such and obtain such and such a result either in this world or the next, or will acquit myself of my duties when such and such actions are done'. This conviction about one's own Self in the form 'I function as an agent and experiencer', that obtained formerly, ceases forever in the case of one who has been enlightened by the text 'That pure Being, the ground of the universe, one only without a second — that thou art'.[57] In his case it has become contradictory. For in the one Self without a second there is no room for differentiated knowledge starting with the conviction 'I am so and so' and proceeding 'I have this other thing to do with such and such an instrument' or 'Having done such and such, I shall enjoy such and such a result'. Thus, when pure Being, the true non-dual Self, is known, conviction as to the reality of the false individual self ceases.[58]

Here an objector might interpose as follows. In the text 'That thou art', he might say, we are enjoined to meditate on the meaning of the word 'thou' *as though* it were pure Being, just in the same way as we are elsewhere enjoined to meditate on the sun and the mind[59] and other worldly objects *as if* they were the Absolute, or as in ordinary worldly practice people take images and the like for deities such as Viṣṇu. It cannot literally mean 'Thou art pure Being'. For if Śvetaketu (the pupil) were really pure Being, how could he not know himself as such and how, consequently, could the teaching 'That thou art' be needed?

But this view is wrong, as there is a difference between the text 'That thou art' and the texts enjoining meditation on the sun as the Absolute and the like. Because the words in such texts are cast in inverted commas, as in '(Meditate on the theme) "The sun is the Absolute" ' we do not take them to mean that the sun literally *is* the Absolute. The sun and the like have colour and perceptible form, and the mind and the ether are mentioned in this context in inverted commas,[60] so we know that none of them can be the Absolute. But here the text begins by showing the entry of pure Being (into the three divinities that constitute the world)[61] and then afterwards declares without equivocation that pure Being is the Self in the words 'That thou art'.

Nor can you say that the text 'That thou art' is merely figurative speech, as when we speak of a man of audacity as a lion. For pure Being has been taught to be real and one only without a second (in the manner of other material causes from which a plurality of effects arise) like clay.[62] Nor could it be taught that 'His delay before liberation will only be so long'[63] if such liberation depended on knowledge of anything merely figurative, for knowledge of a merely figurative 'truth' is error, as in the case of one taking the statement 'Thou art verily Indra and Yama' literally.[64] Nor could the text 'That thou art' be a piece of formal eulogy, as Śvetaketu is not an object of worship (to his father who spoke the words). Nor would it constitute an eulogy of pure Being if the latter were called Śvetaketu, as one does not eulogize a king by calling him a slave. Nor would it be right to circumscribe pure Being to one place (by calling it Śvetaketu), since it is the Self of all. It would be like telling the provincial governor (by way of eulogy) that he was the village-headman. There is in fact no other course in the present context but to interpret the text as a declaration that pure Being is the ultimate Self.

Perhaps you will say that all we have here is an injunction to action, an injunction to meditate on the idea that one is pure Being, and that we are in no way being confronted with a piece of information telling us that we are that pure Being, a fact that has hitherto been unknown. This we counter by quoting the text itself, which declares itself to be 'that through which what was previously unheard is now heard'.[65] Nor can you dismiss this as a mere eulogy promoting fulfilment of the injunction to meditate on the mere *idea* 'I am pure Being'. For the text also says, 'He who has a Teacher *knows* "I shall remain here only till I am released (from the body)".'[66] If the text 'I am pure Being' were part of a mere imaginative exercise to be practised in obedience to an injunction, and not a declaration that the 'Being' that would later be referred to by the word 'thou' was in fact nothing other than pure Being, then the passage would never have gone on to say that it was a means to knowledge that was being presented here, as it does in the phrase 'He who has a Teacher *knows*'. For in any injunction to perform ritual such as 'He should offer the Agnihotra', the fact of the one so enjoined having a Teacher is a foregone conclusion (as it is impossible to carry out the household ritual without having first learned the texts by heart from a Teacher who knew them).[67] Nor could the text have added 'I shall remain here only till I am released'. For if the opponent's view were right, there could very well be release arising from one act of mere imaginative meditation, without pure Being or the metaphysical principle of the Self being known at all. Nor can it be claimed that the conviction 'I am pure Being' that arises when the authoritative text 'That thou art' has been taught to a pupil with the requisite qualifications can be obliterated by any subsequent idea 'I am not pure Being'. It cannot be claimed that it never rises at all, for all the texts of the Upanishads without exception are concerned directly or indirectly to establish this one truth. It is no more possible to say that this metaphysical conviction is wrong, or that it does not arise, than it would be to say that the ideas that we have of enjoined ritualistic duties arising from the texts enjoining the Agnihotra and other ritual were wrong or did not arise.[68]

As for the contention that if the student were the Self as pure Being he would be certain to be aware of this fact without teaching, we refute this with the reminder that living creatures are not even aware of themselves as a soul functioning as agent and experiencer and distinct from the body, mind and senses, which they merely use as instruments,[69] what to say of being aware that they are the Self as pure Being.

Well, you will ask, in these circumstances how do they in fact become aware that they are the Self as pure Being?[70] To explain this, we ask you the counter-question, 'How is it that when the soul, according to your (Mīmāṃsaka) account of the matter, knows itself as separate from body, mind and senses, it still can and does think that it is an agent and experiencer?' It is because such a soul, even though possessing the knowledge that it is separate from the body, mind and senses, continues to identify itself with them that it does not come to know itself as the Self and as pure Being. Hence it stands proved that the function of the text 'That thou art' is merely to end the conviction that one is the individual soul, competent for agency and empirical experience in the realm of illusory modifications.[71]

❖

2. We have such texts as, 'The Self, verily, is to be seen, to be heard about, to be cogitated on, to be subjected to sustained meditation', 'Having come to know that, the man of wisdom should contemplate it', and 'That should be investigated, one should enquire into that thoroughly'.[72] Here the doubt might arise, 'Has one to rise to the conception only once, or has one to return to it repeatedly?'

And one might initially suppose that one had to rise to the conception only once, just as the subsidiary rituals called prayāja have only to be performed once. For that is all that the Vedic texts demand.[73] And to perform a repetition when none was mentioned in the Veda would be to perform something not enjoined in the Veda. Perhaps it would be objected (i.e. by the Advaitin) that phrases like 'It must be heard about, cogitated upon, subjected to sustained meditation' imply repetition. But the text as it stands does not warrant us to go beyond one act of hearing, one piece of cogitation, one piece of sustained meditation, and nothing more. No repetition, for instance, is implied in texts occurring just once and saying 'He knows' or 'He should meditate'.

To all this the author of the Sūtras replies, 'One must affirm the notion repeatedly'. Why? 'Because of the repeated instruction'. Instructions like 'It should be heard about, cogitated over and subjected to sustained meditation' involve repetition and imply repeated affirmation. You will say that you have already explained how we are not justified in going beyond the literal meaning of the text. But this rule cannot be applied in the case of these texts. For they are concerned ultimately with vision, and hence what they teach belongs to the realm of the visible and has to be repeated:[74] as, for example, the rice has to be pounded until it is actually husked.

Moreover, words like worship (upāsana) and sustained meditation (nididhyāsana) both imply continued, repeated action. When, for example, we speak in the secular way of the worship (i.e. service) of a Teacher or of a king, we imply staying permanently in the presence of that Teacher or king. And similarly, when we say of a wife whose husband has gone abroad 'She thinks of her distant husband' we mean the continual lively remembrance of her husband. And in consonance with this we find the words 'knowledge' and 'meditation' used interchangeably in the Upanishads. Some texts begin by speaking of knowledge (vidi) and sum up calling it 'meditation' (upāsanā), as for example in the text 'And I say this of anyone who knows what Raikva knows',[75] followed closely by 'O Raikva, teach me, venerable sir, that deity on which you meditate'.[76] Sometimes we find the text using the root for 'meditate' (upās) at the beginning and the root for 'knowledge' (vid) at the end, as in 'He should meditate (upāsīta) on mind as the Absolute'[77] followed by 'He who knows thus shines and burns bright with an aura of good name and good fame and the lustre of knowledge of the Absolute'.[78] Hence it follows that there can be repetition even in texts which only give an injunction to do something once.

The texts also give overt hints that meditative affirmation should be practised repeatedly. For example, at one point they prescribe meditation on the Udgītha in the words 'The Udgītha is the sun'.[79] They then rescind this as defective, because it only results in the birth of one son, and prescribe repeated meditation on the plurality of its rays as a means to having many sons in the words 'Meditate repeatedly on the rays'.[80] This passage shows that repeated meditations are accepted. If this is the case here, we may assume that the principle holds good in the case of all other meditations, too, as the process of meditation is always basically the same.

Here the opponent might intervene and say that repetition is intelligible in the case of ends that can be gained by active means, as it is possible one might gain more of such ends by more meditation. But what occasion could there be for repetition in the case of the notion of the Absolute in its supreme form, which communicates the Absolute as the Self, eternal, pure, enlightened and liberated by its very nature? And if the Advaitin were to complain that there was a place for repeated affirmation inasmuch as the fact that the Absolute is one's own Self is not intelligible at a single hearing, we reply (i.e. the Advaitin's opponent replies) that nothing would be altered by mere repetition. If a text like 'That thou art'[81] does not engender the idea that the Absolute is one's own Self at one hearing, what hope is there that it will do so when repeatedly affirmed?

Perhaps the Advaitin will say that no sentence can give anyone direct acquaintance with anything, so that what grants one direct experience of the fact that the Absolute is one's own Self is a text supported by reasoning. But even here, replies the opponent, repetition will be useless. For such reasoning will bring direct experience (if it brings it at all) through being performed once.

The Advaitin, however, may persist and say that a sentence supported by reasoning will only yield abstract and general knowledge, not concrete and particular knowledge. Someone else will only have an abstract knowledge of the fact that you have a pain from hearing your sentence 'I have a pain' and from his inference based on such signs as the trembling of your body. He will not have the direct experience of the pain that you have. And it is a concrete experience only that can remove nescience,[82] and so there should be repeated affirmation to secure it.

But the opponent disallows this also, on the ground that mere repeated affirmation will not bring the concrete knowledge. For hearing revealed texts and applying one's reason to them will not yield concrete particular knowledge even if repeated a hundred times over. Hence, whether revelation and reason applied to it are concerned with something concrete and particular (such as the Self of the hearer) or only with something abstract and universal, in either case they yield whatever knowledge they can yield at a single stroke, and there is no room for repetition. Nor can it be roundly affirmed that they never occasion immediate concrete experience in anyone, as people differ widely in their intuitional powers. In the case of a worldly subject, there will be (the division into whole and) parts and a general aspect and a particular aspect. Here repeated attempts to acquire knowledge are in place, as one may become aware of one aspect of such a subject through one act of attention and another through another, as happens, for instance, when one is mastering a lengthy chapter. But the Absolute in its unqualified form is bare Consciousness, without any distinction into general and particular aspects. Hence there is no place for repetition in one's attempts to acquire knowledge of it.

To all this the Advaitin replies as follows. Repeated resort to the appropriate means of knowledge is indeed useless in the case of the person who can attain immediate experience of the fact that his Self is the Absolute from merely hearing the text 'That thou art' spoken once. But it is perfectly appropriate in the case of the person who cannot do so. For in the Chāndogya Upanishad the Teacher first says, 'That thou art, O Śvetaketu',[83] and then the pupil repeatedly says 'Teach me again, revered sir'[84] and the Teacher proceeds to teach him 'That thou art' repeatedly, resolving more of his doubts on each occasion. And we have quoted other Vedic texts which support this general position, such as 'The Self, verily, is to be seen, to be heard about, to be cogitated on, to be subjected to sustained meditation'.[85] True, you have said that if the text 'That thou art' will not yield immediate knowledge of what it has to say when uttered once, it will not do so when repeated. But this cannot affect our position, for one cannot rule out on the basis of mere logic that which is actually experienced to be the case. And we do actually find it to be the case that those who have but a faint idea of the meaning of a text on hearing it once do come to understand it rightly after repeated hearing, through shedding their various misconceptions.

Moreover, the force of the text 'That thou art' is to declare that that which is represented by 'thou' is really of the nature of that which is represented by 'that'. And the word 'that' represents the Absolute, that which 'took thought' and was the main topic of the passage. It is spoken of as the cause of the rise, maintenance and dissolution of the universe, as we know from many texts, such as 'The Absolute is the Real, Knowledge, the Infinite', 'The Absolute is Consciousness and Bliss', 'The Seer, not Himself seen', 'Unborn, untouched by decay or death', 'Not gross, not subtle, not short, not long'.[86] Here, words like 'unborn' show that the Absolute is bereft of the six modifications beginning with birth.[87] Words like 'not gross', etc. show that it is bereft of the substance-attribute relation. Words like 'Consciousness' declare that it is of the nature of Consciousness and Light. Known as the Absolute (brahman), it is of the nature of immediate experience and is bereft of all empirical qualities. This is the meaning of the word 'that' which is recognized by the specialists in the upanishadic teaching.

Similarly, the meaning of the word, 'thou', too, is the inmost Self, the true hearer,[88] that which is distinguishable from all other elements in the empirical personality, from the body onward, as the inmost Self, finally discovered to be pure Consciousness. But there are some who are obstructed by ignorance (ajñāna), doubt or erroneous knowledge[89] and cannot come to a correct understanding of the meaning of these two words 'that' and 'thou', and in their case the text 'That thou art' cannot yield knowledge (pramā) of its true meaning. For one can only understand the meaning of a sentence if one already understands the meaning of the words composing it.[90] In the case of such people, repeated application to the texts and reasoning over them is appropriate in order to get at the meaning of the *words*. It is true that the Self which is being communicated has no parts. But many parts are erroneously attributed to it, such as body, mind, senses, intellect and sensation of objects. Here, one act of attention can dispose of another. In this sense, communication of the Absolute is by stages. But all this is but the preliminary form of apprehension of the Self.

Meanwhile, those gifted persons who are not afflicted by any ignorance, doubt or erroneous knowledge to obstruct the comprehension of the meaning of the *words* can have direct knowledge of the meaning of the *sentence* when it is heard only once. For them, repetition would quite evidently be superfluous. For once the Self is known, this knowledge suppresses nescience. Here we do not admit stages of any kind....

But in the case of the person in whom this immediate experience does not arise at once, we admit that repetition is necessary in order to acquire that immediate experience. But even here, one should not become involved in any departure from the true meaning of the text 'That thou art' through (false ideas about what is implied by) 'repetition'. One does not marry off one's daughter with the idea of killing the bridegroom.[91] One who performed repetition of the text in obedience to an injunction and thinking 'I am an agent with a right and duty to perform this act' will necessarily generate a conviction that is quite contradictory to the conviction that he is the Absolute. But the case is different with the person of dull intellect and who is about to lose the meaning of the text for lack of insight. Such a person is quite justified in working to strengthen his convictions as to the meaning of the text, with a search for the right meaning based on 'repetition' and similar practices.[92] Hence there can be repetition of the preliminary processes leading up to knowledge, even in the case of knowledge of the Absolute in its highest form.[93]

❖

3. The 'appropriator' (*viz.* the ego-sense) always stands in proximity to this Self (which is pure Consciousness) and acquires a reflection of it. Hence arises the undiscriminated complex of the Self and what pertains to the Self, which is the sphere of the 'I' and the 'mine'. Words may designate this complex, because it is associated with a universal and with action. But no word can designate the Self as such, because the latter is not associated with a universal or an action or the other requisite characteristics.[94] Only when there is a reflection (ābhāsa) of the inner Witness (to form the ego-sense) can words, by referring to the reflection, indirectly indicate the Self.[95] They cannot designate the latter directly in any way. For no entity that is not associated with a universal or other such characteristic can be designated by words. Because the ego-sense is a reflection (or appearance, ābhāsa) of the Self,

the words by which the ego-sense is *designated* may also be used to *indicate* the Self, though only indirectly, as their direct meaning is something different. It is the same as when words referring indirectly to fire are applied to torches and the like.[96]

❖

4. *Objection:* It is seen, and is a fact well-known from worldly usage, that act and agent, denoted respectively by root and personal affix,[97] though different in themselves, pertain to one subject (*viz.* the agent himself), as in the case of 'he does' or 'he goes'.[98]

Reply: The personal affix refers to the reflection of the Self in the intellect, the root to the activity of the intellect in knowing. Through a failure to discriminate these two elements one says erroneously 'he knows'. The intellect *per se* has no knowledge: the Self *per se* has no activity. So the expression 'he knows' cannot rightly be applied to either. Nor can the word 'jñapti' (knowledge in the sense of the act of knowing) be rightly attributed to the Self. For the Self does not undergo change, as we know from the (upanishadic) teaching that it is constant.[99] Nor can the Self (as knowledge absolute) be designated by the term 'buddhi',[100] a term which pertains properly to the intellect. For there cannot be an instrument (such as the 'buddhi') without a (separate self using it as) agent. Nor can the Self be regarded as knowledge in the sense of 'that which is known'. Those who hold to the one eternal Self free from pain and not subject to modification, cannot ever maintain that the Self is either expressible in words or knowable as an object. If the ego-sense were the Self, it could be the direct meaning of the term 'Self'. But the ego is not the real Self taught by the Upanishads, since that has absence of hunger and other (super-human) qualities.[101]

Objection: Well then, if there is no direct meaning of a word, there cannot be an indirect one either.[102] So you must explain how words like 'he knows' are used.[103] If words have no meaning, the Veda will cease to be an authoritative means of knowledge. You do not want that, so you had better admit that the phrase 'he knows' (in the Veda) is to be understood in its well-known sense (as referring to the act of knowing).

Reply: If in regard to the meaning of words we accepted what seems self-evident to the foolish people of the world, we would hold to the doctrine of no (transcendent) Self. This would be the view of the Materialists, and something you do not want yourself. And if we accept the scholarly view (of the grammarians), then the meaning of the word 'knowledge' as applied to the Self in the Veda remains hard to make out, as we have already shown.[104] But the Veda is agreed to be an authoritative source of knowledge, and we cannot accept that it falls into an *impasse* here. We explain the matter as follows.

Men take the reflection of the face in the mirror to be the one with the face. For the reflection of the face is seen to have the form of the face. Indeed, wherever there is a reflection of a thing, the thing and its reflection are apt to be identified through lack of proper discrimination. In this way,[105] everyone naturally says 'he knows' as if it were a real act.[106] Superimposing on to the Self the agency pertaining properly to the intellect, we say of the Self 'he knows' and call it the knower. And superimposing onto the intellect the consciousness (that pertains properly to the Self) we speak of the intellect also as the Absolute. In fact, however, we know from the Veda that knowledge is changeless and eternal, the very nature of the

Self. Consequently, it is never in fact produced, either by the intellect or by the Self or by anything else. In the expression 'he knows', people in the world speak of the intellect and the Self as the agent of an act of knowing just in the same (loose) way that they apply the ego-notion to the body. True, the Logicians say 'Knowledge is produced (causally)'.[107] But they are deluded by the presentations of the intellect which are admittedly produced and which have a semblance of consciousness.[108]

Therefore, the words of phrases like 'he knows', the (apparent) experience (corresponding to them), and the (apparent) memory of that experience, all proceed from failure to distinguish from one another consciousness, its reflection in the intellect and the intellect. Just as (when we look at the reflection of a face in the mirror without pausing to reflect that it is not the face) the quality of conforming to the characteristics of the mirror (e.g. being dark or smudged) that belongs properly to the reflection is attributed (momentarily) to the face, so (in popular experience) the quality of conforming to the characteristics of the intellect, which belongs properly to the reflection in it, is attributed falsely to the Self. And thus (i.e. because the intellect, pure consciousness and the reflection are not distinguished) the presentations of the intellect lit by the reflection of the Self, appear to have the power of active cognition, just as torches and the like appear to have the power of burning.[109]

The Buddhists say that the representations are self-luminous and themselves the power of active cognition. They deny the existence of any other power which knows them. Now, unless it be admitted that the representations (are non-conscious objects and) are illuminated by a power radically different from themselves in nature, this theory will be hard to refute.[110] For if it be not admitted that their rise and fall is witnessed by a reality distinct from themselves in nature, then, the view that there is a persistent subject (grāhaka) actively cognizing the various modifications of the intellect and accompanying all of them is not better than the Buddhist theory. For such an active subject[111] would itself be as non-conscious as the mental modifications, and there would be no other perceiver to perceive them. And even if you (admit the radical difference in nature between the Witness and the representations of the intellect but) say that valid cognition can be established through the bare proximity of the Witness to the representations, that also is wrong.[112] For the bare proximity of the Witness (without the mediation of a reflection of consciousness) is of no service to those modifications.[113] And if it could charge them with consciousness it would charge everything with consciousness.[114]

Moreover, we would ask a question of you (i.e. of the Sāṅkhya philosopher who analyses empirical consciousness without recourse to the theory of a reflection of pure Consciousness).[115] The one in pain, the suppliant, the one who listens to teaching — is *he* the Witness or another (*viz.* the agent in empirical experience)? You do not accept that the Witness is a suppliant or undergoes pain. Nor can you admit that, as the agent in empirical experience, the suppliant could grasp the real in the notion 'I am the Witness, the real'.[116] And on this view, the statement in the Veda 'Thou art the real' would be false, which is also incorrect. The statement of the Veda becomes intelligible if it is assumed that it is made (from the standpoint of one) discriminating (the ego, the Self and the reflection of consciousness).[117] If, however, it had discriminated the empirical knowing subject from the pure Witness and said to the former 'That thou art', the above-mentioned faults would have come in.[118] If the intention of the word 'thou' is to indicate the Witness, then you (Sāṅkhya philosopher) will have to determine the relation between the ego-sense (the primary meaning of the word 'thou') and the Witness, through which alone the term 'thou' can indicate the Witness.[119]

If you say, 'The relation is that of seer and seen', we ask, 'How can the act of seeing pertain to the actionless Witness?' And even if the Witness, though actionless, had a relation of non-difference (tādātmya)[120] with the ego-sense,[121] still, without a perception of this relation in the form 'the Witness is my (real) Self',[122] the idea (of the Witness) could not arise (as the indirectly indicated meaning of the word 'thou').[123] If you think that knowledge of a relation (between the ego-sense and the Witness) arises from the Vedic texts,[124] that, too, is wrong. For the three difficulties mentioned above will crop up.[125] And even if they did not, the relation would be grasped in the form 'there is a Witness of mine' (and not in the form 'I am the Witness'). But when (as on our view), the intellect, not itself a conscious seer, *appears*[126] to be a conscious seer, then its representations also (*appear* to be luminous), as sparks from a burning iron (appear to be fire).

The fact that people sometimes experience the presence of a reflection of consciousness (as in waking and dream) and sometimes its absence (as in dreamless sleep) is explicable only if there exists a Witness, itself uncontradictable,[127] (of both these states) — and not otherwise. And on this assumption it becomes explicable how the Witness can be known.[128]

Objection: Well, but on the last-quoted analogy there will still be a real entry of consciousness (into the non-conscious), just as fire becomes really transferred to the lump of iron.[129]

Reply: This idea has already been silenced by our statement (that the entry of consciousness into the non-conscious is) like the reflection of a face in a mirror.[130] (Even in the other classical illustration to which you refer) all that is said is, 'The black iron seems to acquire a glow (ābhāsa) of red colour'. An illustration is never in every respect identical with that which it is cited to illustrate. And, in the same way, the intellect, acquiring a reflection (ābhāsa) of Consciousness, becomes *like* Consciousness, just as a reflection (ābhāsa) of a face in the mirror is *like* the face. And a reflection is said to be illusory. To say that the intellect *is* Consciousness would be to contradict both the Veda and reason. And moreover it is a theory that would imply that the body also was Consciousness, as well as the eye and the other sense-organs. The difficulty here is that one falls into the doctrine of the Materialists (which is anti-Vedic).[131] Nor could there ever be the notion 'I' am the 'Witness' unless there were a reflection of consciousness in the mind. And unless there is the preliminary conviction 'I am the real (I am the Witness)' the teaching 'That thou art' itself will be useless. The text is meaningful to one who already knows the distinction between the Self and the not-self.

Whatever is known as 'mine' or 'this' quite evidently falls within the not-self. What is known as 'I' belongs to the sphere of the Self, and what is known with the feeling 'I am such and such' belongs to the Self and the not-self both.[132] All these notions are accepted as being relatively more or relatively less direct expressions (of the Self). The problem of which of them qualify which and which are qualified by which must also be worked out rationally.[133] The 'mine' and the 'this' are both qualifications of the 'I am such and such'. Just as, in the case of a man having wealth or a man having cows (the wealth or the cows are a qualification of the man as a whole, including his body), so is the body itself (a qualification) of the (bare) ego-sense.[134] All that ever comes into the intellect, including the ego-sense, is on this reasoning the qualification of the Witness. Thus pure Consciousness, itself never coming into contact with anything, illumines all.

All that we have been saying so far on this topic is the reverse of the truth (as seen from the highest standpoint), as we have been speaking from the standpoint of worldly experience. The not-self element only exists for those who lack metaphysical discrimination; it does not exist for those who possess it. But it is only through reasoning over examples of agreement and difference in the case of both words and the things denoted by words[135] that one can determine the meaning of 'this' (the not-self element) and 'I' (the Self)[136] in the present context (and not from the uncritical standpoint of common-sense).

The feeling 'I did not see anything whatever in this my recent sleep' does not deny one's own consciousness in that state, but does deny that any representation occurs in it. The Veda itself, in the words '(Here in dream this Spirit, puruṣa, is) self-luminous'[137] and '(For no break is found in the seeing) of the seer',[138] declared that pure Consciousness (saṃvit) exists and that it is immutable (kūṭastha) and that there are breaks in the mental representations with which it is associated. Consciousness (avagati) and the individual cognitions with which it is associated are (therefore) distinct.

When the meaning of the text ('That thou art') has once been understood on the basis of Vedic and secular grammatical usage, the Veda again says 'That thou art' for the final removal of the hearer's delusion'.[139] It is as when Brahmā removed the nescience of Rāma by his mere words ('O Rāma: Thou art Viṣṇu, not the son of Daśaratha').[140] He did not mention any other task Rāma had to perform in order to become awake to his nature as Viṣṇu (apart from merely listening to the words). It is in this way (i.e. as just stated, without any further work being required) that the word 'I'[141] reveals the Light, the inmost Self. That same revelation is given in the text 'Thou art the real'.[142] The fruit is liberation.[143] If the holy knowledge did not ensue from the mere hearing of the relevant texts, one would certainly have to assume that there was some act that had to be performed.[144] But in fact there is no such contingency. Even before one has experience of it (through the texts such as 'I am the Absolute') one admits the existence of one's own Self.[145] The valid cognition of the meaning of texts like 'That thou art' is generated immediately on hearing them and results in liberation from all evils such as hunger, etc. There is then no doubt as to the truth of their content throughout the past, present and future. There is no doubt that authoritative knowledge of the Self springs up immediately from hearing the texts in the manner described. For the obstacles to an understanding[146] have been removed (by the preliminary method of reasoning by agreement and difference), and the Self is of the very nature of Consciousness.[147]

Does the text 'I am the Absolute'[148] convey 'Verily, I am the real' or something else? If it conveys 'Verily, I am the real' the meaning of the term 'I' will be identical with 'real'.[149] But if anything else is conveyed by the text, then the later conviction 'I am the real' would be false. Therefore it is only by taking the two terms of the proposition as identical that we avoid a contradiction with the experience of liberation.[150]

Now, the empirical cognitions and the intellect which entertains them exist for the sake of that Self which is reflected in them. Since they are both *per se* non-conscious, it is said figuratively that the fruit of the liberating knowledge accrues to pure Consciousness.[151] Indeed, because the two active causes of the fruit of liberation — the preliminary mental activity and the ensuing cognition in its empirical aspect — are (themselves non-conscious and so) not of the nature of that fruit, it is but right to attribute it to the Immutable (even though He is actionless), just as victory (won solely by the acts of his servants) is fitly attributed to a king.[152]

(Or one may also say:) That reflection through which the mirror assumes the form of the face is itself verily the face.[153] And in the same way, that reflection through which the mirror of the empirical cognitions assumes the form of the ego-sense, is itself verily the real 'I'.[154] That is how the text 'I am the real'[155] should be understood, and not otherwise.[156] And without a (similar) bridge (with empirical experience provided by the reflection-theory) the text 'That thou art' would also be useless.[157]

❖

5. In the case of burns, cuts and injuries sustained by the body, there cannot be anyone in pain except through a Self identified with that body, for no one anywhere feels pain from burns and the like sustained by anyone else. Because I (as the inmost Self) am not the body and am ever beyond physical contact, this notion (that the Self is suffering when the body is harmed) must arise from false identification. It is like the false idea that one is oneself dead that might arise for a time on the death of one's son.

Just as the notion 'I am the one with the ear-rings' becomes cancelled for him who discriminates himself from his ear-rings, so does the notion 'I am the sufferer' become cancelled for ever[158] through the rise of the conviction that one is the bare 'I'.[159]

If it were ever proved that the Self was subject to pain, we would willingly grant that some faculty of experiencing pain belonged to it naturally. But in fact the sense of being the sufferer[160] accrues to the Self through false identification. It is only through this false identification that the Self becomes capable of experiencing profit and loss.[161] Just as the sense of contact is attributed to the Self though it is in fact without the sense of contact, and just as movement and other properties of the body are attributed to it though it is without them, even so is pain attributed to the Self though lack of discrimination, though pain belongs properly only to the mind. Pain is rejected, just like movement, through the conviction that one is the Self, which arises through discrimination. The mind 'moves' involuntarily because of its non-discriminatory nature.[162] Then, when the mind is moving, pain is experienced. But when the mind is not in motion, the Self experiences no pain. Therefore that pain cannot exist in the inmost Self.[163]

Because the words 'thou' and 'real' (in 'Thou art the real' taken as the equivalent of 'That thou art') refer to one and the same entity, they function like the words 'the black horse' (that is, each word loses that part of its meaning which is incompatible with the meaning of the other word).[164] Through being brought into apposition with the word 'real' which expresses absence of pain,[165] the word 'thou' (loses its meaning of the empirical experiencer subject to pain and) is left with the meaning 'real' (and without pain). And similarly, through being set in apposition with a word (*viz.* 'thou') signifying 'the inmost Self', the term 'real' (loses the sense of 'something not immediately known' and) is left with the meaning 'inmost Self'. In the sentence 'Thou art the real', the reference is to the inmost Self, as in the sentence 'Thou art the tenth'.[166]

Without (totally) giving up their own (individual) meanings, the words ('thou' and 'real' together) convey a qualified meaning (arising from the mutual qualifications of their individual meanings). And they lead to immediate awareness of the inmost Self. There can be no other meaning than this one (i.e. than the inmost Self), for it would result in a contradiction.[167]

The man whose mind has been led away by the notion of

nine and is not aware of himself as completing the ten requires only to know his own Self.[168] And the one whose intellect is led away by desire because his eyes have been bandaged by nescience fails to see that his Self is pure Consciousness, ever distinct from all else, just as (the other man failed to perceive that he himself was) the tenth. Just as one comes to know himself (as the tenth) simply from hearing the words 'Thou art the tenth', so does the other come to know his own Self as the Witness of all intellects from simply hearing the words of texts like 'That thou art'.

In regard to the texts of the Veda, there is no such rule as 'A sentence must begin with such-and-such an element (e.g. the subject) and proceed to such-and-such an element (e.g. a predicate).[169] One must first determine the mutual relation of the words through reasoning on their meaning through the method of agreement and difference, and then it would be possible to understand the meaning of the sentence.[170] For (knowledge of) the meaning of a sentence results from memory of the meaning of the words heard to compose it. And in the case of sentences which proclaim the eternal truth (i.e. that the hearer is the supreme Self), when once the meaning of the words has been correctly discriminated in order to arrive at an understanding of the meaning of the sentence as a whole, then no further room for questioning the meaning remains.[171] We spoke of reasoning by the method of agreement and difference only in regard to the (preliminary) process of calling to mind the appropriate meaning of the words. No one can understand the meaning of a sentence unless he first calls to mind the meaning of its words.

In sentences such as 'That thou art', the meaning of the sentence will not become clear until there has first been a discrimination of the meaning of the word 'thou' as the pure 'I', ever liberated. Reasoning by the method of agreement and difference is required for discrimination of the meaning of the word 'thou' and not for anything else.[172] For when discrimination has once determined the meaning of the word 'thou', the meaning of the sentence becomes as clear as a bilva fruit held in the palm of the hand. In this way the meaning of the holy text 'That thou art' as bare 'I'[173] becomes clear from the meaning of the words that compose it, since the inmost Self (of the hearer) is determined as the meaning through the cancellation of the false notion of the Self as sufferer (as incompatible with the word 'real').[174] When the meaning (of the text 'That thou art') is capable of being made out (rationally) in this way, it is no longer possible for those genuinely expert in the meanings of sentences and words to assume meanings which are not the meaning of the Veda and which would undermine that meaning.

Perception and other means of empirical cognition might contradict a text (concerned with sense-objects) like that concerned with the cooking of gold particles.[175] But how can mere appearances such as perception and the other means of empirical cognition contradict the texts (which proclaim the Self as the supreme reality)? You may say that as long as (even the appearance of) the feeling 'I am the sufferer' persists on the basis of mere appearances such as perception and the other means of empirical cognition, the conviction 'I am free from suffering' cannot rise from the holy text.[176] But this is wrong, for there is the contrary example (of the conviction on the part of one who has awoken from a painful dream that he was not really related to pain even during the painful dream experience).[177] Here we have the experience 'in a dream I was in pain from burns and cuts and the like'. Well, let us suppose for the sake of argument that this was not negated by words heard during the dream. Even so, when the dream is over, the pain is regarded as non-existent now and as having been unreal before. For pain and error, once cancelled, do not assert themselves again.[178] If a man once comes to know that his own inner Self is the supreme Self through cancellation of the notion 'I am the sufferer', his knowledge is uncontradictable, like that of the one whose erroneous notion that he is the ninth is cancelled by his knowledge that he is the tenth.[179]

The knowledge that one is (really) ever liberated comes from the holy texts and from no other source. And knowledge of the meaning of a text is not possible without first calling to mind the meanings of its component words.[180] It is certain that the meaning of a word is called to mind on the basis of agreements and differences.[181]

The clearest form of authoritative knowledge of the inmost Self (i.e. immediate awareness based on identity-feeling) arises from such texts as 'That thou art'[182] just as it does from 'Thou art the tenth'. Just as all the pain pertaining to a dream ceases on waking, so the notion that one's Self is the sufferer ceases for ever through the knowledge that one is the inmost Self. Authoritative knowledge (pramā) does not arise from such texts as that enjoining the melting down of gold particles,[183] because such texts have to be interpreted metaphorically on account of (conflict with sense-experience which reveals) the fact that gold does not melt. But this (inability to produce authentic knowledge) is not the case with sentences like 'That thou art', because they do not involve contradictions with known truths.

In the text 'That thou art' the meanings of the two words 'that' and 'art' are already known. The sentence will not yield the authoritative knowledge that the meaning of the word 'thou' is 'the real' without their support. The purpose of the word 'art' is to show that 'that' and 'thou' refer to one and the same entity.[184] Thus the word 'that' comes to mean that inmost Self, and the word 'thou' comes to mean the same as the word 'that'. Taken together, they exclude from one another respectively the ideas of 'the sufferer' and 'not being the inmost Self'.[185] Thus the two terms 'that' and 'thou' taken together (as united by the word 'art') express the same meaning as the phrase 'not this, not this'.[186]

❖

6. As knowledge results from the text 'That thou art' when it is understood in this way, how can it be maintained that this text is not an authoritative source of knowledge in itself and that it requires to be supported by action (in the form of further meditation and ritual)? The notion 'do' is incompatible with the meaning of this text, whether at the beginning, end or middle.[187] Hence we do not assume that action is involved here, especially as there is no Vedic warrant for it. To abandon the Veda is useless.

Here you might object that no concrete experience, like the

concrete satisfaction that follows eating, arises from the mere hearing of a sentence. And to analyse a sentence in the hope of getting a concrete experience is like trying to make milk-pudding from cow-dung.[188] To this we reply that it is true that all sentences about the not-self yield abstract knowledge only. But it is not so with sentences about the inmost Self, for there are exceptions, as in the case of the one who realized he was the tenth.[189] One should accept that the Self is its own means of knowledge, which means it is directly knowable to itself (svayam-vedyatva). On our view, when the ego is dissolved, experience of one's own Self is realized. We regard pain as something experienced as an object even by the empirical cognitions. How can there be any connection with pain for the inner Witness, for whom even the cognitions are objects?[190] The Witness, verily, is experienced by itself alone, being of the nature of experience. The rise of a mental cognition in which it is reflected is spoken of as 'the experience of it'.[191]

❖

7. (The Dharma Śāstra) says:[192] 'In order to perform the discrimination necessary to find the meaning of the word "thou" there must be renunciation of all action (saṃnyāsa)'. This is the right means (to Self-knowledge, and not the prolongation of action recommended by the Prasaṅkhyāna Vādins).[193] For the Veda teaches, 'Peaceful, controlled'.[194] First a man must perceive the innermost Self as the Self of his own psycho-physical organism and as the meaning of the word 'thou'. Then he sees all as his own Self alone, which is the meaning of the whole sentence ('That thou art'). When the meaning of the sentence, which is an authoritative means of

knowledge, has been correctly comprehended as 'All is the Self', no other authoritative means of knowledge can remain.[195] How can any injunction to act apply after there has been comprehension of the meaning of the sentence ('That thou art')? For there cannot be the two contradictory ideas 'I am the Absolute' and 'I am the agent'.[196]

❖

8. Does someone cause a person to know that principle which is different (from the empirical cognitions)[197] through a positive means of proof (pramāṇa)? Or is it not rather through the negation of all else other than it, and without a positive means of proof?

If in this context you maintain that there is a negation of all else other than the Self which proceeds through the mere authority of the Vedic texts, we reply that in that case a mere void would result, as there would be no familiarity with the Witness. If you answer (that a person can infer that he is of the nature of consciousness) by saying (to himself), 'Thou art consciousness. How couldst thou be the (non-conscious) body?', we reply, 'No, for one is not familiar (with oneself as transcendent Consciousness)'. This argument (also proceeds through negation of what is contradictory (to the Self as pure Consciousness). It would be valid only if pure Consciousness were already established through some other proof.

If someone were to say, 'The Witness affirms its own self-existence because consciousness is immediately self-evident (aparokṣa)', we reply that (if the appeal is to immediate consciousness) in that case the different view of the one who denied the Self (the Buddhist Nihilist) would be equally cogent.

'Well', you may say, 'people have the memory, "I saw this". This proves that an instrument (i.e. a cognition), an object and an agent (in the act of knowing) are manifest simultaneously (to an abiding self which is the knower)'.[198] But even granting for the sake of argument that memory were a valid means of knowledge,[199] the instrument, object and agent (of the act of knowing) are apprehended successively, and memory, coming later, must likewise reproduce the cognitions as successive. The notion of their simultaneity must therefore be a false one, due to the speed at which they occur.[200] In the idea 'I was aware both of the object and of myself (as knower at the same time)', there is certainly mutual relativity.[201] Where we have distinctions (in cognition) based on mutual relativity, there cannot be simultaneity.[202] Moreover, each of the three factors (i.e. knower, knowledge and object) will be necessary in the act of perceiving each one of themselves. When the knower is engaged in perceiving itself, it will not be available to perceive (simultaneously) knowledge and the known object.[203] And again, it is laid down[204] that an object is that which an agent is striving to obtain. Hence an object relates to an agent, and not to anything other than an agent (such as the Witness).[205] Objects open to direct designation by words (padārtha) are revealed either through speech or inference or by some other means of valid knowledge (pramāṇa) to one who does not already know them, and not in any other way.

Is the Witness (which is not subject to designation by words) also established by a means of valid cognition (pramāṇa), or without one? It is established without one. And yet this knowledge is of no use to (is concealed from) the ignorant person (until enlightenment comes through the Vedic text 'That thou art'). If it be held that it is the Witness Himself who is ignorant of His own true nature, then He will require a fresh cognition (depending on a means of valid cognition) if He is to know that He Himself is knowledge. And if it be one other than the Witness who is ignorant of the nature of the Witness as knowledge, then a fresh cognition will be required all the more certainly.

What is 'being established (siddhi)'? Is it being known? Or coming into being? Or something else? If it is 'being known', you should bear in mind the two views we have just discussed.[206] If 'being established' meant 'coming into being', then all efforts in the matter would be useless. For every one knows that an object comes into being naturally from its proper causes. Consequently, when we are discussing the question of knower, knowledge and known,[207] the phrase 'being established' is used to mean 'being known'.[208] The 'establishment of Witness and witnessed' means their being known, not their coming into being. If you[209] assume that 'being established' is the clear distinction between object, agent and act, evident in the act of knowing, then we reply that clear and unclear pertain only to something other than the Self, and not to the Self. The reason why a pot cannot be 'clear' to a blind man is that he is not a seer. If the agent, instrument and object of the act of self-knowledge are to be 'clear', then there will have to be a seer (Witness) beyond them to apprehend the fact.[210]

❖

4. Meditation (Dhyāna) and Repeated Affirmation (Abhyāsa)

It is clear from Śaṅkara's own Bṛhadāraṇyaka Commentary[211] that a three-fold discipline for the assimilation of the supreme upanishadic wisdom consisting in hearing (śravaṇa), cogitation (manana) and sustained meditation (nididhyāsana) was already accepted and familiar doctrine for his predecessor Bhartṛprapañca. Śaṅkara does refer to the triad,[212] but only very rarely, and he is not very explicit about what he understood by the terms. As Saccid-ānandendra Svāmin points out,[213] it is somewhat remarkable that Śaṅkara does not elaborate on or define the term nididhyāsana even when commenting on the word 'nididhyāsitavya' in the Bṛhadāraṇyaka Upanishad.[214]

The best way to see how Śaṅkara conceived hearing, cogitation and sustained meditation is to read through his Upadeśa Sāhasrī. In the first part of the prose section (paras 1-44) we find the pupil mainly preoccupied with hearing clusters of texts from the Teacher, texts which he already knows by heart but which have to be presented to him by the Teacher in due order and within a broadly sketched framework of cosmological, psychological and meta-physical teaching. In the second part of the prose section (paras 45-111) the Teacher resorts to argumentation to quell the pupil's doubts and shift him, in a kind of Socratic manner, to new viewpoints. The third and concluding part of the prose section constitutes a recapitulatory summary of the earlier teaching, called a 'Parisaṅkhyāna'. This term does not appear to have been much used in Advaita except to introduce these paragraphs in the Upadeśa Sāhasrī, and the practice itself is not common, though the Fourth Book of the Naiṣkarmya Siddhi of Śaṅkara's pupil Sureśvara might be regarded as an example of it. While the first and second parts of the prose section of the Upadeśa Sāhasrī well exemplify what Śaṅkara meant by śravaṇa and manana respectively, it is clear that the third part does not really correspond with what he would have understood by the term nididhyāsana. This is better exemplified by the Extracts gathered below in the present section, taken from the shorter chapters of the *verse* section of the Upadeśa Sāhasrī. They supply the themes for affirmation, reflection and meditation appropriate for those living the life of Adhyātma Yoga, the way of life sketched in the Extracts of the opening section of the present chapter. Saccidānandendra Svāmin considers that for Śaṅkara 'adhyātma-yoga', 'mano-nigraha', 'dhyāna-yoga'[215] and 'nididhyāsana' were almost interchangeable terms.[216]

The appended Extracts are arranged in two groups, covering 'Dhyāna' and 'Abhyāsa' respectively. The Extracts of the first group give some idea of the way in which Śaṅkara conceived the physiological and psychological aspects of meditation, though texts on this subject are spare in his Vedāntic works. The Extracts in the second group consist mostly in verse passages from the second part of the Upadeśa Sāhasrī which are clearly meant to be learned by heart and continually reflected and meditated upon by the highest class of spiritual enquirer. The object is to enable him to affirm and re-affirm over and over again the final spiritual truth, that which he is aiming to become aware of by direct intuition (anubhava). This practice merges with, and can be regarded as an aspect of, reflection (vicāra), the discipline of reflection and meditation whereby the mind is prepared to understand the highest texts and grasp their truth in immediate vision. This discipline is needed by all but the few gifted pupils who immediately understand the meaning of the texts on hearing them for the first time. In their case, it is presumed that reflection and meditation have been performed in an earlier life.

TEXTS ON DHYĀNA

1. The text now goes on to enumerate alternative methods, such as meditation and others, for attaining vision of the Self. Meditation (dhyāna) is the withdrawal of the outward-going perception of the senses into the mind and the one-pointed focusing of the mind on the source of its consciousness. Examples to illustrate it have been given, such as when we say in common parlance 'The crane seems to be meditating' or in such a text as 'The earth seems to meditate, ...so do the mountains'.[217] From these we collect that meditation consists in sustaining one idea uninterruptedly, like an unbroken flow of oil. Some yogins have been able to become aware of the inner consciousness illumining their intellects through meditation with a mind already purified through previous meditation.

Others come to the same result through the discipline (yoga) of speculative enquiry (sāṅkhya). Sāṅkhya is speculative enquiry on the pattern of 'These constituents called sattva, rajas and tamas are perceived by me, therefore I must be different from them, the Witness of their operations, myself changeless and eternal, different in nature from the constituents, and in fact the Self'. This speculative enquiry (sāṅkhya) is a form of discipline (yoga), and through it certain yogis, as the text points out, 'perceive the Self through the mind'.

Others, says the text, achieve the same result through 'karma-yoga'. Here the action (karma) is itself the discipline (yoga). Action (karma) is to be defined as an activity performed as an offering to the Lord, and is figuratively called spiritual discipline (yoga) because it is performed for the sake of spiritual discipline. Other yogins are here said to achieve the same result as those mentioned earlier, this time through the discipline of action, but it is only meant in the sense that action indirectly prepares them for the rise of knowledge through purifying their minds.[218]

❖

2. Having described the external seat, the Lord now goes on to describe how one should hold the body for meditation. Body, head and neck should be held upright and motionless. 'Motionless' is specified because there could still be motion on the part of one holding his body, head and neck upright. The meditator should make his physical position firm. He should be *apparently* gazing at the tip of his nose. We have to understand the word 'apparently' here, because the text does not mean to prescribe gazing at the tip of the nose literally. What it means is the withdrawal of the gaze from objects, and it is assumed that this depends on previous concentration of the mind. If it had really been meant that the gaze should have been fixed at the tip of the nose, it would have followed that the mind would have been concentrated there and not on the Self. But the Lord will teach later that the mind must be concentrated on the Self...[219]

❖

3. In the case of meditations (upāsana) associated with ritual, there is no problem about the posture of the body in which they are to be carried out, as they are not carried out for their own sake, but only as part of the ritual. Nor is there any discussion as to whether they might lead (directly) to right

intuition, as knowledge is conditioned by the nature of the real and not by the action of the subject (in meditation). But in regard to other meditations (upāsana), the question arises whether one may perform them standing, seated or lying down according to one's wish, or whether they should regularly be performed in a sitting posture. And one might initially suppose that, since meditation was a mental act, there would be no restriction as to the posture of the body.

To this the author of the Sūtras replies that meditations must be performed in a sitting posture, because it is only in this way that they can be performed at all. Meditation is the maintenance of a continuous stream of ideas of identical content.[220] No one who is walking or running about can do this, as walking and the like shake up the mind. Even one who is standing still has to occupy his mind with holding his balance and is not able to attend to anything subtle at the same time. And one who is lying down is liable to an unexpected invasion of sleep. But one who is seated easily avoids these difficulties and many others, and is therefore able to perform meditation.

This 'maintenance of a continuous stream of ideas of identical content' is the same thing as is understood by the word 'dhyāna'. One speaks figuratively of 'dhyāna' in the case of beings who have minimized the motions of their limbs and fixed their gaze squarely on one point and whose minds are concerned with one object only, as when one says, 'The crane is in contemplation', 'The woman whose husband has gone abroad sits buried in contemplation'. This can happen effortlessly only when one is seated, so this is another reason why meditation should be considered as an act to be performed in a sitting posture. And another indication that meditation has to be performed in a sitting posture is supplied by the text 'The earth seems to be in contemplation',[221] for contemplation is figuratively attributed to the earth and the like on account of their motionlessness. And there is the tradition amongst the learned that posture is a part of meditation, as expressed in such texts from the derivative literature as 'Having taken up a firm posture in a clean place'.[222] And as a further confirmation, we find that the Yoga System teaches the 'lotus' and other seated bodily postures.[223]

And there is the further doubt as to whether or not there are rules as to time and place and the way one should be facing. And one might initially suppose that since rules as to place and time and direction to be faced are usually found in the case of Vedic undertakings, there would be some kind of rule in the present instance too. But the author of the Sūtras argues against this, and maintains that rules as to time, place and the direction one should face should be made to suit one's own aim. One should meditate in whatever place and at whatever time serves most easily to concentrate the mind. For what is invariably desired by those sitting down to meditate is a one-pointed mind, and that alone. The case with the rituals is different. They are performed for different ends, and consequently there is room for different instructions about facing the east, performing the sacrifice early in the day or on ground sloping towards the east. But in regard to sitting down to meditate, where the goal is always one and the same, no different specifications as to time, place and direction to face are found.

Here you might object that, as a matter of fact,

specifications *are* found. For example, 'He should perform his practices in a clean, level spot, not pebbly or in the vicinity of fire or sand, having features helpful to the mind in meditation such as the sound of waterfalls, not containing any creatures (such as mosquitoes) to afflict the eyes and with opportunities to retire to a windless place such as a cave'.[224] Yes, we agree that there are specifications of this sort. But the Teacher (the author of the Sūtras) declares, in his compassion, that there is no rigid obligation to obey these specifications. And the phrase 'helpful to the mind in meditation' that came in the quoted text shows that the real specification is 'Wherever one-pointedness can be found'.[225]

❖

4. The supreme Self is one, is alone real, is ever pure, enlightened and free by nature, as we know from such texts as 'One only without a second'.[226] All else is unreal. Why then do we find meditations (which imply at least the duality of ends and means) taught in such texts as 'The Self is to be seen', 'That Self beyond sin... (He should be sought)', 'Let him form a resolve (to meditate)', 'The Self alone is to be meditated upon',[227] and also rituals such as the Agnihotra?

Listen to the reason as given by the Teacher (Gauḍapāda). There are three kinds of qualified souls treading the spiritual path within the framework of the castes and stages of life, those, namely, of excellent, middling and weak powers of vision or intelligence. The instructions to meditate and perform ritual are provided by the Veda in a spirit of compassion for the benefit of those of middling and weak powers of vision, not for those of excellent vision who have already acquired the conviction 'The Self is one only, without a second'. They are just means that will help them eventually to come to the highest standpoint from which one sees that all is one, as expressed in such texts as 'That which one does not think with the mind, that, they say, by which the mind is thought — that alone is the Absolute, you must know, and not that on which you meditate', 'That thou art', and 'All this is the Self'.[228]

TEXTS ON ABHYĀSA

1. Whatever is seen, anywhere, at any time, in any intellect, is seen by me (the sole Witness). Therefore I am the Absolute, the Supreme, omniscient and omnipresent. As I am the one witness of the activities of my own mind, so am I the one witness of the minds of others. I can neither be increased nor diminished. Therefore I am the supreme.

The Self is not the mind. It is neither subject to mutation nor impure nor material. Being the Witness of all minds everywhere, it is not of limited knowledge like the mind.

Just as the red hue and other qualities of a jewel stand illumined in sunlight, so do all things stand illumined in me as if by sunlight. Objects exist in the mind, but only when the mind is in manifestation.[229] But the Witness ever remains the Witness. This proves that duality does not exist.

Just as the mind first fails to see the Supreme through lack of discrimination, so, when discrimination supervenes, nothing exists apart from the Supreme, not even the mind itself.[230]

❖

2. O my mind! My nature is pure unadulterated Consciousness, and my connection with the body is but a product of thy delusion. No result whatever accrues to me from all thy activities, as I am ever without distinctions of any kind. Give up thy intense activity, bred of illusion, abandon thy weary struggles and attain the great peace. For I am the Supreme, the Absolute, ever free, unborn, one without a second. I alone exist, ever the same in all beings, all-pervading and indestructible like the ether, undivided, partless, actionless, the supreme Good, the transcendent: no result can accrue from thy activities.

I myself am my own sole possession: I recognize nothing else as my own. Nor do I belong to anyone else, for I am relationless. Yes, I am relationless, and have nothing to do with thy activities, for I am one without a second.

Seeing that people are deeply attached to the idea of cause and effect, I have composed this little dialogue for their benefit, which will throw light on their own true nature. If a man meditates on this dialogue, he will be released from the attacks of the great foe ignorance. He will walk the earth ever free from desire, free from suffering, seeing the same in all, a knower of the Self, joyful.[231]

❖

3. In the causal chain constituted by the elements, which begins with the earth (as ultimate effect) and passes through water, fire, wind and ether to the inmost Self standing beyond the elements as their ultimate cause, each successive member of the chain is recognizable as the cause of those which have gone before because it lacks the distinguishing properties of

its effects, and is hence more subtle and pervasive than they.[232] The earth and other elements in our own bodies demonstrably obey the same laws as the great elements. Just as the all-pervading ether existed before the production of wind and the other grosser elements, so is the one 'I' (aham) (within the body) eternally existent. It is pure, of the nature of unmixed consciousness, omnipresent, one without a second. According to a text of the derivative literature,[233] all living beings from Brahmā to the meanest plant are my bodies. How can lust and anger and other defects arise in me at all, as they would have to come from without? People read defects into Me, seated within the creatures and ever untouched by their defects, like a child reading blue colour into the colourless ether of the sky.

Because the minds of all living beings are ever illumined by consciousness, all living beings form my body, though I am omniscient and free from all taint. Whatever is subject to production and to being known as an object is akin to what is experienced in dream. But the pure principle of knowledge itself is eternal and not to be known as an object. Hence duality does not exist. The knowledge of the knower[234] has been declared to be eternal and unbroken.[235] As knowledge persists in dreamless sleep but with nothing over against it to know, waking consciousness must arise from nescience,[236] and the objects of knowledge are therefore to be taken as unreal. Since knowledge has no form or quality, it cannot be the object of any action, and hence we conclude that the Infinite (the Self) cannot be the object of any act of knowing.

Verily I am ever the transcendent principle of Consciousness in its pure state, one, unborn, indestructible, stainless, omnipresent, subtle like the ether, untainted non-dual, OM! I am the pure Witness, not subject to modification. In my true nature, I have no relation with any object. Established in my own Self, unborn, I am perfect infinitude, extending in all directions, in front, to the sides, above and below. I am unborn and hence immortal, not subject to decay and death. I am self-caused,[237] omnipresent, without a second. I am neither a cause nor an effect, utterly pure, ever content in myself alone and hence free. OM!

None of the experiences of dreamless sleep, waking and dream really belong to me. It is all a delusion. They are not real in themselves and they do not acquire reality from anything else. I am the Fourth,[238] the eternal non-dual Consciousness. The succession of miseries that constitute the body, the senses and the mind are neither me nor mine, for I am not subject to change. No succession of experiences arising from an unreal cause can itself be real. It is all like the visions of one dreaming. What, however, is true is that I am without change of any kind. For there can be nothing to occasion change in me when I am one without a second. Neither merit nor demerit, neither bondage nor liberation, neither caste nor stage of life apply to me, for I have no body. Being beginningless and without empirical qualities, I do no acts and experience no results. I am non-dual and transcendent. Though I exist in the body, I am not touched or tainted, for I am subtle, like the all-pervading ether.

I am ever one and the same in all creatures, their Lord. I am the supreme principle, beyond both the perishable objects of the universe (kṣara) and their imperishable ground (akṣara);[239] I am that principle which is referred to in the Gītā as the supreme Spirit.[240] And although, being the supreme Self, I have no second being over against me, I appear otherwise, on account of nescience. The Self stands alone, untouched by nescience, fancy or action, perfectly pure. The non-dual 'I' stands fixed in its own nature like the immoveable ether, hidden from view (to us) by our (apparent) powers of seeing, hearing, thinking and knowing.

Whoever has a settled vision of the Self in the form 'I am the Absolute in its supreme form' is not reborn, says the Veda.[241] When there is no seed, there cannot be propagation of any fruit, nor can there be birth of any kind where there is no delusion.

Men fall into delusion and imagine vainly, 'This is mine' and 'This is of such and such a kind' and 'I am of such and such a nature, not anyone else and not different from what I think'. No such vain conceptions occur in the Absolute, ever non-dual and transcendent, everywhere the same.

Where there is the supremely pure non-dual knowledge of the great souls, there is neither grief nor delusion. When grief and delusion are absent, there is neither action nor birth. This is the conclusion of those who know the secret of the Veda. He who, though seeing duality, does not see it, like one asleep, on account of his vision of non-duality, and who, though acting, nevertheless does not act (being anchored in the Absolute) — he is a knower of the Self and no one else is, such is the conclusion of the Vedanta. What I have here thus declared is the doctrine of supreme truth, the final conclusion of the Upanishads. If one acquires personal conviction as to its truth, one is liberated. He is pure like the ether, and no more tainted by actions even here below.[242]

❖

4. In the case of all living beings, their nature as a conscious Witness is self-evident, while their notion that they are anything else derives from nescience. Because the notion that they are anything else proceeds from nescience, it can be corrected by hearing the Vedic text, 'That thou art'.

'This is enough for immortality', said Yājñavalkya.[243] No action is needed as an auxiliary to knowledge. In saying this, the Veda ruled out both action and the external emblems of action[244] in the case of the enlightened sage.

How can there be any distinctions in me, the changeless Witness of all the activities of the mind? The mind and its activities are the sole objects of the Witness in waking just as they are in dream. But in dreamless sleep neither the mind nor its activities exist. There is then only pure Consciousness, omnipresent and eternal. Just as a dream is true until awakening, so are the identity with the body and the authority of empirical knowledge that characterize the waking state true until knowledge of the Self.

I stand in the midst of all beings like the ether, untouched by their limitations. I am the Witness, the illuminer, pure, without empirical qualities. I am the Absolute, the transcendent. I am other than name, form and action. I am eternally free by nature. I am the Self, the Absolute, the Supreme. I am pure Consciousness, ever free from duality.

Those who think, 'I am the Absolute' and also 'I am the

agent and experiencer' are lost through the contradictory attempt to adhere to knowledge and action at the same time.[245] They are no better than the free-thinkers. The ritualists accept on the authority of the Veda that their meritorious and sinful deeds will bring unseen future rewards and punishments. They should accept on the same authority that liberation proceeds from knowledge and that the real nature of the Self is the Absolute. The 'saffron robes' referred to in the Veda[246] are the mere visions seen by dreamers here below. He who beholds them, the Witness, is other than they. Just as a sword is revealed when it is withdrawn from its scabbard, so is the self-luminous Witness revealed in dream as separate from the mind, which assumes the form of cause and effect.[247] Just as the realms of a great king and the like seen in dream[248] are mere imaginations in me, so, one should know, are the two forms that go to make up the manifest universe also imagined in me, together with the impressions (vāsanā) that give rise to them.[249] Actions have to be performed by the physical body and by the subtle body, formed of impressions. But the true Self is of the nature of 'Not this, not this' and hence I have no action to perform whatever.

And there is no hope of acquiring immortality through action, as action proceeds from nescience. Liberation proceeds from knowledge, and requires no support from anything that is not knowledge.

My Self which is immortal, which is beyond the sphere of danger,[250] and which is imperishable,[251] is that which I value most dearly.[252] Therefore one should give up everything other than that, including action.[253]

❖

5. Just as, when a person's body is standing in light, he identifies himself with it and thinks it is manifesting on its own account,[254] so also does he identify himself with his mind, which does but reflect the light of the true knower, and think 'I am the knower'. The deluded soul in the world identifies himself with whatever he sees, and this is the cause of his not finding his own true Self.[255] Just as the tenth person regarded himself as included within the nine he was counting,[256] so the deluded world identify themselves with the objects of their experience. Were it not for this, they would be aware of their own Self in its true nature.

How in the name of reason could the two contradictory ideas 'Thou must perform action' and 'That thou art' apply to the same being at the same time? Suffering only occurs to him who identifies himself with such an external adjunct as the body, not to the true nature of a person, which has no body.... This is proved by the invariable absence of pain in dreamless sleep. The Upanishads say 'That thou art' to remove identification with the body from the Self.

When the Yogī has a mental cognition in which the Witness-consciousness is reflected like a face in the mirror, he is apt to think he has seen the Self. But only he is called the best[257] of yogis who has neither this nor any other false notion. 'Thou art the knower of knowing', says the Veda.[258] And this 'knower of knowing' is what is expressed by 'thou' in 'That thou art'. It is itself 'immediate experience' (anubhava); all other experience purporting to be 'of it'[259] is false. How can there be either vision or non-vision of Me, who am of the form of eternal Consciousness? There can be no second experience to experience immediate experience.

Just as the Witness witnesses sunburn from the sun afflicting the body as an object located in the body, so does it witness the passions afflicting the mind as objects located in the mind. I am the Absolute, transcendent, ever-free and unalloyed. I am the knower, homogeneous like the ether, without a second, the negation of any notion of 'this'.[260] There can be no other 'knower of knowing' beyond me. Therefore I am ever the supreme knower in all beings, ever free. He only is a knower of the Self who is aware of himself as unbroken light, void of agency, and who has lost the feeling 'I am a knower of the Absolute'. The discriminative cognition of the mind 'I am the knower, not to be known as an object, eternally pure and free' is itself an object to the Witness and hence transient. The notion that the Self is an agent is false, as it arises from the false idea that the body is the Self. The true notion rising from the appropriate authority (the Veda) is 'I do nothing'. Agency depends on the presence of the factors of action. Non-agency is the natural state. Hence it is but right to say that the notion 'I am the agent and experiencer' is false. When one's own true nature has once been known through the authority of the Veda and reasoning in the way just shown, how could the notion 'I am subject to this or that injunction' any longer hold true?

As the ether pervades from within, so do I pervade the ether from within, changeless, immoveable, pure, beyond decay, ever without a second.[261]

❖

6. Because I am without an eye, I have no sight.[262] As I have no ear either, how could I have hearing? As I have no voice,

I have no speech. As I have no mind, I cannot think. There can be no action on the part of that which has no Vital Energy (prāṇa), and no knowership on the part of that which has no intellect. Nor can there be any alternation of knowledge and ignorance for me who am the light of pure and self-existent consciousness.

There can be no hunger or thirst or grief or delusion or old age or death for me, who am ever free, pure, firm as a mountain peak, unchangeable, immortal, indestructible, ever disembodied. I am bodiless and all-pervasive like the ether.

Because I have no sense of touch, I do not experience touch. Because I have no tongue, I do not experience taste. No alternation of knowledge and ignorance can apply to me who am of the very nature of eternal consciousness. As for the mental idea representing colour coming from the sense of sight, that is itself ever viewed as an object by the eternal vision of the Self. The same is true of all other ideas connected with the senses and representing sense-objects, as well as of the purely mental phenomena, such as memory and longing and dream: all are witnessed by another. Hence the vision of the Witness is eternal, pure and infinite. The Witness is the sole existent entity. But when spiritual discrimination is lacking, the Witness seems impure and changeable. And in the same way, the 'I' seems to become 'happy' and 'miserable' through association with the pure vision of the Self thus misconceived. When it seems to be deluded, the people of the world feel deluded, when it seems to be pure they feel pure. Through this alternation, they remain engulfed in trans-migratory life. But if anyone desires liberation, he should constantly remember the Self declared by the Veda to be without eyes,[263] to be outside and inside everything[264] and to be unborn[265] and eternally free.

The texts saying that the Self is without eyes and the like show that I am ever without sense-organs, and this is confirmed by the text 'Without sense-powers (prāṇa), without mind, pure'.[266] In the Kaṭha Upanishad[267] the Veda declares that I am without sound, touch or colour. Because I am without sense-organs or mind, I am not subject to modification of any kind. I am not at one time distracted and at another concentrated: distraction and concentration are states of the mind, which is subject to modification. How can these two states arise in me who am pure Consciousness and not mental by nature? Being bodiless and all-pervading, it follows that I am non-mental and non-changeable. I only had to perform concentration as long as nescience remained: in my true nature I am pure, enlightened and eternally free. How could there be either concentration or failure of concentration or anything else to be achieved for me? For it is when men meditate on me and become awake to me that they feel that they have done all that there was to do.

I am the Absolute, the all, ever pure, ever enlightened. I am unborn and am everywhere beyond decay, indestructible and immortal. In all beings there is no other knower but me. I distribute the rewards of merit and demerit. I am the Witness and illuminer, eternal, non-dual, without empirical qualities.[268] I am neither being nor non-being nor being and non-being combined. I am the Alone, the Transcendent. I am that eternal Witness in whom there is neither day nor night, neither dawn nor dusk. Like the ether in being subtle and free from all form, I am one without a second. I am the non-dual Absolute, void even of the ether. Just as distinctions are falsely imagined in the one ether corresponding to differences in the various receptacles in which it appears to be enclosed, even though it is always one and undivided, even so is the distinction between 'my Self' and 'the true Self' falsely imagined on account of receptacles like the body and the mind and the ego in which the one Self seems to be enclosed. Distinction and non-distinction, one and many, knower and known, goer and path are all imagined in me who am one. How could they exist truly? I am changeless and therefore subject neither to increase nor diminution, ever free, ever pure, ever enlightened, without empirical qualities, without a second.

In this way, a sage should concentrate his mind and dwell on the fact that his Self is all.When he knows that it is I who am present as the knower in his own body, he will surely be liberated. The yogi who acquires this realization of the metaphysical truth has done all that has to be done and has reached perfection. He is a true Brahmin.[269] If he fails, he is a 'destroyer of the Self'.[270]

What I have given here is a brief exposition of the final conclusion of the Veda. It should be taught only by one whose mind has been educated in the traditional spiritual way and only to renunciates who are possessed of peace.[271]

❖

7. How can there be anything for me to do who am the Witness, without sense-organs or mind, unrelated to aught else, all-pervasive like the ether? I never experience absence of concentration (samādhi) in my Self, which is changeless.[272]

There is nothing to purify in me who am the Absolute and therefore pure and without blemish. Neither have I anywhere to go, since I am omnipresent and motionless. I can go neither upwards nor downwards nor sideways, being partless and void of empirical qualities. I am the eternal light of pure Consciousness, wherein the darkness of nescience cannot penetrate. How could there be any remnant of action left to me, who am eternally liberated? How can there be cares and worries for him who is without a mind? How can there be action for him who is without organs? True were the words of the Veda, 'Without Vital Energy, without mind, pure'.[273]

Because the Self is beyond time, place, spatial direction and occasion, meditation on the Self is never restricted by rules involving these.[274] One should bathe in the holy lake of one's own purified mind, where all the gods and Vedas are united. Having bathed there, one becomes immortal.

Sound and the other great elements of the external world are not self-manifest, and neither do they manifest one another mutually. They are witnessed by one wholly different from themselves: and such also is the case with the component elements of the physical body of man. Similarly, feelings of egoism, possessiveness, desire, effort, change, pleasure, pain and the like are also witnessed as objects. And since they do not witness each other mutually, they must be witnessed as objects by one beyond themselves. Therefore, thou art the Supreme. All the changing forms assumed by the mind beginning with the ego, which are associated with the sense of agency and with the acquisition of results from one's action, are all alike illumined by pure Consciousness as if by the sun. Hence the Self is (different from them and) not bound by the results of action. As pure Consciousness, the (one) Self pervades the minds of all embodied beings, just like the ether. There is no other knower but He. Therefore He is the one Lord, the Supreme.[275]

5. Meditation on OM

The holy syllable OM is not mentioned in the Ṛg Veda, the earliest collection of Vedic texts. It is found in the Yajur Veda as a 'holy syllable' uttered in the course of the ritual, but not yet identified with the Absolute or raised above and distinguished from such other 'holy syllables' as him, hum, svāhā, vaṣaṭ and veṭ.[276] In the Brāhmaṇas it is said to mean 'Yes' in the language of the gods.[277] It was pronounced at the end of a sacrifice by the chief priest in charge as a sign of approval, confirming that the ritual had been correctly carried out. Gradually the syllable began to become more and more of a focus for the meditation and speculation of the early sages. It was pronounced at prominent places in the ritual, by the Ṛg Veda priests at the end of the Anuvākya and by the Sāma Veda priests at the end of the Udgītha. At the beginning of the Jaiminīya Brāhmaṇa[278] of the Sāma Veda it is said that Prajāpati created the three worlds by extracting the essence (sāra) of the three holy 'enunciations' (vyāhṛti) 'bhūḥ, bhuvaḥ, svaḥ', but that he could not extract the essence of the syllable OM. The same text identifies OM with the mysterious 'cow' of Ṛg Veda I.165. 42 and 45, 'from which the "Imperishable" (akṣara) proceeds'. Thus already in the Ṛg Veda period the sages had come to think of speech as having a manifest aspect as the objects of the world and an unmanifest transcendent aspect beyond them. From the time of the Jaiminīya Brāhmaṇa and the Chāndogya Upanishad these speculations are prominently linked with the syllable OM. Since OM came to be regarded as the origin of speech (vāc), it came to be invested with the same wonderful properties that had formerly been attributed to the latter.

A number of the main points about OM taught by the sages of the upanishadic period appear in the group of Extracts to follow, as the latter consist in Śaṅkara's comments upon them. The analysis of OM into A + U + M goes back to the ancient upanishadic period. But the Māṇḍūkya Upanishad correlation of these three elements of the syllable OM with the three states of consciousness, waking, dream and dreamless sleep, with the syllable as a whole correlated with the Self in its transcendent form, is new. Speech (vāk) considered as a metaphysical principle had earlier been identified with other triads, such as the three worlds, and also the three planes of manifestation, those, namely, of man's body (ādhyātmika), the cosmos (ādhibhautika) and the realm of the Vedic ritual (ādhiyājñika),[279] and had also been divided into four 'quarters' of which one was transcendent.

The first Extract on OM to follow concerns the relevance of meditation on OM for the indirect path to liberation. Mention has already been made[280] of how the soul of the man who practises Vedic ritual and meditations and has been able to achieve concentration of the mind in the heart-centre at death may pass along the subtle canal called the suṣumnā which leads (not from the base of the spine but) from the heart-centre to a minute aperture in the skull through which it proceeds along the Path of the Flame to 'conditioned immortality'. The opening Extract below explains the significance of meditation on OM for the person following this path.

The remaining Extracts bring out the importance of meditation on OM for those following the direct path to release as well. As the worshipper of Viṣṇu vividly imagines the invisible deity as present in the visible stone image, so the seeker who desires union with the Absolute uses the syllable OM as a focus where he can picture its presence. Just as the progressive manifestation of his own Self under the guise of the deity under worship appears to the ignorant worshipper as the 'grace' of the deity, so 'grace' in this sense emanates from the Absolute when worshipped through the syllable OM.[281]

Other Extracts point out that the syllable OM is the most appropriate name and the closest symbol of the Absolute, both in its supreme form and also in its conditioned form as Hiraṇyagarbha. One may meditate either on the actual sound of the syllable OM as uttered or else on the written symbol of that sound.[282] All speech is inherent in the initial 'a' of the syllable OM (broken down as A + U + M), because all vowels and consonants can be seen as modifications of an initial 'a' sound.[283] From one point of view the whole Veda can thus be regarded as latent in the 'a' of OM. From another point of view, all mutually separate objects may be regarded as the product of the arbitrary application of names which in turn depend on and derive from the 'a' of OM.[284] The syllable OM not only represents the Absolute, it *is* the Absolute.[285] As an archer concentrates his aim on his prey by means of his bow, so the seeker of the supersensual Absolute concentrates his mind on the latter through the symbol OM.[286]

The final two Extracts treat of different doctrines of meditation on OM found in the texts on which Śaṅkara was commenting. The commentary on Māṇḍūkya Upanishad 8-12 analyses OM, according to the original text, into three parts, A + U + M, connected respectively with the waking state and the world of waking experience, with the dream-state and the dream-world and with the dissolution of these two states and their worlds in dreamless sleep. Then it speaks of OM in its true, partless or transcendental nature, corresponding to Turīya, the awakening to the true nature of the Self which (unlike the state of dreamless sleep) does not contain the seeds of further dualistic experience.

In the last Extract, there is further elaboration on the mystical significance of the elements A, U and M. 'A' stands for the Ṛg Veda. 'A + U' stands for the Yajur Veda, the realm of the mind, the realm of dream, the realm of the moon, the realm intervening between the earth and the 'roof' of the sky. 'A + U + M' stands for the supreme Spirit present in the sun, and whoever meditates on it steadfastly is taken at death by the texts of the Sāma Veda along the Path of the Flame, never to return for further worldly existence. Or meditation on OM may also result in realization of the Absolute in its supreme form.

TEXTS ON MEDITATION ON OM

1. In this connection, the following texts are worthy of notice. When Satyakāma asked of Pippalāda, 'Holy Sir: Whoever amongst men meditates his whole life intently on the syllable OM, withdrawing his senses from external objects, with concentrated mind, identifying OM with the Absolute in reverence — what "world" will he conquer?'[287] Pippalāda began his reply, 'O Satyakāma: Verily, this syllable OM is both the unconditioned and the conditioned Absolute',[288] and eventually continued, 'But he who meditates on the syllable OM taking cognizance of its three elements (A + U + M) and meditates on the supreme Spirit through the symbol of this syllable (becomes identified with the principle of light (the Sun)'. Again, we have the passage in the Kaṭha Upanishad which begins '(O Yama, tell me what thou seest) beyond merit and demerit' and goes on, 'That which all the Vedas declare, that which all the austerities proclaim,[289] desiring which people practise a life of continence and holy vows, that I shall tell thee in brief. It is OM'.[290] These texts refer to the

syllable OM as denoting the Absolute in its supreme (unconditioned) form, and also as symbolizing it like an image. And they declare that meditation on the syllable OM is intended as a means to help men of weak and mediocre minds towards knowledge of the supreme (unconditioned) Absolute and that its fruit will be liberation *at a later time*.

This same idea is taught in the present Gītā passage. The passage about the supreme Being as 'ancient and omniscient and the ruler of the whole world' and as 'that Indestructible Principle taught by those who know the meaning of the Veda' establishes the subject as being the supreme (unconditioned) Absolute. And it proceeds now to explain how meditation on this syllable OM, which is a means to knowledge of the Absolute in the sense just described, has liberation at a future time for its result, adding what is considered necessary in the way of further direct and indirect information.

Closing all the gates of knowledge of the body, and confining the mind within the lotus of the heart and stopping its movement, he passes with controlled mind up from the heart-centre along the upward-going canal, assiduously raising the life-breath to the crown of the head and holding it there. Holding it there, he pronounces the syllable OM which designates the Absolute, and with his thought concentrated on the meaning, Me, he dies. He who leaves the body thus goes to the highest state.[291] 'Leaving the body' is specified to exclude the idea that the soul is destroyed at death.[292]

❖

2. Here the word OM is used as a means to meditate upon the Absolute. To support this statement, we might refer to

other Vedic texts in the same vein, such as 'This is the best support, this is the supreme support', 'One should concentrate on the Self, uttering OM', 'One should meditate on the supreme Spirit through the one syllable OM', 'Meditate on the Self through OM'.[293] And we also know indications which would allow other possibilities. For elsewhere we find texts like 'He sings the hymn with OM' or 'He chants the Udgītha with OM',[294] which show that OM must be regularly used before the beginning and after the conclusion of one's private recitation of one's daily portion of the Veda. But we do not find any such special meaning here. Hence the word OM is here only being taught as a means of meditation.

Though 'Brahman' and 'Ātman' and others are names for the Absolute, yet the authority of the Veda shows that OM is the name which fits closest, which is why it is the chief instrument in the apprehension of the Absolute. It performs its task in two ways, as a symbol (substitute) and as a name. OM has to be taken as non-different from the Absolute, just as an image of Viṣṇu and the like is taken as non-different from what it represents. For the grace of the Absolute descends on him who makes OM his support, as the text 'This is the best support, this is the supreme support, knowing this support one becomes glorious in the world of Brahmā'[295] says.

Now, lest one should think that the ether meant in the phrase 'The ether is the Absolute' (kham brahman) was material ether, the text adds the words 'primaeval', meaning it is the eternal ether or the ether constituted by the supreme Self. This primaeval ether of the supreme Self is not accessible to the eyes or other senses and hence yields no basis or support for meditation. For this reason the meditator must superimpose it on OM with deep spiritual feeling and a compound of faith and devotion, just as people at large superimpose Viṣṇu onto images of stone and the like which are carved with all Viṣṇu's features and limbs....

This (OM) is the Veda, for through it one 'knows (veda) what has to be known'. Hence OM is the Veda and is a name declaring or denoting the Veda. Through that name one knows what has to be known, *viz.* the Absolute; one knows (veda) what has to be known and named; that is, the aspirant knows or perceives it. Hence the knowers of Brahman of yore thought 'This OM is the Veda', and it is in this sense that they think of it both as a name and as an instrument.

Or else it may be that the phrase 'This (OM) is the Veda' is an eulogy. How? OM was first prescribed as a symbol of the Absolute, for the words 'OM', 'ether' and 'Absolute' were placed in apposition. Now it is eulogized as being the Veda. This whole Veda is nothing but OM. It arose from OM and consists in OM, all of it, with all its distinct parts such as the Ṛk, the Yajus and the Sāman. For we have that other Vedic text, 'Just as all the leaves are pierced and held together by a rod,[296] so is all speech pierced and held together by OM'.[297]

Or one might take the eulogy thus. This OM is the Veda because whatever has to be known (veditavya) is known through this OM, which is thus the Veda.[298] On this OM depends the Vedahood even of the other Veda. This OM being something so magnificent, it should definitely be adopted as an instrument of approach to the Absolute.

Or else the eulogy might be. That is the Veda. What is? The OM known to men of spiritual realization.[299] The latter must surely know it in some of its alternative forms such as Praṇava and Udgītha. If it is used as an instrument of approach to the Absolute, it is as good as if the whole Veda had been used.[300]

❖

3. The syllable OM is the most distinctive and intimate name for the supreme Self. When it is used, the Self tends to pour out grace, as people in the world do when addressed by pet-names. But here the presence of the word 'iti' [the Sanskrit equivalent of our inverted commas] shows that it is the mere sound itself that is under consideration, apart from its power of denotation. As such, it becomes (not a word denoting the Absolute but) a symbol of the Absolute like a stone image of a god. It is clear from the Upanishads as a whole that it is the best instrument of approach to the supreme Self, whether as name or symbol. It is indeed well-known that it is the best instrument of approach to the supreme Self, whether as name or symbol. It is so on account of its very frequent occurrence at the end of recitations (of Vedic texts) and rituals and of the repetition of one's own daily portion of the Vedic texts. In the present text the syllable OM is referred to as the 'Udgītha' because it forms part of the Udgītha section of a Sāman.[301]

On this syllable OM occurring as part of the ritual and also symbolizing the supreme Self, one should practise sustained, firm, one-pointed meditation. The present text itself goes on to explain why the syllable OM is called (here) 'the Udgītha'. It is called the Udgītha because the singing of the Udgītha begins with OM.[302]

❖

4. I will tell you in brief, says the text, the nature of the state about which you ask, the goal taught by the Veda as a whole, that which the austerities proclaim, that for the sake of which people live as students in the house of a Teacher seeking realization of the Absolute.

In brief it is 'OM'. That is the goal which you ask. That the text adds the particle 'iti'[303] shows that OM is the word which expresses this state or (taken as a written character) symbolizes it visually.

This syllable OM, continues the Upanishad, is the Absolute both in its 'lower' (apara) form (as Hiraṇyagarbha) and in its supreme (transcendent) form. That is to say, it is the symbol of these two. Whoso meditates on this syllable alone, thinking of it as the Absolute in the form under which it can be meditated on, can obtain whatever he wants, whether it be the Absolute in its supreme form or something lower. If it is the supreme, he will 'know' it; if it is something lower, he will 'attain' it.[304]

❖

5. Now a form of meditation on the syllable OM is laid down, the latter being a necessary prelude to all meditations, whether concerned with the supreme reality or with lesser principles. The mere sound of the syllable OM when meditated on either as the Absolute or as Hiraṇyagarbha is a means to the attainment of the Absolute or Hiraṇyagarbha. It is the support to which one resorts for meditation on the Absolute or Hiraṇyagarbha, as an image is the support to which one resorts for meditation on Viṣṇu. For we have the Vedic text, '(OM, verily, is the Absolute and Hiraṇyagarbha.

Therefore, the wise man) should approach one or the other through this'.[305]

The text begins with the word 'OM' in inverted commas. The force of the inverted commas is to limit the meaning to the sound 'OM' (as opposed to the meaning of OM). One should meditate in the mind on the mere sound 'OM', all sound being pervaded by OM, as we know from another Vedic text, 'As all the leaves are pierced by a rod, so is all sound pierced (penetrated) by OM'.[306] All this (world) is said to be OM because the named depends on the name.[307]

❖

6. That imperishable Principle of Consciousness pervading the Vital Principle and the rest from within is real (says the text) and hence not a delusion. Hence it is indestructible. That is what the mind has to penetrate, to strike into; that is, the mind has to become concentrated on it. Therefore, my dear one, penetrate the Absolute, concentrate your mind on it.

How is it to be penetrated? Take up the great bow found in the Upanishads. Fix in it an arrow sharpened by constant meditation, which means 'trained'. Then draw the bow. That is, withdraw the mind and senses from their natural objects and concentrate them on the one target or goal.[308] The text cannot be taken literally, as if it were saying that a bow literally had to be drawn by a hand. O pupil, take the Absolute, the Imperishable Principle as described above, as the goal, and pierce it with a mind steeped in meditation upon it.

OM is the bow. OM is the instrument that enables the

arrow of the empirical self to pierce the Imperishable Principle, as the bow is the instrument that enables an arrow to pierce its target. The arrow is the Self as associated with external adjuncts. It is the supreme Self that has 'entered' into the body in the sense that the sun and other luminous bodies 'enter' into water when they are reflected in it, and is witnessing from there all the ideas that come into the mind. It is concentrated on its own Self, the Absolute, the Imperishable Principle as if (*qua* concentrating on itself) it were other than itself.[309] And in this sense the Absolute is said to be its target, because those who are trying to concentrate their minds take it as their target and dwell on it as their Self. So the Absolute is the target that has to be pierced by the one who has mastered his senses and rendered his mind one-pointed, having already lost the habit of inattention that results from thirst for experience of sense-objects, and so become indifferent to everything in the empirical realm. And after piercing the Absolute, the empirical self becomes one with it, as an arrow becomes one with a target that it has pierced. As the arrow achieves unity with the target, so the empirical self rises above self-identification with the body and the mind and in this sense 'achieves' identity with the Imperishable Principle.[310]

❖

7. But you might raise the question how it could be shown that this whole world of transmigratory experience, manifest and unmanifest, consisting in action, its factors and results, could be of the nature of name, form and action only, and not of the Self. The Upanishad begins the reply to this question by considering the question of name. Speech (vāc) is the

sound-universal including all names as given in the previous section. As it has already been laid down, 'Whatever sound exists, it is verily (an aspect of) Vāc',[311] it follows that the meaning of the word Vāc is simply sound in general, and this sound-universal is the 'uktha' or material cause of all the various names, as a salt-mound is the material cause of the individual particles of salt which come from it. The Upanishad goes on, 'For from this'.... It means that all particular names such as Yajñadatta and Devadatta proceed from this sound-universal, in the sense of being separated from it like salt particles from the parent mound. And an effect is non-different from its material cause, while particulars fall within the universals they belong to.

But in what sense is Vāc spoken of as the universal, and the names as its particular instances? 'It is their common element', says the Upanishad. A universal is what is common to a number of things, the syllable sāma' in the word 'sāmānya' (universal) expressing 'samatva' or 'being universally present'. For Vāc is common to all names, which are its particular forms, and particular names cannot come into being without it. That which cannot come into being without a certain thing is seen to be non-different from that thing, as clay-pots are non-different from clay.

The Upanishad goes on to explain how particular names receive their being from Vāc. It is because this — that is, the Absolute, the principle referred to here as Vāc — is their Self. Names proceed from it because they can have no being apart from sound. Then the text explains this. The Absolute is sound in its universal aspect because it supports particular sounds and all names in the sense of lending them reality as their essence (svarūpa). And this shows that all particular names are nothing but sound, inasmuch as the latter is their cause and the universal of which they are particular instances and the principle which endows them with an essence and with reality.[312]

❖

8. So far the commentary on the syllable OM has been made from the standpoint that it *represents* the Self with four quarters. Now the Self will be treated of adopting the standpoint that the syllable OM *is* the Self. The 'syllable' here referred to is the syllable 'OM'. The term 'adhimātram' (in the text of the Upanishad) shows that it is to be analysed here into its constituent parts (mātra). The 'quarters' (pāda) of the Self are the parts of OM, the latter consisting of A, U and M.[313]

The text now goes on to state the correspondences more specifically. The Self in the waking state, the Self as Vaiśvānara, is the sound A, the first constituent part of OM.[314] The text states that the point of similarity between Vaiśvānara and the 'A' of 'OM' is their pervasiveness. All speech is pervaded by the sound 'A', as is confirmed by the Vedic text 'All speech is A'.[315] And Vaiśvānara pervades the world, as is shown by the text, 'Of this universal Self, the head is the brilliant light (of the heavens)'.[316]

It has already been remarked that the name and the named are one.[317] As the syllable 'A' forms the beginning, so does Vaiśvānara. It is on account of this point of similarity that Vaiśvānara is known to be the sound 'A'.

Then the text declares the results that accrue to a person

who knows this. He attains all desires and becomes first among the great ones.

The dream-state of the Spirit, called Taijasa, is the second part of the 'OM' or the sound 'U'. What is the point of similarity which shows this? Superiority. The sound 'U' is as if superior to 'A',[318] as Taijasa is superior to Viśva.[319] And the sound 'U' comes between 'A' and 'M', as Taijasa comes between Viśva and Prājña. The Taijasa 'comes between' Viśva and Prājña in the sense that it shares a common character with each.[320]

The fruit of this knowledge is next stated. Whoso knows it prolongs the line of knowledge. His enemies no longer feel any enmity against him any more than his friends do. No one in his family fails to acquire knowledge of the Absolute.

The dreamless sleep of the Spirit, called Prājña, is the sound 'M', the third sound in 'OM'. What is the point of similarity that shows this? It is known through the measuring. Viśva and Taijasa are as if measured by Prājña when they enter and leave it, when they dissolve into it and spring forth from it, like barley being measured with a measuring-ladle. And in a similar way, 'A' and 'U' dissolve into 'M' and later come out of it again (when OM is pronounced afresh).

Or the point of similarity may be dissolution. When the 'M' of 'OM' is pronounced, the 'A' and the 'U' dissolve into it and become one with it. Similarly, Viśva and Taijasa dissolve into Prājña and become one with it at the time of dreamless sleep. So the identity of Prājña and the sound 'M' follows from this additional point of similarity.

Next the text states the fruit of this knowledge. One who knows this 'measures all this'. That is, he has a correct knowledge of all this universe. And he 'dissolves', that is, becomes identical with the cause of the universe. The subordinate fruits here mentioned are but eulogies of the main discipline....[321]

The OM with no constituent parts is the Fourth. It is the pure Self, beyond word and meaning, beyond speech and mind. It represents the final dissolution of the universe, the blissful non-dual principle. When used by one who has this knowledge, OM with its three parts is the Self with its three 'quarters'. Whoso knows this enters his real Self himself. Such a one sees the highest reality and knows the Absolute. In his case, the third 'quarter', the seed-state, has been burnt up.[322] He has entered the Self and is not reborn, as the Fourth (turīya) bears no seeds of further empirical experience. For when the rope and the snake for which it was formerly mistaken in the dark have once been distinguished, the snake disappears into the rope and, being a mere impression of the mind (buddhi-saṃskāra), never again emerges in the case of those possessed of discrimination.

Different, however, is the case with those of average or dull minds whom we call 'aspirants' (sādhaka). They are walking on the right path. They have become monks. They know how the parts of OM correspond to the 'quarters' of the Self. It is right and proper that they should meditate on OM as a symbol of the Absolute for the sake of knowledge of the Absolute. The Teacher will explain this later when he says, 'There are three kinds of qualified souls treading the spiritual path'.[323]

❖

9. Next Satyakāma, the son of Śibi, asked a question. This question is recorded now in order to enjoin meditation on the syllable OM as a means to attain identity with the Absolute in both its conditioned and unconditioned aspects.

The question runs: 'Holy Sir: Whoever amongst men meditates his whole life intently on that miraculous syllable OM, withdrawing his senses from external objects, with concentrated mind, identifying OM with the Absolute in deep reverence — what 'world' will he conquer?' The word 'abhidhyāna' (meditation) in the text implies meditation in which the idea of the Self is sustained without a break like the motionless flame of a lamp protected from the wind, and is not interrupted by any intruding idea of a different kind. It is assumed that this discipline is carried out to the accompaniment of truth-speaking, continence, non-injury, non-acceptance of gifts or rewards, renunciation of possessions (tyāga), withdrawal from household life (saṃnyāsa), inner and outer purity, cultivation of contentment with whatever comes, avoidance of all forms of deception and acceptance of the other rules of ascetic life.[324] What 'world', then, will such a man conquer? Various are the worlds to be conquered by meditation and rituals. Which will a man conquer by meditation on OM in this way?

Pippalāda began his reply, 'This, verily, O Satyakāma!' The sound of OM is verily both this unconditioned and conditioned Absolute. The unconditioned is the real, the Indestructible Principle (akṣara) called Spirit (puruṣa). The conditioned is called the Vital Energy (prāṇa) and the First-born. It is the 'true nature' of the syllable OM in the sense that the syllable OM is its symbol.

The Absolute in unconditioned form, which cannot truly be indicated by sound or other means, and which is without any kind of quality, cannot be fathomed by the mind alone, as it is beyond the reach of the senses. The case with the syllable OM, however, is different. It is a symbol, like the image standing as the symbol of Viṣṇu or some other deity. When it is meditated on as the Absolute with deep reverence, the latter manifests 'grace' and reveals itself to the meditator. This is so in the case of the unconditioned Absolute, and it also holds true of the conditioned Absolute. Hence the text identifies the sound OM with the unconditioned and conditioned Absolute by way of a figure of speech.

Therefore, he who knows this attains either to the unconditioned or conditioned Absolute through meditation on the syllable OM, this means of attaining to the Self. For the syllable OM is the closest symbol of the Absolute there is.

Even if he does not know all the details of the different parts of the diphthong[325] OM when resolved, a person will attain to a high state through the force of meditating on the sound of OM as such. This defect of incomplete knowledge does not cause the one who takes sole refuge in the syllable OM to fall to a lower state because he has neglected the ritual and symbolic meditation on features in the ritual.[326] For even if he knows the separate significance of but one part of the syllable, enlightened by meditation on that he will quickly attain (another) human birth on earth.[327] The text specifies *human* birth, because various other kinds of birth are possible. It is the Ṛk verses which conduct the meditator to the earth, his human 'world'.[328] For meditation on the first element in the syllable OM (the sound 'A') is equivalent to meditation on the Ṛg Veda.[329] Through this he enjoys rebirth as a human and a noble Brahmin, equipped with austerity, chastity and faith, and achieves distinction. He does not lose his faith or indulge in self-willed action. Such a one, though technically 'fallen' on the path of yoga,[330] never descends to a lower condition.

If he knows two elements of the syllable OM (the sound 'A' plus the sound 'U') and meditates on it in this form, he attains to identity with the venerable principle of mind, of the nature of dream (svapna), which springs from the Yajur Veda and has the moon (soma) for its presiding deity. 'Attains to identity with it' means that he has become absorbed in it through dwelling on it one-pointedly. When he has attained identity with it, he is transported at death by the texts of the Yajur Veda, which are equivalent to the second element in the syllable OM (the sound 'U'), to the world of the moon, which corresponds to the second element in the syllable OM and is here referred to as the space intermediate between heaven and earth because it is the support of the latter. In other words, the texts of the Yajur Veda cause him to be born in the 'world' of the moon. And having enjoyed distinction there, he returns again to the world of man.

But he who meditates on the syllable OM taking cognizance of its three elements (A + U + M) and meditates steadfastly on the supreme Spirit within the sun through the symbol of this syllable, ...he becomes identified with the principle of light (tejas), the sun, which is the third element of the syllable OM. In his case, there is no return after death, as there is from the moon and other places. He just remains identified with the sun.

Just as a snake crawls free from its old skin and thereby becomes renovated, even so such a meditator becomes free from all impurity and is taken up to the world of Brahmā (brahma-loka) by the texts of the Sāma Veda which are equivalent to the third element of the syllable OM. The world of Brahmā is the world of Hiraṇyagarbha, called 'satya'. This Hiraṇyagarbha is the Self of all souls in transmigratory life. He is the inner Self (antar-ātman) of all creatures as he is their subtle body (liṅga). For all souls are included as an aggregate in this subtle body. Hence it is the aggregate of the individual souls.

He who knows the three elements of the syllable OM beholds in meditation the supreme Spirit called the highest Self (paramātman), which lies beyond Hiraṇyagarbha, the aggregate of the individual souls. The Spirit (puruṣa) is so called because it dwells in the body (puriśaya), having entered within every body....

The three elements 'A', 'U' and 'M' do not (if taken in isolation from one another) rise above the world of death. But when used in meditation practices and united together and not used to stand for anything particular — what happens then? Then the yogin (meditator) who knows the three elements of the syllable OM as explained above can be said in a special sense 'not to waver' during a particular period of meditation in his three yogic practices consisting in meditation on the Spirit as manifested in waking, dream and dreamless sleep, the latter being external, intermediate and internal respectively.[331] For in this meditation the Spirit as associated with waking, dream and dreamless sleep, together with those three states themselves, are seen as identical with the syllable

OM with its three elements. He who knows thus becomes the syllable OM and the Self of all. What could he waver away from? What could he waver towards?...

A man reaches this (familiar) human world through the verses of the Ṛk. He reaches the intermediate region between heaven and earth, ruled over by the moon, through the texts of the Yajur Veda. Through the verses of the Sāma Veda he reaches the third goal, the world of Brahmā, which is known to the wise only and not to the ignorant. With the syllable OM as his instrument he reaches a world of one of these three kinds, all being the Absolute in its conditioned form.

But it is also through meditation on that very syllable OM that a man attains to the Absolute in its unconditioned form, the real, called Spirit (puruṣa), tranquil, free, bereft of waking, dream or dreamless sleep and their realm of experience, beyond decay, immortal and beyond fear, and hence transcending all.[332]

NOTES TO CHAPTER XV

References to Extracts are in bold type

1 Cp. B.S.Bh. II.i.3, dvaitino hi te sāṅkhyā yogāśca nātmaikatva -darśinaḥ (the followers of Sāṅkhya and Yoga are dualists and do not have the vision of the sole reality of the Self).

2 Kaṭha I.ii.12.

3 *Ibid.*

4 Cp. below, Extract 3. See also Sac, *Intuition of Reality*, 65.

5 Bṛhad. Bh. II.iv.5.

6 Cp. above, Vol.V, 230f.

7 The phrase 'adhyātma-yoga' appears here in the upanishadic text under comment.

8 The meaning of the term 'dissolve' here is explained in the following Extract. When a faculty is restrained, it 'merges' in the higher principle from which it proceeds, which is its material cause.

9 Kaṭha Bh. I.ii.12 and 13.

10 Kaṭha I.iii.12.

11 jñāna-ātman = vijñāna ātman = buddhi.

12 Śaṅkara does not here identify the great Self with Hiraṇyagarbha as he did in the previous Extract. In the present Extract he may be merely following established tradition for the interpretation of the B.S.

13 Kaṭha I.iii.13.

14 B.S.Bh. I.iv.1.

15 Cp. the appearance of the term yoga at Kaṭha II.iii.11 in the last of the verses to come under comment in the present Extract.

16 On the difference between manas and buddhi, cp. above, Vol. III, 33, 34f.

17 Cp. Bh.G.Bh. VI.23.

18 I.e. the text says that the yogi *is* never careless. But this may be taken to mean 'must never be careless' on the analogy of the text 'The sacrificial post is made of acacia wood' which means that it should be or may be made of acacia wood. Sac.

19 The explanation to follow applies to the first of the two alternative explanations of 'Is never careless'.

20 Śaṅkara distinguishes yoga from knowledge. Yoga is a discipline or technique for concentrating the mind. Unless it is maintained, the concentration will lapse. Knowledge is something that can never lapse, once attained. Knowledge is immediate intuition of Reality: yoga is a means to that intuition.

21 Kaṭha Bh. II.iii.9-11.

22 By the measures of truthfulness, etc. Cp. above, Vol.V, 145f.

23 Prāṇa, apāna, etc., cp. above, Vol.III, 35.

24 The consciousness that is ever present in these organs, latent and ready to spring into manifestation at the appropriate stimuli, just as buttermilk always develops in milk when the latter is churned, and fire develops from sticks when they are rubbed together with sufficient alacrity.

25 Muṇḍ. Bh. III.i.8-9.

26 Cp. above, Vol.V, 142f.

27 Vivaraṇa to Ā.D.S., Adhyātma Paṭala I.xxii.1. *Minor Works of Śrī Śaṅkarācārya*, Ed. Bhāgavat, 425.

28 Cp. above, Vol.I, 25.

29 No trace of the term has been found in the Upanishads or in any other Brahminical texts. Cp. S. Mayeda, 'On the Authorship of the Māṇḍūkya...Bhāṣya', 93.

30 G.K.Bh. III.36 *ad fin*.

31 He does not have to pursue spiritual concentration (samādhi). Ānandagiri.

32 When the mind falls asleep, ignorance as the seed of future empirical experience remains intact. Sac, M.R.V. on G.K. III.44, 301.

33 Śaṅkara himself sometimes observes a distinction of meaning between citta and manas, and sometimes ignores it, cp. above, Vol.III, 28ff.

34 Reading cit-svarūpa (not citta-svarūpa as in the G.P. Ed.).

35 G.K.Bh. III. 38-46.

36 Here the word 'karma' is used, as so often in Śaṅkara, in a predominantly ritualistic sense to mean acts enjoined or forbidden in the Veda, not action in general. Only such acts were considered to be of serious consequence for the after-life or for births to come.

37 Manu Smṛti II.3.

38 M.Bh. Śānti Parva 177, 25, G.P. Ed. Vol.III, 512.

39 Bṛhad. IV.iv.5.

40 Manu Smṛti II.4.

41 Bh.G.Bh. VI.4.

42 Cp. above, Vol.I, 8ff. and Vol.V, Chapter XII, sections 3 and 4 *passim*.

43 Cp. Bh.G.Bh. XIII.10, sā (bhaktir) hi jñānam.

44 Sac, Gītā-Śāstrārtha-Viveka, 123-126.

45 Bh.G. X.20.

46 Bṛhad. I.iv.8.

47 Bh.G. VII.18.

48 Bh.G.Bh. XV.1.

49 Bh.G.Bh. XI.54 and 55.

50 Troṭaka, Ś.S.S. 104-106.

51 Ś.S.S. 106, which refers specifically to Draviḍa. On Draviḍa, cp. above, Vol.I, 22ff.

52 Above, Vol.V, 292f.

53 B.S.Bh. I.i.4, Gambhīrānanda, 31, quoted Sac, *Sugamā*, 102.

54 B.S.Bh. I.ii.6, Gambhīrānanda, 115.

55 See Note 189, below.

56 B.B.V. I.iv.1390-2, quoted by Sac, *Sugamā*, 110.

57 Chānd. VI.viii.7.

58 The reading 'ātmani jñānam vivartate' of the Ā.Ś.S. Ed. here should perhaps be dropped in favour of the 'anṛta-jīvātma-vijñānaṃ nivartate' of H.R. Bhāgavat's text, Poona, 1927, 276.

59 Cp. Chānd. III.xix.1, III.xviii.1.

60 Cp. Chānd. III.xviii.1, etc. The word 'iti' in the Chānd. text serves the purpose of our inverted commas.

61 Chānd. VI.iii.2.

62 So that our reason tells us, when applied to the texts on pure Being, that we cannot be anything but pure Being, as the clay-pot cannot be anything but clay. Hence we have no case for figurative interpretations of 'That thou art' since the literal meaning makes sense.

63 Chānd. VI.xiv.2.

64 I.e. if a person mistakes a piece of deliberate flattery for the literal truth.

65 Chānd. VI.i.3.

66 Chānd. VI.xiv.2.

67 It has already been pointed out above, Vol.V, 297, that the Teacher from whom one learned the sacred texts by rote was not necessarily or even probably the Teacher whom one approached for training in the upanishadic wisdom. Here Śaṅkara avers that reference to a Teacher coupled with special emphasis on spiritual knowledge implies that Chānd. VI.xiv.2ff. is not a passage concerned with ritual, as the need for a Teacher from whom to learn the texts necessary for performance of the ritual was so obvious that there would have been no need to have mentioned it.

68 This is a *tu quoque* argument against the Mīmāṃsaka. He bases his ritualistic teaching on the authority of the Veda, and must accept that authority also in the parts of the Veda which go beyond ritual.

69 Another *ad hominem* argument against the Mīmāṃsaka. The latter found it necessary to elaborate a reasoned philosophy to show his pupils that an eternal soul existed independently of the body, without which knowledge they would not have performed rituals for the sake of an after-life.

70 The questioner is a Mīmāṃsaka who cannot appreciate that the texts of the Veda are authoritative if they merely contain plain information. This follows from his belief that the Vedic texts are only authoritative when they enjoin action for the sake of an 'unseen' fruit. The counter-question he receives makes him see that his own view implies that the pupil learning Vedic texts is ignorant about the true nature of the soul. 'That thou art' gives *information* to end that ignorance.

71 Chānd. Bh. VI.xvi.3.

72 Bṛhad. II.iv.5, IV.iv.21, Chānd. VIII.vii.1.

73 I.e. on the *prima facie* view they do not explicitly ask for repetition.

74 If a ritualistic act has an unseen result, then it is only to be performed once unless anything else is specified. This rule holds for the prayāja fore-sacrifices. But if a ritualistic act has a 'visible' result, a result that can be experienced here and now in this world, it has to be repeated until the result is obtained. An example is the pounding of the paddy (uncooked rice) in ceremonies of food-offering which involve this act. Govindānanda.

75 Chānd. IV.i.4.

76 Chānd. IV.ii.2.

77 Chānd. III.xviii.1.

78 Chānd. III.xviii.3.

79 Chānd. I.v.1.

80 Chānd. I.v.2. In his commentary to the passage, Śaṅkara says that meditation on both the rays and the sun is meant.

81 Chānd. VI.viii.7.

82 Cp. Sureśvara, N.Sid. III.57.

83 Chānd. VI.viii.7.

84 *Ibid.*

85 Bṛhad. II.iv.5.

86 Taitt. II.i.1, Bṛhad. III.ix.28, III.viii.11, Muṇḍ. II.i.2, Bṛhad. III.viii.8.

87 Birth, existence, growth, development, decay and death.

88 Cp. Ait. Bh. II.i.1. (introduction), above, Vol.I, 225ff.

89 In the triad 'ignorance, doubt and erroneous knowledge',

ignorance means absence of knowledge, and Śaṅkara uses the word 'ajñāna' for it. It is not here used in the same sense as 'avidyā', which for Śaṅkara usually means superimposition or positive erroneous cognition.

90 See Note 94, below.

91 I.e. if one has has a particular goal or project, one does not engage in any subsidiary activity that would nullify it. Similarly, one does not aspire to know the meaning of 'That thou art' and then undermine this aspiration by practising repeated affirmations conceived as actions performed in obedience to injunctions, since action and knowledge of the meaning of 'That thou art' are contradictory.

92 For the meaning of vāco-yukti here, see Monier Williams, *Sanskrit-English Dictionary*, 937.

93 B.S.Bh. IV.i.1 and 2.

94 Broadly speaking, Śaṅkara accepted the view of the Grammarian Patañjali (2nd cent. BC) that words are significant only by virtue of referring to a genus or universal (cow), or an action (he looks), or a quality (black) or as arbitrarily invented proper names. Śaṅkara agreed with the Mīmāṃsakas that (apart from some proper names) speech can refer to the individual only through the universal. For its power to signify depends on its relation with a meaning and the hearer's knowledge of its relation with that meaning, and the hearer cannot have prior knowledge of all the individuals in a class. The direct meaning of the word must therefore be the universal, and it is the remainder of the words in the sentence in which it occurs that narrow the meaning down to the universal as embodied in a particular individual. Thus for Śaṅkara the word 'I' could quite well designate the Self as revealed in empirical experience in the undiscriminated complex of 'I' and 'mine'. Egos are many, and thus form a class. They act and have qualities, they possess things and have relations. But none of this is true of the Self as

pure Consciousness. It is non-dual and so in no way associated with a class or universal. It is actionless and without qualities or relations. Words, therefore, can only be used to indicate it approximately, by heading off the mind from all else, or by suggestion. They cannot be used to designate it in its true nature.

95 For Śaṅkara, the reflection was non-different from the Self. Cp. this chapter, 136.

96 When words such as 'it burns' are used of torches, the statement has the direct meaning 'The torch burns', but the indicated meaning is 'The fire in the torch burns', since that which burns is the element fire, not the torch, its passive vehicle. Still, the torch has the *appearance* of burning, so we say 'The torch burns'. Similarly, the ego-sense has the appearance of being the Self. Hence the words which mean 'the ego' can be used to indicate the Self. No word can *mean* the Self, as it is beyond the universe of discourse. But words which mean the ego can be used to *indicate* the Self. **U.S. (verse) XVIII.27-31.**

97 In English, by verb and pronoun.

98 I.e. an act must inhere in the agent.

99 Kaṭha I.ii.18, II.ii.13. Śaṅkara is arguing that the Self is knowledge in a sense that escapes direct verbal designation. To 'know', as the word is used in ordinary parlance, implies an act. The Self is knowledge absolute, but is not the knower, knowledge or known of familiar empirical experience. It is the light in which this process takes place.

100 Which means 'knowledge', but only in the sense of the instrument *whereby* a thing is known.

101 Bṛhad. III.v.1.

102 A word needs to have a direct meaning before it can have an indirect meaning because the indirect meaning, settled by

convention, is based on the direct meaning. Cp. Bṛhad.Bh. I.iii.1, trans. Mādhavānanda, 31f. The direct meaning is inherent in the word itself. The indirect meaning is then later established by human convention, and depends on some relation (such as causality, similarity, propinquity, etc.) subsisting between the thing referred to by the direct meaning and that referred to by the indirect meaning. Examples: The king marches against the rebellious city. (Causality: the king causes the army to march without marching with them.) Devadatta is a lion. (Similarity: he has leonine qualities.) The galleries are shouting. (Propinquity: the people *in* the galleries are shouting.)

103 The analysis of knowledge presented in the preceding verses has tended to show that a verbal form meaning 'he knows' is meaningless. The analysis was performed to show that when the upanishadic texts call the Absolute 'knowledge', they do not mean knowledge as we ordinarily understand it in the world. If that is the primary meaning of the word 'knowledge', then the Upanishads are referring to something else by a secondary meaning when they call the Absolute 'knowledge'. Śaṅkara's task in the reply is to show that phrases like 'he knows' do have some intelligible primary meaning from which a secondary meaning can be derived to enable the Upanishads to refer to the Absolute indirectly by the word 'knowledge'.

104 It has been shown at the beginning of the present section that the grammarians' analysis of 'he knows' implies a single agent active in the act of knowing. The Advaita analysis has suggested that the 'agent' in the 'act' of knowing is neither the Self nor the intellect but a false notion arising from the confusion of the two.

105 I.e. by identifying the reflection, which is not a reality, with the Self, which is.

106 It is not a real act because the only possible agent for such an act would be the reflection of the Self in the intellect and it has

been shown cp. above, Vol.III, 16ff. that reflections are not realities. The Self cannot be the agent because the Veda says that it is changeless. The intellect cannot be the agent because it is palpably the instrument that is used by another in knowing.

107 Cp. Hiriyanna, *Essentials*, 91f.

108 Arising from the reflection of the pure Consciousness of the Self in the intellect. The classic text on this is the Extract given above, Vol.III, 58ff.

109 This verse explains further the way in which the Logicians are deluded. Hypnotized by the flow of empirical experience, they fail to see that its three component factors on the objective side (consciousness, reflection and intellect) are distinct from one another in nature, and hence they attribute to knowledge the instability of the intellect. So R.T's Ṭīkā *ad loc.*

110 According to the commentator R.T., this is a stricture addressed against the pre-Śaṅkara Vedāntins of whom Bhartṛprapañca (Cp. Vol.IV, Chapter X, section 3, above) may be cited as the type. For Bhartṛprapañca the one supreme Self (paramātman) went into modification (vikāra) to assume both the form of the individual experiencers and of their mental representations and also of the objects of the external world. Śaṅkara's complaint against this doctrine was that it reduced even the supreme Self to the level of an object and so failed, for lack of a subject, to account for the fact of anything being known. In this they are on a par with the Vijñāna Vāda Buddhists.

111 Being active in cognition, it would be subject to modification. It would therefore fall within the sphere of the object and be just as unconscious as the mental modifications themselves, unless illumined by something else.

112 The reference here is to the Sāṅkhyas, cp. Īśvara Kṛṣṇa, verses 17-20. Unlike the Logicians (the Vaiśeṣikas and the Naiyāyikas) or the Mīmāṃsakas, the Sāṅkhyas grasped the *radical*

difference between the ultimate subject and object in empirical experience, and spoke of the ultimate subject as a mere Witness and not an agent. But they regarded the Witness as illumining the intellect by its bare proximity (sāṃnidhya) and did not speak of a reflection. Cp. Vācaspati's Tattva Kaumudī Commentary on Īśvara Kṛṣṇa verse 20.

113 At U.S. (verse) XVI.49 Śaṅkara complains that since the soul (puruṣa) and Nature (prakṛti) of the Sāṅkhyas have mutually contradictory characteristics, there can be no relation between the two, and hence it is wrong for the Sāṅkhyas, who do not speak of a reflection, to speak of either of them as being of service to the other. The passage has appeared above, Vol.IV, Chapter XI, section 3, Extract 3.

114 I.e. there would be no basis for the worldly distinction between the conscious and the non-conscious, between, say, minds and stocks and stones.

115 By insisting that it was totally different in nature from the intellect, the Sāṅkhyas made the Witness a pure, changeless, actionless principle of consciousness, purified of all objective elements. But because they did not admit a reflection of consciousness in the intellect, they failed to account for agency and experience in the empirical world.

116 Because, on the view attributed to the Sāṅkhya philosopher, the empirical agent must fall on the side of the intellect, considered as being quite independent of and distinct from the actionless Witness. As against the Vedāntins of Bhartṛprapañca's school, the Sāṅkhyas were right on this point. But because they do not accept the view that the empirical experiencer results from a reflection (ābhāsa) of consciousness in the intellect (but try to make do with the concept of mere proximity, sāṃnidhya, of intellect to pure Consciousness) they cannot explain liberation as taught in the Upanishads. The liberating cognition ('I am the Witness'), as well as ordinary empirical experience, is

inexplicable without recourse to the hypothesis of a reflection of Consciousness in the intellect. It cannot pertain either to the Self alone or to the intellect alone. For lack of recourse to the hypothesis of a reflection, the Sāṅkhya is unable to explain either transmigratory experience or liberation.

117 R.T. explains: The seeker of liberation must be one who has not yet discriminated Self, ego and reflection — or he could not be a candidate for knowledge or even perceive the evidence of the Upanishads, which depends on his having fallen into the state of empirical agent and experiencer. In the text 'That thou art', the Veda utters the word 'Thou' in conformity with the ignorant seeker's experience, so that this word is intelligible to him in its primary sense and can serve as a basis for conveying an indirectly indicated meaning. But at the same time, when considered in its place in the sentence 'That thou art' as a whole, the word 'thou' serves to indicate the Witness indirectly. The word 'that' in the sentence 'That thou art' is also intelligible to the ignorant seeker in its primary sense as referring to that which cannot be directly known but which must exist as the cause of 'this', the perceived universe. But when considered in its place in the sentence as a whole, the word 'that', by being identified with 'thou', serves to indicate indirectly the nature of the Absolute as the transcendent Self. Without being able to characterize the Absolute positively, the text 'That thou art' indicates it indirectly by stating that it is not other than the Witness on the one hand or the ultimate cause of the universe on the other. The nature of the Absolute Self defies direct expression in words, or otherwise it would lose its character of being raised above subject and object and be reduced to an object among objects.

118 That is, the Witness would have to be conceived as the suppliant and the one in pain.

119 We have seen that a necessary condition of the metaphorical or indirect use of words is that some relation can be established

between the thing denoted by the word as used directly and the thing denoted by it when it is used indirectly. Cp. Note 102, above. Causality, similarity and propinquity were cited; but some relation there must be, or otherwise any word could be used to indicate anything, which would undermine the utility of language altogether. The Sāṅkhya is here made to say that the 'thou' of 'That thou art' is intelligible in the direct meaning of Witness or 'Puruṣa'. But as his doctrine does not, as here expounded, include a reference to the reflection of consciousness in the intellect, he cannot point to any knowable relation between the ego-sense and the Witness. For on his analysis the ego falls on the side of 'Nature' and between non-conscious Nature (prakṛti) and conscious Spirit (puruṣa) there are no common qualities. Though 'propinquity' between each individual Puruṣa and its intellect was claimed, a plurality of individual all-pervading 'Spirits' is a monstrosity. Hence the Sāṅkhya would not be justified in saying that the word 'thou' meant the ego in its primary sense and was also used indirectly to indicate the Witness. The Advaitin, however, is able to bridge the gap between Spirit and intellect through his hypothesis of a reflection of Spirit in the intellect and so to account for the power of the texts to refer to the supreme Self by indirect indication. Cp. Note 121 below.

120 Non-difference (tādātmya) may be interpreted as non-reciprocal relation under which the ego-sense is non-different from the Self but the Self is not non-different from the ego-sense. Advaita accepts this theory of the relation between the ego-sense and the Self, but points to the need for the reflection theory if it is to be serviceable in accounting for liberation through upanishadic teaching.

121 The relation of non-difference (tādātmya) between ego and pure Self is here offered tentatively as the basis of the indirect indication of the pure Self through the word 'Thou'. Cp. Note 119, above.

122 Such a perception (only possible on the reflection theory as we shall see) is necessary because comprehension of indirect usage of words is possible only when there is prior knowledge of both the direct and indirect meanings.

123 For the Sāṅkhya philosopher, Witness and intellect belong to two different orders of being, having totally disparate characteristics. Advaita agrees as to the disparity, but points to the need for postulating a reflection of consciousness in the intellect to bridge the gap between intellect and Witness and explain the upanishadic doctrine of liberation.

124 The commentator R.T. quotes Chānd. III.xiv.3-4, 'This Self of mine within the heart...this is the Absolute'.

125 The same Commentator says they are: (1) The ego-sense, being non-conscious, cannot grasp any connection. (2) Neither can the Witness, because it is actionless. (3) The Veda cannot enlighten that which is by nature non-conscious.

126 The intellect 'appears to be a conscious seer' by virtue of receiving a reflection of pure consciousness. A reflection, however, is not a reality (cp. above, Vol.III, 16f) and is therefore classed as a false appearance, ābhāsa. On the present view, it becomes clear how the knowledge 'I am the Absolute' can arise in the intellect, which was not clear on the Sāṅkhya analysis.

127 Lit. 'a limit'. The states of 'presence of a reflection of consciousness' and 'absence of a reflection of consciousness' mutually contradict and negate one another. But the fact that we are conscious of both points to the existence of a Witness beyond all contradiction and negation. The Self as Witness is referred to by Śaṅkara and his early pupils as the 'limit' (sīman, avadhi) beyond which negation cannot go.

128 On the Sāṅkhya theory, the upanishadic teaching cannot convey knowledge of the Self for lack of a connection between the ego,

which can be directly designated by words, and the Absolute, which cannot. But on the Advaita reflection-theory it is possible to establish a connection between the ego, designated by the word 'thou', and the Absolute, which is the original of which the consciousness belonging to the ego is a reflection.

129 Reference has earlier been made (above, Vol.III, 17) to pre-Śaṅkara Vedāntins who spoke of a reflection (ābhāsa) of the supreme Self in the individual soul, but regarded it as a reality. Śaṅkara is now explaining that he does not interpret a reflection in this way.

130 A fundamental point in Śaṅkara, cp. Bṛhad Bh. I.iv.7, trans. Mādhavānanda, 84.

131 Cp. above, Vol.IV, Chapter XI, section 2 (intro.).

132 The *bare* notion 'I' or the notion 'I am the real' or 'I am the Witness' is distinguished from all notions of 'I' as associated with particular qualities or with action and identified with the Self. Both these contradictory factors are present in empirical experience. Which is due for negation?

133 That which is qualified is self-existent substance in relation to that which qualifies it, which is a mere supported quality. The qualifying element or quality depends for its existence on that which it qualifies. It has its being and Self through that which it qualifies. In the end it is seen that it *is* what it qualifies, and then it suffers negation.

134 R.T. considers that the wealth and the cows are a 'this' in relation to the man as qualified by his ego-sense and body. Śaṅkara uses the example of a 'man having cows' also at Bh.G.Bh. XIII.12 to illustrate the relation of possession. Cp. above, Vol.I, Chapter III, section 3, Extract 2.

135 R.T. explains that one reasons that words like Self, Consciousness, Massed Consciousness, Absolute, Being, etc. are invariably used of the bare Self, not of things qualified by

anything else or of their qualifications. On the other hand, words like agent, enjoyer, knowing, seeing, hearing, speaking, going, lean, fat, etc., are never used of the bare Self but always of the Self as apparently related to activity dependent on some external factor.

136 Aham ('I'), which here means the Self. The reference is to the preliminary rational discrimination of the Self that has to take place before the proper work of the final texts can begin.

137 Bṛhad. IV.iii.9.

138 Bṛhad. IV.iii.23.

139 Reasoning by the method of agreement and difference on the way in which the texts use words discovers the meaning of the separate words of the text 'That thou art'. From this, the mind progresses to a theoretical understanding of the meaning of the text. After this, the text can be repeated to the pupil, who now understands it, and from this hearing liberation may result if purity of mind and other pre-requisites are present in sufficient measure. No further meditation or reasoning is then either desirable or possible.

140 Cp. Rāmāyaṇa, Yuddha Kāṇḍa, Chapter 119, trans. H.P. Shastri, Vol.III, 339. Reference supplied by S. Mayeda. Cp. Sarva-jñātman II.182.

141 In the text 'I am the Absolute', Bṛhad. I.iv.10.

142 A variation of 'That thou art', Chānd. VI.viii.7.

143 There was a tradition in Vedic exegesis that it must be possible to point to a text in the Veda stating the fruit of the performance of any ritualistic act it enjoined. All knowledge imparted by the Veda was either of service for understanding the nature and results of some ritualistic act or else carried a peculiar 'fruit' of its own. Otherwise there would be texts in the Veda of no use to man, which is absurd. It was formally incumbent on the

Advaitins to show that knowledge arising from the texts proclaiming the existence of the transcendent Self carries its intrinsic fruit, as otherwise other schools could claim that their function must be to explain or stand as an eulogy for some ritualistic act. In the latter case, they would forfeit absolute authority as valid sources of information, as they might be mere eulogies.

144 Or otherwise those texts would have no intrinsic fruit and would have to be dismissed as mere eulogies.

145 R.T. explains that the present passage is concerned with rebutting certain objections that might conceivably be raised against the authoritativeness of the knowledge immediately conveyed by the Veda that one is the transcendent Self. He claims that the words 'one admits the existence of one's own Self' only mean 'There is no evidence to contradict the teaching that one is the transcendent Self'. This disposes of the objection that the teaching is evidently self-contradictory. Sentences to follow show that the teaching that one is the transcendent Self is not without advantage (fruit) and is not associated with doubt, and also that it never fails to arise when the preliminary conditions are fulfilled.

146 According to R.T., the chief obstacle is the failure to understand the meaning of the words of the text, an obstacle which has now been removed through reasoning by the method of agreement and difference.

147 Self-luminous Consciousness always shines forth naturally whenever the obstacles to its manifestations are removed.

148 Bṛhad. I.iv.10.

149 According to R.T., the passage is directed against those who hold that a sentence can only convey a synthetic meaning, i.e. a meaning consisting in a synthesis of the diverse meanings of its different words. It was a commonly held view among the

Vedantins of Śaṅkara's day. Śaṅkara was not troubled by the point as he taught that the texts did not convey knowledge of the Absolute, as a transcendent non-dual principle, directly: they only indicated it indirectly.

150 The rejected view, called Prasaṅkhyāna Vāda, holds that the information conveyed by the text is false or at least seriously inadequate. It has to be converted into right knowledge by the exertions of the hearer in meditation. But, as R.T. shows, Śaṅkara insists that if the holy texts are to be regarded as authoritative, they must actually convey the liberating message themselves. He exposes a self-contradiction in the position of the Prasaṅkhyāna Vādin, who holds that the texts are instrumental in producing liberation, but that liberation cannot arise except in contradiction with the meaning conveyed by the texts. Such a view is self-stultifying because it undermines the authority of the texts. One must therefore accept that the texts convey the final truth immediately, on pain of their forfeiting authority to convey it at all. Whether they do so at the first time of hearing is another matter. Perhaps the student will not have done enough preliminary reasoning on the meaning of the words in them or enough self-purification of the heart to understand them correctly.

151 The statement is figurative because 'fruit' normally accrues to an agent in virtue of his action, whereas pure Consciousness is actionless. But it has to be made, as otherwise the supreme texts would be without fruit and so not authoritative.

152 One must regard liberation as a 'fruit', or the authoritativeness of the texts leading to it cannot be substantiated, as has just been explained. But to whom does the fruit accrue? The only possible repository for the fruit of liberation is the conscious element in man, the Self. One can only attribute the 'fruit' of any action to the Self figuratively because it is not an agent and all its ends are realized. Still, we have the secular example of the fitting attribution of the fruit of his servants' deeds to a king.

153 R.T. remarks: As people in the world are apt to identify the reflection and its original.

154 R.T. relates this to the end of the previous paragraph as follows. In the earlier passage it had been maintained that the 'fruit' called liberation could not really accrue to the Self, but could only be attributed to it metaphorically. According to the theory of the present verse, however, the Self, though changeless, is really (and not just metaphorically) connected with the 'fruit' called liberation in that liberation accrues to the empirical knower, while the latter depends for its existence on the reflection of Consciousness in the intellect, and the latter is in turn (ultimately) nothing different from pure Consciousness. Thus, if we were to interpret the text 'I am the Absolute' according to this line, the term 'I' would refer to the supreme Self because there is nothing ultimately capable of manifesting 'I' except the supreme Self. But one can only pass to this purified conception of the 'I' *via* the ego-sense, as has already been explained above, 127 and Note 94. One can only pass to some notion of the pure 'I' through the reflection of Consciousness in the intellect, because only the latter is knowable as an object and thus subject to designation by a word.

155 Cp. 'I am the Absolute' at Bṛhad. I.iv.10.

156 I.e. the text must be interpreted on the basis of accepting the presence of a reflection of pure Consciousness in the intellect. R.T.

157 The bridge is provided, says R.T., by the word 'thou'. The meaning of the word 'thou' is known already, because it includes the reflection of Consciousness known as the ego and as an object in introspective empirical experience, and one rises to the meaning of the word 'that' from this firm basis in empirical experience. But if the reflection-theory is not accepted and the words are supposed to refer directly to the transcendent Self, the result is that the words come to have no intelligible meaning whatever and the text is useless. The extract is from **U.S. (verse) XVIII.51-110.**

158 Adopting the reading 'sadā' from D.V. Gokhale's footnotes.

159 When the bare notion 'I' stands unrelated to any kind of a 'this', when there is no judgement of the form 'I am such and such', then the highest Self has been realized. Cp. above, 133.

160 Śaṅkara's pupil Sureśvara does not use the word 'jīva' for the individual soul anywhere in the N.Sid. He uses the terms 'the sufferer' (duḥkhin) or 'the one in transmigration' (saṃsārin). Hacker, *Texte*, 40.

161 Cp. Sureśvara, N.Sid. III.60, prose introduction *ad fin*.

162 Unless withdrawn by conscious control, it remains bound up with the physical organism and hence in motion.

163 The mind is motionless in dreamless sleep and also when it is withdrawn from identification with the senses and body through the practice of meditative concentration (samādhi). In neither of these states is any pain experienced. The inmost Self abides unchanged whether the mind is in motion or motionless. Pain is experienced only when the mind is in motion. Therefore pain belongs exclusively to the mind, not to the Self.

164 In the phrase 'the black horse', the term 'horse' excludes all 'non-horse' from the meaning 'black', and the term 'black' excludes all 'non-black' from 'horse'. Nouns considered in themselves and in isolation from their position in a sentence, stand for universals. 'Horse' stands for the universal 'horse-hood' present in all horses, 'cow' for the universal 'cowhood' present in all cows. Cp. above, Note 94. Words only come to stand for particulars when placed in sentences, for once they are placed in a sentence, the range of their meaning becomes restricted by qualifications introduced by other words in that sentence. Within the general system of rules about the restricting influence of word-meanings on other word-meanings within a

sentence, Śaṅkara here refers specifically to a rule laying down how words placed in grammatical apposition restrict one another's meanings. The two commonest and most obvious examples of groups of words in apposition are (1) Nouns and their qualifying adjectives (e.g. 'the black horse') and (2) Words in subject-predicate relation, coupled by the verb 'to be' (e.g. 'The horse is black', 'That thou art'). The rule to which Śaṅkara appeals appears to have been first formulated by the Buddhist logician, Diṅnāga (K. Kunjunni Raja, 193). It says that when words are grouped in a sentence in apposition, each has the function of excluding its own contradictory from the other and so of narrowing the meaning of the other term down. The contradictory of 'black' is 'non-black', of 'horse' 'non-horse'. Thus in 'The horse is black' (or equally in 'the black horse'), 'black' excludes 'non-black' from the meaning of the term 'horse', and 'horse' excludes 'non-horse' from the meaning of the term 'black'. The peculiar application of this rule in the phrase 'That thou art' is explained in the passage immediately following.

165 Cp. Note 163, above.

166 A stupid man in a party of ten is deputed to count the party after crossing a river, and continually counts the other nine but reports one short as he forgets to count himself. When a bystander says 'Thou art the tenth' he immediately recognizes the truth of the statement. Like him, the spiritual enquirer already knows his own true Self in advance, but forgets it under the outward pull of nescience. Yet he is in principle capable of immediately recognizing the truth of the text 'That thou art'. And though the knowledge derives from speech, it is nevertheless knowledge by direct acquaintance and not knowledge through description, since it concerns the Self of the hearer.

167 Śaṅkara's mention of a qualified (viśiṣṭa) meaning refers back to the process just described earlier. It has been said that the meanings of the words 'thou' and 'real' (equivalent also to

'thou' and 'that' in 'That thou art') had to be taken as qualifying each other mutually in the same way that the meanings of the words 'black' and 'horse' qualify one another in 'the black horse'. It was common ground between Mīmāṃsā (P.M. Sūtra I.iii.33) and Vedanta that a word-meaning could only enter a sentence-meaning through becoming qualified by the meanings of other words in the sentence. How this process of mutual qualification occurs in the case of the words 'thou' and 'real' has been sufficiently explained above. Cp. Sureśvara's N.Sid. III.2, 3 and 16, where at III.2 the sentence 'The lotus is blue' is cited as a parallel to Śaṅkara's 'the black horse'. Compare also the Mānasollāsa Commentary to the Dakṣiṇāmūrti Stotra III.15, a Commentary that is attributed to Sureśvara. Śaṅkara's statement that any other interpretation of 'Thou art the real' would result in a contradiction implies that the meanings of 'thou' and 'real' turn out to be identical when purified by mutual qualification. Cp. N.Sid. III.9, Mānasollāsa III.15-16, Sarvajñātman I.195-197 and Sadānanda, Vedānta Sāra paras 148-169. The sentence does not ultimately refer to a substance qualified by an attribute, though it has to be taken as such initially (Sarvajñātman, *loc. cit.*) Taken in this sense, however, it is found to be self-contradictory, and in order to avoid a contradiction, it has to be taken as an identifying statement on the pattern of 'The ether in the pot is the great (cosmic) ether'. N.Sid. III.9. Here, in order to avoid a contradiction, one has to exclude the element of limitation from the ether apparently (but not really) enclosed by the pot and the element of 'greatness-as-opposed-to-smallness' from the great ether, so that the sentence in the end points to, without actually characterizing, the pure ether, which is unconditioned in any way. In a similar way, as already stated earlier in the present passage, the terms 'thou' and 'real' point to, without actually characterizing, the inmost Self.

168 No *action* of any kind is needed. The verse is reproduced by Sureśvara at N.Sid. IV.34.

169 Otherwise, R.T. explains, the Self would have to be taken as the subject in 'I am the Absolute' but as the predicate in 'That thou art'. In fact, it has always to be taken as the subject.

170 One reasons, says R.T., that what is already known must form the subject and that what is not known is predicated of that. Thus the word 'I' is the subject and that which is not known is predicated of that. Thus the word 'I' is the subject in 'I am the Absolute' and the word 'thou' in 'That thou art'. For the words 'I' and 'thou' stand for the hearer's own Self, which is already directly known to him, although his present knowledge of it is overlaid by superimpositions and requires to be corrected by the further information given in the predicate.

171 This is directed against the view of the Prasaṅkhyāna Vādins that one must continue with meditating on the text and reasoning about its meaning till the fall of the body. Cp. above, Vol.V, Chapter XIII, Note 245. Reasoning about the meaning of the words by the method of agreement and difference is necessary until the sentence has been comprehended. But once a text proclaiming the eternal truth has been comprehended, there is no further scope for reasoning.

172 Such as strengthening one's conviction about the truth of the text as suggested by the Prasaṅkhyāna Vādin.

173 As 'I' unassociated with any further notion.

174 Cp. U.S. (verse) XVIII.165.

175 The example comes from P.M. Sūtras X.i.1-3 and X.ii.1-2. The injunction 'He should melt down the gold particles' is contradicted by perception, as it is observed that they do not melt. Here, since sense-objects are involved, perception is competent to contradict the plain meaning of the text, which accordingly has to be explained metaphorically. But perception and the other means of empirical cognition are not competent to establish a contradiction in the texts proclaiming the supreme Self because,

though they have practical validity in the empirical sphere, the empirical means of cognition have no validity in the metaphysical sphere.

176 According to R.T., the objector's argument is that since the two contradictory ideas 'I am the sufferer' and 'I am not the sufferer' are manifesting simultaneously, the knowledge 'I am not the sufferer' received from the text is merely abstract knowledge and so not of itself sufficient to contradict the notion 'I am the sufferer' that has been established through previous experience stretching over limitless time. Śaṅkara himself, a little further on, quotes the example of awaking from sleep, and compares the experience to enlightenment. Cp. Sureśvara's N.Sid. III.47 and III.105f.

177 The experience of enlightenment is itself compared to an awakening from sleep, cp. Sureśvara's N.Sid. III.47 (introductory prose commentary).

178 Thus our attitude to painful dream-experience when we have awoken from the painful dream affords an example of how a conviction can arise that there was no real relation with pain even during the time that the pain was being experienced. Like the one who has awakened from a painful dream, the enlightened one has awoken from the dream of nescience that makes him feel that he is really related to the psycho-physical organism and its experiences. Through this awakening he acquires a parallel conviction that he is not really related to the painful experiences even during the time they are apparently occurring — in his case, the present. Thus the objection raised earlier about the persistence of the feeling 'I am the sufferer' during embodied life even in the case of the enlightened person is answered.

179 Cp. Sureśvara, N.Sid. III.69 and 70.

180 Reproduced at N.Sid. IV.31.

181 That is, agreements and differences noted in (1) the contexts in which speakers use the word and (2) the characteristics of the entities for which they make it stand. Cp. above, Notes 135 and 136. When the present verse is quoted by Sureśvara at N.Sid. IV.32, the commentator Jñānottama says that the reference is to 'the speech usages of the elders'.

182 Śaṅkara actually quotes only 'Being only (existed in the beginning, my dear one)'. Chānd. VI.ii.1. But the immediate awareness he is talking about could not arise from the mere sentence beginning 'Being only...' unsupported by the later reference at Chānd. VI.viii.7 to the inmost Self in the phrase 'That thou art'. Śaṅkara's present verse is quoted at Sureśvara, N.Sid. IV.33.

183 Cp. Note 175 above.

184 Śaṅkara's early follower, the author of the Pañcapādikā, refers to the stock phrase 'This is that Devadatta' to illustrate this type of sentence, and many later Advaitins followed him. It appears that Śaṅkara himself does not quote this particular phrase. Cp. P.P. Eng. trans., 307.

185 The idea of 'the sufferer' is excluded from 'thou', the idea of 'not being the inmost Self' from 'that'.

186 Bṛhad. III.ix.26, IV.ii.4, IV.iv.22. **U.S. (verse) XVIII.163-198.**

187 According to R.T., this means either when the text is first heard or when one is reflecting on its meaning to try to understand it when one does not yet understand it.

188 A proverbial expression for making efforts to procure something with the wrong means, found also in Vyāsa's Commentary to Patañjali's Yoga Sūtra I.32. If speech in general yields not concrete experience but merely abstract ideas, then it is absurd to seek concrete experience from mere analysis of speech, which would keep one at a yet further remove from concrete experience than speech itself.

189 One may know something directly about one's own Self and yet require to be reminded of it. In this one exceptional case, verbal knowledge can be direct knowledge, as in the case of one who is reminded that he is himself 'the tenth' when he is so occupied with counting his nine confederates that he forgets the fact. Cp. Note 166 above. Two or three centuries after Śaṅkara, Vimuktātman summed up the Advaita view as follows (Iṣṭa Siddhi, 122): 'Even verbal knowledge can be direct knowledge, because it can concern that which is immediately and directly known, as in the case of a human sentence proclaiming the self-luminosity of the Self'.

190 Pain is exterior even to the empirical cognitions, since they experience it as an object. But the Witness is even further removed from the possibility of relation with pain, since it witnesses the cognitions themselves as objects.

191 R.T. explains that the Witness, being itself of the nature of experience, could not require any other experience apart from itself to experience itself. But the wise speak also of an adventitious knowledge of the Self consisting in the rise of a mental cognition pervaded by the reflection of the Self. **U.S. (verse) XVIII.199-205.**

192 It is remarkable to find that Śaṅkara can quote the Dharma Śāstra on the analysis of 'That thou art', a text that does not seem to have been emphasized in the B.S. or by other pre-Śaṅkara Vedāntins that we know of, with the marked exception of Draviḍācārya. The Dharma Śāstra text which Śaṅkara here quotes has not been traced, but was evidently authentic, as it is quoted in Viśvareśvara's Yati Dharma Saṅgraha, Ā.Ś.S. Ed. Vol. 60, 156. It is also referred to in Madhusūdana's Bh.G.Bh. III.6. Cp. D.V. Gokhale's Notes to his edition of the U.S, on (verse) XVIII.222.

193 See U.S. (verse) XVIII.9ff.

194 Bṛhad. IV.iv.23.

195 Cp. above, Vol.V, Chapter XIII, section 2, Extract 20.

196 U.S. (verse) XVIII.222-225.

197 That is, the Self.

198 The view of the P.M. Prabhākara. Cp. Frauwallner, G.I.P.Vol.II, 185.

199 It is not, because it bears upon the already known, and it is one of the accepted rules that only that is a means of valid cognition (pramāṇa) which reveals what was previously unknown. Memory may be either clear or confused, but in either case it is not normally accorded the status of a 'valid means of cognition', because it does not bear on what was previously unknown.

200 Therefore the agent of knowing, as proposed in the theory, would not be present at the same time as the instrument and the object, and therefore could not reveal them.

201 One can only know 'this' as 'not me', and 'me' as 'not this' (not external).

202 Because a lapse of time is required, however brief, to apprehend the distinct but related terms.

203 So that it would have to know them in subsequent cognition, and the notion of simultaneity cannot stand. The position also involves infinite regress. If every cognition is analysed into three component factors which cannot be proved to be grasped simultaneously, then the knowledge of each of the factors will have to be analysed as a further cognition implying three factors and thus three further cognitions, and each of these three new cognitions will imply three factors which will have to be known through three further cognitions and so to infinity. Thus cognition can never be accounted for by the mere memory 'I saw this'.

204 Pāṇini Sūtra I.iv.49.

205 The example alleged above of the memory 'I saw this' would

therefore at best prove the existence of an agent in the act of knowing. But U.S. (verse) XVIII.123 has shown that we are in search of a changeless Witness beyond modification and activity. Hence the Self cannot be shown to be self-evident to those in nescience, and consequently requires to be known through a positive means of cognition. The mere negation of the empirical realm would not suffice to reveal it.

206 That is, if 'being established' in the case of the Witness means 'being known', the case is covered by the two alternatives mentioned in the previous verse, as previous Ignorance of the Witness is implied. In either case a means of valid knowledge (pramāṇa) would be required to establish the Witness.

207 Or else: in the theory of those who accept knower, knowledge and known.

208 Reading 'jñātatvaṃ' with Swāmī Jagadānanda.

209 The Bhāṭṭa, the P.M. of Kumārila's school, is meant. R.T.

210 U.S. (verse) XVIII.124-40.

211 Bṛhad. II.v.1, trans. Mādhavānanda, 262f.

212 E.g. at B.S.Bh. III.iv.51, trans. Gambhīrānanda, 808.

213 Sac, M.V., 137, *Vision*, 70f.

214 Bṛhad. Bh. II.iv.5, trans. Mādhavānanda, 247.

215 Cp. above, 155f.

216 Sac, M.V., 146ff.

217 Chānd. VII.vi.1.

218 Bh.G.Bh. XIII.24.

219 Bh.G.Bh. VI.13.

220 Bh.G.Bh. XII.3.

221 Chānd. VII.vi.1.

222 Bh.G. VI.11.

223 Vyāsa mentions 'padmāsana' in his Bhāṣya to Yoga Sūtra II.46. The Vivaraṇa on this Bhāṣya attributed to Śaṅkara describes it as follows: The Padma and other āsanas are described (not in the Yoga Sūtra but) in other traditional texts... In the case of the Padmāsana one should draw up the left foot and place it high on the right (thigh) and place the right foot over the left (thigh) in the same way. Hips, chest and neck should be held firm, the gaze should be staring at the point of the nose like one dead or asleep, the lips closed as if to form a closed casket, the teeth not clenched, and chin held up a fist's length away from the chest, with the tip of the tongue inserted between the front teeth, hands laid over the heels either in the 'Kacchapaka' or 'Brahmāñjali' pose, remaining steadily in the adopted position, continuously refraining from any efforts to modify the position of the body or limbs.

224 Śvet. II.10.

225 B.S.Bh. IV.i.7-11.

226 Chānd. VI.ii.1.

227 Bṛhad. II.iv.5, Chānd. VIII.vii.1, III.xiv.1, Bṛhad. I.iv.7.

228 Kena I.6, Chānd. VI.viii.7, VII.xxv.2. **G.K.Bh. III.16.**

229 I.e. in waking and dream, but not in dreamless sleep.

230 U.S. (verse) VII.1-6.

231 U.S. (verse) VIII.1-6.

232 Cp. above, Vol.II, Chapter VI, section 3, Extract 7.

233 Ā.D.S. Adhyātma Paṭala 4, Bhāgavat, 426, 'All living beings are the dwelling-place of Him who is hidden in the heart of all...'

234 This is a 'subjective genitive' referring to the knower's knowledge, not to the fact of his being known.

235 Bṛhad. IV.iii.23.

236 Cp. above, Vol.III, Chapter IX, section 2, Extract 12.

237 Perhaps the expression can be understood negatively as 'not caused by anything external to itself'.

238 See above, Vol.III, Chapter IX, section 3, intro.

239 Cp. Bh.G.Bh. XV.16.

240 Bh.G. XV.18,19.

241 Cp. Kaṭha I.iii.8.

242 U.S. (verse) Chapters IX and X.

243 Bṛhad. IV.v.15 *ad fin.* You only need to *know* the truth about the Self. You do not need a course of action in addition.

244 In particular, the sacred thread, the sign of a man of one of the three higher castes, eligible to perform Vedic ritual.

245 Cp. above, Vol. IV, Chapter X, section 2, *passim.*

246 Bṛhad. II.iii.6.

247 In the waking state you have external objects, so here the knowing subject might be the mind. But in dream the mind is, when viewed in retrospect, quite clearly the object of the knowledge of a subject. Therefore it is clearer in the dream state than it is in the waking state that there must be something other than the mind illumining the mind, *viz.* the Witness. I owe this explanation to Dr. A.M. Halliday.

248 Bṛhad. II.i.18.

249 See Bṛhad. II.iii.1ff.

250 Taitt. II.7.

251 Bṛhad. III.iv.2.

252 Bṛhad. II.iv.5. It should hardly need pointing out that the ego is not meant here. But there have been European scholars ready to

accuse the Vedanta of 'crude egoism' (l'égoïsme brutal) in this context.

253 U.S. (verse) Chapter XI.

254 I.e. the body could not be visibly manifest without light from some external source, but in ordinary experience we do not reflect on this.

255 The identification is primarily with mind, senses and body. Cp. above, Vol.V, 219f.

256 For this story, see above Vol.IV, Chapter XI, Note 242.

257 Adopting the reading śreṣṭho for preṣṭo from Gokhale's footnotes.

258 Bṛhad. III.iv.2.

259 I.e. experience purporting to bear on immediate experience.

260 Pure Consciousness may be said to affirm 'I am' as long as one does not attribute to it the notion 'I am this'. The 'this' element bespeaks individuality and narrows the Self down to an ego. Cp. U.S. (verse) II.2.

261 U.S. (verse) Chapter XII.

262 Cp. Bṛhad. III.viii.8.

263 *Ibid.*

264 Muṇḍ. II.i.2.

265 Bṛhad. IV.iv.20.

266 Muṇḍ. II.i.2.

267 Kaṭha I.iii.15.

268 Cp. Śvet. VI.11.

269 Understood as a knower of the Absolute brahman. Cp. Bṛhad. III.viii.10.

270 Cp. Īśa 3. Such souls continue to transmigrate because they fail to know the Self.

271 U.S. (verse) Chapter XIII.

272 Hence there is no longer any need or possibility of *pursuing* concentration (samādhi).

273 Muṇḍ. II.i.2.

274 E.g. it is not restricted to dawn and sunset, to holy places, to persons facing the east, to the occasion of an eclipse, etc.

275 U.S. (verse) XIV.34-44.

276 Padoux, 27.

277 *Ibid.* 28. Cp. Ait. Br. VII.18.

278 Ed. and trans. Oertel, J.A.O.S. XVI, 1894, 79ff. The Brāhmaṇa specifies that the final 'm' is only a nazalization (like final 'n' in French 'en' or 'on' before a consonant) and not the full consonant 'm'. Cp. Padoux, *loc. cit.*

279 Padoux, 34.

280 Above, 30f.

281 Cp. present chapter, 183.

282 Kaṭha Bh. I.ii.15 *ad fin.*, oṃ-śabda-vācyaṃ oṃ-pratīkaṃ ca. Cp. present chapter, 175f.

283 V.S. Bhattacharya in Ā.Ś.G., 10 *ad* G.K. I.19 quotes Sāyana on the Taittirīya Āraṇyaka saying 'akāro vai sarvā vāk'. He adds: 'The Aitareyakas also preserve a text Ait. Āraṇyaka II.iii.3 (cp. Note 315 below), saying that all speech is "a". It is this basic sound that undergoes modification in vowels and consonants'. The Taitt. text in question is quoted by Madhusūdana Sarasvatī in his Bh.G.Bh. X.33.

284 See above, Vol.II, Chapter VI, section 2, Extract 5.

285 Below, 179.

286 Below, 176f.

287 Praśna V.1.

288 Praśna V.2.

289 Inanimate beings and even abstract things like parts of discipline are apt to be personified in the Upanishads.

290 Praśna V.5, Kaṭha I.ii.14-15.

291 At a subsequent time, 'after passing through fire and light, etc'. i.e. on the Path of the Flame. See Bh.G.Bh. IX.1, introduction.

292 Bh.G.Bh. VIII.11-13.

293 Kaṭha II.17, Mahānārāyaṇa (ed. Varenne, 136), Praśna V.5, Muṇḍ. II.ii.6.

294 Chānd. I.i.9.

295 Kaṭha I.ii.17.

296 Chānd. II.xxiii.3. Deussen remarks that the reference is probably not to bundles of palm-leaf manuscripts (the popular interpretation of the phrase here), as writing would probably not have been used for religious manuscripts at the time the Chānd. was composed. He suggests the reference may be to bundles of leaves pierced and held together on a stalk, to be used later as plates. Śaṅkara himself speaks of leaves held together by the stalk in his Commentary to the Chānd. passage in question.

297 Chānd. II.xxiii.3.

298 Play on 'veditavya' and 'veda'.

299 On this interpretation, the reading is taken as ' 'yam', not 'yam'.

300 From Bṛhad. V.i.1.

301 Many of the larger sacrifices were accompanied by verses of the

Ṛg Veda re-arranged for singing. Thus re-arranged they formed the Sāma Veda, where the word Sāma is for Sāman = chant. Each chant had four or more sections (bhakti), of which the Udgītha was the second and perhaps the most important. It began with the syllable OM.

302 Chānd. Bh. I.i.1.

303 The equivalent of our inverted commas.

304 Kaṭha Bh. I.ii.15-16.

305 Praśna V.2.

306 Chānd. II.xxiii.3. On the rod, cp. Note 296, above. But Swāmī Gambhīrānanda takes the reference to be to the midribs that hold the leaves together naturally, which may be the correct explanation, superseding earlier ones.

307 Taitt. Bh. I.8.

308 The mere negative practice of withdrawing the senses (and mind) from their natural functions (pratyāhāra) is not enough. The mind has to be concentrated on the Absolute. Sac.

309 Reading 'para iva' with Sac instead of the 'śara iva' of other texts.

310 Muṇḍ. Bh. II.ii.2-4.

311 Bṛhad. I.v.3.

312 Bṛhad. Bh. I.vi.1.

313 At Māṇḍ. 2ff. the quarters of the Self are given as Vaiśvānara, Taijasa, Prājña and Turīya. One must surely take A, U and M as corresponding successively to the first three.

314 The syllable O is analysed by the Indian grammarians into the diphthong A + U. But OM is not very often spelt AUM in modern texts printed in Devanāgarī.

315 Aitareya Āraṇyaka II.iii.3. All speech is a modification of the 'ah' sound we sometimes make when surprised.

316 Chānd. V.xviii.2. The text as a whole equates Vaiśvānara with the universe. Originally the term Vaiśvānara referred to Agni as the progenitor of mankind, from whom Vivasvant (the Shining One) and Manu proceeded. But the universe was also regarded as a manifestation of Agni. Cp. Bergaigne, Vol. I., 19, 38, 47, 70. The connection of Vaiśvānara with Agni in the present passage is attested by the reference to the 'brilliant light'.

317 Cp. above, Vol.II, Chapter VI, section 2, Extract 16 (a passage which belongs also to the present section). The Absolute is not different from OM, and Vaiśvānara is a mere modification of the Absolute, a mere imagination in it. A modification is a mere suggestion of speech: it is nothing without the word which expresses it, and, therefore, in a sense nothing but that word. A clay cart made as a toy is not a cart but simply a lump of clay fashioned in a certain form and arbitrarily called a cart. And even a 'real' cart is only pure Being called a cart.

318 Because it modifies it.

319 Viśva and Vaiśvānara are here synonymous.

320 It is positive wrong perception of reality, like viśva, and it is based on absence of perception of reality, like prājña. Sac.

321 Sac writes: Knowledge of the identity of Viśva with the sound A, etc., are but subordinate disciplines throughout. Although 'fruits' are mentioned for those who gain these items of knowledge, the mention of such fruits does not convert the text into a series of injunctions to meditate on the identity of Viśva with the sound A and so on. For symbolic meditations are not the subject of the section. The subject of the section is liberation, and the mention of subordinate fruits for subordinate items of knowledge is made merely to eulogize the main discipline. This chief discipline is the knowledge that the

syllable OM and the Absolute or the Self are identical, and that neither of them is either a verbal expression or anything expressed. This knowledge is the means to liberation. M.R.V. 124.

322 And *a fortiori* the other two, the dream-state and the waking-state, of which the dreamless sleep state is the seed.

323 The reference is to Chapter XV, section 4, Extract 4, above. **Māṇḍ. Bh. 8-12.**

324 These are laid down in the appropriate sections of the traditional Law Books. There are to this day ascetics in India who live in caves deep in the forest or mountains, wholly devoted to silent meditation. There are others who withdraw from normal household life but maintain contact with humanity as spiritual Teachers. The list of ascetic virtues which Śaṅkara gives here implies some degree of contact with humanity being retained, and not a life almost entirely exhausted in meditation on the Absolute.

325 'O' in OM is pronounced like a deep Scottish 'o', but it was analysed as A + U. It should, however, never be thought of as resembling the English sound 'ow' in 'how'.

326 The latter are only possible in the course of household life, not in a life spent in retirement from the world and largely given over to meditation on OM.

327 I.e. a birth favourable to the further practice of spiritual disciplines.

328 The text on which Śaṅkara is commenting reflects the ancient pre-upanishadic belief that the Vedic texts had a quasi-personal existence and could perform physical acts like a human being, such as leading a person somewhere.

329 The syllable 'OM' 'contains', and is therefore equivalent to, the whole Veda. The first element, the sound 'a', is equivalent to

the Ṛg Veda, the first part of the Veda.

330 In the sense of having given up the household ritualistic duties without attaining to that knowledge of the Absolute that absolves one from rebirth. Cp. Bh.G. VI.41.

331 I.e. viśva, taijasa and prājña.

332 Praśna Bh. V.1-7.

CHAPTER XVI

THE ENLIGHTENED MAN

1. Enlightenment is not a Change of State

The material from Śaṅkara's texts dealing with the enlightened man has been arranged in five sections. Of the four Extracts in section 1, the first points out that it is only from the standpoint of nescience that we, the unenlightened observers, associate the Self with certain modifications of the mind and speak of 'enlightenment' where there has been a mental distinction between Self and not-self. The enlightened person himself does not regard himself as capable of individual thought and action.

Extract 2 shows that, from the standpoint of nescience, we may speak of a discrimination between the Self and the not-self on the part of the enlightened person. It is useful to do so, because it shows that the notion of any distinction between the individual soul and the supreme Self was erroneous. This being so, enlightenment implies no change of state, but only the correction of an error.

The theme that enlightenment implies no change of state is continued in Extracts 3 and 4. In particular, texts which speak of the individual 'reaching' the Absolute or 'being poured into it' are interpreted as being figurative (Extract 3). With enlightenment, all desires are realized (cp. section 3 below) and there is no longer any need for, or possibility of, action (Extract 4).

TEXTS ON ENLIGHTENMENT IS NOT A CHANGE OF STATE

1. The reference is to him who knows the Self as described in the previous verse, that is to say as indestructible, as without the last modification of worldly things called destruction, and as unborn and not subject to decay. How can such an enlightened man, the text asks, be in a position to kill or to cause anyone to kill? That is to say, he cannot kill anyone or cause anyone to kill anyone in any way. The two questions are to be interpreted as being rhetorical, as genuine questions would not be in place in the context. The Lord's meaning throughout the whole section is to deny that the enlightened man can perform any action at all, as he says that he is (identified with the Self and therefore) not subject to modification, which makes him ineligible (not only for killing but) for any action whatever. The denial of his power to kill is meant only as an example.

Perhaps you would like to know what particular reason the Lord had for thinking that the enlightened man was unable to perform action when He said 'How can such a man kill?' We have already said that the particular reason for the Self not being able to perform action is that it is not subject to modification. But you will perhaps object that this does not explain the matter, as the enlightened person who knows the Self is not identical with that unchanging Self. It does not follow that one who knows an unchanging stump of wood is himself incapable of action! But this objection is wrong, as the enlightened person *is* the Self. Enlightenment does not pertain to the body or to other aspects of the psycho-physical organism. So it follows as the only remaining alternative that the enlightened one *is* the Self, not subject to modification entering into relation with anything whatever. For the Lord to deny, in the words 'How can such a man kill?', that the enlightened one so conceived could enter into action was thus correct.

Though the Self is void of all modification, it is imagined through nescience, in the form of non-discrimination from the modifications of the mind, to be the perceiver of sounds and other objects brought before the mind. Similarly, the same Self, which is in reality beyond all changes of state, is called 'enlightened' on account of discriminative knowledge separating the Self from the not-self, even though such knowledge is only a modification of the mind and illusory in character (and implies no real change of state).[1]

❖

2. But how (wonders an objector) is it possible that that which is eternal and raised above all change should 'attain' by itself to its own true nature? In the case of gold and other such substances, it is intelligible that the true forms should be lost through contact with other external substances and that their true qualities should fail to manifest, and that in this condition they could be made to 'attain' to their true nature through polishing with corrosive material. Similarly, in the case of the stars, it is intelligible that their light should be overpowered each day by the sunlight and that they should again 'attain' their real form at night when that which had overpowered them is removed. But nothing can conceivably overpower the eternal and constant light of the Self as Consciousness, as it

is beyond contact with the material objects, just like the ether, and as it would contradict our actual experience to maintain that it did. For sight, hearing, thought and knowledge constitute the very essence of the soul, and these are found in constant association with the soul, even in the case of those souls who have not yet transcended the body. For every soul enjoys empirical experience through seeing, hearing, thinking and knowing, and could not enjoy empirical experience otherwise. If it were contended that this Consciousness, as constituting the essence of the soul, was only 'attained' after transcending the body, that would be in contradiction with the fact that we enjoy empirical experience before transcending the body. What, then, is this 'transcending the body'? And what is this 'attainment of the soul's true nature'?

To this we reply that before the rise of discriminatory knowledge, the true nature of the soul, which is the light which animates sight and the rest, does not seem in any way distinct from such external adjuncts as the body, the senses, the mind in its lower and higher aspects and the sensations arising from the experience of objects. Compare the case of a piece of transparent crystal where, before the introduction of a discriminating cognition, the true nature of the crystal, which is really whitish and transparent, does not seem to be different from such external adjuncts as the red or blue colour of the objects near which it is placed. But after the rise of a discriminating cognition, the crystal becomes distinct, and is said to have 'attained' its true nature as whitish and transparent, although it was really exactly the same all along. In the same way, when the true nature of the soul is not yet discriminated from the body and other external adjuncts, the cognition arising through the Veda that does effect this discrimination is what constitutes 'transcending the body'. And the 'attainment of the soul's true nature' is nothing more than knowledge of the true nature of the Self, the result of the discriminating cognition.

The question of whether the soul 'has' or 'has not' a body depends simply on whether discrimination has or has not arisen. For the Vedic text says, 'Existing in bodies, itself without a body'.[2] And the derivative literature, too, teaches that there is no real distinction between having a body and not having one, in the text, 'Though existing in the body, O son of Kuntī, He does not act and is in no way stained'.[3] Hence we say that when through absence of discriminatory knowledge, the soul's true nature is hidden, it is then revealed through the rise of discriminatory knowledge. But the true nature of the soul cannot really either manifest or lose another form, from the mere fact of being the soul's true nature. Hence the distinction between the individual soul and the highest Lord arises from false knowledge and not from reality. For in reality both are relationless like the ether (and hence identical)....

There are some philosophers of other schools who think that the individual, limited, form of the soul is a reality as such, and some also of our own school (Vedanta) share this opinion. The Brahma Sūtras, however, were composed specifically to enlighten all these people, who are enemies to the right knowledge of the perfect unity and sole reality of the Self.

The one supreme Lord, the sole existent, eternal and

constant and raised above all change, the root of consciousness, appears as many through nescience, as a magician appears as many through his hypnotic power (māyā).

It is true that the author of the Sūtras has just denied that a particular text referring to the highest Lord referred also to the individual soul, in the words, 'No, because it would be impossible'.[4] But that has to be understood as follows. On the supreme Self, eternal, pure, enlightened and free by nature, raised above all change, one and without relation to anything else, is erroneously superimposed the form of the limited individual soul, whose characteristics are the opposite, as impurities and a tent-like roof are falsely attributed to the stainless infinite ether of the sky. The author of the Sūtras therefore emphasized the difference of the supreme Self from the individual soul, knowing that he would be going to negate it later by quotations of Vedic texts teaching the unity and sole reality of the Self, supported by reasoning, and by independent rational refutation of the views of the dualists. There is no question of his teaching that the individual soul is really different from the supreme Lord. All the author is doing is to follow the general worldly notion that the individual soul is different from the supreme Lord, which is based on nescience. It is in the same way that the injunctions to action found in the Veda do not fall into contradiction with the metaphysical statements (denying that the soul in its true nature can act), because these also merely conform to the natural (ignorant) conviction that one is an agent and enjoyer. But in other places he shows that what the Veda really has to communicate is the unity and sole reality of the Self, for instance in such a Sūtra as, 'But statements made from the

Veda's own standpoint (teach the identity of the soul with the Absolute), as in the case of Vāmadeva'.[5] And we have already explained how the notion that there is any contradiction between the metaphysical statements of the Veda and its injunctions to action is to be refuted through recourse to the distinction between ignorant and enlightened souls.[6]

❖

3. The question at issue is: 'He who attains the supreme Light and assumes his true form — does he remain different from the supreme Self or does he stand identical with it?' And one might at first think that the soul in release must stand separate from the supreme Self on account of the implicit mention of containing and contained in the text, 'He moves about *there*'[7] and because of the mention of agent and object of an act in the text 'Attaining the supreme Light'.[8] But the author of the Sūtras corrects this idea by saying that the liberated one stands non-separate from the supreme Self. Why is this so? Because this is the doctrine actually found in the holy texts. For there are texts which show that the liberated one is non-different from the supreme Self, such as 'That thou art', 'I am the Absolute', 'Where he sees nothing else', 'There is no second thing other than that, that he should see anything different'.[9] And it is but right that the result of his meditation should accord with his aim, according to the principle 'Whoso wills the Absolute (attains the Absolute)'.[10] And there are texts which directly describe the nature of the liberated man and say he is non-different from the supreme Self, as for instance, 'O Gautama, as pure water poured into pure water becomes the same as the latter, so it is with the soul of the

enlightened sage'.[11] And the various pieces of imagery like that of rivers mingling with the sea are also relevant in this context.[12] Where the texts taken in their literal sense seem to teach a distinction between the liberated man and the supreme Self, this can be (reconciled with the aforementioned texts by being) understood as a mere manner of speaking, while the non-difference of the two remains the fundamental truth. Examples of this are, '"Sir, on what is the infinite established?" "On its own greatness (or not even on greatness)".'[13]

❖

4. It has been said that only he who is attached to the results of actions transmigrates. Since one who has no desires cannot act, the one who is free from desires is automatically liberated.... How does one become free from desires? By realizing them: but this can only be achieved when one's desire is for the Self alone. The Self is the 'all', a mass of pure Consciousness, homogeneous throughout, with nothing inside, nothing outside, nothing above, nothing to the side, nothing below. All one's desires are realized when there is no other reality apart from the Self that could be an object of desire. What could he desire who has acquired the realization, 'When all has become one's own Self, what could one see and with what, what could one hear, what could one think, what could one know?'[14] Only that which is thought of as other than oneself can be an object of desire, and in the case of the enlightened man who has realized his desires no such thing exists.... 'All has become one's own Self' and 'There is something other than oneself capable of being desired' are contradictory notions. Desire is impossible in the case of him

who sees all as the Self, because there is nothing that could be desired.

In the case of those who imagine that ritual still has to be performed to avoid demerit, there is not yet realization of the fact that all is the Self, even though they may (suppose they) have knowledge of the Absolute. For the demerit they wish to avoid is considered as something other than their own Self. The one whom *we* speak of as a knower of the Absolute is he who knows that Self which is ever beyond hunger and the like and unconnected with demerit.[15] But he who sees nothing to acquire or reject cannot even be connected with action. Nor does our position imply any contradiction with ritualistic Vedic texts. For we admit that he who does not know the Absolute must perform ritual to avoid the demerit of its omission. But the one who has nothing to desire and does not desire is not reborn. Verily, he is liberated.

There being no cause for the departure (to heaven, the moon, etc.) of such a one, his Vital Energies, that is to say his faculties such as speech and the rest, do not ascend upwards from the body at death. The desire of such an enlightened one is for the Self, and through this desire he has become the Absolute. An example was earlier given to illustrate the state of being the Absolute and the Self of all in the words 'This is his form in which he has realized his desires, in which the Self is his desire, in which he is without desire'.[16] And the present passage beginning 'Free from desires' is summarizing the teaching and pointing out what the liberated state symbolized by that example (of a man embracing his wife) actually is.

He who sees his own true nature, the Self, a featureless, non-dual unbroken light of Consciousness, similar to the state of dreamless sleep — he has no desires because he has no objects of desire, and his Vital Energies such as the faculty of speech and the rest do not ascend at the death of his body, for there is no cause for him to depart (to the realm of the moon, etc.). In fact, the enlightened one is already the Absolute here on earth. Though he appears to have a body, yet (as the present text puts it) 'Being already the Absolute, he "goes to" the Absolute'.[17] It is because he has no desires to cause the limitation of feeling himself to be 'not the Absolute' that he is 'already the Absolute' and '"goes to" the Absolute' even here in this world and not after the death of the body. For when the enlightened person passes away he does not acquire any new state different from the one he had while alive. 'He goes to the Absolute' only means he does not pass to any other body. For if liberation meant the acquisition of another state, that would contradict the main truth which all the Upanishad texts conspire to declare — the unity and sole reality of the Self. And liberation would then be achieved through action and not through knowledge, which is not the accepted doctrine. And liberation would moreover then be impermanent, as nothing produced through action is found to be permanent. Liberation, however, is universally recognized to be permanent, for we have the text 'This is the eternal glory (of a knower of the Absolute)'.[18]

Moreover, nothing can be supposed eternal but a thing's true essence (svabhāva). If the essence of the Self is its true nature, like the heat of fire, it cannot be called dependent on human activity. For the heat and light of fire are not dependent on the activity of fire: it would be a contradiction to say that they depended on the activity of fire and also that they were essential properties of fire. Nor can you say that they are dependent for their existence on the burning activity of fire. For it is through the properties of heat and light that fire with its powers of burning and the rest is revealed, through the removal of obstructions (such as darkness), to the perceptions of others: it is not that the heat and light are dependent on fire for manifestation. What happens is that heat and light, though qualities of fire, are at first blocked and not in contact with the senses of the perceiver, and are then revealed to his senses afterwards when the obstruction has been removed through the fire's burning. This is the reason for the illusion that the heat and light of fire only arise with the burning. Or if it should turn out that heat and light were not essential properties of fire, then we should cite whatever property *was* an essential property. You cannot say of any object that it is without an essential property.

Nor is it right to say that liberation is a mere negation, a mere cessation of bondage like the breaking of a fetter.[19] For we have to acknowledge that the supreme Self is one and the sole reality, on account of the Vedic text 'One only, without a second'.[20] There is not any other being who is (really) bound that he could acquire real liberation in the form of cessation of bondage, like the breaking of a fetter. We have explained at length how nothing else apart from the supreme Self exists. And that is why we also said that cessation of nescience is what is loosely spoken of as liberation (although the liberated one is not liberated from any real constriction). It is like the destruction of the imaginary snake that had formerly been projected onto the rope that results when the snake-error is overcome.

There is another school that holds that a new Consciousness and a new Bliss are revealed at liberation.[21] Let them tell us what they mean by 'revealed'. If they mean ordinary perception through encompassing of the object,[22] then let them say whether what is revealed exists or does not exist. If it exists, then it must be the Self of the liberated one and there would be nothing to prevent its being perceived, so that it would be constantly perceived, and to say that it was perceived by the liberated one would be a meaningless distinction. But suppose it was only sometimes perceived, then this would imply some obstacle to its perception and so it would be not-self, for otherwise (i.e. if it were the Self) it would be continually perceived. If it were not-self, it would depend on some instrument or organ for its perception. But as the Consciousness and Bliss will have the same (immediate) basis as the perception, there is no possibility of any temporary obstruction, so that they will either be always revealed or else never revealed at all, and nothing can show that there is any intermediate position between those two extremes.

Now, it is not possible that qualities inhering in one and the same substance can be related to one another as subject and object.[23] Furthermore, that which before the revelation of the special Consciousness and Bliss undergoes transmigration and after it becomes released must be as totally different from the supreme Self, the eternally manifest knowledge, as cold is from hot. And to assume that any changes can occur in the supreme Self is to abandon the Vedic doctrine.

You will object that if liberation was in no way different from our present state, there would be no point in making extreme efforts in pursuit of it, and the Vedic teachings would be useless. But the objection is wrong, as the function of efforts and the Veda is to remove the errors springing from nescience. There is no real distinction between a (supposed) liberated and a (supposed) non-liberated state, for the Self is ever identical. But ignorance about the true nature of the Self can be removed through knowledge arising from the authority of the Vedic texts and the instructions of the Teacher. And before that teaching is received, there is room for efforts to prepare for it.[24]

2. Action During Enlightenment

The state of consciousness of the enlightened person is an enigma to the unenlightened. Nevertheless, from the standpoint of the unenlightened observer he is an embodied person, acting. How is this semblance of embodiment and activity to be explained?

When explaining appearances from the standpoint of nescience, Śaṅkara accepted the current distinction between the total merit and demerit arising from a beginningless series of lives (sañcita karma) and that minute portion of such merit and demerit that initiated the life in which liberation was attained (prārabdha karma). The total stock of merit and demerit is abolished on enlightenment, except for the small portion of it which initiated that birth. The latter is like an arrow which, once shot, cannot be called back. Extract 1 explains this, adding that the 'actions' of the enlightened person create no new merit and demerit, as they are not accompanied by ego-sense. Extract 2 further underlines the same point.

Extract 3 suggests that experience, namely the experience of the enlightened person, shows that prārabdha karma has a peculiar status compared with all other karma. It is compatible with enlightenment, as the experience of the enlightened person shows. But action of any other kind is associated with merit and demerit and is incompatible with enlightenment.

The same point is made at Extract 4. Metaphysical knowledge of the true nature of the Self prevents the creation of new merit and demerit, and so ends involuntary reincarnation. But, from the standpoint of nescience, the prārabdha karma appears to continue. On the plane of nescience and action, nothing has occurred to hinder the working out of the small stock of merit and demerit that initiated the current birth. The enlightened person, for his part, witnesses the experiences brought to him by his prārabdha karma, but is not deluded into taking them for real. One whose sense of direction was formerly wrong but has now been corrected may occasionally be visited by the former wrong impressions, which he effortlessly corrects. We, today, see the sun rising and act accordingly, without being deluded into the firm belief that it is actually rising up in the sky.

Extract 5 speaks of the prārabdha karma as sustained by the impressions (saṃskāra) of nescience. The Extract, like the previous one, emphasizes that the enlightened man is *both* conscious of his embodied state *and* conscious that the experience is an illusion. The last part of the Extract, included here for completeness, refers to a doctrine treated of earlier in the Source Book (Volume V, 103-126) — the doctrine, namely, that performance of the daily obligatory ritual without desire for reward purifies the mind and is thus a remote auxiliary (ārād-upakāraka) for knowledge.

Extract 6 speaks of the power of the liberated person, within the realm of nescience, to return to the world in new bodies if he elects to do so to fulfil some particular office.

Extract 7 may be regarded as a kind of Appendix. It comes from the Commentary on the Adhyātma Paṭala of the Āpastamba Dharma-Sūtra. Professor Hacker and others have held that this is a genuine work of Śaṅkara. The doctrine of 'degrees of knowledge' of the Absolute which it contains is not one that is much stressed by Śaṅkara elsewhere, though no doubt he was conforming to the text on which he was obliged to comment. In other respects, the teaching appears to conform to that of other Extracts in the present section well enough.

TEXTS ON ACTION DURING ENLIGHTENMENT

1. Whoever knows the Spirit (puruṣa) in this way, that is, in immediate identity-feeling of the form 'This am I', and who knows this 'Nature' of the nature of nescience, together with its modifications, to have been reduced to non-existence through knowledge, however he may live in the present life, he is not born again in another body after the fall of the present one. And all the more certainly is he not reborn if he adheres to the duties of his station.

Well, it is quite true, you may perhaps say, that it has been said that there will be no further rebirth after the rise of knowledge. But, you may contend, there is a difficulty here. We have to consider the acts performed in the present life before the rise of knowledge, the acts performed after the rise of knowledge and the acts performed in innumerable previous lives. It is not right that the acts of any of these three classes should be destroyed without engendering their due results. There must therefore be three more lives in which to experience the results of these three different classes of acts. For no acts can be expunged without their engendering their due results. This is admitted in the case of acts performed in the present life for the sake of desired results (in this life), and the same will hold good for all acts whatever. Hence the three classes of acts will either originate three more lives or else coalesce to originate one more life. Otherwise we shall have acts being expunged without engendering their due results, and this will give rise to all-round scepticism as to the truth of the Vedic teaching, and the Veda will be rendered useless. So the statement in the text 'He is not born again' is not right.

But this objection is not well founded, on account of such Vedic texts as 'His acts are destroyed', 'So long only will I continue here (as I am not released from the body)' and 'All his actions are burnt up like a tuft of reeds laid upon a fire'.[25] Here in the present work (the Bhagavad Gītā), too, the Lord has already said, 'O Arjuna, the fire of knowledge burns up all action to ashes, like a well-lit fire burning fuel to ashes', and He will repeat the same thing later.[26] Reason also supports our view. For actions can only give rise to the 'sprout' of another life when they spring themselves from such seeds as nescience, desire and the passions. The Lord has in certain places in the Gītā made clear his view that only works performed with ego-feeling originate further experiences for the performer, not others.[27] And there is (the well-known Mahābhārata verse) 'Just as seeds once burnt by fire do not sprout again, so does the Self stand ever free from passions once they have been burnt up by knowledge'.[28]

Here it might be that you would concede that the acts performed after the rise of knowledge could be burnt up by the fire of knowledge, since they came into existence when knowledge was already present. But you might regard it as unreasonable to suppose that knowledge could burn up those acts of the present life that were performed before the rise of knowledge or those of innumerable previous lives.

Such a view, however, is wrong, as the Lord specified that *all* acts are burnt up in the fire of knowledge.[29] Nor can you supply any reason for limiting the bearing of his words to all acts performed after the rise of knowledge alone.

As for the statement that it was as impossible to expunge acts (of other lives) which had not begun to fructify in the present life as it was to expunge those which had begun to fructify in the present lîfe, and which would bring their fruit to the performer ineluctably even though he had attained knowledge of the Absolute, — that statement was wrong. Why? Because the acts which have begun to fructify in the present life are in a different case. They are already engaged in producing their fruit (at the time of enlightenment), like an arrow that has already been loosed from the bow. Consider the case of the arrow that has already been loosed from the bow against the target. Even after piercing the target, it will cease motion only when it falls to the ground on account of the exhaustion of its original impetus. It is the same with the action (of previous lives) which originates a given body. Even when the purpose for which dwelling in the body takes place (i.e. liberation) was secured, the action which originated the body will continue to produce its effects as before until the force of the impressions (saṃskāra) is exhausted.

But that same arrow, before it has been released and before it has acquired its impetus, can be withdrawn even after it has been affixed to the bow. And in the same way the acts of former lives that have come into play to originate the present life remain in their seat (the subtle body) and are deprived of their seed-force through knowledge of reality. Hence it is shown that the Lord was justified in saying that once the body of one who had attained enlightenment passed away that person would not be reborn.[30]

❖

2. In the present Sūtra the author states a further peculiarity about the text. '(One should hope to live a hundred years) performing work here all the time'.[31] Even if it be connected with the enlightened man on the ground of context and taken to mean that it is the enlightened man who should 'perform work here all the time', the reference to 'performing work' should still be regarded as inserted only for the glorification of enlightenment, as the text goes on to say (in the same verse) 'No work can cling to (such) a man'. The burden of the passage is that, even if a man of enlightenment does work his whole life, the results of his deeds do not cling to him, and that this result is due to the power of knowledge. This is how the text utters an eulogy of knowledge.[32]

❖

3. How can action, which has its seed in the ego-notion and which is located in that which has the ego-notion (i.e. in the individual soul) sprout forth again after it has been burnt in the fire of the notion of no-ego? You may object that the actions of the one who has realized the Absolute have visible results. And you may claim that they will also result in further activity in future lives in the same way as before. But it is not

so. The actions of such a man are due *solely* to his previous actions.[33]

Perhaps you will ask here: If, as you say, in the case of the one who has realized the Absolute the seed of previous activity has been destroyed, what do you now mean by saying that his actions are 'due to it'? We reply that, because it was powerful enough to initiate the present body and its appurtenances, the merit and demerit arising from previous action of which the present body is the result can overcome knowledge of the real in you (who have realized the Absolute) and put forth their fruit. At the end of this process (i.e. at the fall of the body or death of the enlightened person) unobstructed knowledge arises. The seeds of action which initiate the body of the one who realizes the Absolute bring forth these two fruits — namely, empirical experience (during the whole term of that body's existence) and knowledge of the Self. Empirical experience and knowledge of the Self must therefore be mutually compatible. But all other merit and demerit (except that which is responsible for the present body) is contrary (to and therefore negated by knowledge).

Whoever possesses knowledge of the Self, which contradicts the notion that the Self is the body as clearly as the 'knowledge' of the ignorant man affirms it, is liberated whether he wishes it or not. Hence all this (the logical compatibility of spiritual knowledge with empirical experience and its incompatibility with all seeds of future activity except those which initiated the present life) stands proved, and we have declared the manner of the proof.[34]

❖

4. Here an objector might claim that if there were (as the Advaitin of Śaṅkara's school maintains) no sustained stream of cognitions yielding knowledge of the Self, it would have to be the last cognition of the Self (in the case of one liberated in life) that actually destroyed nescience, and not the first, as in his case the presence of contradictory cognitions and of their effects is a matter of empirical observation. But we reply that this theory will not do, for in denying the power of the first cognition of the Self to destroy nescience it precludes the certainty of any cognition doing so. If the first cognition of the Self fails to halt nescience, the last one will also fail, as its object is the same. Nor will it do to say that it is a constant stream of cognitions of the Self and not an isolated cognition that destroys nescience. For there cannot be a constant stream of cognitions of the Self if there is to be life in the world. There cannot be a constant stream of cognitions of the Self while one is thinking of bodily necessities, as the two notions are contradictory.

Perhaps you will claim that a stream of cognitions of the Self is possible if pursued with sufficient assiduity until the time of death, as it will enable the person concerned to rise above his thoughts of bodily necessities and the like. But this theory is also wrong as it fails to specify the exact length of the stream of cognition of the Self required, and so fails to accord the Veda any definite meaning. It does not say how much cognition of the Self is required to terminate nescience, and so leaves the Vedic teaching vague, which is not acceptable.

Nor will it do to say that the Vedic teaching has been made quite precise enough in saying that a stream of cognitions is required. For you have not said whether it is the first or the last. Since it has not been made clear whether it is the first stream of cognitions of the Self that destroys nescience or the last one at the time of death, the difficulties mentioned above in connection with the first and last cognitions still remain. And you cannot say that knowledge of the Self does not put an end to nescience anyway, because this very text (now under comment) says, 'Therefore he became all this', and there are other texts implying that knowledge of the Self destroys nescience, such as 'The knot of the heart is broken' and 'What delusion can there be then?'[35] You cannot say that these texts are mere eulogies of knowledge of the Self (not intended to be taken literally). For this would mean that all the teaching of all the Vedic schools was mere eulogy, as all their teaching has but the one aim of leading on to knowledge of the Self.

Perhaps you (the ritualist) will claim that teaching in connection with knowledge of the Self *is* mere eulogy, because the Self is accessible to perception. But we have already shown that this is not so.[36] And we have also refuted it on the ground that after knowledge of the Self, the cessation of ignorance, grief, delusion, fear and other such defects is a matter of direct experience. Therefore the truth is that all this quibbling about whether it is the first or the last cognition of the Self that destroys nescience, or whether nescience is not destroyed by a member of a stream of cognitions at all, is beside the point. The very nature of knowledge of the Self is to result in the cessation of nescience and all its attendant evils. Whatever cognition produces this result is what we recognize as metaphysical knowledge, whether it be the first or the last of a stream of cognitions or not a stream of cognitions at all. Hence there can be no room for further argument.

As for the assertion that cognitions contradictory to knowledge of the Self, and the effects of such cognitions, are observable in the case of the man who has realized the Self — we deny that this is true. For it is (not ignorance of the Self but) the unexpended portion of the past deeds that have already begun to fructify that keeps (the body and the mind of the man who has realized the Self) in being. The previous deeds through which the body in which the Self was realized was brought into being were caused by the defect of wrong knowledge, and can only bring their results in association with the same defect. It continues to occasion false notions and defects like attachment and so on until the fall of the body, these being included in the experience of their 'fruit'. For the fructification of past acts that has brought this body into being is already under way and must pursue its course, like an arrow that has been loosed from the bow. Metaphysical knowledge has not the power to stop *this*, as it is not in contradiction with it.[37] What then does it stop? It stops any new effects of nescience, contradictory to itself, proceeding from the empirical personality, of which it is the substratum. For these belong to the future, whereas the actions being discussed before belong to the past.

Moreover, no false notions arise in the case of the one who has metaphysical knowledge, there being in his case no scope for them. A false notion arises on the basis of a general notion of an object when its particular nature has not been ascertained, as when the false notion of silver arises in nacre (that has only vaguely been perceived). But in the case of one who knows the particular nature of an object the cause of all false notions in relation to it has been destroyed, and they can no longer arise as before. The silver is no longer seen when a correct idea of the nacre has been obtained.

It can, however, be that memories conveying false knowledge may arise from impressions derived from earlier false notions that came before right knowledge arose, and in some inexplicable way momentarily suggest false notions. This happens, for instance, in the case of one who inexplicably loses his sense of direction momentarily, although really in possession of it. If, however, the one who had right knowledge could still have erroneous knowledge *in the same way as before*, this would undermine confidence in right knowledge and render application to knowledge of the Vedic teaching pointless and invalidate every valid means of knowledge, the distinction between valid and invalid becoming nugatory.

This reasoning also disposes of the objection of those who ask why the body does not fall immediately on acquisition of right knowledge of the Self. The present text denies that any obstacle can intervene to prevent knowledge of the Self immediately yielding its fruit. It thereby shows that, upon knowledge of the Self, all action before and after the rise of knowledge in that birth is eradicated, as well as the accumulated actions of previous births that have not begun to bear fruit in the present one.[38]

❖

5. Now we turn to consider the results of knowledge of the Absolute. One might raise the doubt whether the results of ignorance of the Absolute in the form of demerit were or were not destroyed when the Absolute was known. What is the view that might first commend itself here? One might (tentatively) suppose that, since actions are for the sake of results, they cannot be destroyed until they produce these results (and must necessarily subsist in the form of merit and demerit). We know from the Veda that the special property of ritualistic action is to produce future results. It would render the Veda null and void if the act could be destroyed before its results had been experienced. And we have a text from the derivative literature, 'Merit and demerit are not destroyed'. Nor can you say that if merit and demerit were not subject to destruction, this would make nonsense of the passages in the Veda that deal with penances (which have for their purpose the destruction of demerit). For penances are explicable as merely being acts that have to be performed on various special occasions, like the sacrifice that has to be performed when one's house has been burnt down.[39] And in any case penances are enjoined in connection with some evil, so that in their case the destruction of evil is admittedly conceivable. But knowledge of the Absolute is not enjoined at all.[40] Nor should it be contended that if the actions of the enlightened man are not destroyed, he will necessarily have to experience their results and will not be liberated. For liberation arises according to conditions of place, time and cause in just the same way as the results of action do. Hence demerit does not cease when the Absolute is known.

To this the author of the Sūtras replies that when the

Absolute is known, past demerit is destroyed and there will be no future clinging of demerit, as is known from the teaching of the Veda. For in a passage treating of the knowledge of the Absolute it is declared that demerit that would otherwise be expected to assert itself in the future is no longer connected with the enlightened man, saying, 'Just as water does not cling to a lotus leaf, in the same way evil action does not cling to the man who knows the Self'.[41] And it also teaches that previously amassed demerit is destroyed in the words, 'As the soft fibres of the iṣīkā reed are burned up when laid on the fire, even so are all his sins burned up'.[42] And another passage teaching that the actions of the enlightened man are destroyed is the following: 'When this transcendent principle is known, the knot of a man's heart is cut, all his doubts are destroyed and his actions nullified'.[43]

As for the statement that the theory that action could be destroyed before its results had been experienced would make nonsense of the Veda, we do not accept it as a valid criticism of our position at all. We in no way deny that actions have the power to bring future results that have to be experienced. This power exists. But we say that this power is subject to obstruction by external causes, of which knowledge is one. The Veda is only concerned with affirming the existence of this power, not with the question of whether it is or is not subject to obstruction in particular cases. The statement in the derivative literature that merit and demerit are not destroyed is also merely a general statement, taking no account of exceptions. It merely states the general principle that action does not perish before its results have been experienced, as the results are what it was performed for.

As for the question of whether it is destroyed by penance, we affirm positively that it is. For we have texts from the Veda and the derivative literature to this effect, such as 'He who offers the Aśvamedha sacrifice and who knows this to be so crosses over all sin, crosses over even the murder of a Brahmin'.[44]

As for the statement that penances are merely acts that have to be performed after certain other actions — that statement was quite wrong. For they are prescribed in connection with some evil. And as it is perfectly possible that their result would be the destruction of that evil, other hypotheses are out of place.

Then a further point was made. It was said that, unlike penance, knowledge was not enjoined with a view to destroying evils. To this we reply as follows. There are certainly injunctions to 'knowledge' in the form of meditations on themes associated with qualities (saguṇa). And it is to be declared in the sequel that one who obtains knowledge in this form attains the position of a god (aiśvarya) and the destruction of his sins. As there is nothing to show that these two results are not what the text primarily intends to convey, it can only be accepted that both occur and that such persons first lose their demerit and then acquire a god-like state.

But in the case of knowledge of the Absolute in its supreme, qualitiless (nirguṇa) form, although there is here no injunction, action is burnt up on account of one's becoming awake to the fact that one is the actionless Self. Indeed, the Teacher's phrase 'no longer clings' shows that the knower of the Absolute is not an agent in future acts. The Teacher's words 'is destroyed' refer to the fact that although the enlightened man was once, on account of his erroneous notions (mithyā-jñāna), apparently an agent in regard to his past acts committed before enlightenment, nevertheless his erroneous notions have now been destroyed through right knowledge, and even his past acts are in this way dissolved. For the conviction of one who knows the Absolute is, 'I am the Absolute, by nature a non-agent and non-experiencer eternally throughout past, present and future time, quite contradictory to the agency and experiencerhood that seemed evident before: I am not an agent or experiencer now: and I never shall be in the future'. Only on this basis is liberation intelligible. Otherwise there could be no liberation, as there could be no destruction of action that had been proceeding from beginningless time. Nor is it in any way correct to say (with the exponent of the *prima facie* view) that liberation arises according to conditions of time, place and cause (in just the same way as the results of actions do). For if it arose in this way, it would be transient, and in any case the result of knowledge cannot be anything requiring time to supervene. Hence it stands proved that demerit is destroyed when the Absolute has been known.

In the topic just concluded we have explained how natural demerit, the cause of bondage, is declared by the Veda 'not to cling' in the case of the 'acts' of the enlightened man after his enlightenment. But one might suppose that meritorious acts, because based on the Veda, could not conflict with knowledge derived from the Veda. To dispose of this idea, the rule stated in the course of the previous topic is extended further.

Even the other kind of action, namely meritorious action,

says the author of the Sūtras, is destroyed or 'does not cling' in the case of the enlightened man. We know this because if it brought forth its own results it would prevent knowledge of the Absolute from bringing forth its results. And the Veda expressly teaches that both meritorious and sinful deeds are destroyed in such texts as 'He goes beyond these two'.[45] The destruction of action occasioned by awakening to the fact that one is the actionless Self applies to good and evil action alike, and we have the Vedic text 'And his actions are destroyed'[46] which makes no distinction between good actions and bad actions.

Of course there are passages where only sins are said to be destroyed. But even in these cases it should be understood that meritorious deeds are also included. For even meritorious action is mean in its results compared to knowledge. And there is the Vedic text in which the word 'sin' is actually applied to meritorious action. For the passage which begins 'Over that bridge day and night do not cross'[47] goes on to include 'well-doing' and 'ill-doing' among the things that do not cross that bridge, and concludes by saying, 'Thus all sins turn back from it', which amounts to including meritorious and sinful action under the one heading 'sin'.

Here the author of the Sūtras adds, 'At the fall of the body', using the particle 'tu' (but) for extra emphasis. He wishes to emphasize that liberation comes to the enlightened one at the fall of the body without any shadow of doubt, because his meritorious and sinful actions, the cause of bondage, either 'are destroyed' or else 'do not cling'.

In the two preceding 'topics' (sections of the argument in

the Sūtras) it has been established that meritorious and sinful actions are both destroyed through knowledge of the Absolute. We now raise the question, 'Does this apply to all actions in general, including both those whose effects have begun to fructify and those whose effects have not, or does it only apply to those whose effects have not begun to fructify?' And one might initially suppose that it applied to all action without distinction. For we have texts such as 'He goes beyond both these two'[48] which decry any distinction and suggest that all actions are destroyed without exception (at the time of knowledge of the Absolute).

Against this the author of the Sūtras says, 'But only those actions are destroyed whose effects have not yet begun to fructify'. Meritorious and sinful actions whose results have not yet begun to appear, which accumulated in previous lives and in the present life before the rise of enlightenment — such actions are destroyed through knowledge of the Absolute. But those meritorious and sinful actions whose effects have begun to manifest and have been partially experienced and through which the birth which resulted in the knowledge of the Absolute took place, are not destroyed by knowledge of the Absolute.

How do we know this? Because the text 'The enlightened one knows "the delay will only extend till I am released from the body, then I shall attain union"'[49] shows that final peace comes at the fall of the body. If it were not for the distinction between action the effects of which have begun to fructify (in the life in which enlightenment is attained) and action the effects of which have not at that time begun to fructify, all action without exception would be destroyed by knowledge of the Absolute. And in that case there would be nothing further that could sustain the empirical existence of the enlightened man, and he would enter the final peace forthwith. But then the Veda would not have spoken of the need to wait for the fall of the body.

One might ask how it is that this awakening to one's true nature as the actionless Self, which destroys actions merely by coming about, could destroy some actions while leaving others untouched. Nobody could admit that if fire came into contact with a collection of seeds some would be destroyed and others not. To this we reply that the rise of knowledge presupposes a fund of action the effects of which have begun to manifest. This is presupposed, and there cannot be anything to stop the results of such actions. The actions that have begun to fructify carry on fructifying until their energy is spent, like a potter's wheel revolving on once it has been set in motion. Hence one has to wait until the energy of the action is exhausted. Awakening to the fact that one is the actionless Self admittedly destroys actions by negating erroneous knowledge. But the negated erroneous knowledge continues on for a certain time owing to the force of latent impressions (saṃskāra), like the vision of a second moon (occasionally visiting the one who is cured of squinting). And one should not raise the objection that the knower of the Absolute must either support the body for a certain time after enlightenment or else not support it. For if a person, even though he be only one single person, yet has the conviction in his own heart that he has direct knowledge of the Absolute and is also supporting a physical body at the same time, how can any one else cause him to deviate from that conviction? And this very point is made by the Veda and the derivative literature when they describe the state of the one of steady wisdom (sthita-prajña).[50] Hence it is only those good and evil deeds whose effects have not yet begun to manifest that are destroyed by the power of knowledge.

The rules for the 'non-clinging' and destruction of all evil deeds have now been extended to meritorious deeds. And the suggestion might be made that it extended to *all* meritorious deeds. This the author of the Sūtras denies, beginning by saying 'But the Agnihotra, etc.' The word 'but' serves to contradict the suggestion. The daily obligatory rituals which the Veda prescribes, such as the Agnihotra milk offering, 'have the same purpose', that is, they have the same purpose as knowledge.[51] For we find such Vedic texts as 'The Brahmins hope to know this very principle through repetition of the Vedic texts, through sacrifice and charity'.[52]

Perhaps you will object that since the results of knowledge and action are different in kind, it is wrong to say that they are for the same purpose. But this does not affect our position. For curds (if eaten too cold) will produce fever, and poison will produce death. But curds taken with sugar and poisonous substances treated by magic spells yield delight and nourishment. And in the same way, action can be an (indirect) cause of liberation if knowledge supervenes.

But, you will object, liberation is not anything that could be caused.[53] How can it be said to result from action? But this does not affect our position either. For action promotes the same result as knowledge indirectly. It is only knowledge that actually produces liberation, but action is an indirect aid, and is spoken of as a cause metaphorically. And hence it is also beside the point to say that we are claiming that knowledge and action have the same result. For once the knower of the Absolute has obtained enlightenment, he is no more able to perform the Agnihotra or any other ritual. For when there is knowledge that one's own Self is that Absolute which is beyond the reach of injunctions, one passes beyond the realm of Vedic commands. But in the case of knowledge arising from meditation on themes involving form and quality (saguṇa), the sense of agency is not brought to an end. In its case, therefore, the Agnihotra and other ritualistic action can still follow. For when such ritualistic action is performed by one who is without desire for any personal advantages, it can contribute to knowledge, as it has no other function to perform.[54]

❖

6. We now raise the question whether the man of enlightenment does not undergo another birth after the death of the present body. One might initially object that such a question was meaningless. For if one has obtained enlightenment, which is the means to liberation (from rebirth), it makes no sense to ask whether liberation ensues or not, any more than it would make sense to ask, when all the arrangements for cooked rice had been completed, whether cooked rice will actually be the result or not, or to ask whether it will satisfy the consumer or not, when he has already begun to eat. But the objection is wrong and the enquiry is justified, because we find references in the Epics and Purāṇas to new births even for men of enlightenment. There is the tradition, for example, that Apāntaratamas, a certain ancient sage and Teacher of the

Veda, took birth as Kṛṣṇadvaipāyana in the interval between the Dvāpara and Kali eras, at the command of Viṣṇu.[55] And Vasiṣṭha, a 'mind-born son of Brahmā', having lost his body through the curse of Nimi, was reborn from Mitrā and Varuṇa at the command of Brahmā. And we hear also of the rebirth of Bhṛgu and other 'mind-born sons of Brahmā' at a sacrifice to Varuṇa. Sanatkumāra, who was also a 'mind-born son of Brahmā', was himself reborn as Skanda as a result of a boon granted to Rudra. And in fact on many occasions in the derivative literature we hear of Dakṣa, Nārada and other enlightened souls undergoing rebirth.

We often come across the same thing in the hymns and explanatory passages (artha-vāda) of the Veda itself. Sometimes we hear of enlightened souls acquiring a new body after the fall of the old one. Sometimes they remain in their present body and assume several other bodies at the same time by virtue of their extraordinary yogic powers. And all of them are held to have plumbed the entire depths of the Vedic teaching.

In face of this fact that enlightened beings sometimes acquire new bodies, one might suppose that knowledge of the Absolute was erratic in its results, and sometimes did and sometimes did not cause liberation. To this supposition the author of the Sūtras replies with a negative. For all these figures, like Apāntaratamas and the rest, were appointed to perform various functions that are necessary to keep the world in being, such as the propagation of the Veda and the like, and their acquisition of new bodies was to do with their office. The same is true of that holy Savitṛ (i.e. the sun) which, having presided over the world for thousands of aeons, will experience a state of liberation, without rising or setting, when the world comes to an end, as is shown by the text 'Then, having risen upward, it will neither rise nor fall any more, but will stand alone in the middle'.[56] And it is in the same way that knowers of the Absolute today experience liberation as soon as the portion of merit and demerit that occasioned their present birth is exhausted, as we know from the text, 'His delay lasts only as long as he is not liberated from the body. When this occurs, he attains complete identity'.[57]

In this way, even the great lordly figures like Apāntaratamas and the rest, appointed to perform various functions by the Lord, remain (in the empirical world) for the period of their office, even though right knowledge of the Absolute, the cause of liberation, is theirs, while their merit and demerit remain unexhausted. When the period of their office comes to an end they are liberated. In this way there is no contradiction.They expend only the stock of merit and demerit which began their present life, but in such a way that it enables them to fulfil their office. They move from one body to another with perfect ease, as if they were crossing from one house to another, in order to carry out their work. They do not forget their experiences in one body on attaining the next. Being masters over the body, senses and the forces of nature, they create bodies at will either successively or simultaneously and, having created them, dwell in them. They do not fall into the class of 'those who remember their previous lives', as the traditions say 'These are they in very deed'.[58] There was the case in the Epic (the Mahābhārata) of the lady-metaphysician called Sulabhā, who wished to have a dispute with Janaka, and to this end left her own body and entered Janaka's body, and then returned to her own body after having the argument with him.[59]

Indeed, if when the merit and demerit that had set in motion the present body was exhausted, further merit and demerit would come into play such as would initiate other bodies, then we should have to assume the continued existence of yet more merit and demerit as seeds of further experience not yet burnt (and neutralized by the fire of knowledge). And this would permit the suspicion that knowledge of the Absolute was erratic as a cause of liberation. But this suspicion is not in fact permissible, as both the Veda and the derivative literature show that knowledge burns the seeds of merit and demerit....[60] Nor is it possible to suppose that when the passions (kleśa) such as ignorance and the rest are burnt, one part of the stock of merit and demerit in the form of a seed of further passions is burnt, while the other part continues to sprout. For we do not find that when a grain of rice is burnt by fire, one part continues to sprout. But the fruition of merit and demerit that has already begun to fructify comes to an end when its energy is spent, like the motion of an arrow that has already been discharged. The end of its course is marked by the fall of the body, as the text 'His delay lasts only as long as he is not liberated from the body'[61] shows. Hence the statement that the lordly beings continue to perform their offices as long as their appointment lasts was correct, and yet knowledge of the Absolute invariably produces its effect (of liberation). The Veda accordingly declares that all beings without any exception acquire liberation through knowledge of the Absolute in the text 'Whichever of the gods became enlightened became that (became the Absolute). The same is true of the seers (ṛṣi), the same is true of ordinary men'.[62]

Sometimes even great seers (maharṣi) become attached to other forms of meditation which bring lordly states and other great rewards. In their case, we must suppose that, having been disappointed on finding that their lordly states come to an end, they applied themselves to knowledge of the supreme Self and attained liberation. For we have the text from the derivative literature, 'When cosmic dissolution has come and Hiraṇyagarbha's days are at an end, then they all enter the supreme state along with Brahmā, having realized the Self'.[63]

And because knowledge brings its reward immediately, there can be no question of any delay. In the case of action, the reward, such as heaven, is not immediately evident, and there can be doubt as to whether it will come or not. But the fruit of knowledge of the Absolute is immediately evident, for the Veda speaks of 'The Absolute which is immediately and directly evident' and teaches 'That thou art' as an already accomplished fact.[64] One cannot twist the meaning of the text 'That thou art' into 'That thou shalt be when thou art dead'. And the text 'Seeing that, the seer Vāmadeva knew "I was Manu, I was the sun"' shows that the fruit of this knowledge is 'becoming' the Self of all at the instant of that right knowledge. Hereby the man of enlightenment has been shown to attain liberation with absolute certainty.[65]

❖

7. It might be objected that as the removal of all defects and the destruction of merit and demerit arise through

enlightenment, then, because the removal of defects arises automatically, the phrase in the text (of verse 11 of the Adhyātma Paṭala of the Āpastamba Dharma Sūtra) reading 'Having removed the creaturely defects' is superfluous as it merely reiterates what is already the case naturally. But the objection is not right, as the merit and demerit that has already begun to unfold in the life in which enlightenment is attained must run its course. For actions that have been performed in the numerous births which occurred before that in which enlightenment is attained are divisible into two classes from the point of view of merit and demerit — those that are and those that are not in the course of fructification during the life in which enlightenment is attained. As regards the actions which have begun to fructify in the life in which enlightenment is attained, it implies defects and the experience of the deserts of merit and demerit incurred on the part of the agent concerned. Otherwise, if there were no defects, the merit and demerit could not have begun to fructify at all (and the life in which enlightenment took place could never have begun). For no one is ever found here on earth engaging in action bringing pleasure or pain in the absence of attachment and aversion and other defects. Defects, therefore, arise (even in the case of the man liberated in life) through action performed (in previous births) for the sake of results, and they must be extirpated with efforts proportionate to their gravity. Otherwise they might lead to further interested action.

So what is being said is that the extirpation of psychological defects depends on 'yoga'.[66] This further follows because the situation varies according to whether spiritual knowledge is of lesser quality, average quality or high quality.

Knowers of the Absolute are not all equal in their degree of awareness of the Absolute, for sometimes one will be found with exceptional powers of discrimination. And we know this from the Vedic text, 'This one (i.e. this type) is the best amongst the knowers of the Absolute'.[67] And there is the text from the derivative literature which (distinguishes a certain type of knower and) says 'Possessed of right-knowledge'.

In the case of the knowers of the Absolute whose knowledge is of lesser or average quality, the injunctions to renunciation, dispassion and conquest of the senses are meaningful. In the case of those whose knowledge is of the highest quality these qualities are already present and the injunction merely registers what is already the case. And this also follows from such texts as 'Even the taste leaves him when he has seen the Supreme',[68] which indicates the state of the one who has passed beyond the three constituents (guṇātīta).

Here you might object that on our doctrine even the enlightened man would be liable to further reincarnation on account of the psychological defects arising from the merit and demerit unfolding during the life in which he attained enlightenment, and from the acts resulting from those psychological defects. But in fact no further life can be initiated, because the acts proceeding from the psychological defects of the enlightened one arise merely from merit and demerit that has already begun to fructify (prārabdha) and must complete its course like an arrow that has left the bow. Their power (to cause future rebirth) is destroyed merely by the experience of the results of that merit and demerit already under way, and there is no other possible cause that could lead to rebirth.[69] If it be taken that there still exists a stock of merit and demerit not involved in producing the life in which enlightenment takes place, it cannot produce a new life, as, in the very nature of the case, its seed-power has been burnt by the fire of knowledge of the Absolute. And the Veda and derivative literature confirm this when they say 'and his merits and demerits are destroyed' and 'The sword of knowledge reduces all action to ashes'.[70] Thus it has been shown that the wise man (paṇḍita) attains serenity through extirpating his psychological defects.[71]

3. The Enlightened Man Enjoys All Pleasures

The Extracts in this section correspond to, and are mostly commentaries on, 'enthusiastic' passages in the Upanishads, which speak of the bliss of the enlightened person in positive terms. Extract 1 says he enjoys all the pleasure there is, but that this should not be conceived as the successive enjoyment of a series of pleasures. Extract 2 says that his delight does not depend on anything external. Extract 3 speaks of pleasures enjoyed by the enlightened person on the purely mental plane, on the plane of objective reality and on the plane of 'Brahma-loka' in the after-life. According to Extract 4, the enlightened person wanders about feeling himself the Self of all. He gives out the truth for the sake of the people.

TEXTS ON THE ENLIGHTENED MAN ENJOYS ALL PLEASURES

1. Well, what of this person who knows the Absolute in this way?[72] The answer given is that he enjoys all pleasures without exception.

Does he enjoy them one after another, like us, first the joy of having a son and then the joy of heaven and so forth afterwards? No, he enjoys them all together. He enjoys them instantaneously, all lumped together, in one cognition swift as the light of the sun, which is yet eternal, being no other than the Absolute itself, which is Reality, Knowledge and Infinity, as we have explained. That is what the text means when it says, 'With the Absolute'.

The enlightened man is himself the Absolute, and enjoys all pleasures at once in his capacity of being the Absolute. Ordinary people of the world enjoy pleasures through a (false) self set up by external adjuncts. This transmigrating self stands to the real Self as the image of the sun reflected in water stands to the real sun. And the pleasures it experiences come one after the other, depending on the operation of merit and demerit previously amassed, as also on the functioning of the eyes and the other senses. But the enlightened man enjoys *all* pleasures through his Self as the eternal, omniscient, all-pervading Absolute, without dependence on merit and demerit previously amassed or on the functioning of the eyes and other senses. By 'wise' the Upanishad means that the enlightened man experiences all pleasures through his omniscient nature as the Absolute.[73]

❖

2. Those who lack discrimination speak of the body and the rest of the empirical personality as the 'I'. In order to do away with any such idea, the text now goes on to speak of the Self as being the pure Self alone, transcendent, of the nature of Being, untainted. He who takes delight in the Self, the enlightened man, sees everything on all sides as the Self alone, as the one unborn principle, infinite on all sides like the ether and void of anything else. His delight in the Self alone arises from cogitation (manana) and direct vision (vijñāna). His 'sport' is in the Self. Delight occasioned merely through the instrument of the body without recourse to external instruments is called 'sport', as is shown by the familiar worldly expression 'He is sporting with women or companions'. But the delight and the 'sport' of the enlightened man are not of this kind. Both proceed from his knowledge of the Self alone. The joys of sex-contact depend on the mutual presence of two people, but the joy of the enlightened man is independent of all pairing and coupling. The bliss (ānanda) of the enlightened man is the Self. His bliss does not need to be occasioned by the presence of material objects. In his case, all is bliss, always and in every way, occasioned by the Self. He is independent of all external objects such as a body or life or physical enjoyment.

The enlightened man thus defined is anointed an independent spiritual sovereign in his own life-time, and becomes a sovereign spiritual king on the fall of the body. Because of this independence, he can do as he pleases in all the worlds. In the case of the Cosmic Vital Energy (prāṇa) and other earlier planes[74] (which he reached through meditation) his freedom was always limited to 'such and such', which means he was not sovereign but subject to another. But here the text says that he can do as he pleases and is sovereign, implying that all subjection to another is at an end. But those who do not possess this enlightenment are ruled over by another, and the worlds they attain to prove transient, because that vision which involves distinctions has for its realm the finite, and we have already explained how the finite is the mortal. The worlds of those who see duality are transient. And because their fate is conditioned by their standard of vision, they do not attain to independence of action in any of the worlds.[75]

❖

3. As in the example just cited[76] wind and the rest become indistinguishable from the ether, so this individual soul that attains to utter serenity (samprasāda) in dreamless sleep becomes unable to distinguish himself from the body during the transmigratory state, on account of the force of nescience, and thinks 'I am so and so, born as a son, now decrepit and about to die'. But when he becomes enlightened through the teaching, introduced according to the gradual method by which Indra was taught by Prajāpati,[77] affirming 'Thou hast no connection with the attributes of the body, that thou art', then he rises above the body, just as the wind and the rest rise above the ether in the example. By this the Upanishad means that he gives up identifying himself with the body and becomes aware that the true Self is utterly different in character from the body, the senses and the mind. How he emerges in his true form as the Self or pure Being has already been explained.[78] That true form in which he ultimately emerges, is utterly serene (samprasāda) and the 'emergence'

is an 'emergence' (of the Self) in its true nature from the erroneous conception of that nature that obtains before enlightenment, like the 'emergence' of a rope that had 'become' a snake through error and 'emerged' later as a rope when illumined by a light.[79]

Thus the 'utterly serene one' is also the supreme Spirit (uttama-puruṣa).[80] The Spirit-in-the-eye (akṣi puruṣa) and the Spirit-enjoying-dreams[81] are manifest. The spirit-in-dreamless-sleep is unmanifest, utterly serene, disembodied, and (here the Spirit) has emerged in its true form. But the Spirit that has become permanently established in its true form (through knowledge) is called the supreme Spirit, being supreme in relation to the manifest and the unmanifest, the perishable and the imperishable, as has been explained in the Gītā.[82]

This utterly serene Spirit, having emerged in its true form,[83] being established in its own true nature as the Self of all, is said in the text to 'move about'. Sometimes it laughs — or the word may also mean 'eats', 'eats dainties of various kinds like an Indra'.[84] Sometimes it sports with women and other objects of delight,[85] whether in the form of mental creations or of objects present in the world of Brahmā or in this world, not remembering his body of this world. The word 'upajana' in the text means his body of this world — 'upajana' either referring to the fact that it is born of a woman through proximity to a man, or else to the fact that it proceeds from the Self and exists through the proximity of the Self.[86] He does not remember his body of this world as that would only cause pain, since the latter is pain by nature.

Nor would it be correct to say that if the liberated one did not remember his physical body, he would not be omniscient. For the body was only brought into being by wrong knowledge and its concomitants in the first place, and, when the latter have been eradicated by right knowledge, is known never to have been an object of (genuine) experience at all. Not to remember such a trifle as that does not affect the omniscience of the liberated one. One is not expected to remember what one experienced when one was in the grip of a delusion or of an evil spirit after the madness passes away. And in the same way, what is 'experienced' by those undergoing transmigration through the affliction of nescience does not touch him who is bodiless and the Self of all.[87]

❖

4. The meaning of the text 'Reality, Knowledge, the Infinite' was sufficiently explained in the section of the Taittirīya Upanishad called the Ānanda Vallī, which is in fact no more than an elaboration of that text.[88] But the text declaring the fruit of that knowledge in the words 'He obtains all desires through identification with the omniscient Absolute'[89] has not been explained at any length. We now go on to explain what those desires are, and also the meaning of 'identification with the Absolute'.

In this context, the text has already taught how self-discipline[90] is the means to realization of the Absolute in a little story that was added by way of an appendix to the teaching of the earlier book. It has also been explained how those effects which begin with the Cosmic Vital Energy and end with the ether can be divided into food and eater of food,[91] and some forms of meditation on the Absolute have also been taught. And it has been explained how all these desires each have their appropriate means of fulfilment and how their objects belong to the world of distinct effects which begins with the ether. But when all has become one, it becomes impossible to entertain desires, for all distinctions have then become one's own Self. In what sense, then, does the one who knows he is the Self of all attain all desires at once through identification with the Absolute in its true form? The reply is that this is intelligible when he is the Self of all.

In what sense can one be the Self of all? He does so by attaining to the Absolute as Reality, Knowledge, the Infinite, as natural bliss associated with 'invisibility' and other traits,[92] as unborn, immortal, beyond fear, non-dual — and this by gradually passing beyond the five 'selves'[93] beginning with the self of food and ending with the self of bliss, negating all differences of grade through realizing his identity with the Spirit (puruṣa) resident in the sun.[94] In this condition he wanders about in these worlds such as this earth (bhū) and the rest. He eats whatever food he wishes and assumes whatever form he wishes. 'Wandering about' here implies feeling himself to be the Self of all and experiencing the worlds as his own Self.

When the text says 'He goes on singing this chant (sāman)', the 'chant' means 'the Absolute', as the latter is perfectly homogeneous (sama). He sings the chant of non-difference from all. That is, he enunciates the unity and sole reality of the Self for the benefit of the people. And he goes on singing the chant that means that one has attained the fruit of realization and achieved all that has to be achieved. The chant runs 'Haaavu! Haaavu! Haaavu!' It is like an 'Aho!' expressing one's utter astonishment.

What is it that causes such astonishment? Though I am the non-dual Self and unsoiled by the world, yet I am food and the eater of food. I am that which unifies food and the eater-of-food, their conscious creator. Or else it means 'I am he who reduces food to unity, though it is many, as is clear from the mere fact of its existing for the sake of another, the eater of food'.[95] The three repetitions of the phrase are to emphasize the sense of astonishment.

I am the First-Born (Hiraṇyagarbha) of this world of gross and subtle objects. I existed before the gods. I am the hub (lit. the navel) of immortality: the immortality of living beings rests in me.

Whoever gives me as food to those who desire food, who speaks of me as though I were the Self of food, he 'protects' me, intact as I am. But that other person who eats food without giving food to those who ask for it at the proper time, I take for food and myself eat.

You will say that in that case a person will be afraid of liberation and becoming the Self of all, because when liberated he would become the food of food itself and be eaten. Would it not be better to remain in transmigratory life? But in fact you need not fear. For he whom we are talking about has passed beyond the empirical experience set up by nescience which comprises food and the eater, and all realization of desires falls within this realm. He has destroyed nescience and attained the Absolute through knowledge. He has no second thing over against him which could occasion fear. So there is nothing to fear from liberation.

But if this is so, why did the text say 'I am food and the eater of food'? We answer: Empirical experience comprising food and the eater of food is an effect. It is only empirical experience and not ultimate reality. Being thus, and having the Absolute for its cause, it must be taken as other than the Absolute and so not real. 'I am food and the eater of food' is a mere eulogy of the state of having become the Absolute through knowledge of the Absolute. Therefore there is not a trace of fear or other such defects arising from nescience for the one who has become the Absolute by uprooting nescience.

I am the whole world (bhuvana). The world is here called 'bhuvana' because it is shared by living creatures (bhūta) from Brahmā on, or else because living creatures exist (bhavanti) in it. I engulf this whole world with my true nature as the highest Lord. My light is eternal like the sun.

This concludes the holy knowledge (upaniṣat) expounded in the two books (the Ānanda Vallī and Bhṛgu Vallī of the Taittirīya Upanishad) devoted to knowledge of the supreme Self. Whoever comes to know this holy knowledge here expounded, and who is possessed of inner and outer control, absence of personal desires, will to endure hardship and undertake spiritual self-discipline, and who performs great austerity like Bhṛgu, will acquire this result, namely liberation of the kind here described.[96]

❖

4. The Enlightened Man as Actionless

Extract 1 says that when devotion to knowledge leads to the 'realization of the actionless state' (naiṣkarmya-siddhi) spoken of in the Bhagavad Gītā,[97] the devotee becomes directly aware of his identity with the Absolute already here in this present life. This is called 'sadyo-mukti' or immediate liberation, in contrast to that form of liberation which occurs only at the end of the world-period (krama-mukti) expounded above in Chapter XIV.

Extracts 2-4 explain how the enlightened man sees inaction in action and *vice versa*. The sage is aware that his true Self does nothing. He witnesses 'the constituents' playing on the 'constituents'. Extract 5 explains how such a person has 'transcended the constituents'. But he can only put himself in a position to do so through strenuous cultivation of good qualities first, followed afterwards by the worship and service of Lord Nārāyaṇa, seated in the hearts of all creatures. The last discipline is called Bhakti Yoga.

The last three Extracts explain how realization of the actionless state automatically brings one the status of a true renunciate, irrespective of the particulars of one's body and dress as seen by others. If, while still in the state of ignorance, one desires enlightenment, it is better to adopt the life of 'renunciation' in the sense of religious mendicancy, as the requisite qualities of self-control are not usually obtainable in the householder's state. The enlightened man has no debts or duties in the world, which is a mere appearance produced by metaphysical ignorance. There is Vedic authority for this. The texts which speak of renunciation of action and of ritual are not merely intended for cripples, as the ritualists would like to make out. Although no rules apply to the enlightened person, he cannot behave in an irregular way, as all such behaviour depends on nescience, which he has finally overcome.

TEXTS ON THE ENLIGHTENED MAN AS ACTIONLESS

1. The next verse is uttered to explain that 'realization of the actionless state' (naiṣkarmya-siddhi), of the nature of devotion to knowledge, which arises out of the great new quality of 'fitness for devotion to knowledge', that itself arises from the disinterested performance of action.

He whose mind is not attached to sons and wife and the like, whose mind is under control, who is without thirst for body, life and pleasures — such a one, a knower of the Self, is actionless because he is awake to his own identity with the Absolute. This actionless state is a perfection (siddhi) — or else the phrase may refer to the *realization* (siddhi = niṣpatti) of this actionless state, the normal state of one's own true actionless Self. This is the supreme perfection, and it differs from any perfection that can be attained through action, being of the nature of immediate liberation (sadyo-mukti).[98] This he establishes through right knowledge of the Self or through that (automatic) renunciation of all action which is associated with right knowledge of the Self.[99]

❖

2. By 'action' is meant here bodily activity in general,[100] and the text says, 'Whosoever sees absence of action in bodily action and sees action in bodily inaction, he is wise among men, he is a man of true discipline (yoga) and has performed all action'. Both action and withdrawal from action depend on a sense of agency. All the play of action and its factors and results, that takes place before one realizes one's true nature

as the Absolute, belongs to the realm of nescience.[101] The one who sees action as inaction and inaction as action is eulogized as 'One who has performed all action'.[102]

But is it not a self-contradiction to say 'Whosoever sees absence of bodily action in action and action in bodily inaction'? Action is not inaction, neither is inaction action. How could anyone perceive such a contradiction? Well, but the truth is that inaction, which is the final reality, appears in an illusory way to the bemused eye of the people of the world as action. And action (which is illusory) appears, in the same way, to be (the ultimate reality which is in fact) inaction. The Lord says, 'Whoever sees absence of action in bodily action...' with a view to help people to see the truth rightly. Hence He is not guilty of any contradiction. Our interpretation is supported by the (immediately preceding) text, '(He among men is) wise' and the Lord's previous statement that more had to be learned. Liberation from evil cannot arise through false knowledge, as the text, 'knowing which thou shalt be liberated from evil'[103] shows. Hence the Lord's statement 'Whoever sees absence of action in bodily action...' was only made to help put an end to the wrong notion about the nature of action and inaction which is naturally held by all living beings. It is not that inaction exists *in* action in the spatial sense, like plums in a dish. Nor does action dwell *in* inaction, as inaction is simply absence of action. Hence the meaning is that action and inaction are wrongly apprehended by people in the world, like the wrong apprehension of water in the case of the mirage or the wrong apprehension of silver in nacre.

Well, you will say, action is always action for everybody and never anything else.[104] But this is not so. Consider the case of a person on a moving boat. The motionless trees on the bank will seem to him to be moving in the opposite direction. And very distant objects, even when actually moving, appear to be motionless. In the same way, in the context of worldly notions about action, we find the notion 'I am doing it' applied to inaction and the notion of inaction wrongly applied to action.[105] It was to remove these wrong conceptions once and for all that the Lord said, 'Whosoever sees absence of action in bodily action...'.

The Lord repeats this reply again and again and again, both because He perceives that the matter is difficult to understand and also because the people of the world labour under great delusions over the point, and forget the truth that they have been taught, and repeatedly raise new and quite unfounded objections, misunderstanding the answer that has been given to them even though it has been given many times. The absence of action in the Self has already been taught many times in such passages as 'He is unmanifest, unthinkable' and 'He is not born, He does not die';[106] it is already familiar from the Veda, the derivative literature and reason, and will be repeated in the Gītā again later. But the notion that action is to be found in this actionless Self, that is, in inaction, is deeply engrained; hence it will be said, 'Even sages are deluded as to what is action and what is inaction'.[107] Equally deeply engrained is the feeling 'I am the agent, this is my act and I shall experience this fruit resulting from it', a notion which results from superimposing onto the Self the action which pertains properly only to the body and senses. Similarly, the people of the world have the idea, 'Now I am staying quiet so that I may be untroubled, actionless and happy'. Here they superimpose onto the Self the non-performance of action and the happiness resulting from this which pertain properly to the body and senses, and think 'I am doing nothing' or 'I was happy in my quietude'. It was to remove this false impression that afflicts the world in general that the Lord said, 'Whoever sees absence of action in bodily action...'

Consider further. Action, conceived as retaining its nature as action located in the body and senses, is superimposed onto the Self by all. Even sages think 'I am acting'. Hence the meaning is as follows. The verse first refers to him (i.e. the true sage) who sees inaction in that action which all feel to be associated intimately with the Self, like one (a person of discernment) seeing absence of motion in trees on the bank of a river, which appear (to his companions) to be moving in the opposite direction to that in which he is himself moving when travelling on that river in a boat. And then it speaks of the same person (the sage) as seeing action in inaction, the latter conceived as cessation of activity of the body and senses, which is itself falsely superimposed on the Self just as much as action is, because the notion 'I was happy doing nothing' is connected with the ego-sense.[108] Whoever can distinguish between action and inaction in this way 'Is wise among men, is a man of true discipline and has performed all action'. He has 'performed all action' in the sense of being liberated (by his spiritual knowledge) from having to experience the fruits of action any more, and so has done all that has to be done.[109]

❖

3. The text then goes on to praise the vision of inaction in action (and action in inaction). He whose actions are all void of desires and purposes, which cause desires, whose acts are mere reflexes performed without any purpose — if such a person engages in action, it is as an example and for the good of the world, and if he practises renunciation, he acts only (just enough) to keep the body alive. He who so lives is called, by the enlightened ones who know the Absolute, a sage. He sees action as inaction and inaction as action. This knowledge is the fire whereby he burns up good and bad actions (so that he does not have to experience their future effects).

Because he has this insight into action and inaction, he is beyond action and a renunciate, one who acts for the mere maintenance of the body. He does not engage in action any longer, even though he may have done so before he acquired discrimination into the nature of action and inaction. As for the one who, though first engaged in action, subsequently acquires right knowledge of the Self, he no longer sees any purpose in action and gives it up, together with the means to it.[110] If for any reason he is not able to give up action, he may remain engaged in action as before as an example and for the good of the world, yet, because he has no purposes of his own to serve, and is without attachment either for action or its fruits, he does nothing. And to show that the action of such a man is verily inaction, because it has been burnt by the fire of knowledge, the Lord adds a further verse.

He, verily, does nothing at all who satisfies the following conditions: who has given up all self-identification with actions, who has given up all attachment to their fruits and is perfectly content and without desire for objects on account of having attained the spiritual knowledge just mentioned, and who seeks nothing whereby he might attain any individual human end, whether of this world or another.

The action done by a man of enlightenment is in the deepest sense inaction, as he has acquired vision of the Self beyond action. One might suppose that a person of this kind would renounce both action and the means to action because it could have no purpose for him. But if he found that he could not escape from action, then, even if he continued to act as before, either to set an example to the people or for their own good or to avoid the censure of right-thinking people, he would yet 'do nothing', for he would have attained vision of the Self beyond action.

However, the case with the renunciate is somewhat different (as the following verse goes on to point out). He has already felt the identity of his own inmost actionless Self with the Absolute, present within all, before he has taken up work.[111] Such a person sees no point in action at all, whether for fruits in this world or the next, as he is without any desire for reward here or hereafter. He renounces work and the means to work.[112] He is already released and lives as an ascetic (yati), devoted to knowledge and acting only just enough to maintain the body. To indicate all this the next verse runs as follows.

The one who no longer has any desires, whose mind and body are under his control, who has renounced all personal possessions, acts only to support his body without identifying himself with it, and acquires no merit and demerit. From the standpoint of the one desiring release, even merit is a 'stain' as it makes for further bondage (transmigratory life).

One might raise the question whether the phrase about doing 'bodily work only' in the text meant 'work done by the body' or 'work done merely to sustain the body'. For if it meant 'work done by the body', then, when the text went on to say 'he would not be "stained"', this would apply to *all* work done by his body for ends in this world or the next, including forbidden deeds, and this would involve contradiction with the Veda.[113] If the text only meant that work done by the body for ends in this world or the next world would not involve 'staining' if it were done in accordance with Vedic command, this would make it (the text) into a mere negation of something no one would ever proclaim.[114] Moreover, the special qualification 'bodily' and the use of the word 'only' would result (on this interpretation) in the suggestion that a person would receive 'staining' (demerit) from *all* acts of speech and thought[115] whether they were enjoined or prohibited, whether they represented merit or demerit. In so far as the performance of enjoined acts of speech and thought (as well as prohibited ones) would be declared to bring 'staining' (demerit), this would result in a further contradiction. And even in so far as prohibited acts of speech and thought would be declared to bring demerit, the text (on this interpretation) would add nothing to what was already known and would therefore be useless.[116]

But if the phrase 'bodily work' meant work done merely to sustain the body, then the text would mean that no other work was being done with an end in this world or the next, either by the body, speech or mind, either prescribed by the

Veda or prohibited. A person so behaving, and at the same time, from the worldly standpoint, carrying out reflex actions of body, speech and mind for the mere maintenance of his body, does not identify himself as the agent of such actions, as the use of the word 'only' shows. Such a man is not 'stained'. Such a man, being beyond 'staining' which is synonymous with demerit, acquires no further demerit in the form of bondage to further transmigration. It means that, since all his actions have been burnt by the fire of knowledge, he is under no further bondage (to further empirical experience arising from them) and is released. This is in fact a mere repeated statement of the fruit of right-knowledge of the Self which has already been declared earlier. On this interpretation, therefore, the phrase 'bodily work' is perfectly intelligible.

An ascetic who renounced all acceptance whatever would renounce even food and other necessaries to sustain the body. He might therefore feel the need of sustaining his body through begging and the like. The Lord now proceeds to point out the way in which food and the like may be accepted for the maintenance of the body, as permitted by such texts as 'Whatever is received by chance or without demand or special arrangement (is lawful)'.[117]

Content with what comes by chance (the text goes on), with a buoyancy of spirit which extremes like heat and cold can do nothing to diminish, void of jealousy and of all enmity in the mind, indifferent whether chance bring him anything or nothing — (such a man is not bound, even if he acts). An ascetic of this kind does not feel any special elation if he gets what he needs to sustain his body, nor is he in any way depressed if he fails to get it. He sees inaction in action, and so forth, as described above. He is intent on direct vision of the Self as it really is. Even in begging and other such actions performed with body, speech and mind for the mere maintenance of the body, he always feels 'I do nothing' and 'The constituents are acting on the constituents'.[118] Such a one perceives his own non-agency and in fact, properly speaking, does not 'do' any action like wandering round with a begging bowl at all. From the standpoint of ordinary worldly experience, he seems to be the agent in such acts, because worldly people falsely credit him with agency. But in his own direct experience, which arises through the authoritative Vedic texts and other such sources, he is in every respect a non-agent....

The text spoke above[119] of the one who had given up all attachment to the fruits of actions. The reference was to one who was continuing to act. When such a person has attained direct awareness of his identity with the Absolute, he will perceive that agency and action are irrelevant to his true Self, and one would expect him to give up action. But this may for some reason be impracticable, and he may continue in his action as before. It has already been shown how such an one does not act, because he feels 'I do nothing'. With regard to a person of this kind, the text now proceeds further.

In the case of one in whom all attachment for anything anywhere has subsided, and who is released in the sense of no longer being in bondage to merit and demerit, whose mind is established in knowledge, and whose whole action is conceived as sacrifice, all his actions, together with their latent future results, are dissolved.

The next verse explains how this is possible. Such a

knower of the Absolute (brahma-vit) sees even the ladle with which he pours oblations into the fire as verily the Absolute. He sees it as non-existent except as the Self. When a person who has been under the illusion that a piece of nacre is silver perceives the absence of silver in that piece of nacre, he says, 'This silver is only nacre'. It is in this sense that the liberated one says, 'The ladle is only the Absolute'. The two words 'ladle' and 'Absolute' in the text are not to be taken as forming any kind of grammatical compound, but as meaning 'The ladle *is* the Absolute'. That is to say, what the world takes as a sacrificial ladle is to the knower of the Absolute only the Absolute. Similarly, what is taken by the world as the oblation is only the Absolute to the knower of the Absolute. Again, the words 'the Absolute' and 'the fire' are to be taken as a grammatical compound meaning 'into the fire which is (also) the Absolute'. Where an oblation is made into the fire, which is the Absolute, by the Absolute, there the agent is the Absolute.[120] The act of oblation is itself also the Absolute. The goal is also the Absolute, and he who has realized that action is the Absolute has the Absolute as his final destiny. Thus, even one who wishes to perform action for the good of the world performs action which is in reality non-action, as it is cancelled by his realization that it is in reality the Absolute.

Even in the case of one who has given up action and become a complete renunciate, it was quite proper on the part of the text to speak figuratively of spiritual realization as a 'sacrifice'[121] in order to eulogize spiritual realization. In the case of the one who has seen the ultimate reality, the ladle and the like, well known to all in the context of ritualistic sacrifice, are but his own inner realized Self (adhyātma), the

Absolute. Otherwise, apart from this special vision, when everything was the Absolute, it would have been meaningless to have spoken of the ladle, etc., specially as the Absolute. Hence, in the case of the enlightened man who is aware that 'All this is the Absolute alone', there is complete absence of action.

A further reason is that in his case there is no idea of the existence of separate factors of action. Action (karma), also called sacrifice (yajña), is never found in the absence of any notion of the existence of the factors of action. Every sacrifice (karma), such as the Agnihotra oblation, is invariably performed as associated with a particular deity as recipient, to whom the sacrifice is offered through a spoken formula. There is also invariably a person supposing himself to be the agent, performing the sacrifice for the sake of some reward. Never is any sacrifice found to be performed when all notion of the distinction between action, its factors and results has been effaced, or when there is no one fancying himself to be the agent and desirous of a reward. But this action (of the man of enlightenment) we are here discussing is an 'action' or 'sacrifice' where all notion of the distinction between action, its factors and results has been effaced by the notion that all is the Absolute. And the Lord has Himself affirmed this in such texts as 'Whoso sees inaction in action', 'Though engaged in action, he does nothing', 'The "constituents" act upon the "constituents",' 'He who practises yoga and knows the reality thinks "I am doing nothing".'[122] And here and there the Lord negates the notion of the distinction between action, its factors and results.[123]

It has been seen earlier[124] how, when such a ritual as the

Agnihotra is being performed for an individual end, it ceases to be a 'ritual performed for an individual end' if desire for that end subsides in the sacrificer in the course of performing it. And we have seen how actions are responsible for different results according to whether they are performed deliberately or otherwise. Hence it is quite intelligible in the present context if the 'action' of the enlightened man is non-action. It consists only in external reflex activity, and in his case the notion of the distinct existence of the factors of action, such as the ladle, and the act itself, and its results, has been effaced by the conviction that all is the Absolute. Hence the text says that all his action dissolves.[125]

❖

4. In the next verse the Lord explains the condition of one who knows the ultimate reality. 'Having renounced all actions mentally, the embodied one rests happily in the nine-gated city of the body in self-control, neither acting nor causing to act'. 'Having renounced all action' implies renunciation of the obligatory and occasional and optional ritual as well as forbidden deeds. Renouncing them mentally means renouncing them by seeing inaction in action and so on,[126] through intellectual discrimination. The idea is that the embodied one rests happily having given up all activity of body, speech or thought, without putting forth any effort, contented at heart, thinking of nothing but the Self. 'In self-control' means 'with his senses under control'. The nine-gated city of the body refers to the seven apertures in the head through which the soul exercises perception, plus the two lower ones for the expulsion of excreta and urine. The body is called a city

because it is like a city, with the soul for its only master. The latter is in charge of the higher and lower mental faculties[127] along with the senses and their objects, which procure for it various results and experiences and stand as its 'subjects'. The embodied one rests happily in this nine-gated city, renouncing all action.

What meaningful qualification is introduced by the text in saying 'rests in the body'? For every human being rests in a body, whether he be a renunciate or not. The answer is that the spiritually ignorant embodied soul identifies itself with the psycho-physical organism only, and thinks that it does its 'resting' in a house or on the ground or in a seat. He who identifies himself with the body and restricts himself to that can never think 'I rest in the body like a person resting in a house'. But a person who is aware of himself as other than the psycho-physical organism can have this conviction. And in these circumstances the 'mental renunciation' of actions is possible. For actions pertain to the body, and it is through ignorance that they are falsely superimposed onto the Self, which is other than the body. And they can be 'renounced' through discriminative knowledge that the Self is different from the body and its works.

He in whom this discriminative knowledge has arisen, who has renounced all action, continues nevertheless to rest in the nine-gated city of the body, undergoing experiences conforming to the (unexhausted) remainder of the impressions of that portion of his past deeds which initiated the present birth. For it is only in the body that particular cognition is possible. Therefore a meaningful qualification *is* introduced when the text says 'rests in the body', for the meaning is '*only* rests in the body', and this implies a distinction between the experiences of a man of enlightenment and a spiritually ignorant person.

Though a man may be resting in the body renouncing duty and action and instruments of action as mere false superimpositions onto the Self, yet might not agency and the power to prompt others to act reside in his Self by nature all the same? The text denies this, saying he neither acts himself nor prompts others to act.

Does the text mean that the agency and the power to prompt others to act that one finds in an embodied soul belong to his Self by nature and are only absent because he gives them up, in the way that walking is 'absent' in a person who for the moment has stopped walking? No, it means that agency and the power to prompt others to act are by nature absent from the Self. For we have such texts as 'It is said to be beyond modification' and 'O son of Kuntī, even though stationed in the body, it does not act and is not stained'.[128] And there is also the upanishadic text, 'It only *seems* to think, it only *seems* to stir'.[129]

❖

5. The man who has passed beyond the constituents (guṇātīta) does not feel any special dislike for the effects of sattva, rajas or tamas[130] when they emerge in the form of objects and confront him. For example he does not feel: 'An idea arising from tamas has come into my mind which has made me feel deluded and confused. Likewise, a painful drive towards action has arisen in me from rajas, driven on by which I have fallen from my true nature and have undergone much suffering. Likewise, a luminous state has come upon

me, arising from sattva, and bringing a new power of discrimination but at the same time causing attachment to a new kind of happiness and so causing bondage'. A man without enlightenment feels distaste for the products of tamas, rajas and sattva in this way, but the man who has gone beyond the constituents (guṇātīta) does not.

Nor does the one who has gone beyond the constituents feel longing for them when their products have ceased to come before him, as men of sattva, rajas or tamas do when they have once perceived the products of sattva, rajas and tamas and these are later withdrawn.

This mark is not one that can be perceived by anyone except the one who has gone beyond the constituents himself. For no other person can perceive a person's private dislikes and desires.

Next the Lord answers the question as to the behaviour of the one who has crossed beyond the constituents. 'He sits like one indifferent'. He takes no sides. He is well settled on his path leading beyond the constituents. In this condition, the knower of the Self, the renunciate (saṃnyāsin), is not made to depart from his discriminative insight by the constituents. The Lord goes on to clarify this further and to say that whoever is convinced that the constituents, transformed into the bodies and organs and objects of experience, act upon each other... does not move. That is, he remains established in his true nature.

To such a person, pleasure and pain are the same. He is happy, established in his own Self. A clod of earth, a stone and a piece of gold are all alike in his eyes. The pleasant and the unpleasant, praise and criticism are all alike. He remains unchanged whether treated with praise or disrespect. He not only practises indifference on his own but maintains it even in the presence of well-wishers and ill-wishers. He acquires the habit of giving up all action for personal ends, either in this world or the next. In fact he gives up all activity except the bare minimum needed to support the body. Such a man is said to have 'gone beyond the constituents'.

The qualities that are mentioned after the phrase 'He sits like one indifferent'[131] have to be tirelessly cultivated by a renunciate until they become second nature to him as a seeker of liberation. Once they have become his second nature, they become evident to him, and, as such, marks whereby he can know himself to be an ascetic who has gone beyond the constituents.

Finally the Lord answers the question, '*How* does a person go beyond the constituents?' Whatever ascetic or man of works serves Me, the Lord Nārāyaṇa seated in the heart of all living creatures, with unswerving yoga of devotion (bhakti) — where the devotion *is* the yoga — goes beyond these constituents and becomes fit for attaining the Absolute or liberation.[132]

❖

6. This also establishes that the enlightened man must become a renunciate (parivrājaka)[133] through the mere fact of his firm knowledge of the Absolute as his Self, and without any (need or possibility of an) injunctive text, in the manner already shown.[134] For the Absolute is void of birth and other modifications, including the factors of (ritualistic) action, such as the being (deity) to whom a sacrifice is offered.[135]

The fact that a knower of the Self becomes a renunciate has already been explained at an earlier passage in the words 'This Self is our world'.[136] The enlightened ones of old renounced household life as they did not desire progeny. The renunciation of the enlightened ones arose from their mere awakening to the world of the Self.

And the fact that even the one who *desires* knowledge of the Self may also become a renunciate is established by the same text in the words 'Verily, desiring this Self for their world, they wander forth from their homes'. We have already explained how action[137] belongs to the sphere of those ignorant of the Self. Actions are for the purpose of producing, transforming, preparing and purifying within the realm of nescience.[138] We have already shown how those who (as yet only) *desire* knowledge of the Self perform sacrificial action for the purification of their souls, and how action is in this sense a remote auxiliary to knowledge of the Self.[139]

❖

7. Here[140] an objector might interpose and say that (although there can be no reason for further action after enlightenment) there can be no reason for renouncing action either. For we have the text from the derivative literature, 'He has nothing to gain from renouncing action'.[141] Those, therefore, who say that a man should renounce the world immediately upon attaining enlightenment suffer from the same fundamental fallacy as affects those who say he should continue with ritual — the absence, namely, of any purpose for the proposed course.

This objection, however, is wrong, because renunciation is not something one does. Any end or purpose is a product of wrong-knowledge, and not a characteristic of anything real, as is visible in the case of all living beings. For speech, thought and physical action are seen to be (universally) prompted by thirst for an end. We have the teachings from the Vājasaneyi Brāhmaṇa[142] in the passage beginning 'He formed the desire "Let me have a wife" '[143] and 'Both these[144] are but desires'[145] which affirm that the ritual which requires the five accessories[146] is based on desire alone.

That speech, thought or physical deed which is associated with the five accessories proceeds from the defects of ignorance and desire, and cannot occur in the case of the enlightened man, as he is without such defects as ignorance. In his case, therefore, renunciation is mere absence of action; it is not a positive course that he has to follow, as performance of the ritual or the like would be. It is simply the *characteristic* of the enlightened man, so there is no need to establish any prompting cause for it. If somebody goes out at night and then the dawn supervenes, there is no need to enquire into the prompting causes that enable him to avoid falling into pits or mud or brambles.

You may object that if renunciation comes of its own accord immediately on enlightenment in this way, then it cannot be enjoined, and that if supreme enlightenment should dawn on anyone when he was in the householder state, he should stay in that state without acting, and should not go on to abandon his home and depart elsewhere. But this is not right, the householder's condition being entirely prompted by desire, as is shown by the declarations 'That is the range of desire' and 'Both these (desire for sons and desire for wealth) are but desires'.[147] Renunciation means merely the absence of relationship with sons and wealth and the like based on desire. It does not mean abandoning one's household and moving off elsewhere. So the one in whom enlightenment has arisen while he is in the householder state does not remain in that state, sitting still doing nothing. These considerations also suffice to show that service of the Teacher and asceticism are not possible in the case of the enlightened person.

In this connection there is a certain householder[148] who is afraid of the life of wandering about and living on alms and of the humiliation to which he might be subjected, and who wishes to make a parade of the subtlety of his intellect, and who maintains that because there are rules governing the alms-begging of a monk, a householder, too, if his only wish and aim is to go on supporting the body, and he is free from desire for ends and means, can remain in his house, if he eats and dresses solely to maintain the body in being. This, however, is wrong. For we have already explained how the adoption of a particular house as one's own is based on desire. And if one does not adopt any particular house as one's own, and accepts no particular thing as one's own, and eats and dresses solely to maintain the body, then this is virtually mendicancy.

Now, rules are laid down for the monk when he walks about begging alms for the maintenance of his body, as well as for his acts of personal cleanliness, etc.[149] Will not there also be the rule for the enlightened person, even if he be a householder, without desire, that he must continue to perform his obligatory daily ritual, because of the Vedic texts saying man should perform ritual all his life, and also to avoid the demerit of omitting them? But this idea is wrong, first because we have already shown that this cannot be enjoined on the enlightened person, and secondly because he is beyond the range of all injunctions anyway.

You will object that this argument renders useless the Vedic injunctions to perform ritual regularly the whole of one's life. But this is wrong, for the latter have their utility in the sphere of those afflicted with nescience. As for the rules regulating the behaviour of the mendicant who is working only for the bare maintenance of his body — such rules do not promote activity but only regulate it. When a man is engaged in sipping water for ceremonial purposes, it may be that his thirst is also incidentally assuaged. But we do not thereby conclude that he had any other reason for sipping than that of carrying out the ceremony. (Similarly, if a mendicant decides to walk abroad asking alms, he finds himself involved in certain regulations: but the regulations are not what impel him to walk about and beg.) But rituals like the Agnihotra are not actions which prompt themselves to a man naturally and which are merely *regulated* (and not enjoined) by rules.

Of course, one could not obey rules regulating natural activity unless there were some motive for obeying them. But in the case of the enlightened person, obedience to such rules comes naturally through previous habit, and it would actually involve an effort of will to contravene them. And the fact that the enlightened man should obey such rules is further confirmed by the text 'Having given up the three desires, the Brahmins take up the life of living on alms'.[150]

Even the man still afflicted with nescience should renounce home and worldly life if he desires liberation. The authorities for this statement are the texts like 'Peaceful, self-controlled'.[151] The qualities of inner and outer control and so on, pursuit of which is the means to vision of the Self, are not attainable in any other stage of life except that of mendicancy. And this is confirmed by the Śvetāśvatara Upanishad, which says, 'He (i.e. the enlightened man Śvetāśvatara) gave the right teaching to those in the highest stage of life about this supreme Principle, the Absolute, which is such a delight to the assemblies of Seers'.[152] And the Kaivalya Upanishad says, 'Some few obtained immortality, but it was not through ritual or wisdom or wealth, but through renunciation alone'.[153] And there is the passage from the derivative literature, 'Having obtained enlightenment, one should practise actionlessness (naiṣkarmya)', and also 'One should stay in the stages of life that conduce to the realization of the Absolute'.

Continence and other means to knowledge can only be perfectly observed in the higher stages of life,[154] and not in the stage of householder, and nothing can be completed if the necessary means for its completion is not available. It has already been stated in a passage of recapitulation that the highest result of the 'knowledge' (meditation) to which ritual is an auxiliary is becoming one with all deities,[155] and this falls within the realm of transmigratory life. If (as the opponent thinks) it were only the active ritualist who could attain knowledge of the Self, the final recapitulation would never have declared that the (highest) reward (for ritualistic meditation) was one which fell within the realm of transmigratory life.

Nor can it have been meant that becoming one with all deities was only an incidental reward. For knowledge of the Self, which is the principle of reality, is *in contradiction with* the idea of dissolution in a deity. The means to immortality is that knowledge which bears on the Self as supreme principle of reality, to the negation of all name, form and action. If knowledge were connected with incidental rewards, it could not be such as to bear on the Self as supreme reality, to the negation of all particular distinctions. But the fact that knowledge bears on the highest reality has to be accepted. For the text, 'But where for him everything has become the Self alone'[156] negates all empirical notions of the enlightened one, including action and its factors and results. And the Vājasaneya Brāhmaṇa (i.e. the Bṛhadāraṇyaka Upanishad) makes the opposite point that the one who is not enlightened but ignorant enjoys only transmigratory life in the form of action, its factors and fruits, in the words, 'But where he sees duality, as it were'.[157] And so in the present work (the Aitareya Āraṇyaka with the Aitareya Upanishad enclosed within it), the text first sums up the reward of following the teaching (of the part of the Āraṇyaka that precedes the Upanishad) as becoming one with all deities, which falls within transmigratory life, as the gods are afflicted with hunger and thirst.[158] And now (at the beginning of the Aitareya Upanishad) the text goes on to say, 'From here on I will teach the knowledge which bears on that reality which is the Self of all in its pure form, a knowledge which leads to immortality'.

The obstacle of the debts which one owes to man, ancestors and gods affects the aspirations of the ignorant man to attain the worlds of man, ancestors and gods, but it does not affect the enlightened man at all. For the Veda says, 'This world of man, verily, is attained only by a son',[159] and lays down the means for attaining these three worlds. But in regard to the enlightened man desirous of the world (state of consciousness) of the Self it says, 'What shall we do with progeny, (we whose world is this Self)?'[160] Then there is the text, 'The enlightened Seer, Tura (Kāvaṣeya), verily, said "Why should I recite texts?",' and also the text of the Kauṣītaki Upanishad, 'Knowing this, indeed, the ancients did not perform the Agnihotra'.[161]

But would it not follow from this that an ignorant man could never adopt the life of mendicancy without first discharging his three afore-mentioned debts? By no means. For until one enters into the householder's state, one cannot have any debts. If any one could be a debtor before he was in a position of responsibility for a debt, the unwelcome conclusion would follow that anyone could be in debt (irrespective of whether he had contracted a debt or not). And there is a text which shows positively that renunciation of home life and mendicancy is a necessary requirement for knowledge of the Self even in the case of one who has assumed the householder's state, namely, 'Having first left home and become a forest-dweller, he should proceed next to adopt the life of mendicancy, or else he may jump straight out of studenthood or the householder's life or forest life and become a wandering monk'.[162] As for the Vedic texts speaking of performing ritual for one's whole life, they referred to those souls who are not enlightened and do not seek release. In some versions of the Chāndogya Upanishad[163] there is mention of abandoning the Agnihotra after performing it for twelve nights.

As for your view that renunciation of ritual is *only* for those who are physically unable to perform it, this view is wrong. For this class of persons is specially mentioned (*along with* householders, etc., as eligible for mendicancy) in such texts as, 'He whose sacrifical fire has gone out or who has no sacrificial fire'.[164] It is well-known, too, that throughout the derivative literature mendicancy is recommended both as a direct leap from any of the other stages of life and also as the final stage of an orderly progress through all four.

There is also a view that, as the enlightened man is automatically prompted to renounce the world by the mere fact of his enlightenment, the question of whether he in fact does so does not fall within the scope of Vedic injunctions, and it does not really matter whether he remains at home or goes off into the forest. This view is wrong, as he is unable to alter the fact that he is a renunciate, seeing that his renunciation results automatically from his enlightenment. We have already explained how descent from the natural condition of renunciation to householderhood is the result of previous actions and desire. Renunciation is nothing other than the absence of these.

Irregular behaviour, however, is not part of the enlightened man's make-up, because we see that irregular behaviour proceeds from crass ignorance. Even the actions enjoined by the Veda do not apply to the knower of the Self, as for him they are just a grievous and useless burden — what to say, then, of irregular behaviour, always the result of total lack of discrimination? What is seen in a fit of frenzy or as the result of squinting vision (timira) does not stay on unaffected when the evil state departs. For its very existence was conditioned by frenzied or squinting vision. Hence it stands proved that the knower of the Self remains a renunciate, that he does not indulge in irregular behaviour, and that he has no further duties.

As for the reference to the passage 'He who knows that ritualistic action (avidyā) and knowledge (vidyā) go together crosses death through ritual and obtains immortality through knowledge'[165] — this passage does not imply that ignorance (avidyā) and knowledge (vidyā) co-inhere in one and the same enlightened person. On the contrary, it means that they cannot both pertain to the same person at the same time, any more than one and the same person could see both a piece of (real) silver and a piece of nacre in a single piece of nacre. The Kaṭha Upanishad (I.ii.4) says, 'Wide apart, contradictory and divergent are ignorance (avidyā) and that which they call knowledge (vidyā)'. Therefore there cannot be ignorance (avidyā) if there is knowledge (vidyā).

As is clear from the Vedic text, 'Seek to know the Absolute through asceticism (tapas)',[166] asceticism and the other aids to spiritual knowledge, as well as such acts as keeping the company of the Teacher and serving him and so forth, are called nescience (avidyā), because they are of the nature of nescience.[167] Through these acts one attains knowledge and crosses beyond death in the form of desire. To show that a person later attains immortality through knowledge of the Absolute after first renouncing all desire, the text says, 'He crosses death through ignorance (avidyā) and obtains immortality through knowledge'.[168]

❖

8. Is it, then, that acceptance and avoidance are altogether meaningless for the man of enlightenment? No, it would be better to say that he has gone beyond them by realizing all his ends.[169] When anyone is subject to commands, the commands he receives relate to things which have to be eliminated or acquired. How, then, can anyone who sees only the Self, and nothing beside it that can be eliminated or acquired, be subject to any command? He cannot be commanded to perform any action on his own Self.[170]

Perhaps you will say that it is precisely the one who sees that he is separate from the body who is subject to the Vedic injunctions.[171] But this is wrong, for the one you have in mind conceives himself as entering into composition with the body, though separate from it. It is true that one who takes himself to be distinct from the body in this sense is subject to injunctions. But only he is subject to injunctions who fails to see that he no more enters into composition with the body than the ether (enters into composition with the pots within which it appears to be enclosed). For we see that no one who dissociates himself completely from the body is subject to injunction, what to say of one who perceives the unity and sole existence of the Self.

But it does not follow that, because the man of enlightenment is not subject to injunctions, he just behaves as he likes. For it is always self-identification with the body and the like (the senses, etc.,) that prompts undisciplined behaviour, and this is absent in the case of the man of enlightenment.

On these grounds, the author of the Sūtras says that

acceptance and avoidance depend on (the sense of) relation with the body, 'as in the case of light and the like'. As an aspect of the principle of light, fire is everywhere one. But the fire that has consumed bodies on the cremation-ground is avoided (as impure), while other fire is not. Similarly, sunlight, as light, is always the light of the one sun. But sunlight falling on impurities is avoided, while sunlight falling on a pure place is not. Again, one is eager to collect diamonds and crystals, which are aspects of earth, while one avoids human corpses and the like, which are likewise (predominantly modifications of) the earth element. Similarly, one is eager to get hold of the urine and excreta of a cow, since they are regarded as holy, but one avoids the urine and excreta of other species. Thus (acceptance and rejection do not depend on the nature of the thing to be accepted or avoided, but on the nature of that with which it is related).[172]

5. The Enlightened Man as Bodiless: His Glory

Extract 1 explains that the notion that one has a body is due to wrong knowledge. Extract 2 explains that the enlightened person does not feel identified with a body and does not experience suffering. Extract 3 explains how the enlightened one is 'dis-embodied' while still alive, because embodiment is an illusion caused by nescience. This Extract declares that he sees all beings as his own Self, and that, for him, all delusion is eradicated. Extracts 4-7 explain how the enlightened one does not 'go' anywhere at the time of the death of his body. The individuality of such a person has already been 'extinguished like a lamp'. The gods, if hostile, cannot affect him. All his family comes to know the Absolute.

Extract 8 shows how, though the means to liberation may vary, the experience of liberation is always the same. The final metaphysical knowledge is not capable of variations of degree. Extract 9 explains the sense in which 'childishness' is spoken of as a characteristic of the enlightened person. Extract 10 explains how he has no defect. Extract 11 remarks that the knowledge which produces enlightenment is uncontradictable. Such knowledge produces indifference to any conceivable object.

Extracts 12-15 speak of the glory of the enlightened person. He sees all as the Self. He has burnt up all merit and demerit in the fire of vision of the Self and will not suffer involuntary reincarnation again. He has 'done all that has to be done'. He knows that the transcendent Self alone exists and that duality and pain do not exist. He is a 'Brahmin' in the sense of a 'knower of Brahman'.

TEXTS ON THE ENLIGHTENED MAN AS BODILESS: HIS GLORY

1. An objection is here[173] raised to the effect that it is not so clear that the metaphysical statements of the Upanishads serve a purpose as it is that statements explaining to those who are imagining a rope to be a snake that it is only a rope have a purpose. For it is seen that even those who have heard the metaphysical statements about the Absolute remain entangled in transmigratory life exactly as before.

We reply that no one can show how one who has understood that the Absolute is his own true Self can be entangled in transmigratory life any more. For transmigratory life stands in contradiction with the knowledge that one's own Self is the Absolute, derived from the authority of the Veda. In the case of one who is still identified with the body and its organs, pain and fear and the like are certainly found. But one cannot conclude from this that when a person has realized that his Self is the Absolute through the authority of the Veda, and when identification with the body and organs has consequently ceased, he still continues to experience the pain and fear that arose from that erroneous identification before.

Take, for instance, the case of a wealthy householder, identified with his possessions. It is clear that the loss of them will cause him pain. But one cannot on this ground assert that when that same householder has gone forth as a wandering ascetic and had disidentified himself from his possessions, he will experience the same pain at the fact that he is parted from them! Hence the Upanishads say, 'The pleasant and the unpleasant do not touch the one who no longer has a body'.[174]

Perhaps you will say that disembodiment can only occur when the body falls at death, and not in the case of a living person. But this is not correct. For the notion that one has a body at all is prompted simply by wrong knowledge. One cannot suppose that the Self possesses a body except through erroneous knowledge, taking the form of identifying the Self with the body. For we have already explained how the bodilessness of the Self is eternal as it is not the result of any act.[175]

Nor can we admit that its meritorious and vicious action constitute its embodied state. For there is no way of establishing the connection of the Self with a body, seeing that it is impossible to establish even that the Self is the agent of meritorious or vicious actions. Indeed, to attribute an embodied state to the Self, and to ground that embodied state on the performance of meritorious and vicious actions, is to commit the fallacy of begging the question,[176] so that speaking of a 'beginningless cycle' in this context is like speaking of a beginningless chain of blind men.[177]

Further, the Self cannot be an agent, as it has no connection with action. Nor will it avail to say that agency is sometimes seen to accrue from mere proximity, as in the case of kings and the like.[178] For it is quite intelligible why kings should be spoken of as agents, since they are connected with servants whom they have collected by gifts of money and the like. But in the case of the Self, one cannot make out any relation of master and servant with the body and organs, based on money-gifts or the like. Quite the contrary, it is false identification that is clearly the cause of the relation.[179]

❖

2. Therefore,[180] because possession of a body is conditioned by erroneous thinking, it stands proved that the enlightened one is disembodied while still alive. All this is confirmed by the Vedic texts dealing with the knower of the Absolute. For example, 'Then, just as the slough of a snake lies on the ant-hill dead and cast off, so does this body lie cast off in the same way. But the liberated man stands forth as bodiless, as immortal, as the supreme Self, verily as the Absolute, verily as light (tejas)'.[181] Or, 'Without eyes, but appearing to have eyes; without ears, but appearing to have ears; without a voice, but appearing to have a voice; without Vital Energy,

but appearing to have Vital Energy'.[182] And there are also passages in this vein from the derivative literature, such as that beginning, 'How does the one of steady wisdom talk?',[183] which states the marks of the man of steady wisdom and shows how the enlightened man severs connection with self-interested action entirely. Hence we may say that he who has known the Absolute is not entangled in transmigratory life as he was before. He, on the other hand, who remains entangled in transmigratory life as before has not known his Self as the Absolute. Hence our position is unassailable.[184]

❖

3. That seeker of liberation who has assumed the life of a wandering monk (parivrāṭ) sees all beings, from the Unmanifest Principle[185] to the meanest plant, in his own Self, and sees nothing but the Self. He sees his own Self in all those beings and identifies himself with their Self. He sees the one undifferentiated Self in all beings, with the feeling 'Just as I am the Self of this body, this assemblage of instruments and organs, and also the Witness of all the ideas of the mind, the illuminator, transcendent, without empirical qualities, so am I also, with the same nature, the only real Self of all the things of the world from the Unmanifest Principle to the meanest plant'. Possessed of this vision, one feels no horror at anything.

This is but a statement of fact. All violent feelings of dislike occur to one seeing something evil that is other than himself. But it is clear that for him who sees only the extremely pure Self and nothing else there is nothing else outside him that could excite feelings of dislike. So it is but right to say that he feels no horror.

The next verse develops the same theme. The word 'yasmin' either means 'at that time' or else refers back to the previous verse and means 'in that Self'. When, in the case of one who has seen the supreme Reality, all those beings have become his own Self through this vision, what delusion or what pain could there be at that time or in that Self? Delusion and pain, seeds of desire and action, pertain to the ignorant man, not to the one who sees the unity and sole reality of the Self, pure and ethereal.

By asking rhetorically 'What delusion or what pain could there be?' the text rules out delusion and pain, effects of nescience, and thereby proclaims the total eradication of transmigratory experience.[186]

❖

4. The liberated person does not depart on any further journey at death. It has already been laid down[187] that he altogether vanishes, that only his name is left, that it is like the extinction of a lamp. The bodies and organs of those who are still in the grip of transmigration and of those who are set for liberation both alike rest in their (material) causes, whereas the bodies and organs of the liberated ones can never be produced again. As for the cause which prompts the bodies and organs of those who are still transmigrating to undergo repeated reproduction, it has been laid down after a discussion that it is merit and demerit (karma). When that is exhausted only the name is left and all else has vanished — and this is liberation.[188]

❖

5. The text now describes how the process whereby the ordinary transmigrating soul goes to death is the same as that whereby the enlightened one merges with pure Being. It remarks that when the principle of fire (tejas) in a man merges with the supreme deity (pure Being), the dying man has no knowledge of it. The ignorant man re-emerges from pure Being and enters the state of a tiger, a man or a god in accordance with his past thoughts. But when the enlightened man emerges from pure Being, the Absolute, the Self, the latter has already been illumined for him by the lamp of the knowledge he has obtained from the Veda and the instructions of the Teacher. And he does not return (to embodied life).

Others say that the enlightened souls emerge from the body through a subtle canal leading upward through the crown of the head, and proceed to pure Being by way of the sun. But (in the case of the fully liberated man) this is demonstrably wrong. For we find that 'going anywhere' is invariably an action performed for an end conditioned by place, time and cause (occasion). But the man who perceives his identity with the eternal Self and whose sole end is real, cannot be expected to pursue unreal ends, such as those conditioned by time, space and cause (occasion).[189] For this would be a contradiction, since in his case the causes for going, which would be nescience, desire, merit and demerit, would all have been consumed in the fire of the knowledge of pure Being, so that 'going' of any kind would be impossible anyway. In the Atharva Veda it is said, 'But of him who has his desires fully satisfied, who is a perfected soul, all desires vanish even here (on earth)'.[190] And there is also the text giving the example of the river entering the sea.[191]

❖

6. The text refers to those who have acquired the true conviction about the main topic of the Upanishads, the supreme Self. Through their practice of renunciation (saṃnyāsa), that is, through their abandonment of all activity and ritual, through their exclusive devotion to the Absolute in its true form, these men of great effort, whose minds have been purified by their strict life of renunciation, are all liberated.

When worldly people die, the death of the physical body is not the end of their experiences as an individual. By contrast, the death of the seeker of liberation, if it brings his transmigration to an end, is what the Upanishad here calls a 'final end'. The reference to the 'World of Brahman' means the 'world' that *is* the Absolute (brahman). It is referred to in the plural as the *worlds* of Brahman because there are many pupils who strive for it. Though one, it is here conceived as being seen or attained in different ways. Yet the expression only refers to the one Absolute (brahman).

The liberated ones here described are spoken of as 'utterly' immortal because they are identified with the Absolute, which is 'utterly' immortal in comparison with other immortality (for example, immortality implying dwelling in the World of Brahmā until final absorption at the end of the world-period). They have become the Absolute even while alive. They are liberated 'all-round', that is, they simply come to an end,[192] like the flame of a lamp when it is extinguished (nirvāṇa) or like the fragments of ether apparently enclosed in different pots, which disappear when the pots are broken. There is no question of their having to depart on a journey to another 'place'. 'Just as birds leave no footprints in the sky and fish no tracks in the water, so also do the men of enlightenment leave no trace behind'.[193]

As flowing rivers disappear in the sea and lose their name and form,[194] so does the enlightened one, free from name and form set up by nescience, attain to the divine Spirit (puruṣa), which lies beyond that (lower) 'supreme' known as the Indestructible Principle.

You will object that it is very well known that obstacles of various kinds stand between us and the attainment of the highest good, so that even the knower of the Absolute will find himself obstructed either by one of the passions or by a deity,[195] and will go to some other destination and not the Absolute. But this objection is wrong, as enlightenment destroys all obstacles by its mere rise. It is only nescience and nothing else that is the obstacle to liberation: for liberation is eternal and is one's own true Self.

Hence the text goes on to say that if there is anyone who has immediate experience of the Absolute in its highest form and feels 'Verily, I am that and that alone', that person goes to no other destination but the Absolute. Not even the gods can prevent it by obstacles, for he now becomes their own Self. So the knower of the Absolute becomes the Absolute.

Further, there is no one in the family of such an enlightened man who fails to know the Absolute. Not only this, he goes beyond grief, which means that he rises above all mental suffering which arises from being deprived of desirable objects. He crosses beyond 'sin' in the form of merit and demerit. Freed from the knots of nescience that afflict the heart, he 'becomes immortal', that is to say, the knots of the heart and so forth are cut, as already mentioned.[196]

7. The Seer (ṛṣi) Vāmadeva had knowledge thus (i.e already in the womb)[197] of the Self of the nature already described. The Upanishad says next 'after separation from this body'. It means after separation, achieved through heroic power arising from the nectar of the knowledge of the supreme Self, from the notion of being connected with the body, a notion which is only imagined through nescience and which is yet impermeable as iron and productive of many hundreds of evils like birth and death. It means after the (virtual) destruction of the body through the destruction of nescience, together with its seed and cause — and then becoming the supreme Self and rising above the low level of this transmigratory life, becoming the Self of all, illumined by the light of pure knowledge. It means that he became extinguished (nirvāṇa) like a lamp in the one homogeneous savour (rasa) of pure Consciousness previously described — immortal, beyond decay, beyond danger, omniscient, infinite, without a before or an after, without anything outside.

By the words 'in the world of heaven' (svarga-loke) the Upanishad means 'in his own Self'. The words 'was born' mean that the soul 'was born' in his own true nature through knowledge of the Self. He had previously, while yet alive, attained all desires.[198]

❖

8. An account of the various higher and lower means to knowledge has been given at Brahma Sūtra III.iv.26.[199] The question now raised is whether the fruits of knowledge only arise here below in the present birth, or whether they sometimes arise in another birth.

One might initially suppose that they could only accrue in the present birth. For knowledge results from such practices as hearing. And nobody listens to teaching with the idea 'This will lead to enlightenment in a later life'. Even sacrifices and the like only generate enlightenment in association with such disciplines as hearing, cogitation and meditation. For knowledge is produced only by authoritative means of knowledge. So we conclude that enlightenment arises here in the present life only.

On this the Teacher observes, 'Knowledge arises here in this life if the afore-mentioned obstructions do not occur'. What he means is as follows. When there is no obstruction arising from the maturation of the fruit of previous deeds, then the means of knowledge, if put into operation, produce knowledge here in this life. But if there is such an obstruction, they only produce enlightenment in another birth. The maturation of the fruit of one's previous deeds is conditioned by particulars of time, place and occasion. And the conditions of time, place and occasion that produce the maturation of one deed will not necessarily produce the maturation of another. For deeds may well produce mutually contradictory merit and demerit.[200] And the Veda only says that this or that deed will have such and such a result, and does not descend into the details of time, place and occasion. In fact, however, what happens is that in the case of one previous deed an occult power will manifest (and produce a new experience) on account of the intensity of effort with which the work was done and the aptness of the means resorted to, while this very manifestation will block the manifestation of the occult power latent in another deed.

The *prima facie* view was also wrong to maintain, that desire for the dawn of knowledge can only occur if the dawning is to come in this life. For people can quite well think, 'Let me have knowledge either in this birth or another'. And even though the rise of spiritual knowledge depends on the discipline of hearing, cogitation and sustained meditation, yet it also depends on the destruction of obstacles. The Veda itself is witness to the difficulty of achieving knowledge of the Self, saying 'Many do not have the chance to listen to this Truth, many who listen do not understand. He who proclaims it is himself a wonder, he who understands it a man of wisdom. He who knows it is a wonder, even when taught by a man of wisdom'.[201]

And when the Veda teaches that Vāmadeva knew himself to be the Absolute already in his mother's womb,[202] this is already a proof that enlightenment can come in a later life out of the deeds performed in an earlier life. For no one can do any effective work in this life while he is still in the womb. Consider also the teaching of the derivative literature, when the Lord Vāsudeva is asked by Arjuna 'What is his fate, O Kṛṣṇa, if he does not attain perfection in this life?' He first replies, 'My dear one, no one who does good acts receives an evil fate',[203] and then speaks of his rebirth in a pious family, and finally teaches the very doctrine we are advocating here, in the passage beginning 'There he acquires that control of the mind which he had gained in his former birth'[204] and ending 'After acquiring perfection through many lives, he finally reaches the supreme state'.[205] Our view was therefore correct when we said that one obtains enlightenment in this birth or a later one according to whether the obstructions are destroyed or left in force.

We have seen, then, that there is a law in the case of the one desiring liberation and pursuing the discipline that leads to it which states that the question whether his enlightenment occurs in the present birth or in a future one is decided by the intensity of his effort and the aptness of the means to which he resorts. This might suggest that the quality of his liberation might depend on similar factors. To dispel this idea, the author of the Sūtras proceeds, 'There are no different kinds of liberation (resulting from different degrees of effort)'. Why not? Because there is no variation in the account of the state of liberation in any of the upanishadic texts. For the state of liberation is equated with the Absolute, and the Absolute cannot assume any variety of form, as it is always characterized in the same way. We can see this from such texts as 'Not gross, not subtle...'[206]

...Furthermore, variations of degree in the intensity of effort with which the means of knowledge were pursued would affect knowledge, which is the immediate result arising from such means, but not liberation, which is (not their immediate result but) the result of knowledge. For liberation is not subject to production by resorting to means. It is ever in being by its very nature, and is only to be *known* through knowledge, as we have many times explained. Nor is knowledge itself subject to variations of degree: for anything less than knowledge is not knowledge, and anything more is still only knowledge. We might allow that knowledge was better or worse in the sense of arising more quickly or more slowly, but in any case there cannot be any variations of degree in liberation.

The fact that there are no variations in knowledge as such

is a further proof that there are no variations in its result, liberation. The case with knowledge in the form of meditations on the Absolute associated with qualities, as expressed in such texts as 'Made up of mind, with the Vital Energy for its body'[207] is quite different. Here there can be intensification or diminution of quality and a proportionate difference in results accruing from action. The Veda itself gives a hint of this in the text, 'Under whatever form he meditates on Him, that form he becomes'.[208] But this is not the case in qualitiless (nirguṇa) knowledge, as there is no quality (which could vary in intensity).[209] On this point the derivative literature also agrees, when it says 'The state of liberation does not admit of degrees: it is only when qualities come in that the wise speak of differences'.[210]

❖

9. In the passage 'Therefore the Brahmin, weary of the posture of a wise man, should adopt the attitude of a child',[211] adoption of the attitude of a child is recommended.[212] Here the word 'childishness' is an (etymological) derivative, and one might wonder in what sense the text meant adoption of the nature of the activities of a child. And as one cannot summon up the nature of a child at will, the doubt resolves itself into whether the text means literally behaving like a child and going about soiling one's clothes, or whether it only means being like a child in point of undeveloped sensuality and absence of pride and hypocrisy. And one might initially suppose that it meant saying whatever one liked, eating whatever one liked and defecating according to impulse, as this is what is universally understood as the (infantile) state of a child. Nor would such untramelled behaviour yield demerit

for the renunciate. For as he is an enlightened man, he has been expressly exempted from any fault in these matters by the texts of the Veda, just as the Veda exempts the sacrificer from any sin in slaughtering animals for sacrifice.

We reply, however, that this is wrong, as the texts of the Veda in this matter may be differently interpreted. It is not right to assume a meaning for the word 'childishness' that implies the contravention of other injunctions (e.g. as to cleanliness) when another interpretation which does not involve such contradictions is possible. Moreover, the incidental recommendations found in any passage are intended to forward the main purpose. The main discipline of the ascetic at this stage is affirmation of truth. It would by no means forward affirmation of truth if childishness was adopted *in toto*. Hence it is the adoption of some particular features of the childish state which is being recommended, namely undeveloped sensuality and absence of pride and hypocrisy.

Hence the author of the Sūtras says, 'He should not show off'. That is, he should be free from pride and hyprocisy and should not display his knowledge, learning or righteousness. He should be like a child, who does not display himself in front of others because his faculties are not yet developed. When interpreted in this way, the text forwards the main purpose in view.

And in consonance with this we find the following in the derivative literature: 'He is a (true) Brahmin about whom no one knows whether he is pious or impious, learned or ignorant, of a good way of life or a bad one. The enlightened one should hide his spiritual practices and see that his real actions remain unknown. He should walk the earth like one blind, stupid and mute'. And there is that other text, 'With his true nature unmanifest, with his real character hidden'.[213]

❖

10. The sages who see the same everywhere, whose minds are motionless and concentrated on the Absolute, that one identical principle present in all beings, have conquered birth. Though the Absolute may appear to fools to have blemishes, on account of the appearance in the world of beings like outcastes who have blemishes, the fact is that it is untouched by such blemishes. Nor does Consciousness contain any internal distinctions on account of special qualities, as it is without qualities altogether. The Lord Himself will be saying later that desire and other such qualities pertain to the empirical personality, not to the Consciousness illumining it, and will also say of the latter 'Because of its being beginning-less and without qualities'.[214] And there are no 'ultimate particularities' (antya-viśeṣa) distinguishing the Self and making it different in each body, it being impossible to prove their existence.[215]

Hence the Absolute is one and uniform (the text proceeds), and such sages are established in it. They are not associated with even the suspicion of a defect, as they do not identify themselves with the psycho-physical complex.[216]

❖

11. This true knowledge (vidyā) 'I am the Absolute' is not contradicted by the notions 'I am the agent', 'I have desires', 'I am in bondage'. For these arise from the mere semblance

(ābhāsa) of a means of knowledge.[217] When once the notion derived from the Veda 'I am the Absolute and no other' becomes firm, the notions that one is an agent, has desires and is in bondage become as unreasonable as the notion that the body is the Self. One who has once with effort attained to a place of safety from a place of danger does not wish to return to that place of danger if he is free in the matter. How can one who has awoken from his previous ignorance as to the meaning of the words (of the sentence 'That thou art') and is searching for the direct experience (anubhava) of the meaning of the sentence as a whole consider himself free to behave as he likes, particularly when he has accepted the injunctions to become a renunciate, etc.[218] Hence all that we maintained above has been well and truly established. For a man does not engage in action for the sake of obtaining anything when he has become indifferent to the three worlds. For the sake of what could the one desirous of liberation strive? Even if he be afflicted by hunger, a man will not desire to eat poison knowingly. He, then, whose hunger has already been appeased by delightful food will not desire to eat poison unless he is an utter lunatic.[219]

❖

12. The duties laid down for a particular caste and stage of life, when performed without desire for personal rewards, are the highest and only real duties and lead to the acquisition of high states such as that of a deity and the like. Duties when intermixed with acts contrary to the spiritual law form the middle class, as they lead to rebirth as a man. The lowest class of acts are those performed impulsively and against the spiritual law, and these lead to rebirth in animal and other

lower wombs. All these acts are mere imaginations of nescience. One who knows the one Self without a second, void of imagination, is simply not aware of them, any more than a man of discrimination is aware of the contaminations that children suppose to afflict the pure ether of the sky. When this state arises, the mind (citta)[220] is no longer reborn in the form of god, man or beast according to one's deeds. For no result can arise when the cause is removed, any more than a grain can sprout when there are no seeds.

But what exactly does this 'non-rebirth of the mind' mean? When the highest reality is seen, the merit and demerit of the mind, which are the cause of its rebirth, are destroyed. The state of non-birth of the mind constitutes liberation. It is eternal, identical in all states, featureless and without subject-object duality. The reference is to the mind as unborn, unproduced, constituting all reality and non-dual even before (the appearance called liberation supervened). For even before enlightenment duality and birth were mere visions of the mind.[221] The mind (in its true nature) is unborn and ever the whole of reality. Its 'not being produced' is its continual true state, void of subject and object duality. There is no question of it sometimes existing and sometimes not existing: it is ever the same.

Because there is no cause of rebirth, in the manner explained above, the enlightened one, knowing that absence of causality is alone real, has no further cause such as merit or demerit to take him to birth in a divine, human or animal womb. He has by now lost all desire for anything external and is free from lust and grief. Free also from nescience and other hindrances, he reaches the state beyond danger. That is to say, he is not reborn.

It is through blind clinging to the unreal that one becomes certain of the existence of duality, even though it does not in fact exist. It is on account of this infatuation arising from nescience that the mind creates objects corresponding to its desires. But when one becomes awake to the fact that no second reality exists, then one loses this attachment and dependence, and turns away from the realm of clinging to the unreal. When the mind has withdrawn from the realm of duality, and is not active in any other realm because it perceives that no such realm exists, it then assumes a motionless state, being the Absolute in its true form, a homogeneous mass of pure Consciousness. This is the realm of the enlightened ones who see reality. It is the realm of pure identity, unborn, non-dual, featureless, transcendent.[222]

❖

13. The verse says, 'When a man has attained total omniscience and the "Brahmin's" state of non-duality, which has no beginning, middle or end — then what more has he to do?' The reference here is to the texts 'He is a Brahmin' and 'This is the eternal glory of the Brahmin'.[223] After attaining this final goal of the Self, what more has one to do? There is then no motive for doing anything further. For there are such texts from the derivative literature as 'Action then serves him no more'.[224]

The disciplined behaviour of the 'Brahmin' is natural, as also is his inner control of the mind (śama). There is nothing contrived about it, it is just the result of remaining in his natural state as the Self. The same is true of his control of his sense-organs. For the 'Brahmin' is at peace by his very nature. And the enlightened man adheres to his natural peace, issuing from his nature as the Absolute. That is, he adheres to his nature as the Absolute.

Now, we have shown how the world-views of secular philosophies actually *promote* further transmigratory experience because the clashes that occur between them provoke attachment and aversion. And after first exposing the falsity of these various world-views with arguments borrowed from their own mutual recriminations,[225] we have summed the matter up by stating that the only right world-view is the world-view of Non-Duality (advaita), because it is above the four possibilities of (1) affirmation, (2) negation, (3) both affirmation and negation and (4) neither affirmation nor negation. Hence it does not provoke attachment or aversion. So we now proceed to outline our own teaching.

That which exists with empirical reality (saṃvṛti-sat), and of which an idea is formed, constitutes that worldly duality of subject and object which is the basis of all empirical dealings, from the teachings of the Veda down. Here the reference is to the world of waking experience.

There is another sphere consisting of that which does not even have empirical being as an object, but of which an idea is nevertheless formed. This is called 'private' because it is different from the common realm of waking experience. Yet it is said to constitute a 'world' as it is common to all living beings. This is called dream.

But there is another phase of being, which is neither an

object nor an idea and which neither knows nor is known in the empirical sense. This is 'the beyond'.[226] A world is a sphere of subject-object experience. Where this is absent, but the seeds of all future activity are present, we have dreamless sleep.

That is called 'knowledge' whereby one comes to know the supreme reality indirectly, first as the realm of waking experience, then as the world of dream and finally as 'the beyond'.[227] The 'realm of the knowable' of the verse means these same three objects of knowledge. For nothing apart from these three can be 'known' since everything ever thought of by any philosopher falls within them. But that which is knowable through spiritual intuition (vijñeya) is different. It is the final reality, called 'the Fourth' (turya), the Self as a metaphysical principle, non-dual, unborn. This doctrine of knowledge in its three stages, and of spiritual intuition beyond them, is ever proclaimed, says the verse, by those who see reality, those who know the Absolute (brahma-vid).

To begin with, there is knowledge of the three kinds of knowables in order. First comes the gross world. Afterwards, when this is absent, there comes the private world. Then, when this is absent, comes 'the beyond' (i.e. experience of dreamless sleep). Then, when these three have been eliminated one after the other, one knows the ultimate reality, the Fourth, non-dual, unborn, beyond danger. When this occurs, that man of great intellect, being now himself the Self, attains to omniscience here in this very world. As his mind now comprehends that which transcends all empirical knowledge, his knowledge never leaves him. When reality is once known, that knowledge never departs. He who knows the supreme reality does not first acquire knowledge and then find he has to revise it in the manner of the secular philosopher.

Because the three 'worlds' have been taught as having to be known in sequence, the idea might arise that they were real. The author (Gauḍapāda) now shows that from the standpoint of the highest reality they do not exist. The three worlds of waking, dream and dreamless sleep have to be rejected as non-existent in the Self, as an imaginary snake has to be rejected as non-existent in the rope in which it is imagined. What really has to be known is the principle of supreme reality beyond all the four modes of judgement.[228] The true discipline is to become a monk and give up the three desires for a son, wealth and a 'world' (after death), and then to cultivate the qualities of wisdom (pāṇḍitya), child-like simplicity and sagehood (mauna).[229] Psychological defects like attachment, aversion, infatuation and the like have to be ironed out. The monk must know from the beginning[230] what he has to reject, what he has to know, what he has to cultivate and what he has to eliminate, as this is the means to success.

Amongst the things that have to be rejected, cultivated or eliminated, the Absolute that has to be intuitively known forms an exception, and (unlike the others) is real from the standpoint of the final truth. The rest are mere figments of nescience. The knowers of the Absolute do not accept that absolute reality attaches to the other three classes, namely what has to be rejected, cultivated or eliminated.

Seekers of the Absolute must recognize that all souls are subtle, pure and all-pervading like the ether by their very nature. They are also beginningless and hence eternal. To obviate the idea that, because he has spoken of them in the plural, the souls must be many, the author (Gauḍapāda) goes on to say that there is no atom of difference in them anywhere.

Souls are only knowable as objects from the empirical standpoint, not from the standpoint of the highest truth. As the sun is ever luminous by nature and of the nature of eternal light, so also are the souls by nature luminous from the first. It is not necessary to establish their existence, as they are eternally self-established. When they are considered in their own intrinsic nature, there is no room for doubt whether they are of this form or that. When a seeker of liberation finds that, just as the sun shines eternally without dependence on any other light to illumine itself or anything else, so has he himself no need to establish that his own nature or any one else's is always pure consciousness in the above-described sense, then he has achieved the state of blessed abstraction in which he feels no need of acquiring further knowledge or fulfilling further duties. Then he becomes fit for liberation.

There is no need for taking active steps to achieve peace (liberation) in the Self. All souls are eternally at rest, unborn, and completely withdrawn by nature, homogeneous and non-different from one another. That is, the Self, as a metaphysical principle, is unborn, homogeneous and pure, and hence there is no need to produce the state of blessed abstraction or liberation in them. Action can have no effect on that which is eternally of the same nature.

The author (Gauḍapāda) then goes on to explain how in the whole world only those people who have attained the highest reality avoid misery. All the rest are miserable.

Those who hold fast to the reality of distinctions, those who conform to the standards of transmigratory life, dualists who declare that reality is multiple — wandering about on the path of duality imagined by nescience and remaining there permanently, lack purity and are said to be miserable. And this characterization is right.

Next the author goes on to explain how those who are not men of high soul (mahātmā) or wise (paṇḍita) and who are outside the upanishadic tradition, or of low standing and little learning, cannot plumb the depths of the highest principle of reality.

If there should be some few souls, whether they be men or women, who acquire a fixed conviction about the existence of the unborn, all-homogeneous principle of reality, they alone will be the people of true metaphysical knowledge. Their path and their metaphysical knowledge will be quite incomprehensible to other people of ordinary intellect. For there are such texts from the derivative literature as 'Even the gods will be bemused if they try to follow the path of those who have become the Self of all living beings and who are intent on the welfare of all beings, without any aims for their own personal advantage. They will no more be able to track them than to track the flight of birds in the sky'.[231]

The knowledge of unborn, unmoving souls is itself unborn and unmoving, like the brilliance and heat of the sun. Such unborn knowledge does not bear on any external object. Hence it is called relationless, and is like the ether.

But if anyone admits, in accordance with the views of the secular philosophers, the rise of any new reality within or without, even if it be minute in size, a man so lacking in discrimination will never attain the relationless state (of identity with the true Self). All the less could we speak of his ignorance being destroyed.

Very well. But if you say that the ignorance will not be destroyed, does that imply that we accept that souls are ever really ignorant? By no means, says the author. Souls are not by nature in bondage to nescience, desire and the like. They are free by nature, enlightened and liberated from the first.

How, then, do we say of some of them, 'They "become" enlightened'? The enlightened spiritual masters use such expressions metaphorically (for purposes of communication within the phenomenal world), rather as we say 'The sun is shining' although it never ceases to shine, and we say 'The mountains are standing still' even though they never move.[232]

❖

14. Because in ancient times the true Brahmins knew this Self which is neither the instrument nor the result of action, and, knowing it, withdrew from all pursuit of ends, which is characterized by instruments and results, and lived on alms, rejecting ritual and its instruments, whether directed to visible or invisible ends, even so, therefore, should the true Brahmin, the knower of the Absolute, plumb the depths of wisdom even today, perfect his Self-knowledge with the help of the Teacher and the traditional doctrine and withdraw from the pursuit of ends. Wisdom is never complete until there has been

withdrawal from the pursuit of ends, for wisdom arises from contempt of the pursuit of ends and is contradictory to it. Since wisdom concerning the Self cannot arise without contempt for the pursuit of ends, withdrawal from the pursuit of ends is virtually 'enjoined' by knowledge of the Self. This is emphasized in the Vedic text here under comment by the use of past participles relating to one and the same agent.[233] His aim should be to withdraw from the pursuit of ends and stand firm through the power of his knowledge, his state of knowledge. In the case of others, who do not know the Self, strength depends on the instruments and results of action. But the enlightened man should reject all resort to the strength deriving from instruments and ends, and should resort to knowledge of that Self which is neither an instrument nor a result of action. *This* should be his strength. He should *be* that knowledge. When he resorts to *this* power, his senses no longer have the power to drag him down and keep him in the realm of the pursuit of particular ends. The senses can only accomplish this in the case of a fool who is devoid of the strength of knowledge: they prompt him to pursue ends in the realm of the visible and invisible.

Strength, indeed, is defined as the contempt of all vision of objects, achieved through knowledge of the Self. So a man should desire to adhere firmly to that state. The Veda says, 'He attains heroism through the Self' and 'This Self cannot be attained by one who is devoid of strength'.[234]

When he has acquired perfect strength and wisdom, the yogi becomes a sage (muni) through reflection (manana). The true Brahmin does indeed have one 'task' to perform — he has to rise above all representations of the not-self. When he has done this, the yogi has done all that has to be done.

Non-sagehood consists (negatively) in ignorance of the Self[235] and (positively) in vision of the non-self. 'Wisdom' (pāṇḍitya) and strength (bala) are the two technical names for rising above ignorance of the Self and vision of the not-self respectively. Perfection of these represents sagehood (mauna). Sagehood represents the culmination of power to rise above vision of the non-self. When the Brahmin has perfected that, he has done all that he has to do, and the conviction 'All is the Absolute' arises.... The Brahminhood of such a Brahmin is in no sense figurative (as that of the ordinary 'caste' Brahmin is). When it is said that he behaves as he likes, this is an eulogy of the high state of Brahminhood. It does not mean that the true Brahmin is careless in his behaviour. This high state of Brahminhood consists in identity with the Self. It is above 'hunger and thirst, sorrow and delusion, old age and death'.[236] It consists in eternal beatitude. All else belongs to the domain of nescience, is a particular end, is perishable and beset with miseries and about as real as a dream or a display worked by a hypnotist's magic or a mirage in the desert. Only the Self is ever free.[237]

❖

15. Since this glory of the Brahmin (who has realized the Self) is unconnected with action and transcendent in nature, it follows that one who has this realization becomes 'peaceful' (śānta), which means desisting from the activities of the external senses,[238] 'controlled' (dānta), which means above the thirsts of the mind, 'withdrawn' (uparata), which means a renunciate (saṃnyāsin) who has given up all desires, 'ascetic' (titikṣu), which means able and willing to bear extremes of the

pairs of opposites such as heat and cold, 'concentrated' (samāhita), which means concentrated in one-pointedness after withdrawing from all movement of senses or mind. This has already been taught in the text 'Growing weary of the states of "strength" and "wisdom", he becomes a sage'.[239] That means that he sees the Self, the inner illuminator, in his own 'self' or body, the latter being an organism dependent on the Self for its existence. Nor does he see his Self as limited to that. He sees all as the Self, without so much as a tip of hair that is not the Self. He becomes a sage (muni) through reflection (manana), passing beyond (identification with) the three states called waking, dream and dreamless sleep. Sin, which here includes both merit and demerit, does not touch such a Brahmin who can see the Self. And the Brahmin himself goes beyond 'sin' in the form of merit and demerit, which he does by pervading them in the form of the Self. Sin, whether through omission or commission, does not trouble him, either by occasioning or by obstructing empirically desirable fruits. It is he, the knower of the Absolute, who causes trouble to sin by burning it up in the fire of his vision of the Self. He who has this realization becomes 'sinless', that is, free from merit and demerit, free from the dust of desire, free from doubts, convinced 'I am the Self of all, the Absolute (brahman) in its highest form'. In short, he is a true Brahmin.

In this condition he is a Brahmin in the true sense of the word: before attaining to the nature of the Absolute (brahman) he had only been a Brahmin in a figurative sense. 'This, O King, is the World of the Absolute',[240] the world that is the Absolute in a literal and not a figurative sense. 'It is the state of being the Self of all, O King. Thou hast attained unto this

"World of the Absolute"' said Yājñavalkya, 'the realm of "absence of fear" and of transcendence'....

Now the topic of man's highest end has been dealt with and finished. This is the whole duty of man. This is his highest attainable summit, the topmost value (niḥśreyasa). Having reached here, the Brahmin has done all that he has to do (he is kṛta-kṛtya). With this the teaching of the Veda stands complete.[241]

NOTES TO CHAPTER XVI

References to Extracts are in bold type

1 **Bh.G.Bh. II.21.**

2 Kaṭha I.ii.22.

3 Bh.G.XIII.31.

4 B.S. I.iii.18.

5 B.S. I.i.30.

6 **B.S.Bh. I.iii.19.**

7 Chānd. VIII.xii.3.

8 *Ibid.*

9 Chānd. VI.viii.7, Bṛhad. I.iv.10, Chānd. VII.xxiv.1, Bṛhad. IV.iii.23.

10 B.S. IV.iii.15, cp. above, 65.

11 Kaṭha II.i.15.

12 Chānd. VI.x.1, Muṇḍ. III.ii.8, Praśna VI.5.

13 Chānd. VII.xxiv.1, VII.xxv.2. **B.S.Bh. IV.iv.4.**

14 Bṛhad. II.iv.14.

15 Bṛhad. III.v.1.

16 Bṛhad. IV.iii.21. The illustrative example was the famous one of a man embracing his wife.

17 Bṛhad. IV.iv.6.

18 Bṛhad. IV.iv.23.

19 The view of the P.M.

20 Chānd. VI.ii.1.

21 A sub-school of those who taught liberation through knowledge and action conjoined. B.B.V.S. IV.iv.170.

22 Cp. above, Vol.III, 58f.

23 So that, although the Self *is* Consciousness and Bliss, it cannot *have* Consciousness of itself as Bliss. Hacker, *Kleine Schriften*, 226f., cites this passage as evidence that the Bṛhad. Bh. came later in Śaṅkara's output than either the Taitt.Bh. or the G.K.Bh.

24 Bṛhad. Bh. IV.iv.6.

25 Muṇḍ. II.ii.8, Chānd. VI.xiv.2, V.xxiv.3.

26 Bh.G. IV.37, XVIII.66.

27 Bh.G. XVIII.17.

28 M.Bh. Vana Parva 200.110.

29 Bh.G. IV.37.

30 Bh.G.Bh. XIII.23.

31 Īśa 2.

32 B.S.Bh. III.iv.14.

33 He does not identify himself with the acting process. Hence he merely witnesses the actions that result from his previous actions and does not act. Hence, also, he does not create the seed of future activity that would bind him to further lives to come.

34 U.S. (verse) Chapter IV.

35 Muṇḍ. II.ii.9, Īśa 7.

36 Cp. above, Vol.V, Chapter XIII, section 1, Extract 4.

37 Cp. above, previous Extract.

38 Bṛhad. Bh. I.iv.10.

39 This does not annul any past action, but serves to make a repetition of the event less likely. Deussen refers to T.S. II.ii.2.5.

40 Cp. above, Vol.IV, Chapter X, section 1, Extract 9.

41 Chānd. IV.xiv.3.

42 Chānd. V.xxiv.3.

43 Muṇḍ. II.ii.8.

44 T.S. V.iii.12.1.

45 Bṛhad. IV.iv.22.

46 Muṇḍ II.ii.8 (in some editions 9).

47 Chānd. VIII.iv.1.

48 Bṛhad. IV.iv.22.

49 Chānd. VI.xiv.2, cp. above, Vol.V, Chapter XIII, section 3, Extract 3.

50 Bh.G. II.54-5.

51 I.e. They contribute to liberation.

52 Bṛhad. IV.iv.22.

53 According to the familiar argument that if liberation were caused it would have a beginning and so an end likewise, and would not be eternal.

54 B.S.Bh. IV.i.13-16.

55 Kṛṣṇadvaipāyana is Vyāsa, the sage to whom Śaṅkara attributes the authorship of the M.Bh. including the Bh.G. and of the Purāṇas, though not of the B.S. The attribution of the B.S. to Vyāsa has not been traced earlier than Vācaspati Miśra, opening benedictory verse 5 to the Bhāmatī.

56 Chānd. III.xi.1.

57 Chānd. VI.xiv.2.

58 There are some who reincarnate under the force of karma but remember their previous births. The enlightened person does not fall into this class if he manifests in several bodies, as he is the conscious and deliberate controller of the whole process.

59 M.Bh. XII.320.3ff, G.P. Ed. Vol.III, 676ff.

60 Śaṅkara quotes Muṇḍ. II.ii.8, Chānd. VII.xxvi.2, Bh.G. IV.37.

61 Chānd. VI.xiv.2.

62 Bṛhad. I.iv.10.

63 Gambhīrānanda cites Kūrma Purāṇa, Pūrva Bhāga, XII.269.

64 Bṛhad. III.iv.1, Chānd. VI.viii.7.

65 For Vāmadeva, see Bṛhad. I.iv.10. **B.S.Bh. III.iii.32.**

66 Cp. above, Vol.V, Chapter XII, section 4, Extract 6.

67 Muṇḍ. III.i.4.

68 Bh.G. II.59.

69 Because the enlightened person does not identify himself with these acts with ego-feeling and they therefore leave no saṃskāra leading to rebirth.

70 Muṇḍ. II.ii.8, Bh.G. IV.37.

71 **Vivaraṇa to Ā.D.S., Adhyātma Paṭala I.xxii.11.** *Minor Works of Śrī Śaṅkarācārya*, Ed. Bhāgavat, 433.

72 This passage leads on from that which began above, Vol.V, Chapter XIII, section 1, Extract 13.

73 **Taitt. Bh. II.1.**

74 Cp. Chānd. VII, especially VII.xv.3.

75 **Chānd.Bh. VII.xxv.2.**

76 Drawn from Chānd. VIII.xii.2.

77 Chānd. VIII.vii-xi.

78 At Chānd. VIII.iii.4.

79 I.e. an 'emergence' caused by a change of view-point on the part of the observer, not by a change in the thing observed.

80 Chānd. VIII.xii.3.

81 Cp. Chānd. VIII.x.1.

82 Bh.G. XV.16-18.

83 I.e. through metaphysical knowledge as imparted by Prajāpati to Indra in Chānd. VIII.vii-xiii, and not just through passing into a state of dreamless sleep from which one awakens willy-nilly into a condition where one identifies oneself with body and mind through nescience.

84 Indra, the chief of the gods, was conceived as a pleasure-loving warrior living in luxury in a celestial palace.

85 The Upanishad mentions 'chariots' or 'coaches' and 'relatives'.

86 Thus 'upa' signifies proximity and 'jana' birth.

87 I.e. the liberated person. **Chānd. Bh. VIII.xii.3.**

88 Cp. above, Vol.I, introduction to Chapter IV.

89 Taitt. II.1.

90 Cp. above, Vol.V, Chapter XII, section 4, Extract 7.

91 Taitt. III.vii.1.

92 Taitt. II.vii.1.

93 Cp. above, Vol.III. Chapter VIII, section 2, Extract 11.

94 Taitt. III.x.4.

95 Food is 'many' because it exists for the sake of another. Whatever exists for the sake of another has been brought into being by him, and whatever has been brought into being consists of parts that have been brought together.

96 Taitt. Bh. III.x.5-6.

97 Bh.G. XVIII.49.

98 Śaṅkara's 'sadyo-mukti' is broadly speaking equivalent to the 'jīvan-mukti' of his followers (liberation in life). Indeed Śaṅkara uses the term jīvan-mukta, but only once in the probably authentic works (Bh.G.Bh. VI.27).

99 Bh.G.Bh. XVIII.49.

100 I.e. not ritualistic action alone, according to the common meaning in Shāstrika works.

101 That is, the Gītā phrase 'One who has performed all action' is not to be taken literally, but only means 'one who has a right insight into action'.

102 Bh.G. IV.17, which shows that the context is one of insight or knowledge.

103 Bh.G. IV.16.

104 So that the question of wrong apprehension does not arise.

105 A familiar example used in Indian philosophy is that of slow growth, not recognized as action or change at all, as in 'Two years later Tommy still had the same mop of red hair'.

106 Bh.G. II.25, II.20.

107 Bh.G. IV.16.

108 Which is already itself a superimposition on the Self.

109 Bh.G.Bh. IV.18. The following Extract constitutes the sequel in the Commentary.

110 The reference is to ritualistic action, and the means to it are a home and a sacrificial fire within the household precincts, and insignia such as the sacred thread.

111 I.e. while still a student brahmacārin and not yet a householder. The term 'work' means primarily ritualistic sacrifices offered by a householder, these being considered work *par excellence* because their fruits extend pre-eminently to future lives.

112 The means are house, householder's sacrificial fire, sacred thread, etc.

113 Which teaches that forbidden deeds stain the soul with demerit, which leads inevitably to painful experiences in future lives.

114 Such an interpretation of a Vedic text must be wrong because it would render it redundant, and no Vedic text can be accounted useless.

115 It involves saying that meritorious actions bring demerit.

116 And so redundant, cp. Note 114, above.

117 M.Bh. XIV.46.19 (Anu Gītā).

118 Bh.G. V.8, III.28.

119 Bh.G. IV.20.

120 Implying that there is really no agent or act.

121 Though such renunciates do not perform sacrifice.

122 Bh.G. III.28, IV.18, IV.20, V.8.

123 Cp. Bh.G. XVIII.16.

124 Cp. above, Vol. IV, Chapter X, section 2, Extract 5.

125 Bh.G.Bh. IV.19-24.

126 Cp. Bh.G. IV.18.

127 Buddhi and manas, cp. Vol.III, Chapter VIII, section 3, Extract 4.

128 Bh.G.XIII.31..

129 Bṛhad. IV.iii.18. **Bh.G.Bh. V.13.**

130 On the constituents, cp. above, Vol.II, Chapter V, section 5, Extracts 2 and 6.

131 Bh.G. XIV.23.

132 Bh.G.Bh. XIV.22-25.

133 The term 'parivrājaka' means one who leaves home and wanders about. But Śaṅkara distinguishes two forms of monasticism (parivrājya). Formal monasticism, the assumption of the insignia of a monk with threefold staff, water-pot and sacred thread, represents a discipline that can at best lead to release by stages, as on the indirect path. Śaṅkara's critic Bhāskara followed this path, M.V., 536ff., cp. 257f. The renunciation required by Śaṅkara for the direct path and immediate liberation while yet alive is the inner renunciation of all desires. Cp. Bṛhad. Bh. III.v.1, trans. Mādhavānanda, 338f. See also the present work, above, Vol.V, 134.

134 At Bṛhad. IV.iv.23, 'He who knows thus, having become peaceful, controlled, withdrawn, ascetic and concentrated, sees the Self in himself'.

135 Ritualistic action is thus impossible for him who has realized the Absolute, because it implies caste (birth) and a deity to whom offerings are made.

136 Bṛhad. IV.iv.22.

137 Especially ritualistic action is meant in the present context.

138 This analysis of the potentialities of action, which treats it essentially as ritualistic action, derives from the P.M. It is found at Kṛṣṇa Yajvan, 42. Śaṅkara adopts it at U.S. (verse) XVII.50 and B.S.Bh. I.i.4, trans. Gambhīrānanda,.32. Cp. also Sureśvara N.Sid. I.53 and Mānasollāsa I.25.

139 Bṛhad.Bh. IV.v.15.

140 This passage leads on from that which began above, Vol.V, Chapter XIII, section 2, Extract 9.

141 Bh.G. III.18.

142 The Brāhmaṇa of the Vājasaneya school of the White Yajur Veda, which is the Ś.B., of which the Bṛhad. is the continuation.

143 Bṛhad. I.v.17.

144 Desire for sons and desire for wealth.

145 Bṛhad. III.v.1.

146 Wife, son, spiritual wealth in the form of meditation on the symbolic significance of the various elements of the sacrifice, earthly wealth for procuring the materials for ritual and the performance of the ritual itself.

147 Bṛhad. I.iv.17, III.v.1.

148 One is tempted to wonder if this could be a reference to Maṇḍana Miśra, but the doctrine that the liberated man, though remaining a householder, eats and dresses solely to maintain the body, does not appear to come in the B.Sid.

149 In the Law Books, such as those attributed to Manu, Yājñavalkya, etc.

150 Bṛhad. III.v.1.

151 Bṛhad. IV.iv.23.

152 Śvet. VI.21. The highest stage of life is that of the wandering monk, parivrājaka.

153 Kaivalya 2.

154 Studenthood, retired life in the forest and mendicancy.

155 Cp. above, Vol.IV, Chapter X, section 2, Extract 2.

156 Bṛhad. II.iv.14.

157 *Ibid.*

158 Cp. Ait. I.ii.1.

159 Bṛhad. I.v.16.

160 Bṛhad. IV.iv.22.

161 Found in the Ṛg Veda at Kauṣītaki Upan. II.5.

162 Jābāla 4.

163 This injunction survives in later upanishadic texts, cp. Deussen, *Sechzig Upanishad's*, 700f. (= Kaṭharudra 4)

164 Jābāla 4. Cp. Deussen, *op. cit.*, 709.

165 Īśa 11.

166 Taitt. III.2.

167 Being acts, they depend on the sense of agency, which depends in turn on the confusion of the Self with the not-self. Cp. above, Vol.I, Chapter II, section 3, Extract 1.

168 Ait.Bh. I.1 (introduction).

169 That is, they are insignificant now, but were significant before enlightenment from the 'standpoint of ignorance' that then obtained.

170 One and the same being cannot be agent and object of the same act.

171 The P.M. view, according to which the Veda exists primarily to enjoin ritual which will ensure happiness in the life to come. Such injunctions will only be obeyed by those who know that they have an immortal soul separate from the mortal body.

172 Hence nothing can be accepted or avoided by the enlightened person, as he is not related to the body and hence not related to any other object mediately through that. **B.S.Bh. II.iii.48.**

173 The passage leads on from that which ended above, Vol.IV, 35.

174 Chānd. VIII.xii.1.

175 Cp. above, Vol.IV, 26ff.

176 The only proof offered that the Self undergoes embodiment is that it performed meritorious and vicious acts in previous lives. But this itself would only be possible if it were already embodied. A question-begging argument, like the present one, is one in which the truth of the proof depends on the truth of the thing to be proved, which, by definition, has not yet been proved.

177 The argument can never get started for lack of a firm base anywhere. Sac quotes the present passage from Śaṅkara to refute the question-begging theory of nescience of Vācaspati Miśra, M.V., 559.

178 The king, for instance, might be said to take decisions in council when it was really his chief minister who did so.

179 **B.S.Bh. I.i.4.**

180 The present passage leads on from that which ends above, Vol.V, 216. It is referred to by Maṇḍana as pūrva-pakṣa at B.Sid., 34.

181 Bṛhad. IV.iv.7.

182 Untraced. This sentence is puzzling. If translated literally, as by Deussen and Thibaut, it goes against the context. Ānandagiri and Govindānanda re-interpret the sentence according to the context. Here we follow them, in agreement with Swami Gambhīrānanda.

183 Bh.G. II.54.

184 B.S.Bh. I.i.4.

185 On the Unmanifest Principle, cp. Vol.II, Chapter VI, section 2, Extract 10.

186 Īśa Bh. 6 and 7.

187 At Bṛhad. III.ii.12.

188 Bṛhad. Bh. III.iii.1.

189 Thus those who go to liberation by the indirect path (Chapter XIV, above) are not liberated or enlightened at the death of the body but only at the end of the kalpa.

190 Muṇḍ. III.ii.2.

191 Muṇḍ. III.ii.8. **Chānd. Bh. VI.xv.2.**

192 There is no creation from nothing and no extinction into nothing for the Advaitin. If we burn a piece of paper, nothing is lost from the standpoint of physics — there has just been a change in the pattern of energy. Still, there is a change. In the case of enlightenment there is not even a change, only a new vision. Imagine looking at a newspaper photograph under an immensely powerful microscope. It will become clear that one is looking at black and white blobs, and the objects depicted will disappear from view. In this sense, the world and himself as individual in it disappear for the enlightened person in the light of a clearer perception of reality. Even the image of the extinction of a flame is only meant to illustrate 'extinction' in this sense.

193 M.Bh. XII.239.34, G.P. Ed. Vol.III, 584.

194 On the expression 'name and form', see above, Vol.II, 136ff.

195 We have seen how and why the gods place obstacles in the path of the serious spiritual enquirer above, Vol.V, Chapter XII, section 1, Extract 2.

196 Muṇḍ. Bh. III.ii.6-7.

197 Ait. II.i.5.

198 Ait. Bh. II.i.6.

199 Cp. above, Vol.V, Chapter XII, section 3, Extract 17.

200 Cp. above, Vol.V, Chapter XII, section 1, Extract 20, *ad fin.*

201 Kaṭha II.7 (or I.ii.7).

202 Ait. II.i.5, Bṛhad. I.iv.10.

203 Bh.G. VI.40.

204 Bh.G. VI.43.

205 Bh.G. VI.45.

206 Bṛhad. III.viii.8.

207 Chānd. III.xiv.2.

208 Untraced.

209 Vol.IV, 30ff.

210 Probably M.Bh.XII.285.45, G.P. Ed., 636, though the readings are a bit different. **B.S.Bh. III.iv.51-2.**

211 Bṛhad. III.v.1.

212 The word 'bālya' may mean either 'strength' or 'childishness'. In his B.S.Bh., as here, Śaṅkara interprets it as childishness, in his Bṛhad. Bh. cp. 323 below as strength. He was possibly following earlier commentators in each case.

213 Both texts are untraced, but it is always interesting to find Śaṅkara able to quote earlier authors on the state of liberation in life. **B.S.Bh. III.iv.50.**

214 Bh.G. XIII.31.

215 The Vaiśeṣikas held that to be distinct was to be totally distinct. Cp. Praśastapāda, 321ff, trans. Ganganath Jhā, 671ff. Each soul has an 'ultimate particularity' or 'fundamental distinction' whereby it differs from all other souls and from God. The Vaiśeṣikas claim that these 'distinctions' are perceptible to yogis (cp. Frauwallner, G.I.P., Vol. II., 247), but Śaṅkara maintains that their existence has never been proved.

216 **Bh.G.Bh. V.19.**

217 Cp. above, Vol.V, Chapter XIII, section 2, Extracts 20 and 21, and Vol. I, Chapter II, section 3, Extract 1.

218 At B.S.Bh. III.iv.20 Śaṅkara argues that becoming a monk is the subject of an injunction, as also are the subsidiary disciplines that go with this state, such as śama, etc.

219 **U.S. (verse) XVIII.226-32.** Two of the verses are reproduced at Sureśvara, N.Sid. IV.65,66.

220 The use of this term here reflects the Vijñāna Vāda terminology of the fourth book of the G.K. on which Śaṅkara is here commenting. On the hypothesis of Professor Hacker, the G.K.Bh. might well be an early work of Śaṅkara, *Kleine Schriften*, 222.

221 Speaking from the standpoint of ultimate truth, Gauḍapāda and Śaṅkara deny that the mind either comes into being or undergoes changes. G.K.Bh. IV.28, cp. above, Vol.IV, Chapter XI, section 5, Extract 8, *ad fin.*

222 **G.K.Bh. IV.76-80.**

223 Bṛhad. III.viii.10, IV.iv.23.

224 Bh.G. III.18.

225 G.K.Bh. IV.83.

226 Gauḍapāda and Śaṅkara borrow the Buddhist term lokottara, but interpret it to refer to the state of dreamless sleep.

227 I.e. as 'massed consciousness' in dreamless sleep.

228 Is, is not, is and is not, neither is nor is not.

229 Cp. Bṛhad. III.v.1, also B.S.Bh. III.iv.47-50. See also Note 212, above.

230 The term really means 'from the Mahāyāna', see V.S. Bhattācharya, Ā.Ś.G., 199f.

231 M.Bh.XII.239.23-4, G.P. Ed. Vol.III, 564.

232 G.K.Bh. IV.85-98.

233 Cp. Bṛhad. III.v.1, the passage at present under comment, 'Having known this Self, the true Brahmins renounce...'

234 Kena II.4, Muṇḍ. III.ii.4.

235 Read ātmājñāna.

236 Bṛhad. III.v.1, the passage under comment.

237 Bṛhad. Bh. III.v.1.

238 The 'śānta' and 'dānta' of this Bṛhad. text under comment are the origin of the familiar couple 'śama' and 'dama', cp. above, Vol.V, Chapter XII, Note 330. Śama means inner control of the mind, dama control of the external senses. Sureśvara B.B.V. IV.iv.1203 commends Śaṅkara for mentioning dānta before śānta, against the letter of the text, since one has to acquire control of the senses before one can control the mind. We know that the six requisites beginning with internal restraint (śama) were referred to by a standard formula before

Śaṅkara's day, on account of the use of the phrase 'śama-damādi' at B.S. III.iv.27, cp. above, Vol.V, Chapter XIII, section 3, Extract 17.

239 Bṛhad. III.v.1.

240 'Brahma-loka' in the sense in which the term is used in the Bṛhad. — namely, to mean the realm of the Absolute, the realm that is the Absolute.

241 Bṛhad. Bh. IV.iv.23.

LIST OF GENERAL ABBREVIATIONS

In principle, works are referred to under their authors' names throughout the Notes, and the abbreviations occasionally used to distinguish between an author's different works should not cause any difficulty. Except for the two entries R.T. and Sac, the following list comprises those abbreviations that are used independently of any author's name. The list excludes the names of Upanishads on which Śaṅkara wrote commentaries, which are listed under his name in the Bibliography and readily identifiable there.

A.B.O.R.I.	*Annals of the Bhandarkar Oriental Research Institute*, Poona
Ā.D.S.	*Āpastamba Dharma Sūtra*
Ā.S.S.	Ānanda Āśrama Sanskrit Series, Poona
Ā.Ś.S.	*Āpastambīyam Śrauta Sūtram*, Mysore University
A.V.	*Atharva Veda*
B.B.V.	*Bṛhadāraṇyakopaniṣad Bhāṣya Vārtika* (Sureśvara)
B.B.V.S.	*Bṛhadāraṇyakopaniṣad Bhāṣya Vārtika Sāra* (Vidyāraṇya)
Bh.	*Bhāṣya* (i.e. Commentary)
Bh.G.	*Bhagavad Gītā*
Bh.G.Bh.	*Bhagavad Gītā Bhāṣya* (Śaṅkara)
B.S.	*Brahma Sūtras*
B.S.Bh.	*Brahma Sūtra Bhāṣya* (Śaṅkara)
B.Sid.	*Brahma Siddhi* (Maṇḍana Miśra)
C.P.B.	*The Central Philosophy of Buddhism* (T.V. Murti)
G.I.P.	*Geschichte der indischen Philosophie* (E. Frauwallner)

G.K.	*Gauḍapāda Kārikās*, included in Gambhīrānanda, *Eight Upanishads*, Vol.II
G.K.Bh.	*Gauḍapāda Kārikā Bhāṣya*
G.O.S.	Gaekwad's Oriental Series, Baroda
G.P.	Gītā Press, Gorakhpur
I.H.Q.	*Indian Historical Quarterly*
I.I.J.	*Indo-Iranian Journal*
J.A.	*Journal Asiatique*
J.A.O.S.	*Journal of the American Oriental Society*
J.B.O.O.S.	*Journal of the Bihar and Orissa Oriental Society*
J.O.I.B.	*Journal of the Oriental Institute*, Baroda
J.O.R.M.	*Journal of Oriental Research*, Madras University
J.R.A.S.B.B.	*Journal of the Royal Asiatic Society of Great Britain and Ireland, Bombay Branch*
J.U.B.	*Jaiminīya Upanishad Brāhmaṇa*
M.Bh.	*Mahābhārata* G.P. Mūla-mātra Ed., 4 Vols.
M.K.	*Mādhyamika* (or *Mūlamādhyamika*) *Kārikās* of Nāgārjuna
M.R.V.	*Māṇḍūkya Rahasya Vivṛtiḥ* Saccidānandendra Svāmin
M.V.	*Method of the Vedanta* Saccidānandendra Svāmin
N.S.	Nirṇaya Sāgara Press
N.Sid.	Naiṣkarmya Siddhi (Sureśvara)
N.Sū.	*Nyāya Sūtras*
P.D.	*Pañcadaśī* (Vidyāraṇya)

P.E.W.	*Philosophy East and West*, Honolulu
P.M.	Pūrva Mīmāṃsā
P.P.	*Pañcapādikā* Padmapāda
R.T.	Rāma Tīrtha (17th century commentator)
R.V.	*Ṛg Veda*
Sac.	Saccidānandendra Svāmin (modern author d.1975)
Ś.B.	*Śatapatha Brāhmaṇa*
S.B.E.	Sacred Books of the East Series, Oxford University Press, Oxford (reprinted by Motilal Banarsidas, Delhi)
Ś.Ś.P.B.	*Śuddha-Śaṅkara-Prakriyā-Bhāskara* (Saccidānandendra Svāmin)
Ś.V.	*Mīmāṃsā Śloka Vārtika* (Kumārila Bhaṭṭa)
T.S.	*Taittirīya Saṃhitā*
T.B.V.	*Taittirīya Bhāṣya Vārtika* (Sureśvara)
U.S.	*Upadeśa Sāhasrī* (Śaṅkara)
V.P.	*Viṣṇu Purāṇa*
V.V.S.	*Viśuddha Vedānta Sāra* (Saccidānandendra Svāmin)
W.Z.K.S.O.	*Wiener Zeitschrift für die Kunde Süd- und Ostasiens*
Y.D.	*Yukti Dīpikā*
Y.S.	*Yoga Sūtras* (Patañjali)
Z.D.M.G.	*Zeitschrift der Deutschen Morgenländischen Gesellschaft*
Z.I.I.	*Zeitschrift für Indologie und Iranistik*
Z.M.R.	*Zeitschrift für Missionswissenschaft und Religionswissenschaft*, Münster/Westfalen

BIBLIOGRAPHY

I. Texts of Śaṅkara

Aitareya Upaniṣad Bhāṣya, G.P. Ed., n.d. See Venkataramiah, D.

Bhagavad Gītā Bhāṣya (Bh.G.Bh.), ed. D.V. Gokhale, Poona, 1931. See also Śāstrī, A. Mahādeva.

Brahma Sūtra Bhāṣya (B.S.Bh.), ed. with the *Ratna Prabhā Ṭīkā* of Govindānanda, the *Nyāya Nirṇaya Ṭīkā* of Ānandagiri and the *Bhāmatī* of Vācaspati, by Mahādeva Śāstrī Bākre, N.S. Press, Bombay, 1934. See also S.S. Sūryanārāyaṇa Śāstrī.

Bṛhadāraṇyaka Upaniṣad Bhāṣya, ed. H.R. Bhāgavat, Ashtekar Company, Second Ed., Poona, 1928. Also consulted: Ā.S.S. Ed. of the same work, with the *Ṭīkā* of Ānandagiri.

Chāndogya Upaniṣad Bhāṣya, Ā.S.S. Ed., Poona, 1890. Also consulted: H.R. Bhāgavat's Ed., Ashtekar Co., Poona, 1927.

Īśa Upaniṣad. See Saccidānandendra, *Īśāvāsya*. Also consulted: G.P. Ed. of Śaṅkara's *Īśa Bhāṣya*.

Kāṭhaka (usually referred to as *Kaṭha*) *Upanishad*, ed. with Shri Shaṅkara's Commentary and Sanskrit Notes by Saccidānandendra Svāmin, Adhyātma Prakāśālaya, Holenarsipur, South India, 1962. Also consulted: G.P. Ed. of same work.

Kena Upanishad, with the *Pada* and *Vākya* Commentaries of Shri Shaṅkara, ed. with Sanskrit Notes by Saccidānandendra, Holenarsipur, 1959. Also consulted: G.P. Ed.

Māṇḍūkya Upaniṣad and Gauḍapāda Kārikā Bh.(G.K.Bh.), G.P.Ed., n.d.

Muṇḍaka Upanishad, ed. with Shri Shaṅkara's Commentary and Sanskrit Notes by Saccidānandendra, Holenarsipur, 1960. Also consulted: G.P. Ed.

Praśna Upaniṣad Bhāṣya, G.P.Ed., n.d.

Taittirīya Upaniṣad. See Sac, *Taittirīya Upanishad Shikshāvallī* and *Ānandavallī-Bhṛguvallī*, with Shaṅkara's Commentary and Editor's Notes and Commentary. Also consulted: G.P. Ed. of *Taittirīya Bhāṣya*.

Upadeśa Sāhasrī with gloss of Rāmatīrtha, ed. D.V. Gokhale, Bombay, 1917. Also consulted: *Upadeśa Sāhasrī* with Hindi trans. of Munilāla, Banaras, 1954. See also Jagadānanda, Mayeda and Alston.

Vivaraṇa on the *Adhyātma Paṭala* of the *Āpastamba Dharma Sūtra* in H.R. Bhāgavat, *Minor Works of Śrī Śaṅkarācārya*, 2nd Ed., 1952 (422ff).

(Attributed) *Vivaraṇa* on *Yoga-Bhāṣya* of Vyāsa on Patañjali's *Yoga Sūtras*, Madras Government Oriental Series, 1952.

For TRANSLATIONS: see under Alston, Deussen, Gambhīrānanda, Hacker, Jagadānanda, Jhā, Leggett, Mādhavānanda, Mayeda, Nikhilānanda, Śāstrī, A.M., Thibaut and Venkataramiah.

II. List of other authors and works quoted

('trans.' denotes English translation unless otherwise stated.)

ABHINAVAGUPTA, *Īśvara Pratyabhijñā Vimarśinī*, 2 vols, Bombay, 1919 and 1921.

AITAREYA ĀRAṆYAKA: see Keith, A.B.

AITAREYA BRĀHMAṆA: ed. Aufrecht, Bonn, 1879.

ALSTON, A.J. (trans.), *The Thousand Teachings of Śaṅkara*, Shanti Sadan, London, 1990.

— , *Realization of the Absolute*, Shanti Sadan, London, 2nd. Ed. 1971.

ĀNANDABODHENDRA: see *Yoga Vāsiṣṭha*.

BIBLIOGRAPHY

ĀNANDAGIRI: standard sub-commentaries (ṭīkā) on Śaṅkara's commentaries and Sureśvara's Vārttikas consulted in Ā.S.S. Ed.

ĀNANDAPŪRṆA, *Nyāya Kalpa Latikā*, ṭīkā on B.B.V., Tirupati, Vols.I and II, 1975.

ANANTAKṚṢṆA ŚĀSTRĪ (ed.), *Two Commentaries on the Brahma Siddhi*, Madras, 1963. (Being the *Bhāvaśuddhi* of Ānandapūrṇamuni and the *Abhiprāya Prakāśikā* of Citsukha).

ANNAMBHAṬṬA, *Tarka Saṅgraha*, ed. and trans. Athalye, 2nd ed., Bombay, 1930.

ĀPA DEVA, *Mīmāṃsā Nyāya Prakāśa*, ed. (with comm.) V. Abhyankar, Poona, 1937. Ed. and trans. F. Edgerton, New Haven (Yale), 1929.

ĀPASTAMBA DHARMA SŪTRA: See Cinnaswāmī Śāstrī, Bühler, and Bhāgavat, *Minor Works*.

ĀRYA DEVA, *The Catuḥśataka*, ed. V. Bhattacharya, Calcutta, 1931.

ASHTEKAR: see Bhāgavat, H.R.

ĀTMĀNANDA, Swāmī, *Śaṅkara's Teachings in his own Words*, Bombay, 2nd. Ed., 1960.

AUGUSTINE, St., *Confessions*, trans. Sir Tobie Matthew, Loeb Ed. London, 1923.

— , *De Trinitate*, text and French trans. Mellet, Desclée de Brouwer, 2 vols, 1955.

BELVALKAR, S.K., *Lectures on Vedānta Philosophy*, Part I, Poona, 1929.

— , *The Brahma Sūtras of Bādarāyaṇa*, Poona, 2 vols, 1923 and 1924.

BERGAIGNE, A., *La religion Védique* (3 volumes), Paris, 1883.

BHĀGAVAT, H.R., *Upaniṣadbhāṣyam* (of Śaṅkara) Vols I and II, Ashtekar Company, Poona, 1927 and 1928.

— , *Minor Works of Śrī Śaṅkarācārya*, Poona, 2nd Ed. 1952.

BHĀMATĪ: See Śaṅkara, *Brahma Sūtra Bhāṣya*.

BHĀRAVI, *Kirātārjunīyam*, ed. with Mallinātha's comm. and Hindi trans., Śobhita Miśra, Banaras, 1952.

BHARTṚHARI, *Vākyapadīya*, complete text ed. K.V. Abhyankar and V.P. Limaye, Poona, 1965.

BHĀSKARA, *Brahma Sūtra Bhāṣya*, Banaras, 1915.

BHATT, G.P., *Epistemology of the Bhāṭṭa School of Pūrva Mīmāmsā*, Varanasi, 1962.

BHATTACHARYA, V.S., *Āgama Śāstra of Gauḍapāda*, Calcutta, 1943, (Abbreviated Ā.Ś.G.).

BIARDEAU, M., *La définition dans la pensée indienne*, J.A., 1957, 371-384.

— , (Contribution on Indian philosophy to) *Encyclopédie de la Pléiade, Histoire de la philosophie*, I, Paris, 1969.

— , *La philosophie de Maṇḍana Miśra*, Paris, 1969.

— , *Quelques réflexions sur l'apophatisme de Śaṅkara*, I.I.J., 1959, 81-100.

— , *Théorie de la connaissance et philosophie de la parole dans le brahmanisme classique*, Paris and the Hague, 1964.

— , *La démonstration du Sphoṭa par Maṇḍana Miśra*, Pondichéry, 1958.

BOETZELAER, J.M. van, *Sureśvara's Taittirīyopaniṣad Bhāṣyavārttika*, Leiden, 1971.

BÖHTLINGK, O., *Sanskrit-Wörterbuch*, 3 vols, St Petersburg, 1879-89, reprinted Graz, 1959.

BUDHAKAR, G.V., '*Is the Advaita of Śaṅkara Buddhism in Disguise*?', Quarterly Journal of the Mythic Society, Bangalore, several parts, *incipit* Vol. XXIV, 1933: 1-18, 160-176, 252-265, 314-326.

BÜHLER, G., Eng. trans. of *Āpastamba Dharma Sūtra*, S.B.E.

BUITENEN, J.A.B. van and DEUTSCH, E., *A Source Book of Advaita Vedānta*, Hawaii, 1971.

CAMMANN, K., *Das System des Advaita nach der Lehre Prakaśātmans*, Wiesbaden, 1965.

CANDRAKĪRTI: see Nāgārjuna.

CHATTERJI, S.K., *Indo-Aryan and Hindi*, 2nd Ed., Calcutta, 1960, reprinted 1969.

CHATTOPADHYAYA, D.P., *History of Indian Philosophy*, New Delhi, 1964.

CINNASWĀMĪ ŚĀSTRĪ (Ed.) *Āpastamba Dharma Sūtra*, Banaras,1932.

CITSUKHA, *Abhiprāya Prakāśikā* (Comm. on Maṇḍana's *Brahma Siddhi)*, see Anantakṛṣṇa Śāstrī.

CRESSON, A., *Les courants de la pensée philosophique française*, Vol. 2, Paris, 1927.

CURTIUS, G., *Principles of Greek Etymology*, trans. A.S. Wilkins, London, two vols, 1875 and 1876.

DAKṢIṆĀMŪRTI STOTRA, ed. A. Mahādeva Śāstrī and K. Raṅgācārya with Sureśvara's *Mānasollāsa* and explanatory ṭīkās by Svayamprakāśa and Rāmatīrtha, Mysore Oriental Library Publications, 6, 1895.

DAṆḌIN, *Daśakumāra Carita*, ed. and trans. M.R. Kale, 3rd Ed., Bombay, 1925, reprinted Delhi, 1966.

DARŚANODAYA: see Lakshmīpuram Srīnivāsāchār.

DAS GUPTA, S.N., *History of Indian Philosophy*, Vol. V, Cambridge, 1955.

DE, S.K., *Aspects of Sanskrit Literature*, Calcutta, 1959.

DEUSSEN, P., *Erinnerungen an Indien*, Kiel and Leipzig, 1904.

—, *The Philosophy of the Upanishads*, trans. Geden, 1906, reprinted New York, 1966.

—, *Sechzig Upanishad's des Veda*, Leipzig, 3rd Ed. 1921, reprinted Darmstadt, 1963.

— , *Die Sūtra's des Vedānta*, Leipzig, 1887, reprinted Hildesheim, 1966.

— , *The System of the Vedānta*, Chicago, 1912. Abbreviated D.S.V.

— , and Strauss, O., *Vier Philosophische Texte des Mahābhāratam*, Leipzig, 1906.

DEUTSCH, E., *Advaita Vedānta*, Honolulu, 1969. See also van Buitenen, J.A.B.

DEVARAJA, N.K., *An Introduction to Śaṅkara's Theory of Knowledge*, Delhi, 1962.

DEVASTHALI, G., *Mīmāṃsā*, Vol. I, Bombay, 1959.

— , *Śaṅkara's Indebtedness to Mīmāṃsā*, J.O.I.B., 1951-2, 23-30.

DHARMAKĪRTI, *Pramāṇa Vārttikam*, ed. Dvārikādāsa Śāstrī, Varanasi, 1968. See also Prajñākara Gupta.

DĪGHA NIKĀYA, ed. Rhys Davids and Carpenter, Vol. II, Pali Text Society, London, 1966 (reprint).

DOWSON, J., *A Classical Dictionary of Hindu Mythology*, reprinted London, 1968.

ECKHART, Meister, *Sermons and Treatises*, ed. and trans. M. O'C. Walshe, Vol. II, Watkins, London, 1981.

EDGERTON, F., *Buddhist Hybrid Sanskrit Grammar and Dictionary*, Yale University, 1953, two vols. Reprinted Delhi 1970 and 1972.

FOUCHER, A., *Le Compendium des Topiques*, Paris, 1949.

FRAUWALLNER, E., *Geschichte der indischen Philosophie*, Vols I and II, Vienna, 1953 and 1956. Abbreviated G.I.P.

— , *Materialien zur ältesten Erkenntnislehre der Karma-mīmāṃsā*, Vienna, 1968.

— , *Die Philosophie des Buddhismus*, Berlin, 1958.

GAIL, A., *Bhakti im Bhāgavata Purāṇa*, Wiesbaden, 1969.

GAMBHĪRĀNANDA, Swāmī (trans.), *Brahma-Sūtra Bhāṣya of Śaṅkar-ācārya*, Calcutta, 1965.

— , (trans.) *Chāndogya Upaniṣad with the Commentary of Śaṅkarācārya*, Calcutta, 1983.

—, (trans.) *Eight Upaniṣads with the Commentary of Śaṅkarācārya*, Calcutta, two vols 1957 and 1958. (Vol.I comprises Īśa, Kena, Kaṭha, Taitt; Vol.II, Ait., Muṇḍ., Māṇḍ.with G.K. and Praśna.)

GARBE, R., *Die Sāṅkhya Philosophie*, Leipzig, 1917.

GAUTAMA DHARMA SŪTRA, trans. G. Bühler, S.B.E.

GELDNER, K.F., *Der Rigveda*, Harvard, four vols, 1951-57.

GHATE, V. S., *Le Vedānta*, Paris, 1918.

GLASENAPP, H. von, *Entwicklungsstufen des indischen Denkens*, Halle, 1940.

—, *Die Philosophie der Inder*, Stuttgart, 1949 (abbreviated as '*Einführung*')

—, *Stufenweg zum Göttlichen*, Baden Baden, 1948.

GOKHALE, D.V. see under Texts of Śaṅkara, *Bhagavad Gītā Bhāṣya* and *Upadeśa Sāhasrī*..

GONDA, J., *Inleiding tot het Indische Denken*, Antwerp, 1948.

—, *Les religions de l'Inde*, Vols I and II, Paris, 1953 and 1956.

GOUGH, A.E. see *Vaiśeṣika Sūtras*.

GOVINDĀNANDA: see Śaṅkara, *Brahma Sūtra Bhāṣya*.

GROUSSET, R., *Les philosophies indiennes*, two vols, Paris, 1931.

HACKER, P. Most of Paul Hacker's important articles on Advaita Vedanta were assembled in *Kleine Schriften* (see below). These can now be read in English translation in *Philology and Confrontation*, ed. and trans. Wilhelm Halbfass, State University of New York Press, 1995.

— , *Eigentümlichkeiten der Lehre und Terminologie Śaṅkaras*, Z.D.M.G., 1950, 246ff. (Halbfass, 57ff).

—, *Die Lehre von den Realitätsgraden im Advaita-Vedānta*, Z.M.R., 1952, 277ff. (Halbfuss, 137ff).

— , *Jayanta Bhaṭṭa und Vācaspati Miśra, ihre Zeit und ihre Bedeutung für die Chronologie des Vedānta* included in *Beiträge... Walter Schubring dargebracht* (see Schubring) 160-169.

— , *Kleine Schriften*, herausgegeben von L. Schmithausen, Wiesbaden, 1978.

— , *Prahlāda*, Wiesbaden, 1960.

— , *Śaṅkara der Yogin und Śaṅkara der Advaitin*, W.Z.K.S.O. 1968/1969, 119ff. (Halbfass, 101ff).

— , *Śaṅkarācārya and Śaṅkarabhagavatpāda*, New Indian Antiquary, April-June 1947. Preferably consulted in the corrected version in *Kleine Schriften*, 41ff. (Halbfass, 41ff).

— , *Untersuchungen über Texte des frühen Advaita Vāda*, I, Wiesbaden, 1951. (abbreviated 'Texte').

— , *Upadeshasāhasrī, Gadyaprabandha* (Prose Section) übersezt und erläutert, Bonn, 1949.

—, *Vedānta Studien* I, Die Welt des Orients, Wuppertal, 1948, 240.

—, *Vivarta*, Wiesbaden, 1953.

HALBFASS, W. (ed. and trans.), *Philology and Confrontation*, State University of New York Press, 1995. (See above, under Hacker)

HAUER, J.W., *Der Yoga*, Stuttgart, 1958.

HAZRA, R.C., *Studies in the Purāṇic Records*, Dacca, 1940.

HEIMANN, B., *Studien zur Eigenart indischen Denkens*, Tübingen, 1930.

HIRIYANNA, M., *Essentials of Indian Philosophy*, London, 1949.

—, *Outlines of Indian Philosophy*, London, 1932.

—, *Indian Philosophical Studies*, Vol. 1, Mysore, 1957.

HUME, R.E., *The Thirteen Principal Upanishads*, 2nd Edition of 1931, reprinted Madras (O.U.P.), 1958.

INGALLS, Daniel H.H., *Śaṅkara on the Question 'Whose is Avidyā?'* in P.E.W. 1953, 68ff.

— , *Śaṅkara's Arguments against the Buddhists*, in P.E.W., 1954, 291-316.

ĪŚVARA KṚṢṆA, *Sāṅkhya Kārikās* with *Tattvakaumudi* Commentary of Vācaspati Miśra, text and trans. Gaṅgānātha Jhā, ed. H.D. Sharma, Poona, 1934.

IYER, K.A. Subramania, *Bhartṛhari*, Poona, 1969.

JACOB, Col. G.A., *A Handful of Popular Maxims*, in three Parts, Bombay, 1900, 1902 and 1904.

—, *A Concordance to the Principal Upanishads and Bhagavad Gītā*, 1891, re-issued Delhi, 1963.

— see also under Sadānanda and Sureśvara.

JAGADĀNANDA, Svāmī, *A Thousand Teachings* (the *Upadeśa Sāhasrī* of Śaṅkara), text and trans., Madras, 2nd Ed. 1949.

JAIMINI: see under Śabara.

JASPERS, K., *The Way to Wisdom*, London, 1951.

JAYA DEVA, *Gītagovinda Kāvyam*, ed. Nārāyaṇa Rāma Ācārya, Bombay, 9th Ed., 1949.

JHĀ, Gaṅgānātha, *Pūrva Mīmāṃsā in its Sources*, Banaras, 1942.

— , *Chāndogya Upanishad and Śrī Śaṅkara's Commentary* (2 volumes), Madras, 1899

— see also under Īśvara Kṛṣṇa, Kumārila Bhaṭṭa, Śabara, Praśastapāda.

JHALAKĪKARA, B.J., *Nyāya Kośa*, Bombay, 3rd Ed., 1928.

JOHNSTON, E.H., *Early Sāṅkhya*, London, 1937.

JOSHI, L.M., *Studies in the Buddhistic Culture of India*, Delhi, 1967.

JOŚĪ, T.L. (= Jośi, Tarkatīrtha Lakṣmaṇaśāstrī), *Vaidika Saṃskṛti kā Vikāsa* (Hindi trans. from the Marathi), Bombay, 1957.

—, *Dharma Kośa Upaniṣat Kāṇḍa*, Wai (Maharashtra), 1950.

KAṆĀDA: see Vaiśeṣika Sūtras.

KAVIRĀJ, Gopināth, *Bhūmikā* (Introduction to Acyuta Grantha Mālā Ed. of Śaṅkara's B.S.Bh.), Banaras, 1937.

KEITH, A.B. (ed. and trans.), *Aitareya Āraṇyaka*, Oxford, 1909.

—, *A History of Sanskrit Literature*, Oxford, 1920.

—, *The Karma-Mīmāṃsā*, Calcutta, 1921.

—, *The Sāṃkhya System*, Calcutta, 1924.

—, (trans.) *Taittirīya Saṃhitā*, Harvard Oriental Series, 2 vols, 1914.

KṚṢṆA MIŚRA (ed. and trans.), *Prabodha Candrodaya*, Sita Krishna Nambiar, Delhi, 1971.

KṚṢṆA YAJVAN, *Mīmāṃsā-Paribhāṣā*, text and trans. Mādhavānanda, Calcutta, 1948.

KULLŪKA: see under Manu Smṛti.

KUMĀRILA BHAṬṬA, *Mīmāṃsā Śloka Vārttika* (abbreviated Ś.V.), Banaras, 1898-1899; trans. Gaṅgānātha Jhā, Calcutta, 1900-1908.

—, *Tantra Vārttika*, ed. Gangādhara Shāstrī, Benares, 1882-1903; trans. Gaṅgānātha Jhā, Bibliotheca Indica, Calcutta, 1903-24.

KUNJUNNI RAJA, K., *The Date of Śaṅkarācārya and Allied Problems*, Brahma Vidyā (= Adyar Library Bulletin) Vol. 24, 1960, 125-48.

—, *Indian Theories of Meaning*, Adyar, Madras, 1963.

KŪRMA PURĀṆA, Bombay, 1927.

LACOMBE, O., *L'Absolu selon le Védanta*, Paris, 1937.

LAKSHMĪPURAM SRĪNIVĀSĀCHĀR, *Darśanodaya*, Mysore, 1933.

LEGGETT, T., *The Chapter of the Self* (translation and exposition of Śaṅkara's *Vivaraṇa on Praśna I, Paṭala 8 of Āpastamba Dharma Sūtra)*, London, 1978.

LEHMANN, A., *Aberglaube und Zauberei*, 3rd Ger. Ed. Stuttgart, 1925.

MĀDHAVĀNANDA, SVĀMĪ (trans.), *The Bṛhadāraṇyaka Upanishad with the Commentary of Śaṅkarācārya*, Calcutta, 6th Ed. 1985.

MADHUSŪDANA, see Sarvajña Muni.

MĀGHA, *Śiśupālavadham*, Chowkamba Vidyā Bhavan, Banaras,1955.

MAHĀBHĀRATA: G.P. Ed. (Mūlamātra). Also consulted, critical ed. V.S. Sukthankar, Poona, 1933-72. See also Deussen and Strauss.

MAHADEVAN, T.M.P., *Gauḍapāda*, Madras, 1952.

—, (ed.) *Word Index to the Brahma-Sūtra Bhāṣya of Śaṅkara*, Madras, two Parts, 1971 and 1973.

MAHĀNĀRAYAṆA UPANISHAD, ed. and trans. J. Varenne, Paris, 1960.

MAṆḌANA MIŚRA, *Brahma Siddhi* (abbreviated B.Sid.), ed. Kuppuswami Shastri, Madras, 1937. See also Anantakṛṣna Śāstrī, Biardeau, Schmithausen and Vetter.

MANU SMṚTIḤ, with Comm. of Kullūka, Bombay, 1902.

MATICS, Marion L., *Entering the Path of Enlightenment*, London, 1970. See also Śānti Deva.

MAYEDA, S., *The Authenticity of the Upadeśa Sāhasrī*, J.A.O.S., 1965, No.2, 178-196.

—, *On the Authorship of the Māṇḍūkya and the Gauḍapādīya Bhāsya*, Brahma Vidyā (= Adyar Library Bulletin), 1967-8, 74ff.

—, *On Śaṅkara's Authorship of the Kenopaniṣadbhāṣya*, I.I.J., X (1967), 33-35.

—, *The Authenticity of the Bhagavadgītābhāṣya ascribed to Śaṅkara*, W.Z.K.S.O. IX (1965), 155-197.

—, *Śaṅkara's Upadeśa Sāhasrī*, critically edited with Introduction and Indices, Tokyo, 1973.

—, *A Thousand Teachings, The Upadeśasāhasrī of Śaṅkara*, trans. with Introduction and notes, Tokyo, 1979.

MONIER-WILLIAMS, Sir M., *Sanskrit-English Dictionary*, Oxford, 2nd Ed., 1899.

MORICHINI, G., *Early Vedānta Philosophy* (being a short summary of H. Nakamura's work on that subject) in the periodical *East and West* (Rome), 1960, 33-39.

MÜLLER, Max, *Sacred Books of the East* (abbreviated S.B.E.), Vol. XV, Oxford, 1884. Reprinted Delhi.

MURTI, T.R.V., *The Central Philosophy of Buddhism* (abbreviated C.P.B.), London, 1955.

— , *The Two Definitions of Brahman in the Advaita*, in *Krishna Chandra Bhattacharya Memorial Volume*, Almaner, 1958, 135-150.

MUS, P., *Barabadur*, Hanoi, 1935.

NĀGĀRJUNA, *Mūlamādhyamika Kārikās*, ed. with *Prasannapadā* Commentary of Candrakīrti by de La Vallée Poussin, St. Petersburg, 1903-1913.

NAKAMURA, H., *A History of Early Vedanta Philosophy*, Part One, New Delhi, 1983.

— , *The Vedānta Philosophy as was Revealed in Buddhist Scriptures*, in *Pañcāmṛtam*, Dr. Maṇḍan Miśra (ed.), Delhi, 1968, pp 1-74..

—, *Vedanta Tetsugaku No Hatten (Development of Vedānta Philosophy)*, in *Indian Philosophical Thought, Vol. III*, Tokyo, 1955.

— : see also Morichini, G.

NARENDRADEVA, *Bauddha-Dharma-Darśana*, Patna, 1956.

NIKHILĀNANDA, *The Māṇḍūkyopaniṣad with Gauḍapāda's Kārikā and Śaṅkara's Commentary*, Calcutta, 4th ed., 1955.

OLDENBERG, H., *Die Lehre der Upanishaden und die Anfänge des Buddhismus*, Göttingen, 1923.

— , *Die Weltanschauung der Brāhmaṇa-Texte*, Göttingen, 1919.

ÖPIK, E.J., *The Oscillating Universe*, Mentor Books, N.Y., 1960.

OTTO, R., *Mysticism East and West*, N.Y., 1932.

PADMAPĀDA, see PAÑCAPĀDIKĀ

PADOUX, A., *Recherches sur la symbolique et l'énergie de la parole dans certains textes Tantriques*, Paris, 1964.

PAÑCAPĀDIKĀ (abbreviated P.P.), a work attributed to 'Padmapāda', ed. S. Shrīrāma Shāstrī and S.R. Krishnamūrthi Shāstrī, Madras, 1958. For trans. see Venkataramiah.

PANDEY, S.L., *Pre-Śaṅkara Advaita Philosophy*, Allahabad, 1974.

PĀṆINI, *The Ashṭādhyāyī of Pāṇini*, ed. and trans. S.C. Vasu, two vols, 1891, reprinted Delhi, 1962.

PARAMĀRTHA SĀRA: ed. with *Vivaraṇa* of Rāghavānanda by Pt. Śrī Sūrya Nārāyaṇa Śukla, Banaras, 1933. For trans., see also S.S. Śāstrī, below.

PASSMORE, J., *A Hundred Years of Philosophy*, Pelican Books, Harmondsworth, 1968.

PATAÑJALI, *Yoga Sūtras* with Comms. of Vyāsa and Vācaspati, Bombay, 1892.

—, (trans.) J.H. Woods, Harvard, 1914, reprinted Delhi, 1972.

— : see also Śaṅkara for (attributed) *Vivaraṇa* on Vyāsa's Comm. (Bhāṣya) to *Yoga Sūtras*.

POTTER, Karl, *Bibliography of Indian Philosophies*, Delhi, 1970.

PRAJÑĀKARA GUPTA, *Pramāṇa Vārtika Bhāṣyam*, ed. Rāhula Sāṃkṛtyāyana, Patna, 1953.

PRAKĀŚĀTMAN, *Vivaraṇa*, ed. S. Shrīrāma Shāstrī and S.R. Krishnamūrthi Shāstrī, Madras, 1958. See also Cammann, above.

PRAŚASTAPĀDA, *Praśastapāda-Bhāṣya* (or *Padārthadharma Saṅgraha*), with *Nyāyakandalī* of Shrī Dhara, Banaras, 1895. Eng. trans. Gaṅgānath Jhā, Banaras, 1916.

PŪRVA MĪMĀṂSĀ SŪTRAS: see under Śabara.

RADHAKRISHNAN, Sir S., *Indian Philosophy*, London, two vols, 1927.

—, *The Principal Upanishads*, London, 1953.

RĀGHORĀM, B. Shivprasād: (Publisher) *Hundred and Eight Upanishads*, Banaras, 1938 (Sanskrit text only).

RĀMA DEVA: see Jaiminīya Upanishad Brāhmaṇa.

RĀMĀNUJA, *Śrī Bhāṣya*, ed. Vāsudeva Śāstrī Abhyaṅkar, Bombay, 1914.

RATNAPRABHĀ: see Śaṅkara, *Brahma Sūtra Bhāṣya*.

RENOU, L., *Grammaire et Védanta*, J.A., 1957, 121-132.

RENOU and FILLIOZAT, *L'Inde Classique*, two vols, Paris and Hanoi, 1947 and 1953.

ṚG VEDA, Rig Veda (Abbreviated R.V.): see also Geldner.

— , *Ṛg Veda Saṃhitā*, with Comm. of Sāyana, Vedic Research Institute, Poona, 5 vols 1933-51.

RITTER, H., *Das Meer der Seele*, Leiden, 1955.

RUKMANI, T.S., *Yogasūtra-bhāṣyavivaraṇa of Śaṅkara*, Delhi, 2000.

RŪMĪ, Jalālu'ddīn, *Mathnawī*, trans. R.A. Nicholson, London, Vol.I, 1926.

RÜPING, K., *Studien zur Frühgeschichte der Vedānta Philosophie*, Wiesbaden, 1977.

ŚABARA, Jaimini's *Pūrva Mīmāṃsā Sūtra Bhāṣya*, Calcutta, two vols, 1873 and 1887. Trans. Gaṅgānātha Jhā, G.O.S., 3 vols, 1933, 1934 and 1936. See also Frauwallner.

SACCIDĀNANDENDRA SVĀMIN (abbreviated as Sac.) All Sac's works are published by the Adhyātma Prakāśa Kāryālaya, Holenarsipur, Karnataka, India, unless otherwise stated.

—, *Brahmavidyā Rahasya Vivṛtiḥ*, 1969.

—, *Gītā-Śāstrārtha-Vivekaḥ*, 1965.

—, *Intuition of Reality*, 1973.

—, *Īśāvāsya Upaniṣad* with Śaṅkara's Bhāṣya and author's Sanskrit *ṭīkā* (written under the lay name of Y. Subrahmanya Śarmā), 1937.

—, *Māṇḍūkya Rahasya Vivṛtiḥ*, 1958.

— , *The Method of the Vedanta* (abbreviated M.V.), London, 1989 (Translation by A.J. Alston of *Vedānta Prakriyā Pratyabhijñā*, q.v.).

—, *Misconceptions about Śaṅkara*, 1973.

—, *Śaṅkara's Clarification of certain Vedantic Concepts*, 1969.

— , *Śuddha-Śaṅkara-Prakriyā-Bhāskara* (abbreviated Ś.Ś.P.B.), quoted from Sanskrit Ed. in 3 parts, 1964. Available in English, 3 parts

1965-1968, subtitled *Light on the Vedantic Method according to Śaṅkara.*

— , *Sugamā* (Sanskrit exposition of Śaṅkara's Adhyāsa-bhāṣya), 1955.

—, *Taittirīya Upanishad Shikshāvallī,* ed. with Shaṅkara's Commentary and editor's Sanskrit notes, 1961.

— , *Taittirīya Upanishad Ānandavallī-Bhṛguvallī,* ed. with Shaṅkara's Commentary and editor's *Bhāṣyārtha Vimarśinī* sub-commentary, 1962.

— , *Vedānta Prakriyā Pratyabhijñā*, 1964. For an English translation of this work, see *The Method of the Vedānta*, previous page.

— , *Viśuddha Vedānta Sāra*, 1968. (Abbreviated V.V.S.)

SADĀNANDA, *Vedānta Sāra*, ed. with two commentaries, Col. G.A. Jacob, 5th revised Ed. 1934.

— , text and Eng. trans. Nikhilānanda Svāmin, Calcutta, 1947.

SADĀNANDA YATI, *Advaita Brahma Siddhi*, Calcutta, 1888-90.

ṢAḌVIṂŚA BRĀHMAṆA, ed. K. Klemm, Gütersloh, 1894. Trans. W.B. Bollée, Utrecht, 1956.

SAHASRABUDDHE, M.T., *A Survey of Pre-Śaṅkara Advaita Vedānta*, Poona, 1968.

SĀṄKṚTYĀYANA, Rāhula, *Darśana Dig-Darśana*, Allahabad, 2nd Ed. 1947. (Hindi).

ŚĀNTI DEVA, *Bodhicaryāvatāraḥ*, ed. P.L.Vaidya, Darbhanga, 1960. See also M.L. Matics.

SARVAJÑA MUNI, *Saṅkṣepa Śārīrakam* with the Commentary of Madhusūdana, Banaras, 1924

Sarvajñātman and Sarvajñātma Muni: alternative forms of the above name.

ŚĀSTRĪ: sometimes interchanged with Shāstrī, q.v.

ŚĀSTRĪ, A. Mahādeva, *The Bhagavad-Gītā with the Commentary of*

Śaṅkarācārya, Madras, 1897. Reprinted, Madras, 1977.

— , *Dakshiṇāmūrti Stotra of Śrī Śaṅkarāchārya*, Madras, 3rd Ed., 1978. Contains Sanskrit text and Eng. trans. of the *Mānasollāsa Vārttika* attributed to Sureśvara. See also Dakṣiṇāmūrti Stotra above for Sanskrit edition of text and commentaries.

ŚĀSTRĪ, Maṅgaladeva, *Bhāratīya Saṃskṛti kā Vikāsa*, Part II, *Aupaniṣada Dhārā*, Banaras, 1966. (Hindi).

ŚĀSTRĪ, Rāmānanda Tivārī, *Śrī Śaṃkarācārya kā ācāra darśana*, Allahabad, 1950. (Hindi)

ŚĀSTRĪ, S.S. Sūryanārāyaṇa, *The Paramārtha Sāra of Ādi Śeṣa*, Bombay, 1941.

— and C.K. Rājā, *The Bhāmatī: Catussūtrī*, Adyar, Madras, 1933.

ŚATAPATHA BRĀHMAṆA, trans. Eggeling, S.B.E. (in 5 parts).

SCHMITHAUSEN, L., *Maṇḍana Miśras Vibhrama Vivekaḥ*, Vienna, 1965.

SCHUBRING, W. (Festschrift) *Beiträge zur indischen Philologie... Walther Schubring dargebracht*, Hamburg, 1951.

SHARMA, L.N., *Kashmir Śaivism*, Banaras, 1972.

SHĀSTRĪ : sometimes interchanged with Śāstrī, q.v.

SHASTRI, Hari Prasad: see Vālmīki and Vidyāraṇya.

SILBURN, L., *Instant et Cause*, Paris, 1955.

SOGEN, Yamakami, *Systems of Buddhistic Thought*, Calcutta, 1912.

ŚRĪ HARṢA, *Śrī Harṣa's Plays*, ed. and trans. Bak Kun Bae, Bombay, 1964.

SRĪNIVĀSĀCHĀR: see Lakshmīpuram Srīnivāsāchār.

SRĪNIVĀSĀCHARĪ, P.N., *The Philosophy of Bhedābheda*, Madras, 1934.

STAAL, J.F., *Advaita and Neoplatonism*, Madras, 1961.

STCHERBATSKY, Th., *The Conception of Buddhist Nirvāṇa*, revised and enlarged edition by Jaidev Singh, Bhāratīya Vidyā Prakāśana Edition, Banaras, n.d.

—, *Buddhist Logic*, Vol. II, Leningrad, 1930.

—, *Central Conception of Buddhism*, London, 1923.

—, *La théorie de la connaissance et la logique chez les Bouddhistes tardifs*, Paris, 1926.

STRAUSS, O., *Indische Philosophie*, Munich, 1925. See also Deussen.

SŪRA DĀSA, *Sūra Sāgara*, ed, Vājapeyī, Vārāṇasī, 2 vols, 1953 and 1956.

SUREŚVARA, *Bṛhadāraṇyaka Bhāṣya Vārttikam* (abbreviated B.B.V.) ed. with Ānandagiri's ṭīkā in the Ā.S.S. ed., three vols, Poona, 1892-1894. See also Ānandapūrṇa.

—, (Attributed) *Mānosollāsa*. Commentary on *Dakṣiṇāmūrti Stotra*, q.v.

—, *Naiṣkarmya Siddhi* (abbreviated N.Sid.), ed. with Jñānottama's Commentary, by Col. G.A. Jacob and revised by M. Hiriyanna, Bombay,1925. Trans. by A.J. Alston as *The Realization of the Absolute*, Shanti Sadan, 2nd Ed. 1971.

—, (Attributed) *Pañcīkaraṇa Vārttika* in *Panchīkaraṇam of Shree Shankarāchārya*, Ed. with six comms, Gujarati Printing Press, Bombay, 1930.

—, *The Saṃbandha Vārttika*, text and Eng. trans. T.M.P. Mahadevan, Madras, 1958.

—, *Taittirīya Bhāṣya Vārttika* (abbreviated T.B.V.), Ā.Ś.S. Ed. with ṭīkā of Ānandagiri, 1911. For Eng. trans. see Boetzelaer, above.

TAITTIRĪYA ĀRAṆYAKA, Ā.S.S., Poona, Vol. I, 1926.

TAITTIRĪYA BRĀHMAṆA, ed. Rājendralāl Mitra, Calcutta, 1870.

TAITTTIRĪYA SAṂHITĀ: see Keith.

THIBAUT, G., *The Vedānta Sūtras with the Commentary of Śaṅkarācārya* (= Brahma Sūtra Bhāṣya, B.S.Bh.), Eng. trans., Parts I and II.

TROṬAKA (or Toṭaka), *Śruti Sāra Samuddharaṇa*, Ed. Kevalānanda Svāmin, Ā.S.S. Ed., Poona, 1936.

UDDYOTAKARA, *Nyāya Vārttikam*, ed. Dvivedin and Dravid, Benares, 1916-7.

UI, Hakuju, *Vaiśeṣika Philosophy according to the Daśapadārtha-śāstra* Chinese Text, English translation and notes. Banaras, 1962.

UPĀDHYĀYA, Baladeva, *Śrī Śaṃkarācārya*, Allahabad, 1950. (Hindi).

—, *Śrī-Śaṃkara-Dig-Vijaya*, Sanskrit text with Hindi trans., Hardwar, 1944.

UPĀDHYĀYA, B.S., *Bauddha Darśana tathā anya Bhāratīya Darśana*, 2 vols, Calcutta, 1954 (Hindi).

UPĀDHYĀYA, Rāmajī, *Bhārata kī Saṃskṛti-Sādhanā*, Allahabad, 1967. (Hindi).

VĀCASPATI: see under Texts of Śaṅkara, *Brahma Sūtra Bhāṣya, Bhāmatī sub-commentary*. See also Īśvara Kṛṣṇa.

VAIŚEṢIKA SŪTRAS, with Comm. of Śaṅkara Miśra, ed. and trans. A.E. Gough, Benares, 1873, reprinted New Delhi, 1975.

—, ed. Jīvānanda, Calcutta, 1886.

VALLABHĀCĀRYA, *Aṇu Bhāṣya*, text and *Bālabodhinī*, Commentary, 2 vols, Bombay, 1921 and 1926.

VĀLMĪKI, *The Ramayana of Valmiki* (trans. H.P. Shastri), three vols., London, 2nd revised Ed. of Vol. I, 1962.

VĀSIṢṬHA *Dharma Sūtra*, trans. G. Bühler, S.B.E.

VĀTSYĀYANA, *Nyāya Sūtra Bhāṣya*, Poona, 1939. Eng. trans. Gaṅgānāth Jhā, Poona, 1939.

VENKAṬANĀTHA, *Tattva Muktā Kalāpaḥ* with *Sarvārtha Siddhi* and *Bhāva Prakāśa*, Mysore, Vol. II., 1940.

VENKATARAMIAH, D., *The Pañcapādikā of Padmapāda*, G.O.S., Baroda, 1948.

— , *Aitareyopaniṣad with Śaṅkarācārya's Bhāṣya*, text and Eng. trans., Bangalore, 1934.

VETTER, T., *Maṇḍana Miśra's Brahmasiddhiḥ, Brahmakāṇḍaḥ*,

annotated German trans., Vienna, 1969.

— , *Zur Bedeutung des Illusionismus bei Śaṅkara*, W.Z.K.S.O. 1968/69, 407-423.

—, *Erkenntnisprobleme bei Dharmakīrti*, Vienna, 1964.

VIDYĀRAṆYA, *Bṛhadāraṇyaka Bhāṣya Vārttika Sāra* (B.B.V.S.), Acyuta Grantha Mālā Ed., Banaras, two vols, 1941 and 1943.

— , *Panchadashi* (= Pañcadaśī, abbreviated P.D.), text and trans. by H.P. Shastri, 2nd revised Ed., London, 1965.

VIJÑĀNA BHIKṢU, *Sāṃkhya Pravacana Bhāṣya*, ed. R. Garbe, Cambridge, Mass., 1895.

VIMUKTĀTMAN, *Iṣṭa-Siddhi*, ed. Hiriyanna, G.O.S., Baroda, 1933.

VIṢṆU PURĀṆA: G.P. Ed. with the Hindi trans. of Śrī Munilāla Gupta, 1937.

VIVARAṆA: see Prakaśātman.

VYĀSA: see Patañjali.

WARDER, A.K., *Outlines of Indian Philosophy*, New Delhi, 1971.

WOODS, J.H: see Patañjali.

YĀJÑAVALKYA SMṚTI, with Mitākṣarā Commentary and Hindi trans., Umesh Chandra Pandey, Banaras, 1967.

YAMAKAMI, S: see under Sogen, Y.

YĀSKA, *Nirukti*, Calcutta, 4 vols, 1882-91.

YOGA VĀSIṢṬHA, with the Commentary of Ānandabodhendra, two vols, Bombay, 1937.

YOGA SŪTRAS: see Patañjali.

YUKTI DĪPIKĀ, ed. Ram Chandra Pandeya, Banaras-Delhi, 1967.

INDEX OF ŚAṄKARA'S TEXTS

The Index shows what texts have been used in the Source Book and what place in it they occupy. The list is arranged in alphabetical order of the texts cited. The Extracts usually cover only a part of the texts specified. References are to volumes and pages, all in Arabic numerals. Thus 4.29 = Volume IV p.29.

Adhyātma Paṭala Vivaraṇa, see Āpastamba Dharma Sūtra — Adhyātma Paṭala Vivaraṇa

Aitareya Upanishad Bhāṣya

I.i.1 intro.	5.261, 6.288
I.i.1	2.151
I.i.2	2.87, 2.150
I.ii.1	2.196
I.iii.11	1.210
II.i.1 intro.	1.148, 1.225, 2.217
II.1.6	6.307
III.i.1-2	3.51
III.1.3	2.181

Āpastamba Dharma Sūtra
— Adhyātma Paṭala Vivaraṇa

I.xxii.1	6.100
I.xxii.11	6.259
I.xxii.12-14	5.141

Bhagavad Gītā Bhāṣya

I.1 intro.	2.92, 5.85
II.11 intro.	4.67, 5.119
II.16-17	1.200
II.18	1.126
II.20	2.241
II.21	5.219, 6.225
II.69	5.291
III.1 intro.	4.75
III.3-4	5.86
III.27-28	2.83

Bhagavad Gītā Bhāṣya (cont.)

III.33-34	5.131
IV.6	2.93
IV.11	5.124
IV.18	6.272
IV.19-24	6.276
IV.34	5.308
IV.37-39	5.309
V.1 intro. & 6	5.120
V.13	6.283
V.19	6.313
VI.4	6.104
VII.4	2.77
VIII.11-13	6.170
VIII.17-19	2.166
VIII.23-26	6.43
IX.1-3	5.151
IX.10	2.30, 2.88
X.10-11	5.153
XII.1-5	5.154
XII.3	2.80
XIII.2	1.70
XIII.7-11	5.135
XIII.12	1.146, 1.153
XIII.13	1.153, 5.337
XIII.14	1.209
XIII.18	5.156
XIII.19	2.76
XIII.23	6.238
XIII.26	1.103

Bhagavad Gītā Bhāṣya (cont.)

XIV.3 2.78
XIV.5-13 2.81
XIV.22-25 6.285
XV.1-4 5.14
XV.7 3.22
XV.16 2.79
XVI.1-4, 7-8 & 18 5.138
XVII.14-16 5.143
XVIII.10 5.88
XVIII.14-16 5.3
XVIII.17 2.243
XVIII.18 5.8
XVIII.19 4.228
XVIII.41-48 5.107
XVIII.48 4.224, 4.266
XVIII.49 6.272
XVIII.50 1.122, 5.218
XVIII.51-55 5.147
XVIII.67 intro. 1.69, 3.164, 4.41, 4.66, 5.8, 5.205, 5.210, 5.251
XVIII.67 5.310

Brahma Sūtra Bhāṣya

I.i.1 1.94, 1.125, 4.10, 5.64
I.i.4 1.134, 4.12, 4.17, 4.31, 5.66, 5.209, 5.216, 6.4, 6.299, 6.301
I.i.5 1.233, 3.67
I.i.11 6.5
I.i.12 5.336
I.i.17 3.81
I.i.20 2.94

Brahma Sūtra Bhāṣya (cont.)

I.ii.17 2.191
I.ii.18 2.46
I.ii.21 5.74
I.iii.19 6.226
I.iii.27-28 2.193
I.iii.28 4.119, 5.248
I.iii.29 5.247
I.iii.30 5.246
I.iii.33 2.195, 5.288, 5.322
I.iii.34, 36-38 5.71
I.iii.42 3.107
I.iv.1 2.187, 4.227, 6.96
I.iv.2-3 2.156
I.iv.9 2.151
I.iv.14 2.215
I.iv.18 3.154
I.iv.22 3.64
I.iv.23-7 2.18
II.i.1-3 5.273
II.i.4 5.284
II.i.4-6 2.33
II.1.6 5.203
II.i.7 2.116
II.i.8-9 2.39
II.i.9 2.85, 3.159
II.i.11 5.198
II.i.13-14 2.41
II.i.14 1.110, 1.111, 2.6, 2.11, 2.150, 2.221, 4.92, 5.236
II.i.15 2.117
II.i.16 2.118
II.i.17 2.158
II.i.18 2.119
II.i.22-23 2.7
II.i.24-25 2.22

Brahma Sūtra Bhāṣya (cont.)
II.i.27 2.25
II.i.28 2.84
II.i.30-1 2.29
II.i.32-33 2.31
II.i.34-36 2.62
II.ii.1 4.174
II.ii.1-10 4.200
II.ii.11 4.179, 4.236
II.ii.12 4.241
II.ii.13-16 4.245
II.ii.17 4.251
II.ii.18-27 4.286
II.ii.25 4.178
II.ii.28-31 4.303
II.ii.31 4.328
II.ii.32 4.285
II.ii.33-36 4.345
II.ii.37-41 4.129
II.ii.42-45 4.136
II.iii.6 2.176
II.iii.7 4.271
II.iii.9 1.206
II.iii.16 3.9
II.iii.17 3.10
II.iii.18 3.3
II.iii.29 3.23
II.iii.30-31 3.4
II.iii.32 3.31
II.iii.40 3.46
II.iii.41-47 3.74
II.iii.48 6.297
II.iii.50 3.21, 4.224
II.iii.50-53 4.261
II.iv.6 3.31
II.iv.12-13 3.35
II.iv.14-16 3.36

Brahma Sūtra Bhāṣya (cont.)
II.iv.20 2.10
II.iv.20-21 2.168
III.i.1 5.35
III.i.2 5.37
III.i.6 5.39
III.i.8 5.42
III.i.13-15 5.48
III.ii.3-4 & 6 3.107
III.ii.5 3.83
III.ii.7-9 3.131
III.ii.10 3.162
III.ii.14 5.320
III.ii.17 5.238
III.ii.21 4.109
III.ii.38-41 2.49
III.iii.9 1.89
III.iii.10-13 5.326
III.iii.32 6.255
III.iii.33 5.331
III.iii.53-54 4.181
III.iii.59 6.9
III.iv.8-9 4.13
III.iv.14 6.241
III.iv.15-17 4.15
III.iv.26-27, 33, 36-39 5.111
III.iv.50 6.311
III.iv.51-52 6.307
IV.i.1-2 6.120
IV.i.3 3.84
IV.i.4 6.10
IV.i.5-6 6.12
IV.i.12 6.19
IV.i.13-16 6.247
IV.i.18 5.93
IV.ii.1-8 5.49

Brahma Sūtra Bhāṣya (cont.)
IV.ii.9-11 3.45, 5.55
IV.iii.1-15 6.47
IV.iii.14 2.222, 3.82, 4.48
IV.iv.4 6.230
IV.iv.15-18 6.66
IV.iv.22 6.70

Bṛhadāraṇyaka Upanishad Bhāṣya
I.i.1 intro. 5.12, 5.204
I.ii.1 2.123
I.iii.1 5.18, 5.263
I.iii.9 6.8
I.iv.6 5.283
I.iv.7 1.167, 2.158, 2.221, 4.9, 4.274, 5.65, 5.65, 5.68, 5.222, 5.250
I.iv.8 1.239
I.iv.10 1.108, 1.230, 4.102, 5.5, 5.19, 5.224, 6.243
I.iv.16-17 5.78
I.v.1-2 5.83
I.v.2 5.9, 5.41
I.v.3 3.30, 3.36, 5.246
I.v.20 6.23
I.v.23 6.25
I.v.1 6.177
I.vi.1 2.163, 6.177
II.i.1 5.333
II.i.15 3.6
II.i.17 3.141
II.i.18 3.114
II.i.19 3.142
II.i.20 2.223, 3.68, 4.93,

Bṛhadāraṇyaka Upanishad Bhāṣya (cont.)
II.i.20 5.212, 5.253, 5.340
II.iii.1 1.154
II.iii.2-3 2.185
II.iii.6 1.147, 2.187, 4.96
II.iv.1 5.122
II.iv.5 6.95
II.iv.9 1.200
II.iv.10 2.151
II.iv.11 2.172, 3.29
II.iv.12 3.11
II.v.19 2.89
III.ii.13 4.103
III.iii.1 intro. 4.61, 4.178, 5.89,
III.iii.1 5.321, 6.303
III.iii.1-2 2.189
III.iv.2 1.223
III.v.1 1.107, 6.322
III.vii.2 2.190
III.vii.23 2.48
III.viii.9 2.59
III.viii.12 4.90
III.ix.28 1.241
IV.iii.6 4.184
IV.iii.7 3.58, 3.112, 4.314
IV.iii.9-10 3.118
IV.iii.14 3.113
IV.iii.15 2.242, 3.114
IV.iii.20 1.68, 3.45
IV.iii.21 3.146
IV.iii.22 5.283
IV.iii.30 4.99
IV.iii.32 1.236, 3.152
IV.iv.1-2 5.56
IV.iv.6 1.83, 6.231
IV.iv.20 1.130

Bṛhadāraṇyaka Upanishad Bhāsya (cont.)
IV.iv.22 5.121
IV.iv.23 6.324
IV.iv.25 2.226, 5.337
IV.v.15 5.128, 6.287
V.i.1 1.112, 4.84, 6.171
VI.ii.9 5.40
VI.ii.15 6.45

Chāndogya Upanishad Bhāṣya
I.i.1, intro. 6.7
I.i.1 6.174
III.xix.1 2.154
IV.xv.5 6.33
V.i.15 3.39, 5.334
V.x.1-2 6.35
V.x.3-8 5.22
V.xi.7 & xii.1 5.335
VI.ii.1 2.155, 4.270
VI.ii.1-2 4.338
VI.ii.2 2.134
VI.ii.3 1.205
VI.iii.2 3.15
VI.iii.3 2.168
VI.v.1 3.32
VI.viii.1 3.150
VI.viii.4 1.198
VI.ix.1 - x.2 3.154
VI.xii.1-2 5.156
VI.xiv.1-2 5.303
VI.xiv.3 6.116
VI.xv.2 6.304
VII.i.3 1.149
VII.xxiv.1 1.136, 2.160
VII.xxv.2 6.264
VII.xxvi.2 5.130

Chāndogya Upanishad Bhāṣya (cont.)
VIII.i.1 intro. 4.332
VIII.i.1 6.22
VIII.iii.2-3 3.156
VIII.v.4 2.259
VIII.vi.3 3.158
VIII.xii.3 6.265
VIII.xv.1 5.247, 6.41

Gauḍapāda Kārikā Bhāṣya
see Māṇḍūkya Upanishad — Gauḍapāda Kārikā Bhāṣya

Īśa Upanishad Bhāsya
6-7 6.302
8 3.46

Kaṭha Upanishad Bhāṣya
I.ii.5-6 5.11
I.ii.15-16 6.175
I.iii.12 2.91
I.iii.15 1.199
II.i.1-2 5.126
II.i.3 3.50
II.iii.1 5.10
II.iii.9-11 6.97
II.iii.12-13 1.134
II.iii.16 6.30

Kena Upanishad Bhāṣya
I.1 intro. 5.96
I.2 1.221
I.3 (vākya) 1.124
I.3-4 1.168
II.1-4 5.225
II.4 4.101
III.1 (vākya) 2.54 3.74
IV.5 5.336

Kena Upanishad Bhāṣya (cont.)
IV.8 5.146

Māṇḍūkya Upanishad Bhāṣya
1 2.161
3-6 3.169
7 3.175
8-12 3.188, 6.179

Māṇḍūkya Upanishad — Gauḍapāda Kārikā Bhāṣya
I.2 3.181
I.7 2.86
I.11-16 3.185
I.17 2.230
II.4-9 2.248
II.11-17 2.255
II.17 1.88
II.19 2.84
II.32 1.132
III.3-4 3.22
III.5 4.225, 4.258
III.14 5.339
III.15 2.219
III.16 6.153
III.17 4.177
III.19 2.231
III.24 2.90
III.25 4.79, 5.97
III.26 1.150, 5.338
III.27 1.208
III.28-31 2.247
III.29-33 1.162
III.32-33 5.216
III.34-35 3.160
III.36 1.88
III.37-38 1.171
III.47 1.240

Māṇḍūkya Upanishad — Gauḍapāda Kārikā Bhāṣya (cont.)
IV.1 intro. 5.286
IV.14-23 2.232
IV.24-28 4.328
IV.28 4.333
IV.34-39 2.252
IV.42 2.227
IV.47-52 2.246
IV.58 2.86
IV.76-80 6.314
IV.82-84 1.139
IV.85-98 6.316
IV.87-98 3.191
IV.99 4.285

Muṇḍaka Upanishad Bhāṣya
I.i.4-5 5.75
I.i.6 1.159
I.i.7-8 2.182
I.ii.11 6.40
I.ii.12-13 5.305
II.i.2 2.180
II.i.3 2.172
II.ii.2-4 6.176
II.ii.9-10 1.231
III.i.2 5.301
III.i.5 5.145
III.i.8-9 6.98
III.ii.1-5 5.132
III.ii.6-7 6.305

Praśna Upanishad Bhāṣya
I.9 5.21
IV.5 3.123
IV.9 3.16
V.1-7 6.182

Praśna Upanishad Bhāṣya (cont.)
VI.2 4.333
VI.3 4.175, 4.217
VI.4 2.170

Taittirīya Upanishad Bhāsya
I.i intro. 4.36
I.vi-vii 6.26
I.viii 6.175
I.ix 5.99
I.xi 4.39, 4.57, 5.100, 5.104
II.i. 1.167, 1.188, 2.171, 5.20, 5.222, 6.263
II.ii-II.v 3.40
II.vi 1.203, 2.153
II.vii 1.239
II.viii.i 1.237
II.viii.5 2.160, 3.145, 5.287
III.i 5.144
III.vi 1.238
III.x.5-6 6.267

Upadeśa Sāhasrī (prose)
2-13 5.298
18-19 2.149
20-23 3.7
42 5.262
45-61 1.97
64-74 3.13
86-111 1.211

Upadeśa Sāhasrī (verse)
II.1-3 1.159
III.1-4 1.158
IV 6.241
VII.1-6 1.164, 6.154
VIII.1-6 6.155

Upadeśa Sāhasrī (verse) (cont.)
IX and X 6.155
IX.1 2.172
XI 6.159
XII 1.165, 6.161
XIII 6.162
XIV.1-8 3.57
XV.11-34 3.54
XVI.1-10 3.33
XVI.17-18 1.89
XVI.20-22 3.48
XVI.23-29 4.301
XVI.45-50 4.223
XVI.51-55 4.265
XVII.9-12 2.160
XVII.13-21 2.254
XVII.25-26 3.159
XVII.25-31 2.88
XVIII.3-26 5.292
XVIII.27-31 6.127
XVIII.32-50 3.17
XVIII.51-110 6.128
XVIII.111-117 3.20
XVIII.124-140 6.144
XVIII.141-152 4.326
XVIII.153-157 3.58
XVIII.158-162 5.235
XVIII.163-198 6.137
XVIII.199-205 6.142
XVIII.2O6-214 4.66
XVIII.215-221 5.290
XVIII.226-232 6.313
XIX.13-24 2.238

SELECT INDEX OF NAMES AND CONCEPTS

(References are to volume and page, all by arabic numerals, e.g. 4.39 = Volume IV p.39, 4.325n = Volume IV p. 325 (Note). Page references, unless bracketed, refer to a different aspect of the idea contained in the head-word of the entry, and may be followed by a sub-heading specifying their content. If they are enclosed in brackets and follow immediately after a sub-heading, they refer to further material under that sub-heading. Only a few cross-references are given. It is hoped that the abbreviations will be self-explanatory. Ś = Śaṅkara, s/a means 'see also', qv means 'which see', a semi-colon amidst page-references is sometimes inserted to mark the transition to a new volume.)

A

ābhāsa
(s/a reflection, ābhāsa)
light of consciousness, 3.186
Absolute, the (Brahman)
(s/a bliss, cause and effect, cause (material), knowledge (metaphysical), modification, Self)
actionless but appears to act on account of accident of adjuncts (qv) as instruments, 4.222
as efficient cause, does not resort to instruments, 4.206
associated with bliss, but not with joy, of which there are grades, 5.328ff
Bhartṛprapañca on, 4.81f
called Brahman because greater than all else (5.11), 1.231f
cannot be known through reason, 5.202f
cannot be the subject of any argument by analogy, 5.244
definition of as sac-cid-ānanda not found in Prakāśatman (qv), 5.373n
gross and subtle forms of, 1.154f
how known, (1.108f, 122-172), 1.107
identifiable with Lord (qv), 2.14f
identified with Viṣṇu, 1.13
imperishable because qualitiless, 1.199
is referred to as Consciousness only as a result of adjuncts, 5.228
is knowledge and bliss, 5.228
is without attributes, only appearing to have them through adjuncts, 5.228

Absolute, the (Brahman) cont.
knowable only through Veda, 2.25ff and 29f
knowledge by nature, 1.234
material cause of world, 2.44
material and efficient cause of world, 2.16f
none of the forms of judgement apply to it, 1.140f
not known as an object among objects (5.231), 1.5
partless, changeless, indestructible (2.26ff), 1.203
properly only referred to by negations, 1.147f
reality, knowledge, infinity (5.373n), 1.185ff
revealed in experience as consciousness, 5.232
self-luminous, 1.232f
the ground in and through which manifestation takes place, 1.5
there are a supreme and a lower Absolute, 6.63ff
abstraction, blessed state of (kṣānti), prelude to liberation (qv) 3.194f
acosmic teaching, 2.228-260
action
(s/a deities, ego-sense, enlightened person, knowledge, knowledge (metaphysical), merit and demerit, occult force, prārabdha)
all action preceded by nescience, 5.205f
apparent action of an enlightened person is not action., 4.72
at best an indirect cause of rise of knowledge, 5.103f
can lead to liberation in next life, 6.309
can purify for devotion to knowledge (qv under knowledge), 6.272
cause of action is a psychological defect, 4.131
depends on a gross body, 2.242
depends on knowledge, etc., 5.8
in relation to Sat-kārya-vāda, 2.122f
its factors, 5.3ff and 5.8
its four effects, (6.288), 5.306f
its results do not perish for millions of world-periods, 2.183f
karmic consequences of all action burned up by metaphysical knowledge (qv under knowledge), 6.240
modifies the character, 5.60
momentary in itself but big with future results, 2.50ff
name, form and action all relative, 2.160f

action cont.
only action performed with ego-feeling has karmic consequences (6.241f), 6.239
produces results, 1.69, 113
promotes liberation indirectly, 6.254f
prompted by desire, 2.255
purifies for knowledge (6.288)
takes place in a body but depends on consciousness, 4.204f
term karma (action) often confined to ritual in Ś, 6.189n
true action is ritualistic action because of its powerful effect on lives to come, 6.333n
actionless state, naiṣkarmya
(s/a knowledge, devotion to,)
action seen as inaction, inaction as action in Gītā, 6.272ff
defined, 5.87
of enlightened person, 6.271
is one's true natural state which can be realized, 6.272
is the normal state in enlightenment, 6,291
actor, as simile for root cause of world, 2.123
adhyātma yoga, see '**yoga, adhyātma**'
adjuncts, external (upādhi)
(s/a power)
actionless Absolute acts through adjuncts, 4.222
Bhartṛprapañca on, 4.81f
definition, 1.71, 111; 2.3f
name and form (qv) adjuncts of Self, 3.65
soul with adjuncts compared with ether in a pot, 2.8, 43; 3.2, 23
Advaita system
when truth of Advaita is known there is no Advaita system, 4.221
affirmation, repeated (abhyāsa), described, 6.154-167
agent, illusory character of (6.313f), 3.46f, 6.250
aggregates (Buddhist theory of), statement and refutation, 4.287f
agrayāṇataḥ, 3.210n, 6.341n (Note 230)
agreement and difference, observation of,
description of the process, 1.177n
the way to determine the meaning of words 6.134f, 139-141
āhavanīya fire, 3.169, 5.40
Ajāta Vāda, see **Gauḍapāda**

ākṛti, see below under **'word and its meaning'**
analogy, argument by
Absolute cannot be the subject of any, 5.244
must keep within experience, 4.171
Āpastamba Dharma Sūtra Adhyātma Paṭala Vivaraṇa, 1.44, 3.101n, 4.151n
Ārya Bhaṭṭa, 3.91n
Āśmarathya, 3.64f, 4.81
asparśa-yoga,
(s/a under yogin)
1.25, 1.55n, 6.101, 6.188n
association (sāyujya) of soul with Lord rejected 3.2
asura, 5.153, 5.193n
described, 5.18f
person of asuric nature, 5.140,
atoms
before Ś Uddyotakara argues matter cannot be infinitely divisible, but Buddhists attack Vaiśeṣika atom, 4.230
Śaṃkara's attack on Vaiśeṣika's categories and atoms, 4.251-258
sketch and refutation of whole Vaiśeṣika atomic theory, 4.236-251
attribution, false (adhyāropa) and denial (apavāda)
applies to creation-texts (qv) of Veda, 2.2
established traditional method of interpreting Upanishads before Ś, 1.6
exemplified by teaching of plurality of souls, 6.319f
exemplified by teaching of three states of waking, dream and sleep (3.105), 6.318f
exposition of in light of 'neti neti', 5.338
function of texts attributing colour of sun to Absolute is only to deny darkness, 5.218
fundamental text and example for, 5.337f
illustration from image of sparks and from attribution of modification (qv) to Absolute, 5.341f
other illustrations of, 1.143ff
required for teaching the Fourth (qv), 3.168
Ś's main theological method, 1.22
technique already used in B.S., 6.229f
Auḍulomi 3.65f, 4.81

avākyārtha, 1.188, 195f
avatāra see **'descent'**
awareness (avagati) see **'knowledge, right'**

B

Bādarāyaṇa, 2.53,
probably not final author of B.S, 6.90n
Being
as genus merely 'indicates' Absolute, 1.195
before manifestation of the world, Being was not a 'this' (see 'name and form, unmanifest'), 2.156f
cannot arise from non-being, 1.206f
is the object of all perception, 1.205
on doctrine of Upanishads, is conscious, 1.205
on time-space plane, Being persists through successive forms, 2.135
sattā of Vaiśeṣikas, 2.121
the Absolute as, 1.200ff
undergoes no birth, modification or destruction, 1.185
Bhagavad Gītā
doctrines and merit of, 1.13ff
merit of Ś's commentary on, 1.14f
Bhagavān (as epithet), 4.167n
bhakti see **'devotion'**
Bhartṛhari, 1.22f, 26; 4.117, 4.158n, 5.296, 5.344n
Bhartṛmitra, 4.81, 5.198
Bhartṛprapañca
(s/a Difference in Identity, Hiraṇyagarbha, modification, merit and demerit), 1.21 (cp.6.196n), 2.225, 4.81-96, 5.350n, 6.147
Bhāskara, 1.21, 45; 4.81; 6.334n
bliss
Absolute as bliss, (3.44,5.217), 1.182, 235ff
Absolute not often explicitly characterized as bliss by Ś, 2.13
always to be associated with Absolute, 5.329ff
bliss-self described, 3.43
formula sac-cid-ānanda not found in Ś (or even in Prakāsātman 5.373n), 1.182
joy is not bliss, 5.329ff

bliss cont.
limited bliss of dreamless sleep, 3.173f
bodilessness
(s/a enlightened person, liberation)
1.243, 253n; 4.26f, 31; 6.300
body (causal, kāraṇa śarīra)
not specifically associated with deep sleep by Ś, 2.108n
only once mentioned by Ś, 3.27f
Self has no causal body, 3.46
body (physical)
(s/a Piṇḍa, Viśva, Vaiśvánara)
a modification of the elements, 1.219
comes from earth element, 3.7f, 26
considered with its organs comes from all five elements, 3.33f
has contact only with gross objects, 2.242
is the food-formed self pervaded by the Vítal Energy self, 3.40
not immediately evident in the way the Self is because awareness of it lapses in sleep,1.219
not available in experience apart from the Self, 1.93
water predominates in it, 5.38
body, subtle (liṅga śarīra)
(s/a Hiraṇyagarbha, Taijasa)
Bhartṛprapañca on, 4.96f
constituted of impressions qv (cp.5.lf), 3.167
constitution of (3.45f), 3.26f
cosmic form of, 2.188f
death as proof of existence of, 5.56
first taught by the Sāṅkhyas, 3.27
Jainas lack any conception of, 5.37
bondage
an illusion, 1.67 and 76ff
not a reality that exists and comes to an end, 6.234f
Brahmā, (= Hiraṇyagarbha qv)
imagined through nescience, 1.236f
derives his powers from the Lord, 2.11
is Hiraṇyagarbha, 5.247
first saw Veda, 5.247

Brahmā, (= Hiraṇyagarbha qv) cont.
the creator, 5.249
taught Rāma he was Viṣṇu, cp. Rāmāyaṇa (Bombay ed.) VI.120.16, 6.113f, 135
Brahma Sūkta of Atharva Veda, 3.100n
Brahma Sūtras
conception of liberation probably different from that of Ś, 6.88n
content and function: refutation of Sāṅkhya dualism (cp. 4.175f): affirmation of pariṇāma-vāda, 1.20f
date, 1.15
final redactor a bhedābheda-vādin, 4.81
logical fallacies to which the Brahma Sūtras draw attention, 4.170f
on watery body in the after-life, 5.1f
opening Sūtra shows their topic is not that of PM injunctions, 4.13
Ś goes behind them to ancient Upanishadic texts (cp. 2.114f), 1.16
Ś silently develops and corrects them in places, 2.114f
teach (against PM) that supreme goal is knowledge, 4.13f
their teaching of upāsana leads only to Brahma-loka, 1.16
use of Law of Contradiction in them tends to confirm Ś's interpretation of the work, 4.388n
Brahmadatta, 4.81
brahma-loka
Brahma Sūtra discipline leads to it, 1.16
culmination of Northern Path, 6.43, 51f and often
description of path to, 6.50ff
reached through OM (qv), 6.185f
results from ritual and meditation, 5.13
term can mean the Absolute in the Upanishads, 6.81n, 87n, 251, 342n
Brahmanandin, taught illusory character of world, 1.29f
Brāhmaṇas, nature of these texts, 1.3f
Brahmin, 6.316
term may mean 'one who knows Brahman', 6.322ff.
Buddha
(s/a Kumārila)
4.285 and 376n

Buddhism
(s/a aggregates, Buddha, Dharmakīrti, Gauḍapāda, indeterminable, momentary, Vijñāna Vāda, Witness)
Advaitin's doctrine of self-luminous Witness not contradictory, 4.309f, 327
anti-Vedic, hence attacked by B.S., 1.19
Buddhist (arguing from perception and inference alone) should accept waking as real (see below under 'dream, argument for the unreality of waking'), 4.321f
Chāndogya refutes Mādhyamika's view that world arises as an appearance from non-being, 4.338f
defilement and cleansing of consciousness, as also liberation, are all inexplicable on the Buddhist view, explicable on the Advaita view, 4.325f
denies material cause, affirms the world arose from non-being and that all is momentary, the notion of continuity being due to the similarity of one moment to the next — brief refutation of these points by sat-kārya-vādin, 2.116, 124ff
derided Veda, 4.127
example of dream does not support its subjective idealism, as dream is different from waking and depends on it, 4.311ff
fact of memory refutes Buddhist's theory of momentariness, 4.172
from the standpoint of metaphysical truth it is wrong to say, like the Vijnāna Vādin, that the mind even appears in the form of objects, 4.331
from the standpoint of metaphysical truth, (as opposed to that of perception and inference) the Advaitin also denies an external object, like the Vijñāna Vādin, 4.330
general refutation of Buddhism, 4.277-341
if consciousness be reduced to empirical cognitions, Buddhist cannot assert that they are painful, etc. or, if really painful, etc., there could be no liberation, 4.324f
in denying the self, the Buddhist disproves PM view that self separate from body is universally known, 5.204f
in teaching momentary pulses of self-luminosity, Buddhism implies there is no Self and contradicts Veda, 5.235
its influence on Gauḍapāda (2.228f), 1.23ff

Buddhism cont.
its Mādhyamikas cannot claim non-existence of knowledge without self-contradiction, 4.334f
its Mādhyamikas cannot show logically that world could arise from non-being, 4.340
its Mādhyamikas right to deny that the mind assumes the form of objects, wrong to say that the remainder is a void, 4.332f
its theory of momentariness contradicted by our perception of material causality, in which cause and effect co-exist, 4.302
its theory of momentariness contradicted by Self taught in the Upanishads, 6.112
its theory of momentariness refuted by doctrine of Witness, 6.130f
patronized by foreign kings after Alexander's invasion, evoking Brahminical reaction, 1.8
refutation of Sarvāstivādins: see under Pratītya Samutpāda, also under Skandhas, aggregates, momentariness, suppression, momentariness of perceiver, non-existence (problem of origination of being from non-being), 4.286-302
refutation of its Law of Simultaneous Apprehension (see under 'Sahopalambha-niyama'), 4.304, 307f
refutation of Mādhyamikas, 4.332-341
Ś and Buddhist subjective idealism, 1.85ff
sat-kārya-vāda (qv under 'effect') as platform against Buddhist scepticism, 2.113
statement and refutation of Vijñāna Vāda subjective idealism, 4.303-332
subjective idealist's version of self-luminous cognition is self-contradictory, 4.308f
we are aware of knowledge in absence of knowable retrospectively after sleep, 4.336
what is apprehended as external is, as such, external, whether it is logically explicable or not, 4.306f

C

canals, subtle (nāḍi)
exit at death from nāḍi at crown of the head on the path of liberation by stages, 6.30

canals, subtle (nāḍi) cont.
the beginning of the Northern Path (qv) is nāḍi at crown of the head, 6.38
refined part of food rises through nāḍis to become mind, 3.32
role of nāḍis in dreamless sleep, 3.131f, 143, 158f
those enlightened in life do not depart by nāḍi at crown of the head at death, 6.304
cancellation of error (apavāda, bhāda), 1.89, 159; 2.8;
Candrakīrti, 1.55n 4.387n
carpenter, image of, 3.47f
categories
s/a atoms, Bhartṛprapañca, Vaiśeṣikas
the six categories of the Vaiśeṣikas (padārtha), 4.232f
the three rāśis of Bhartṛprapañca, 4.83
causal body see **body, causal**
cause and effect, causality in general
Absolute undergoes transformation without an efficient cause, 2.16
causality unreal, 6.315
cause and effect perceived as co-existent (against Buddhist), 4.302
unreality of cause and effect does not undermine Vedic ritualistic teaching, 1.77
whole notion of causality refuted from standpoint of ultimate truth, 2.234ff
cause, material
Absolute as material cause and sole reality (2.44), 1.186, 200ff, 204
Absolute as root of tree of saṃsāra, 5.14f
effect non-different from material cause (no Dualism), 2.41
material cause not non-different from effect (no Pantheism), 2.37ff
characterization
(s/a definition)
1.189f, 193
childishness, child-like state, 3.193; 6.311f
Citsukha, 1.48, 51n, 5.186n
cognition, resultant (phala, pramāṇa-phala), 1.219
cognitions, empirical (vijñāna)
attributed in ignorance to the Self, 1.194

coma, 3.3, 129, 159, 162ff, 203n; 5.32f, 56
Consciousness (metaphysical) and consciousness (empirical)
(s/a Absolute, Materialists)
action depends on consciousness (against Materialists), 4.181-199
does not exist for the sake of another, (cp. below under 'value'), 3.13f
is always and everywhere one, differentiated only by adjuncts (qv), 4.337
is constant, 1.209f, 220
is not a property of the Self, 3.25
is not an object of perception, 3.180
is not subject to inference, 3.180
is reflected in the mind, 3.2
is self-luminous, 1.213ff, 231ff
is self-established, 1.220
is that through which things are known, 3.50f, 58
is the inmost principle, illumining even the light of the sun, 4.185f
is the hearer of hearing, 1.221
must be self-luminous or we fall into infinite regress, 4.336f
refutation of Buddhist theories of consciousness, see above under 'Buddhism', 4.324f
the non-conscious exists for the sake of the conscious, 3.13f
there is no particularized consciousness after death, 3.65f
consciousness, massed see **prajñāna-ghana**
constituents (guṇa)
(s/a enlightened person, Māyā, Sāṅkhyas)
called pleasure, pain, delusion, 1.220
called joy, misery, despondency, 2.34
constitute the world of transmigration, 5.16
described, 2.81ff
enlightened person is beyond the guṇas (guṇātita), 6.285ff
mentioned frequently, 4.202ff
one cannot infer a Nature consisting of pleasure, pain and delusion from the pleasure, pain and delusion of the mind (i.e. contrary to the Sāṅkhyas, one cannot establish a real entity called Nature on basis of perception and inference), 4.201f
possible origins of theory of, 4.196f

constituents (guṇa) cont.
Sāṅkhyas authoritative on topic of play of, 4.173
the enlightened one thinks 'The constituents work on the constituents, I do nothing' 6.282
Contradiction, Law of
taken in an ontological sense, 4.157n
its presence in B.S. as strong point in favour of Ś's interpretation of that work, 4.388n
cosmological argument for the Self, 1.135, 198, 203f, 208f
creation as sport of the Lord, 2.32f; 4.3 (PM reject this B.S. view)
Creation Hymn (Ṛg Veda), 2.148
creation-texts (not concerned with relating historical fact)
(s/a device)
2.33, 213-227; 5.340, 5.377n (even on PM's tenets they are only 'eulogy' qv)
Creator (Lord as), 2.6ff, 15
Crest Jewel of Wisdom, 1.44, 235
cruelty, problem of in relation to Lord, 2.63f

D

death
process of death, 5.49ff, 54f
Vital Energy persists unmanifest after death, 3.183
withdrawal of intellect and organs from body at death, 3.26
defects of character
(s/a asura)
5.141f
definition, what
(s/a characterization)
1.182ff, 189f, 193.
sāvaśeṣa, svarūpa, taṭastha, 1.196f
deities
are aspects of one deity, prāṇa, 3.40
as cosmic powers, 5.228f
Bhartṛprapañca on, 4.82
constant oscillation of Vital Principle is 'vow of deities', 6.25f
he who meditates on a deity becomes one with it, 3.54

deities cont.
impalpable, so only known through Veda, 5.266
not the governing factor in action, 5.6f
preside over senses (5.191n), 3.36ff
proceed from words of Veda, 4.126
spring from Prajāpati, 5.18
subordinate forms of Lord, 2.15, 37, 47
their existence denied by PM, 4.5f
deity, chosen (iṣṭa-deva) 5.289, 311
delimitation (avaccheda, theory of soul), 3.2, 22f
demon, demoniac see **'asura'**
derivative texts see **'Smṛti'**
descent (avatāra), 3.54
design, argument from, 2.30f, 2.54ff
desires
(s/a enlightened person)
a bandage to the eyes, 6.139
attributed to the Self also by Bhartṛprapañca, 5.283f
freedom from desire = liberation, 6.232
impossible in liberation (6.314), 6.268
no scope for personal desires in adhyātma-yoga (qv) (6.104), 6.103
not attributes of Self as Vaiśeṣikas hold, 5.283f
self-knowledge through purging desire, 6.99f
device (upāya), 2.219f creation-texts a device to teach the Self
devotion (bhakti), 1.11f, 13f; 5.153ff, 169n; 6.105-107
dharma, duty
(s/a householder's duties, merit)
as obedience to Vedic injunctions and merit therefrom, 4.23
as duty, duties classified, 5.105ff, 109ff, 6.314f
no duties for the enlightened (qv)., 5.291f
rise of metaphysical knowledge (see under 'knowledge, metaphysical') dependent on duty, 5.111f
Dharmakīrti, 1.26, 39; 4.280f, 282f chief Buddhist opponent attacked by Ś
dhvani, 4.118, 122-125
dialectic (tarka), 4.169-179

Difference in Identity
(s/a Bhartṛprapañca)
Auḍulomi on, 3.65
Bhartṛprapañca on, 4.80-105
Name of school carrying systematization beyond that of B.S., 1.21
typical view of those in metaphysical ignorance, 2.185
discipline, sixfold, beginning with restraint
comes automatically to liberated person, 6.324f
proximate cause of rise of knowledge, 5.115
recommended by B.S., 5.113f
discrimination
is seeing action in inaction, etc., 6.283
is the final goal of Advaita, 1.93
peculiar difficulty of discriminating Self and intellect, 3.61ff
of enlightened person effective even in sleep, 3.128
of Knower of Body (qv), 1.104
of Self implies cancellation (qv) of not-self, 5.236
of Self negates even the mind, 1.164f
the mere mental cognition 'I am the knower' is transient, 1.166
true discrimination means self-identification with the Witness (6.227f), 1. 232
dissolution, cosmic (pralaya),
compatible with transcendent Absolute, 2.39f
seeds of nescience persist in dissolution, 3.5
Draviḍa
(s/a That thou art)
function of Veda is to negate, 1.28f
importance of 'That thou art', 2.223ff
on 'That thou art' quoted by Troṭaka, 6 .190n
pre-Ś emphasis on 'That thou art' also in Dharma Śāstra, 6.212n
dream
(s/a next entries and 'Buddhism' and 'states (three)')
detailed treatment of, 3.103-127
dream-experience proves self-luminosity of Self, 5.283, 5.362n
dream-experience is through illusion (māyā qv), 2.253ff
not real because transient, 1.209, 211f, 220
soul free from objective sphere in dream, 3.142

dream cont.
subject-object experience labelled dream, 3.191f
waking and dream both dream in metaphysical sense, 1.162, 220f; 3.7, 187
what is remembered in dream is material from waking experience, 2.88
dream as argument for the unreality of the world of waking experience
(s/a Buddhism, idea and object)
from the higher Buddhist and Advaita standpoint external objects are denied for waking and dream, 4.329f
since Vijñāna vādins only accept perception and inference and reject Witness they can only deny the reality of dream on the assumption that waking is real, 4.321
Vijñāna Vāda form of this argument rejected, 2.244-260; 3.57, 4.311ff
dream, waking from, the analogy that explains liberation, 1.86f, 88f
dream, reflection on, metaphysical importance of
consideration of facts of dream undermines Materialism, 4.185ff
known in waking state to have had no external objects (3.119ff), 3.57
metaphysical significance of dreams of the blind, 4.189
shows that Witness is different from the mental modifications because it is seen retrospectively that it was illumining them, whereas in waking the light might have been coming from the sun (6.216n), 3.21
duality
(s/a enlightened person)
all dualists are miserable, 3.195
cannot arise either from the real or the unreal, 2.240
condemned by the Veda, 4.88
duality of waking and dream has no existence apart from our awareness of it, 1.220
duty see **dharma**

E

Eckhart, Meister, 5.174n, 297
effect
(s/a Sat-Kārya-Vāda)
not different from its material cause, 1.136; 2.42f, 110ff, 116ff; 2.124ff

effect cont.
refutation of Vaiśeṣika view, 4.266-270
Sāṅkhya's version of Sat-Kārya-Vāda untenable, 4.224
Sat-Kārya-Vāda a springboard for the acosmic teaching (qv), 2.267n
Self not an effect, 1.127
Vaiśeṣikas attack Sat-Kārya-Vāda, 4.235
ego-sense, ego-feeling, ego-notion
Bhartṛprapañca on, 4.83
cannot reveal Self, 5.295
cosmic ego-sense in Gītā, 2.105n
not a character of the Self, 3.54
object of ego sense is individual experiencer, 4.30f
only actions performed with ego-sense have karmic consequences, 6.239
unenlightened person deluded by ego-sense, 2.84f
Veda may indicate true Self through the ego sense. (6.127, 135), 6.110f
eka-vākyatā, 2.206n; 3.91n
elements
all five elements enter into food, 3.7f
all other elements come from ether, 2.149f
are latent in the mind-stuff (Gauḍapāda's conception), 2.256
are objects, their effects are non-different from them, but both are mere modifications due to the activity of speech in naming, 2.41ff
constitute the objective side of our experience, 2.183
described, 2.165-177
enter into the composition of body, mind and senses (qv), 3.51
enter into the composition of sheaths (qv), 3.41
ether and wind not eternal, 1.207
parts of a hierarchy, 1.199
sense-organs are composed of elements, 3.11, 33
emerald, simile of, 3.59f
enlightened person
(s/a canals, constituents, ego-sense, liberation, prārabdha, renunciate)
bodilessness of, 6.299-307
cannot misbehave, as misbehaviour is due to nescience (6.315, 324), 6.295ff

enlightened person cont.
difference between enlightenment and dreamless sleep, 3.157, 160f
does not undergo a change of state, 6.224-236
does not pursue samādhi as he always has it, 6.165
empirical means of knowledge are cancelled for him, 5.293, 6.143f
enlightenment usually comes in celibate stages of life, 4.16
experiences 'false notions' by which he is not deluded, 6.245f
feels no dislike or horror: all is his own Self, 6.302f
general account of, 6.277-326
gods cannot prevent his liberation as he is their own Self, 6.306
has awoken from his dreams of duality, 1.88f
has conviction he is actionless (cp 2.84), 6.249f
has no desire for action or enjoyment, 1.79
hides his knowledge and powers, 6.312f
his apparent action is not action, 4.72
his state is not comprehensible to others (6.321), 3.195; 6.286
is beyond the constituents (guṇātita), 6.285ff
is not a householder even if he lives in a house, 6.295
is not different from Self, 6.230
is not subject to injunctions (qv), 6.297f
is rare, 1.78, 140
is worthy of worship, 5.132
knows that the constituents act on the constituents while he himself is actionless, 2.84
loses all worldly desires, 5.128
many enlightened persons abandon ritual, 4.14f
nature and glory of, 6.298-326
nature of, 5.133ff
nature of his action during enlightenment, 6.238-262
perceives the world but is not deluded into belief in its reality, 1.105
remnant of nescience in one sense persists for him till death and in another sense does not persist, 6.77n
sees duality and yet does not see it, 6.158
unites with Absolute at death, 3.157f
women eligible for enlightenment, 6.321

entry of Lord into body as soul (praveśa)
(s/a reflection)
as a myth, 1.210f; 2.10f, 25, 43, 139, 215ff
is of the nature of a reflection, 6.133, 177
Kāśakṛtsna's view, 3.64
Self not reflected in mind in deep sleep, 3.150
escape (apavarga)
Bhartṛprapañca on, 4.64
refuted, 4.104f
establishment (siddhi), the product or resultant of a cognition, 1.219f
ether (element)
as ether pervades all world from within, so Self pervades ether from within, 6.162
comes into being (against Vaiśeṣikas), 1.207, 2.12 4.271-274
conceived as first manifestation of name and form, followed by wind, 3.7, 3.22f
conceived as source of name and form, 2.12
is itself a modification, other elements are modifications of it, 1.207, 2.149
ether in cave of heart
(s/a Absolute, Hiraṇyagarbha, Self, sleep)
Absolute known in the heart, though not limited to that organ, 5.222, 6.22, 95, 97
is locus for meditation on Hiraṇyagarbha, 6.26
is not intrinsically all-pervading, 4.100
is partless, Self therefore partless, 2.25
is seat of soul in dreamless sleep, 3.7, 132f, 141, 158
objects of all desires present there, 3.157
we begin with knowledge of body and progress to knowledge of ether in the heart, 1.238f
ether of the sky (= space)
(s/a delimitation)
apparent delimitation of Self into individual souls is like apparent delimitation of ether by pots and other cavities, 2.4, 6, 43, 44; 3.22; 4.225, 6.297
apparently differentiated, actually undifferentiated (as already previously established by the Vaiśeṣikas, 5.347n), 5.232, 339

ether of the sky (= space) cont.
as focus for meditation on the Absolute, 6.6
is relationless and so an image of knowledge of the Self, 6.321
Knower of the Body (qv) partless like the ether, 1.103
limitations falsely imposed on Self are like impurities on sky, 6.229
eulogistic passages (arthavāda)
are true if they lead on to truth, 5.253
cannot also convey information, 5.372n
different forms of, 5.324f
mythological passages in Veda may be explained as eulogies, 2.218, 261n
PM interpretation of 'Agni wept' as a eulogistic passage, 4.145n
exegetical criteria
attributes affirmed of anything in one text hold good in all other references to that thing, except where specifically denied, 5.329
prakaraṇa, liṅga, śruti, etc., 5.315
existence, affirmation of, constant in all perceptual judgements, 1.201f, 209f; 2.39
fictitious (cp. above under 'agent'), 5.8; 6.128ff
experience, immediate (anubhava), 1.166
experience, uncontradictable, 1.109f
experiencer, individual
considered a reality in some pre-Ś and non-Ś Vedanta schools, 6.228

F

fainting see **coma**
faith, 5.157, 310; 6.35, 40, 46
figurative use of language
(s/a indication)
false claim of PM that we refer to the Self as the ego figuratively, 5.207
figurative meaning may be close to or far from primary meaning, 6.18
figurative interpretation of the Veda to be resorted to only when the surface meaning is contradictory, 5.372n, 6.60
Self can only be indicated figuratively, 6.111f

figurative use of language cont.
use or understanding of figurative meaning implies knowledge of direct or primary meaning, 6.194fn
Five Fires , Meditation on (pañcāgni-vidyā)
can be used as a means to liberation by stages (qv), 6.3
enhances the karmic effect of ritual, 5.40
frequently a theme for meditation, 6.32
promotes disgust for world, 5.35
fivefold — meditation on all as fivefold, 6.29
(s/a meditation, ritualistic and symbolic)
Flame, Path of, see **Northern Path**
Fourth, the (turya, turīya)
corresponds to magician in rope-trick simile (qv), 2.87
implies conscious awareness of Absolute (contrast sleep), 3.166
implies transcendence (qv), 3.175ff
only called 'the Fourth' from the standpoint of nescience, 3.104
relation to OM (qv), 3.191, 6.181
void of non-perception and wrong-perception, 3.185ff
what has to be realized, 6.318

G

generation, spontaneous, 2.24
Gauḍapāda
(s/a mentalism and under Māṇḍūkya and Gauḍapāda Kārikās in the Index of Extracts)
Buddhist influence on his subjective idealism, 3.128f
date, 1.15
debt to Buddhism, 1.23ff, 2.228f
doctrine, 1.22ff
his subjective-idealism or mentalism, 1.85
refutes Sarvāstivādins from standpoint of Vijñāna Vāda and Vijñāna Vāda from standpoint of Ajāta Vāda, 4.330ff
Sarvajñātman and Prakāsānanda revert to his phenomenalism, 1.49f
gods
(s/a deities, enlightened person)
cannot prevent the liberation of the enlightened person, 6.306
create obstacles, 5.6

gods cont.
general account of, 2.178-197
possess powers of projection, 2.16, 23f, 84,
ritualists as their food but protected by them, 5.23, 79f
good works (iṣṭā-pūrte), 5.21
grace, 3.84, 5.117f, 6.172, 174, 183
ground, positive, for all illusions, 3.175

H

hearing, cogitation and sustained meditation
(s/a injunction)
already taught by Bhartṛprapañca, 6.147
strictly speaking, cannot be enjoined, 4.64f
heaven (svarga), 5.110
a future reward less certain than that brought by knowledge, 6.259
Hiraṇyagarbha (= Brahmā, Prajāpati, qv.)
(s/a Taijasa)
Bhartṛprapanca on, his faulty doctrine about realizing identity with, 4.82, 84, 105
corresponds to Taijasa on cosmic plane, 3.171
etymology of name, 2.178ff
first 'saw' hymns of Ṛg. Veda, 5.246, 247f
highest 'worldly' bliss, 1.238
identification with, also practised on the direct path to liberation in life (qv), 6.96
is Cosmic intellect, 2.105n
is Brahmā, 5.247
is Cosmic Vital Energy, 2.184
is world-soul, 5.10
is highest goal of ritual, 5.20
realization of identity with, 6.21-31
the creator, 5.249
totality of all impressions (qv), 3.167
Veda itself proclaims that Hiraṇyagarbha does not exist (5.98), 4.79
householder's duties, 5.79
householder's sacrifices, 5.176n

I

idea and object, distinction between, common to waking and dream, 2.255f
Identity, Law of, appeal to, 3.68
ignorance = nescience (qv)
impressions of previous experience
Bhartṛprapañca on vāsanā, 4.83
constitute memory images, 3.182
constitute the subtle body (qv), 3.167, 5.2
dreams are brought forth from them by nescience, desire and past action, 3.126
dreams consist of impressions, 3.118, 172
from previous lives account for unqualified people attaining metaphysical knowledge (qv under 'knowledge'), 5.118
lie in heart or mind, 4.98
pūrvaprajñā described, 5.61
rope-snake (qv under 'snake') an impression of the mind (buddhi-saṃskāra) and there is no external snake, 3.191
the distinction between saṃskāra and vāsanā, 3.204n
vāsanās condition rebirth, 5.26f
indeterminable
(s/a Maṇḍana Miśra, name and form, unmanifest)
2.5f, 12, 28, 143-164, 264n; (Note 61)
instances of early Buddhist use of the term, 4.288, 304
indication
(s/a figurative use of language)
1.188, 193, 195
inference
(s/a inferential sign, mark, reason)
cannot bear on pure Consciousness, 3.180
cannot contradict Veda, 5.212ff
cannot establish any differentiation in the Self, 5.214f
depends on inferential sign (qv), 5.244
is inductive, 5.344nf
its range is confined to name and form (qv), 5.215
legitimate functions of, 5.245

inferential sign (liṅga or lakṣaṇa)
lakṣaṇa, characteristic mark, 3.180
infinite, 1.191ff
inherence, intimate (samavāya)
(s/a Vaiśeṣikas)
4.172, 233, 259f; 5.283
injunction
(s/a enlightened person, hearing, etc., Pūrva Mīmāṃsā)
bearing on the enlightened person to practise repeated affirmation may be accepted if interpreted as a restrictive injunction (niyama-vidhi), 5.62-69
can sometimes be implicit, 5.114
even the injunctions to hear, cogitate and meditate refute the PM's view that the Veda is only concerned with action, 4.40f
except when interpreted as a restrictive injunction (niyama-vidhi) it does not apply to the enlightened person, 6.249, 297
for the six-fold spiritual discipline beginning with restraint (see above under 'discipline, six-fold'), 5.113f
knowledge of the Self cannot be enjoined, 4.12f, 115f; 5.115f; 6.247f
strictly there can be no injunction for hearing, cogitation and sustained meditation about the Self, 4.64f
'the Self should be seen' means 'turn away from all else', 4.114f
to adopt the path, 5.62-69
Vedic ritualistic injunctions lead to pleasure in varying degrees but also to further transmigration, 4.25f
Vedic texts conveying metaphysical knowledge not subordinate to ritualistic injunctions, 4.14f
wrong PM view that a person is invariably subject to injunctions when he knows that his soul is separate from his body, 6.297
intellect (buddhi)
(s/a mind)
connection with it lasts throughout transmigration, 3.5
its function (as opposed to that of the wavering mind) is fixed determination in knowledge and will, 3.33
its qualities are desire, aversion, limitation, finitude, 3.25
its role in perception described, 3.58

intellect (buddhi) cont.
its similarity to Self, 3.61
objects manifest in it through the help of the sense-organs, 1.194
intellect (cosmic)
(s/a Hiraṇyagarbha), 2.105n, 178
as taught in Vedic tradition accepted, 6.41
theory of Sāṅkhyas not accepted, 5.279
Īśvara Kṛṣṇa, 4.195, 198

J

Jābāla Upanishad, 3.102n
Jaimini, 2.51f, 6.60ff
Jainism
(s/a syād-vāda)
anti-Vedic stance attacked by B.S., 1.19
derided Veda, 4.126
faulty view of transmigration (no subtle body), 5.37
helped call forth Brahminical reaction, 1.8, 17
illogically affirms existence and non-existence, 1.140
its influence on Mahatma Gandhi, 4.344
refutation of its main doctrines, 4.345-352
untenable view that soul is of size of body, 4.349ff
Janaka, alternative interpretations of Gītā III.20: either he knew the truth and abstained from formal renunciation (qv), or else he merely sought perfection through action, 4.72f
japa, usually refers to Vedic texts in Ś, 5.186n
joy see **bliss** and **sheaths**

K

karma-yoga, 5.310
Kāśakṛtsna, 1.15; 3.64; 4.81
Kashmir Shaivism, 1.12, 45
Knower of the Body (Knower of the Field, kṣetrajña), 1.73ff, 79ff, 103f, 153, 211; 2.82; 3.182f
knowledge, as characteristic of the Absolute, 1.195f; 2.48f, 5.218ff
knowledge, devotion to (jñāna-niṣṭhā)
an 'actionless activity', 5.192n

knowledge, devotion to (jñāna-niṣṭhā) cont.
an actionless state, 4.66f
conditions for, 5.110
ends transmigration, 5.85
rendered possible by purifying action, 5.86
requires effort and is a means to liberation, 6.305
results in Self-knowledge, 5.150f
knowledge, empirical
(s/a enlightened person)
cannot know the Self (as an object), 5.225f
depends on a reflection of Consciousness, 1.186f, 190ff, 223f; 6.112, 128ff
implies as its prior condition that the Self is already self-evident, 1.127
is all valid in its sphere before enlightenment, 1.106, 110f; 5.216
is at best a kind of dream, 1.139
is not an attribute of the Self as claimed by Bhartṛprapañca and Vaiśeṣikas, 4.100, 160n
is transient, whereas Self's knowledge is constant, 1.228f; 5.233
rests on superimposition (qv), 1.96
knowledge, means of, empirical
(s/a enlightened person, reflection, ābhāsa)
all are valid in their sphere before enlightenment, 5.242f
all are mere appearances (ābhāsa), 5.292f
apply only before enlightenment, 3.86; 5.293
lists of them, 4.62, 5.306
not competent to know the Self, 1.130f
Self-realized person is not bound to respect his empirical data as the rationalist is, 4.132
one means of knowledge (i.e. the Veda) establishes that the Self is beyond the three states (qv), 3.177
only remove ignorance, do not also illumine, 3.178
knowledge, metaphysical
(s/a man)
degrees of it are taught in Ā.D.S., 6.260f
destroys action and its factors, 4.16

knowledge, metaphysical cont.
destroys power of actions to bring future experience, 5.309, 6.240f
external marks of, 5.135ff
Gītā account of, 5.152
implies direct experience, 5.77
implies automatic sustained remembrance, 5.67
is compatible with continued empirical experience, 6.242
is critical, not constructive, 6.110
is itself the Absolute, 5.217
is motionless and relationless, 3.196
is not attained through learning, 5.133
is open to all mankind, 5.117f
is rarely achieved, 1.139
is the final goal of man, 3.192
is the supreme knowledge (parā vidyā), 1.161; 5.74-78
is uncontradictable, 5.253
is what metaphysical enquiry seeks, 1.182
may come gradually, but leads to immediate liberation, 6.265
negates the non-self, 4.65
normally implies formal renunciation (qv), 5.123
sense in which doctrine that it has degrees is acceptable, 6.310
some texts imply practice of spiritual discipline in addition, 5.68
knowledge-power (jñāna-śakti), 2.93
knowledge, right (avagati, pramā)
is eternal, 1.219f
is not a form of action because it is passively conditioned by its object, 6.4
is only figuratively referred to as a product, 1.219f
same in nature whether transient or eternal, whether object-directed or turned in on Self, 1.217
knowledge, verbal
direct when it concerns self of hearer, 6.108
example of Brahmā and Rāma, Rāmāyaṇa VI.120.7ff, 6.113f, 135
usually abstract and indirect, 5.365n
Kumārila
(s/a Maṇḍana, Prabhākara)
attacks pre-Ś theory of nescience, 1.37f

Kumārila cont.
constructed world-view that contradicts Upanishads, 4.2
his opinion of the Buddha, 4.376n
mistaken view that there has to be knowledge of knowledge, 1.124
wrong view that nescience implies duality, 3.102n
kūṭastha, 2.80,
special sense of word, 2.106n, 262n

L

law, universal (vyāpti, based on anvaya and vyatireka, agreement and difference), 2.266n
liberation
(s/a Brahma Sūtras, enlightened person, knowledge (metaphysical), liberation (gradual), liberation in life, Pūrva Mīmāṃsā, ritual)
an uncontradictable experience, 5.290
Bhartṛprapañca on, 4.83f
cannot be achieved through ritual and meditation combined, 4.55-80
cannot be achieved through ritual alone, 4.36-54
means absorption in one's own Self beyond change, 5.151
not the result of an act, 6.250
results of, 6.310
(usually) presupposes formal renunciation (qv), 4.78
liberation, gradual or by stages (krama-mukti)
(s/a canals, Five Fires, meditation (symbolic), Northern Path)
comes through meditation on the Five Fires (qv), 6.3
results from Vedic meditations, 5.312, 6.2
liberation in life (sadyo-mukti)
(s/a Hiraṇyagarbha, last entry)
no implication of 'reaching' or time, 6.44
term 'jīvan-mukta' appears once in Ś, 6.84n, 332n
logical maxims; fallacies and laws of thought
appeal to Law of Excluded Middle (here the guṇas of the Sāṅkhyas must either be or not be capable of change), 4.211
begging the question, 6.301
example of begging the question, 6.337n
Excluded Middle, Law of Identity (qv under 'Identity'), 5.318
fallacy of mutual dependence or vicious circle qv below, 4.131, 133

logical maxims; fallacies and laws of thought cont.
Law of Contradiction, 5.317f
Law of Identity appealed to, 3.68
one must examine the sense in which a term is being used before one refutes or adopts it, 4.228
refutations must accept opponent's premises, 4.178f
short list of fallacies cited in B.S., 4.170f
some logical maxims cited by Ś, 4.171
when refuting an opponent from his standpoint and using his criteria, one's argument need not agree with one's own doctrine: Ś refutes Materialists from standpoint of Vaiśeṣikas, 4.173
Lord, the (Īśvara)
(s/a association, Creator, cruelty, deities, Māyā, Ruler (Inner), soul)
and soul, 2.6ff
appears as many through nescience 'like a Māyā (magic display or illusion)', 6.228f
as controller of karma, 1.210f
as Controller of World, 2.2f
as efficient and material cause of universe (B.S. view), 4.129ff
as Ruler (Inner) qv, 1.106f
deities preside over sense-organs but Lord presides over deities, 3.39
experiences no pleasure or pain, 3.72, 78ff
faulty world-architect theory of, 4.128ff
first imagines Cosmic Vital Principle, imagines the rest as modification of that, 2.257f
has constant knowledge, unlike the soul, 3.70
His existence cannot be established on rationalist basis: if He is not embodied He cannot act, if embodied He would suffer pain, 4.133
His Lordship is due to adjuncts (qv), 1.111
His nature as expounded in B.S.Bh., 2.13ff
identified with Vāsudeva, 5.309
is 'agent', in all acts through his mere actionless presence, 3.74f
is Knower of the Body (qv), 1.71f
is not cruel (cp. above under 'cruelty'), 3.75
is not mere efficient cause on analogy of potter, 4.133
is true Self of individual soul, 3.84

Lord, the (Īśvara) cont.
must be assumed, to account for the order and purpose in the world, 1.64
no argument by analogy from the soul as controller of the senses to the Lord as controller of the world, 4.133
one must accept the notion of His existence as a reasonable hypothesis to explain the world-order, but Sāṅkhyas reject it, 4.22
projects all objects and ideas, 2.256
soul not different from, 2.4
sun is abode of, 2.186
works through deities, 2.245

M

Madhusūdana, 1.29, 48
magician
(s/a māyā)
is the reality behind the unreal effects he produces, 1.208
magnet, image of, 3.71
man (humanity in general),
(s/a knowledge, metaphysical)
is superior to animals, 5.20
metaphysical knowledge (qv under 'knowledge, metaphysical') is open to all people irrespective of caste qualification, 5.117f
Maṇḍana Miśra
(s/a pantheism)
champions a form of Prasaṃkhyāna Vāda (qv), 3.205n and 5.364nf
gives (with Ś) loss of sense of direction as an example of error, 5.364n
his critique of perception, 5.347n
his reply to Kumārila's attack on nescience, 1.38
his theory of indeterminability as 'indeterminable as real or unreal', 2.144ff
notices and attacks Prapañca Vilaya Vāda (qv), 4.108f
possible reference to him by Ś, 6.335n
teaches (with Ś) that the Veda, though illusory, may awaken to reality even as dreams have a practical effect on waking experience, 5.198

Maṇḍana Miśra cont.
treats of many topics from Advaita that are left unmentioned by Ś, 1.48f
tries to argue away the reality of the world, 1.106
mark, characteristic (lakṣaṇa), sometimes equivalent to inferential sign, (qv), 3.180
Materialists
(s/a dream, reflection on,)
claim that consciousness emanates from the body, 4.181ff
derided Veda, 4.127
even though perception is invariably accompanied by the body it does not follow that perception is a property of the body, 4.184
further arguments against the Materialist to show that consciousness is other than body and mind, 4.188ff
general refutation of, 4.179-192
if consciousness belonged to the body, blind people could not see dreams, 4.189
if the body were the experiencer it would experience when dead, 4.189f
memory proves that the experiencer is not the body, 4.189
refuted by Ś from standpoint of Vaiśeṣikas, 4.173
Ś argues against them, 'If consciousness is a property of the elements, how could it know the elements?', 4.183
māyā
(s/a nescience, Lord, power)
alternative theory to account for the mythological wonders in the Vedas and spiritual traditions, 2.218
dream-experience is 'through illusion (māyā)', 2.254 and 3.107
in Ś's authentic texts, 2.66-94
Lord appears as many through nescience 'like a hypnotist's magic display (māyā)', 6.228f
māyā-śakti = indeterminable (qv) unmanifest name and form (qv), 2.12
metaphysical sleep (qv) is a beginningless illusion (māyā) of the nature of ignorance (avidyā-lakṣana), 1.88
term māyā is used in pre-Ś works to mean illusion, 1.36
term māyā is used sparingly by Ś, 1.34

māyā cont.
tree of saṇsara compared to the magic display (māyā) of a mass-hypnotist, 5.17
Vidyāraṇya on, 1.38f
waking and dream experience an illusion (māyā), 3.187
world can be born through māyā like the illusory products of the magician (mass-hypnotist), 1.208
world-periods (qv) intelligible on hypothesis of Lord and his power of māyā, not on that of the Nature of the Sāṅkhyas, 4.206f
means of knowledge see **knowledge, means of**
meditation
(s/a following two entries,)
adherence to one, 6.9f
nature and goal, 6.8
terms knowledge and meditation sometimes interchangeable, 6.121
meditation for Self-knowledge
(s/a ether of sky, OM)
general account, 6.149-154
on OM a necessary prelude to all other meditations, 6.175
on OM as the Absolute, 6.171f
only those of weak and middling vision require meditation, 6.153f
posture described, activity defined, 6.150ff
meditation, ritualistic and symbolic
(s/a Five Fires, fivefold, pratīka, sampat)
beauty and power as foci for meditation on the Lord, 6.6
different goals of meditation, 6.5
even fanciful meditations on the Absolute imply the existence of the Absolute, 5.265
except when evidently fanciful, Vedic meditations are to be taken as true, 5.264f
in symbolic meditation one meditates on a higher entity as present in a lower (e.g. on Viṣṇu as present in a stone image) not vice versa, 6.3, 12-19
in the context of ritual not the means to liberation in life, 4.55-80
is different from ritualistic action on one hand and from knowledge on the other, 6.1, 4f
it may lead to Brahma-loka (qv), 5.13

meditation, ritualistic and symbolic cont.
it may lead to the Northern Path (qv), 5.34, 53ff
it may take one higher than the realms of the gods, 5.92, 98
its function is to purify the mind, 4.79, 5.98
its purpose is attainment of the realm of a deity, 4.64, 6.3, 6.7-10
leads to bliss in varying degrees, 3.43
may be pursued either for particular ends or for self-purification, 6.1f
may be used for enhancing the effects of the ritual, but also for purification, 6.7f
one becomes one with a deity on whom one meditates, 2.197, 3.54
one tends to become that on which one meditates, 6.5
texts enjoining meditation on the Absolute under finite forms cannot contradict the texts saying He is formless, 5.320f
the Absolute is one, but can be meditated on in different ways, 5.330f
memory, metaphysical significance of
(s/a Buddhism, Materialism)
4.189
mentalism (subjective idealism)
(s/a Buddhism, Gauḍapāda)
1.85ff, 163, 250n; 2.116, 247ff, 259f
merit and demerit
are beginningless, 5.9
condition experience after death, 5.59
Bhartṛprapañca's faulty theory of, 4.96f
merit does not cling to an enlightened person (qv), 6.251
remnant of merit, 5.25ff, 43ff
Mīmāṃsaka see **Pūrva Mīmāṃsā, ritualism**
mind
(s/a canals, discrimination, elements, intellect, mind as no-mind)
as instrument of cognition, 3.52
as no-mind, 3.160f; 5.216f; 6.315f
at death, 5.49
attributes of, 3.52f
cannot know its own true Self as an object, 1.169

mind cont.
composed ultimately of food, 3.8, 32
constituted of a subtle phase of matter, 2.16
contrasted with intellect (qv) as wavering, 6.96
depends on light of Consciousness within, 1.223
embraces both knowledge and will, 3.93f (note)
higher and lower, 3.48
inferred to exist as that which co-ordinates the senses, 3.31, 3.33f
its role in perception (qv), 3.58
its state in liberation (qv), 6.94, 103f
its states immediately perceived, 5.192f (note)
natural but erroneous self-identification with the mind, 6.161
not eternal and atomic as Vaiśeṣikas claim, 3.32f
part of Vaiśvānara (qv), 3.169f
modification (pariṇāma, vikāra)
Bhartṛprapañca's view, 4.81f
dreamless sleep evidence that Self is free from modifications, 1.211
is a mere appearance set up by name (qv), 1.185; 2.44, 231f, 259f; 5.216f
is accepted as real in certain contexts, 1.112, 2.7, 16, 21ff
is illusory as modification, but real as the Self, 3.16
modifications are illusory despite Bhartṛprapañca, 4.92
modifications are introduced from without and do not affect the essence of the real, 3.145f
modifications are unreal as they consist in their material cause, 1.201
real modification of Sāṅkhyas implies something coming from nothing (which is absurd), illusory modification of Advaitin does not, 4.224
soul not a modification of Self, 4.93
teaching about the Absolute undergoing modifications. is preliminary to affirming that the Absolute lacks all modification, 2.27ff, 222f; 5.340f
the Absolute undergoes modification only through illusion, 2.231f

momentariness, momentary
(s/a Buddhism)
Buddhist cannot establish similarity to save momentariness, 4.322f
fact of recognition implies universals and refutes momentariness (i.e. Buddhist not entitled to say that *everything* is momentary on basis of mere perception and inference), 4.321
of perceiver refuted (difficulties over recognition, memory, uselessness of Buddhist scriptures), 4.296ff
refutation of Vaiśeṣikas' asat-kārya-vāda (qv above under 'effect') includes refutation of Buddhist's 'momentariness', 2.122f
statement and refutation of Vaibhāṣika Buddhist's theory of momentariness, 4.291ff
the objects of the world (as opposed to the Self) are momentary on Ś's own view, 2.67
would render communication impossible, 4.323f
monk (saṃnyāsī) see **renunciate**

N

nāḍi see **canals, subtle**
Nāgārjuna, 1.55n
name, names
(s/a speech, word and its meaning)
are falsely applied to Being, 1.206; 2.44
modifications are appearances arising through names, see below under 'speech', 2.139ff, 163ff
name and form
(s/a name and form, unmanifest)
are indeterminable (qv), 2.28
arise through ignorance of the Absolute, 1.89
devaluation of from their early status, 2.140ff
do not touch the soul in its true nature, 3.65
evolution of to form the world, 3.7
Lord conforms to name and form like ether (qv) to pots, 1.111
Lord, not soul, unfolds name and form, 2.10ff
range of inference confined to name and form, 5.214f
name and form (unmanifest), 2.2f, 10ff, 28, 89f, 136-164, 3.183
terms used for name and form in Vedic and Smṛti texts, 1.64f

Nārāyaṇa, 2.91ff, 4.128; 6.287
importance of for Ś, 1.9ff
Nature
(s/a pradhāna, Sāṅkhyas)
a real principle for the Sāṅkhyas, 4.176
all activity implies a conscious being in control (against Sāṅkhyas), 4.205f
of Sāṅkhyas not Vedic, 2.12, 80ff, 88, 111ff
Sāṅkhya infers existence of Nature as real non-conscious substance composed of the constituents (qv) — refutation of this, 4.200ff
negation
bare negation without affirmation impossible, 2.116f
implies a positive substratum for the corrected illusion, 1.132, 156f
the Witness as limit beyond which negation cannot go, 6.113
Vedic negation of not-self is affirmation of Self, 2.239f
nescience
(s/a Kumārila, Maṇḍana, name and form, sleep, standpoints, superimposition, Yoga School of Patañjali)
absent in dreamless sleep, 2.255; 3.145
Bhartṛprapañca on, 4.83
detailed account of Ś's conception of, 1.62-113
example of sleep cited by post-Ś Advaitins to 'prove' the existence of nescience, 3.129f
ignorance sometimes means absence of knowledge in Ś (avidyā more often ajñāna), 6.192nf
in post-Ś Advaita, 4.171f
is not a reality afflicting the soul, 3.196
Lord appears as many through nescience 'like a hypnotist's magic show (māyā)', 6.228f
nescience, desire and action as realm of death, 1.200
not a property of soul for Bhartṛprapañca, 4.97
not a property of soul for Sāṅkhyas, 4.97
on enlightenment nescience is known never to have existed, 6.322
pre-Ś theory attacked by Kumārila, 1.37f
seed of nescience present in deep sleep, 3.5
Self is separate from nescience in dreamless sleep, 3.147f
the 'two kinds' of the realm of nescience, 2.184

nescience cont.
to whom does nescience belong? (to you who ask), 3.87
unmanifest name and form 'a seed-power of the nature of nescience', 2.137
use of term in pre-Ś works, 1.37f
nescience, remnant of (avidyā-śeṣa,-leśa,-saṃskāra), see under Prārabdha Karma
nescience (avidyā), seed of
in dreamless sleep, 3.5, 130, 161f
is not material, 3.147
is not real, 3.172
not an entity, but only 'not being awake to the real', 3.185
we are aware of the seed (only) of nescience in sleep as expressed later in 'I knew nothing', 3.162
neti neti
(s/a attribution, false)
negates the gross and subtle forms apparently assumed by the Absolute, 1.154f and 157f
Nimbārka, 1.1, 4.81
nirvāṇa
empirical knowledge extinguished (extinction = nirvāṇa) on enlightenment, 6.23
enlightened person disappears at death of body like the extinction of a lamp, 6.304-6
Ś's etymology of, 1.240
non-existence
(s/a Vaiśeṣika)
before world-creation not admitted, 2.154, 158
not accepted as a category, 1.206f
refutation of Vaiśeṣika theory, 4.266-270
there are no different kinds of non-existence (cp. 4.268f), 1.140; 2.133
treated as a kind of reality by Vaiśeṣikas (cp. 4.234), 4.337
unintelligible, 2.120f
Upanishadic text saying that the world arose from non-being is not unintelligible (as PM holds) but is followed by a negation, 4.338f

Northern Path
(s/a canals, Southern Path)
4.25; 5.21f, 34, 53, 306; 6.31-38

O

occult force of action (adṛṣṭa)
important place in Vaiśeṣika system, 4.231
occult force of action in Vedic tradition (apūrva)
explains laws of Nature, 5.6f
flows from ritual (qv), 5.39; 6.99
wrong view of Jaimini that it functions without guidance of the Lord, 2.51f, 61f
odour, implies presence of earth-element, 3.24f
OM
(s/a meditation for self-knowledge, speech, Veda)
a necessary prelude to all meditations, 6.175
as good as whole Veda as means of approach to the Absolute, 6.174
as source of grace, 6.172, 183
effective both as sound and as written character, 6.175
general account of meditation on OM, 6.167-186
identified with speech qv (vāc), 6.168, 177f
meaning of 'All this world is the sound OM', 2.162f
meditate on OM as the Absolute, 6.172f
meditation on OM at death as an indirect path to the supreme, 6.171
names and objects depend on OM, 6.169
principal topic of G.K. Book I, 5.286
pronunciation of OM, 3.208 (Note 158)
recitations of the Veda begin and end with OM, 6.172
references to OM in Veda, 6.167f
relation of OM to viśva, taijasa and prājña (qv), 6.179f
represents Absolute both in its conditioned and unconditioned forms, 6.182f
results of meditation on the mātrās of OM — A, AU and AUM, 6.179ff, 183ff
the chief instrument in apprehension of the Absolute, 6.172f, 174f
treatment of OM in Māṇḍūkya Upanishad, 3.165
used in mantras of Vaishnavas and Shaivas, 1.9

OM cont.
used to mean 'yes' by pupil to Teacher, 1.221
omnipotence
comes to him who identifies with Hiraṇyagarbha, 6.23f
omniscience
(s/a vicious circle)
of Absolute, 1.194f
there are texts affirming omniscience of the Lord, 2.33

P

pain
(s/a Lord, Witness)
a quality of mind for Advaitin, of soul for Vaiśeṣika, 3.94n
all experience of pain based on false identification with body and mind, 3.79f; 6.137
avoidance of, 5.136; 6.101f
cancelled at liberation, 5.235f, 268, 302f; 6.95, 141, 300, 303
external to cognitions, let alone to the Witness of them, 6.143
he who identifies with Hiraṇyagarbha crosses beyond pain, 6.25
no pain in pure Consciousness, 5.124
Sāṅkhya cannot explain pain: Advaita admits it as perceived, 4.213ff, 6.131f
terrible pain-giving ocean of saṇsāra, 2.196
Pāñcarātras, 4.128, 136ff
Pañcaśikha, 4.197
Pāṇini, 6.213n
pantheism, (effect has nature of material cause, material cause does not have nature of effect) so pantheism not attributable to Ś or Maṇḍana, 2.41, 100n, 113f
Paramārtha Sāra, a pre-Ś work exhibiting some of his characteristic doctrines, 1.33f
parameśvara
(s/a Lord)
use of this term in Ś, 2.13f

passions, kleśa
(s/a Yoga school of Patañjali)
are objects for the Witness, 1.166
Pāśupatas, 4.127f, 129ff
Patañjali, grammarian
(s/a Yoga school of Patañjali)
as early exponent of pūrvapakṣa-siddhānta pattern of argument, 5.315
followed by Ś over pattern of argument, significance of words, 6.193n f
penances, 6.247f
perception
(s/a intellect, Maṇḍana Miśra)
Bhartṛprapañca on, 4.83
cannot contradict metaphysical texts of Veda, 3.86; 5.212ff; 6.140f
cannot contradict Veda in latter's own sphere, 5.244, 321f
is the most direct and authoritative empirical means of knowledge, 5.243
light shoots out through the senses to the objects in perception, 3.55, 57-59
non-veridical perception is only an appearance of perception, 5.322
ultimate object of all perception is Being, 1.206
piṇḍa, 3.167f, 171
Bhartṛprapañca on, 4.82
power, śakti
(s/a knowledge-power, māyā)
Absolute possesses no powers, 2.222
apparent powers of Absolute due to adjuncts (qv), 5.228
non-different from what has the power, 2.114
one of the alternative names for unmanifest name and form (qv under 'name and form unmanifest') 2.137, 151
possible reference to Bhartṛhari's doctrine of infinite powers, 4.163n
refutation of Bhartṛprapañca's view that Absolute has powers, 4.90
Prabhākara, 4.2, 150n
pradhāna, prakṛti
(s/a Nature, 1.205)
non-conscious pradhāna cannot be cause of the world, 2.16, 19, 25f

Prajāpati
(s/a Brahmā, Hiraṇyagarbha, 2.71f, 142; 166)
as the year, 2.204n
prajñā, self-luminous light,
is state of soul in dreamless sleep, 3.152
is what experiences gross objects in dream and waking also, 3.172
Prājña,
as Consciousness associated with the totality of nescience in its seed form, 3.28
compared, along with Viśva and Taijasa (qv) to the magician's double in rope-trick (qv), 2.86f
in dreamless sleep as massed-consciousness withdrawn into the ether of the heart and as 'the Lord' but limited by non-perception of the real, 3.173ff, 182, 184ff
in relation to Viśva and Taijasa, etc., 3.166, 167f, 171, 176
relationship to OM (qv), 3.190
spoken of by later Advaitins (e.g. Sadānanda) as 'devoid of Lordship', 3.204f (note)
prajñāna-ghana, massed consciousness, 3.173f, 177, 179, 182; 4.91, 99
Prakāśānanda, 1.50, 2.67
Prakāśātman, 1.48, 61n; 2.99n, 148
formula sac-cid-ānanda not found in his work, 5.373n
Prapañca Vilaya Vāda
(s/a Maṇḍana Miśra)
4.106-117
prārabdha karma
(s/a enlightened person)
distinguished from sañcita karma, 4.8; 6.236ff
implies defects and different degrees of knowledge, 6.260f
is taught in the Ā.D.S., 6.259ff
of an enlightened person may include passing from one body to another to fulfil an office, 6.256f
'overcomes' the knowledge of the enlightened person, 6.242
Upanishadic authority for doctrine of, 6.252f

Prasaṅkhyāna Vāda
(s/a Knowledge, Verbal; Maṇḍana Miśra)
3.205n (Note 128), 4.56, 5.293ff
Praśastapāda, 4.128, 229, 363n, 369n; 6.340n
pratīka, 6.10f
pratītya-samutpāda
(s/a Buddhism)
4.289f
presumption (arthāpatti), its difference from inference (qv), 5.347n
product (phala) see **cognition, resultant**
pupil
(s/a spiritual qualities)
a Brahmin, ideally, 5.298
but 'Brahmin' (qv) may only mean true enquirer, 5.306
spiritual qualities needed, 5.296-311
Purāṇas
not authoritative where not supported by Veda, 5.323
not favoured by (suspect to) the PM, 4.5
probably uniformly attributed to Vyāsa by Ś, 6.82n
Ś and the Purāṇas, 1.7, 9
some Purāṇic teachings based on experiences no longer available to us, 5.288f
study of Purāṇas recommended by Bhartṛhari, 5.296
Pūrva Mīmāṃsā
(s/a deities, eulogistic passages, exegetical criteria, figurative use of language, injunctions, Jaimini, Kumārila, Prabhākara, occult force, ritual, Śabara, Self, World-periods)
devalues Vedic polytheism, 1.8; 5.372n
example cited by Pūrva Mīmāṃsā for figurative interpretation of Veda, 6.209nf
has to admit that his self is only known through instruction, 6.119f, 191n
its debt to Vaiśeṣikas, 4.2
refutation of its wrong view that Veda was solely concerned with action, 4.19ff, 24ff, 31ff
rejected B.S. doctrine that the Lord created the world in sport (qv under 'sport'), 4.3

Pūrva Mīmāṃsā cont.
rejected Īśvara and theism of Epics and Purāṇas, 4.2f
rejects doctrine of world-periods (qv), 5.240
rejects metaphysical teaching of the Upanishads, 4.1
Ś agrees with the Pūrva Mīmāṃsā view that nouns mean universals, 6.207nf
Ś partially indebted to PM, 4.3, 5; 5.315
tries to explain away 'That thou art' (qv), 6.109
why the Pūrva Mīmāṃsā attacked the sphoṭa (qv), 4.118
wrong theory of liberation, 4.1-54
wrong to say that the word 'knowledge' in the Veda only meant knowledge of the meaning of the texts, as the injunctions for cogitation and sustained meditation also show, 4.40
wrong view that person who thinks he is a soul separate from the body is subject to injunction for that reason, 6.297
wrong view that Vedic texts on renunciation of ritual were for cripples, etc., 6.295
wrongly believed that we are aware of a soul separate from the body, 4.321; 5.205ff, 251f; 6.120
wrongly held that Veda was solely concerned with action, 4.17ff, 31ff; 5.267ff

R

Rāhu, the eclipse, 3.18
Rāmānuja, 1.1, 4, 14, 27f, 35f; 3.128; 4.141n; 5.70; 6.88n, 90n
Rāmāyana, Brahmā's words to Rāma, 6.135, 202n
Rāvaṇa Bhāṣya (on Vaiśeṣika Sūtras) 4.363nf
reality
implies temporal and causal coherence, 3.107
what is uncontradicted in past, present and future, 2.264n
reason
(s/a inference, Veda)
cannot establish God, 4.134f
demands absence of self-contradiction, 4.86f
its positive use in Vedanta is only for interpretation of Veda, 2.52
limitations of, 5.198-203
opponent's view that Self can be known through reason, 5.283f

reason cont.
rationalists always contradict one another, 4.177f., 5.227, 283, 286ff, 6.317
reflection, in a reflecting medium
(s/a reflection, ābhāsa, and the earlier heading 'entry, praveśa')
apparent multiplication through reflection, 2.88f
Consciousness is reflected in the mind, 3.2
dream-experience a.reflection (pratibimba) of waking experience, 3.116f
entry of Self into its creation as reflection (cp. above under 'entry'), 3.15f, 22
explains variety of karma amongst different individuals though Self is one, 3.21
of light of Self in organs, 3.60f
reflection-theory not found in early Upanishads (before Brahma Bindu), 3.91 (note 47)
with the removal of any factor in a reflection it disappears, and the original remains, 3.12
reflection (ābhāsa)
all are aware of Self as a reflection in mind, body and sense-organs, even if some interpret it erroneously, 5.219
empirical means of knowledge (qv under 'knowledge, means of') are mere appearances (ābhāsa), 5.292f
nature of, 3.16f
reflection-theory required to explain 'he knows', 6.129ff
reflection-theory required to explain 'That thou art', 6.112
regarded as real by some pre-Ś Vedantins, 3.90n
reflection, critical thought (vicāra), 5.245
relation, can only subsist between two existent things, 2.119f
remnant see **merit and demerit**
renunciate, saṃnyāsī
(s/a enlightened person)
does not necessarily incur sin omitting ritualistic duties, 4.78
enlightened person a renunciate even if he lives in a house, 6.295
enlightened person is automatically a renunciate, 6.287f
enlightened person as mendicant follows 'regulations' (niyama) not formal injunctions (vidhi), 6.290f

renunciate, saṃnyāsī cont.
liberation (usually) presupposes formal renunciation (becoming a monk), 3.193, 4.77, 5.123, 125f, 129, 148ff, 6.292, 319
the highest form of renunciate (parivrāt), 6.302
renunciation, formal and total
(s/a renunciate)
as the characteristic of the enlightened person (qv), 6.287ff, 293f,
of sense of agency taught in Gītā and all tradition, 5.151
one may renounce the world without discharge of one's householder's debts, 6.294
the two forms of renunciation not the same, 5.120f
with and without insignia, 6.334n
repetition, repeated practice (abhyāsa)
not needed by him who understands the highest metaphysical texts immediately, 6.124
required in the final discipline, 6.121
repetition, verbal, of Name of God
taught before Ś, 1.9
regarded by Ś as suitable for widowers and outcastes and as
preliminary practice in Vedanta, 1.51n
revelation
(s/a Veda)
not an authority for knowledge of Spirit unless confirmed by experience, 1.105f
ritual, ritualism
(s/a ritual, rituals, obligatory, Yājñavalkya)
after-life of those who do not perform ritual, 5.34f, 48f, 91f; 6.314f
and son as means to the three worlds of humans, 4.69f
as such, rituals do not lead towards enlightenment, 5.12f
based on desire promotes transmigration, 5.83f
effective only when allied to good conduct, 5.33
Hiraṇyagarbha the highest goal of, 5.19f
knowledge of ritual is lower knowledge, 5.75
leads to higher forms of activity, 5.253
leads to a sojourn on the moon, 5.21
may be a remote auxiliary to the rise of enlightenment, 5.92f, 114ff

ritual, ritualism cont.
particular ritual may be optional or obligatory according to the spirit in which it is performed, 5.271f; 6.282f
performed selflessly purifies the heart, 5.85f, 87f
Prapañca Vilaya Vāda (qv) on ritual, 4.106-117
renunciates do not incur sin in omitting ritualistic duties, 4.78
ritualist creates new body and world, 2.209n
ritualist denies that gods have bodies (cp.1.8), 2.193f
ritualist acts on faith in ritualistic texts of Veda: he should have equal faith in its metaphysical texts, 6.160
ritualists as food of gods, 5.23
Veda teaches many rituals because men have many desires, 5.103
world as transformation of oblations, 5.41f
ritual, rituals, obligatory
after-life of those (except renunciates) who neglect them, 5.91, 96
for purification, 5.89f, 91ff
only known through Veda, 5.265f
wrong view of PM that liberation comes from daily and occasional obligatory ritual, 4.7; 5.36-54
rope-trick (Indian), 2.86f
Ṛṣis, source of pravṛtti and nivṛtti mārga in Veda, 1.10f
Ruler, Inner (antaryāmin)
(s/a Lord)
2.45ff

S

Śabara, 2.45, 4.33, 118; 5.243, 315f
Sadānanda, 3.204f (note); 6.208n
sahopalambha-niyama
(s/a Buddhism)
proves, against the intention of its authors, that the object is external to the cognition, 4.304f, 307f
restatement of the theory by Buddhist and further refutation by Advaitin, 4.319ff
Śakti, see power

samādhi
bracketed with dreamless sleep, 3.145, 159
difference of samādhi.from sleep, 3.129, 161
enlightened person does not pursue samādhi as he always has it, 6.165
even before samādhi joy comes to the yogi, 6.103
samādhi-yoga (Gītā teaching), 5.310
the Self called 'samādhi' by Gauḍapāda, 1.171
Śaṅkara
and Purāṇas, 1.7, 9
chronological note, 5.363n
his attitude to Buddhism and the Buddha, 1.24ff, 4.285
his devotion to Nārāyaṇa, 1.9ff, 41f
his life, 1.39ff
his realization of the Self, 1.43
his relation to Gauḍapāda, 1.27ff, 31
his works, 1.43ff
was his Bh.G.Bh. later than his B.S.Bh.? 6.84n
Sāṅkhyas
(s/a body (subtle), constituents, effect, intellect (cosmic), Lord, māyā, modification, Nature, nescience, pain, reflection (ābhāsa), Sat Kārya Vāda, soul, That thou art, Veda, world-period)
and all rationalist systems fall into conflict, 4.176f
cannot account for liberation, 4.224f
cannot establish relation between Nature and soul, 4.208ff, 218ff, 223
cannot establish their doctrine of a plurality of souls, 4.226, 5.277f
cannot explain 'That thou art' for lack of a reflection-theory, 6.112f
cannot explain 'the sufferer' taught in their own system for lack of a reflection theory, 6.131f
cannot rationally account for pain: Advaitin merely admits it as perceived, 4.212ff
Cosmic Intellect as described by Sāṅkhyas not acceptable, 5.279
denied joy in liberation, 1.242
did not regard nescience as a property of the soul (puruṣa), 4.97
faulty view of transmigration, 5.37
forced to pluralism by Vaiśeṣikas, 3.100n; 5.125

Sāṅkhyas cont.
founder of Sāṅkhya philosophy had no right to gainsay Veda, 5.275, 278
had no reflection-theory, 3.91n
had tried to systematize Upanishads before B.S., 1.17
held each soul to be all-pervading yet limited to one body, 3.170
misquote Upanishads, 4.175
only paid lip-service to Veda, 4.126f
other views of Sāṅkhyas which contradict Veda, 5.278
Sat Kārya Vāda in the Sāṅkhyas and in Śaṅkara, 2.111ff
soul-theory criticized, 5.74
statement and refutation of Sāṅkhya system, 4.192-228
system already defunct in Ś's day, 4.229f
the first to establish theory of subtle body, 3.26f
the pleasure-pain-delusion in the mind does not imply the Nature of the Sāṅkhyas, 4.201f
the Unmanifest of the Kaṭha Upanishad not the Unmanifest of the Sāṅkhya, 4.227f
their account of play of constituents acceptable, 4.173
their different schools have different conflicting theories, 4.212
their non-conscious Nature fails to account for the element of purpose in the world, 4.201ff
their non-conscious Nature not the true material cause of the world (which is the Absolute), 2.12, 17, 33ff, 156f
their radical distinction between conscious and non-conscious lost in Vaiśeṣika world-view, 1.18
their theory of elements and sense-organs acceptable, 5.279
their theory of real change implies absurdity that something comes out of nothing, 4.224
their 24 Tattvas not in Veda, 5.279
their view that souls are many already criticized in M.Bh., 5.277f
their wrong view that soul acts by its mere presence, 5.210f
Vedic and rationalist schools of Sāṅkhyas, 1.18
why Sāṅkhya is criticized, 5.281f
world-periods unintelligible through non-conscious Nature of Sāṅkhya, intelligible through Māyā of Lord of Vedic tradition, 4.205, 211

Sāṅkhya-standpoint in Gītā, 4.68f, 5.86, 6.149 (speculative enquiry)
sampat, symbolic meditation (qv),
based on correspondence, often numerical correspondence, 4.28
saṃskāra see **impression**
saṃvṛti
(s/a subject-object distinction) 4.383n, 6.317
Sarvajñātma Muni, 1.29, 49
Sarvāstivādins see **Buddhism**
Sat Kārya Vāda see **Buddhism, effect, Sāṅkhyas, Vaiśeṣikas**
satyam-jñānam-anantam, 1.182
Śaunaka, 4.4; 5.75, 246
scepticism
total scepticism makes argument impossible, 4.178f
seed of world
name and form (unmanifest) (qv), 2.137f, 149
totality of ignorance, desire and action, 2.163
Self
(s/a Absolute, cognitions (empirical), cosmological argument, dream, ego-sense, ether, intellect, knowledge (empirical), knowledge (means of), reflection (ābhāsa), soul, value)
as ether pervades all within, so Self pervades ether within, 6.162
as highest value, 1.92, 123, 240; 3.53
as thread (Sūtra), 4.82; 5.59
attaining Self means knowing Self, 5.223f
cannot know itself as an object, 1.186f, 190f, 224; 5.234f; 6.145
consistently affirms itself as real, 3.180
consists of a kind of ether, the 'kham' of 'kham brahma', 6.172f
different from matter, senses and mind, 3.55
difficulty of discriminating Self and intellect, 3.61ff
disagreement about its nature, 1.126
does not have consciousness as a separate quality, 3.25
does not have empirical consciousness as its attribute (against Bhartṛprapañca), 4.99f
enters into living beings as their living soul, 1.5
etymologies of Self as Ātman, 5.127
ever attained, 1.167f; 4.9
identical with Absolute, 3.70

Self cont.
imagines the distinctions that make the world, 2.255
immediately evident, 1.122f
inference cannot show that Self is different from anything else, 5.214f
intellect can assume a form like purity of Self to meditate on it, 5.219
is self-luminous consciousness, 1.214ff
its own means of knowledge (svayam-vedyatva), 6.143
like ether — imperceptible and all-pervading, 3.22f
limitations falsely imposed on Self like impurities on sky, 6.229
not different in each body, 6.313
not immediately evident in its true nature, or Buddhist could not deny it, 6.144f
not in any sense an agent, 6.300f
not known actively, it is knowledge, 1.194f
not known through organs but naturally familiar, 1.103; 5.204f
not revealed by ego-sense, 5.295
not subject to acceptance or rejection, 1.171, 221; 5.216
not the agent in cognition, 3.56; 4.101f
not to be known as an object, 5.215; 6.320
not unknown or unknowable, 1.122f
not 'understood', must be the unbroken Witness of transient empirical knowledge, 5.225ff
omniscient, 3.51
only knowable through Veda, 5.265
relationless, 1.211f
self-evident: Veda does not have to teach it positively as anything new, 1.121, 214; 6.320
Self's knowledge is constant: through illusion the secular philosophers (Vaiśeṣikas, etc.) think it is intermittent, 1.229f
sense in which Self can be known, 3.81
sleep shows Self free from modifications, 1.211f
soul not a modification or part of Self, 4.94f
that for whose sake mind functions, 3.53
that *through which* cognition takes place, 3.58
the transmigrant is not a being separate from the Self, 3.70
unaffected by Māyā, 2.78

Self cont.
Veda can communicate knowledge of Self, 5.220
Veda may use ego-sense (qv) to indicate Self, 6.111f, 127
self-discipline (tapas), 5.143ff
selves, the five, see **sheaths**
sense-organs and mind
(s/a deities, elements, perception, Vaiśvānara, Vital Energy, Vital Principle)
are material objects, capable of contact and disjunction, 1.228
composed of elements and dependent on food, 3.11f, 32
each sense-organ composed of the element it apprehends, 3.28ff, 33, 94n
fate of sense-organs at death, 5.50ff
finally dissolve into Self through knowledge, 3.12
part of Vaiśvānara (qv), 3.169f
quarrel amongst themselves about which is superior, 5.327, 334f
sense-organs are animated by deities, 3.37ff, 41
sense-organs are controlled by mind, 3.143
sense-organs as deities, 2.37f
sense-organs non-conscious, as they exist for another (cp. entry 'value' below), 1.211
their function, 3.3
their role in perception, 3.55
they perceive only gross objects, 2.242
servant and master image, 2.57f, 61; 3.14f, 71, 77; 6.301
Shaivism
brings new spiritual techniques not found in Veda, 1.8
Shaivas adopted Ś, but only long after his death, 1.42
Shaivism not purely Vedic, hence attacked in B.S. and by Ś, 4.126ff
sheaths
(s/a elements, selves, five)
ascending beyond the five sheaths, 6.268
bliss-sheath identified with the Absolute (by exception), 5.336f
doctrine of five sheaths introduced to show ultimately that Self has no sheaths (Sureśvara), 3.28f
joy an attribute of the bliss-sheath not of the Absolute, 5.329ff

similes, as method of teaching, 5.336, 341f;
a simile is never identical with what it illustrates, 6.133
Śiva, doubtful if Ś worshipped Śiva, 1.12
skandhas, statement and refutation of Buddhist theory of, 4.287f.
slaughter, sacrificial, does not cause demerit, 5.33
sleep, dreamless
(s/a Buddhism, canals, dream, enlightened person, nescience, Prājña)
absence of nescience in dreamlesss sleep, 3.145, 152f
after awakening, we express our consciousness of the seed of nescience by saying 'I knew nothing', 3.185; 6.134
as 'the beyond', 3.192; 6.318, 340n
as the natural state of the soul, 3.146, 154
as unity with the Absolute, 3.131-154
Consciousness present in dreamless sleep or we could not make statements about it, 1.213; 3.4ff
described as darkness, 3.56
difference of dreamless sleep from enlightenment, 3.157f
dreamless sleep and metaphysical sleep, 3.173
dreamless sleep a state higher than that of the gods, 1.237
general account of, 3.127-164
in dreamless sleep 'the Veda becomes no Veda', etc., 5.241
is a state of utter serenity (samprasāda), 6.265f
is free from modifications, 1.211
limited bliss in dreamless sleep, 3.174
nescience absent in dreamless sleep, 1.236f
persistence of seed of nescience (qv under 'nescience, seed of') in dreamless sleep, 6.189n
Spirit lies in subtle canals in pericardium during dreamless sleep, 3.125
wrong to think knowledge ceases in dreamless sleep when there are no objects to know, as evidenced by 'I knew nothing', 4.334, 336
sleep, metaphysical, not being awake to the Self, 3.179f
Smṛti,
(s/a reason, Veda)
fallible because of human origin, 1.7
not authoritative unless supported by Veda, 5.77
scope and limits of Smṛti relative to Veda, 5.273-284

Smṛti cont.
what comprises Smṛti, 5.242
snake, illusory, rope-snake
(s/a superimposition)
it illustrates how the Veda communicates knowledge of the Self , 3.177
it does not exist apart from the awareness of it, 1.220
its cause (nimitta) is non-determination of the rope, 1.88
knowledge of rope immediately abolishes rope-snake, 3.178
rope is not snake, yet rope and snake not two distinct entities, 3.181
rope-snake is only an impression of the mind (not an objective phenomenon), 3.191
soul
(s/a association, delimitation, Jainas, Lord, Sāṅkhyas, soul (avaccheda theory of), states, Vaiśeṣikas)
Advaita interpretation of, 4.91
and Lord, 2.6ff, 14, 15
as agent in knowing is not true Self, 1.224f
as mere reflection (see under 'reflection, ābhāsa') of the Lord, 3.15f
as Self qualified by intellect (vijñāna-maya, vijñāna-ātman), 3.59, 81f
Bhartṛprapañca's peculiar conception of soul (jīva); 4.82
does not 'become' the Lord, 3.68
general account of, 3.1-210
has free-will, 3.76
identical with Lord, 3.84ff; 6.229
is imagined and is root of all other imaginations, 2.258
is never distinct from the Lord, 3.71
Jaina's untenable view that soul is of size of body, 4.349ff
Kāśakṛtsna, qv, identifies soul with the Lord, 3.64
name and form (qv) do not rest in true nature of soul but in its adjunct, 3.65
non-different from Absolute, 1.112
not a modification of Self, 4.95
not a part of Self, like spark of fire, 4.95f
not minute, 3.23ff
not subject to origination and dissolution like the elements (qv) and sense-organs (qv) that develop from them, 3.9ff, 23
not the creator of the world, 2.5

soul cont.
notion of soul arises through non-determination of Self in its true nature, 1.88
only appears to be a part of the Self, 3.22
pre-B.S. theories on soul, 3.64ff
refutation of Sāṅkhya's plurality of souls, 4.225
refutation of Vaiśeṣika theory of soul, 4.259-266
souls are not mutually distinct, 3.73f
soul, avaccheda theory of
(s/a delimitation)
3.67f, 80
Southern Path
(s/a Northern Path)
4.25; 5.21ff, 96, 306; 6.36ff, 43ff
sovereignty (svārājya)
limited sovereignty through identification with Hiraṇyagarbha, 6.28,68f
sovereignty of enlightened person (qv) unlimited, 6.264f
space, 1.92 , 102 , 195; 6.64
speech, activity of, as source of phenomenal world
(s/a modification, name, OM)
1.185, 198; 2.141, 160f, 163f
identification of vāc with Absolute, 6.168
Sphoṭa Vāda, 4.117-126
Spirit (puruṣa)
as name for Absolute in its transcendent form, 6.186, 306,
etymology of puruṣa as pūrṇa, 3.17, 60
in right eye as Vaiśvānara (qv), 3.181; 5.57. 226; 6.266
is that which has ultimately to be known, 5.18; 6.182
taught in Upanishads not subject to action, 4.31
spiritual law (dharma), 2.92f
spiritual qualities to be cultivated
(s/a discipline, sixfold)
general account of the virtues needed on the path, 5.129-157
no cultivated virtue is finally real, 3.194
sport (līlā) see **creation**
Śrī Harṣa, 1.48; 4.172

stages of life (āśrama)
are states of the body due to ceremonies, 3.8
different stages of life conditioned by impulses deriving from former lives, 5.100ff
knowledge depends for its rise on performance of duties of caste and stage of life, 5.110ff
members of all stages of life have right to metaphysical knowledge, 5.104, 117f
standpoints, the two (nescience and knowledge),
1.104ff, 110f; 2.6f, 17, 43; 6.229f
states, the three see **dream, sleep, transcendence of the three states, waking, waking-dream-sleep**
stories, value of, 5.333ff
strength
(s/a childishness)
of 'Brahmin' (qv) is his knowledge of the Self, 6.323
subject-object distinction, empirical
ceases on enlightenment, 3.178f
is labelled saṃvṛti-sat (qv) (illusory, true from nescience standpoint only, see under 'standpoint'), 3.191
sense in which it is possible when subject and object are both non-different from the Absolute, 2.41f
waking and dream both called (metaphysical) dream because both have the illusory subject-object distinction, 2.249
subjective idealism see **mentalism**
substratum of illusion see **ground**
subtle body see **body, subtle**
Śūdras, 5.70ff, 108
Sundara Pāṇḍya, 1.27, 33; 5.348n
superimposition, 1.63, 65, 73, 84, 90ff, 109, 120, 252n; 2.258 and see next entry.
superimposition, mutual, of Self and not-self, 1.92ff, 99ff; 3.13
suppression (pratisaṃkhyā-nirodha)
statement and refutation of Vaibhāṣika Buddhist theory, 4.293ff
Sureśvara, 1.12, 48ff, 94; 3.29, 94n, 100f (note), 200n, 205n, 207n; 4.109; 5.62, 349n; 6.78n, 108, 206n, 208n, 210n, 211n, 335n, 340n

suṣumnā
importance for indirect path to liberation, 6.87n
Upanishadic suṣumnā not that of Haṭha Yoga, 6.22
Sūtra see **thread**
svādhyāya see **Veda, private recitation of**
Śvetāśvatara Bhāṣya, 1.46
syādvāda (of Jainas), 4.346

T

Taijasa
(s/a Hiraṇyagarbha, Piṇḍa, Prājña, Vaiśvānara)
2.87; 3.144, 159
in relation to OM (qv), 3.166
tanmātra, 2.105n
Tantra
Ś not associated with Tāntrika worship, 1.12f
Ś knew of and disapproved of 'left-handed' cults, 5.169n
'Tantra' used as term referring to the Sāṅkhya system, 5.273
tapas see **self-discipline**
Teacher
main account, 5.296-343
Teacher's use of Veda, 5.312-343
other references, 1.62, 65, 121, 122, 123, 170, 188, 230; 2.5f; 4.1, 4.89f; 5.4, 71, 75, 97, 105, 126, 135, 182n, 225 and often, 6.42, 92, 121, 147, 191n, 296
temple-worship, 4.128, 137
tenth man, the,1.161f, 165, 167; 4,373f (note); 5.221f; 6.138, 141, 161, 207n
That thou art
(s/a Draviḍa, reflection (ābhāsa), Sāṅkhyas)
detailed explanation, 6.107-146
other references, 1.29, 124f; 2.8; 3.176f, 181, 188, 205n; 4.92; 5.65, 198, 292, 363n, 6.159,161, 207n, 230, 314
thread (Sūtra),
Bhartṛprapañca on, 4.82
Self as, 5.59
time, 1.195; 2.58, 256f

torch, whirling, image of, 1.229, 251n; 2.67, 246f
traces see **impressions**
tradition (sampradāya),
1.170; 3.195; 4.1; 5.296, 298f
need for, 1.123
transcendence, metaphysical
(s/a Fourth)
account of the state of, 6.162ff
called 'kaivalya', 1.240 f.
cannot be associated. with ritual, 4.66ff
devotion to knowledge (qv under 'knowledge, devotion to') transcends action, 4.66
dominant note in Ś's philosophy, 1.1
implies self-identification with the Witness (qv), 6.166f
in transcendence, as in dreamless sleep, there is no subject-object consciousness, 6.68
reality stands beyond the four modes of judgement, 3.193; 6.317
the Absolute is beyond all predicates, 2.114
the alpha and omega of present Source Book, 6.326
the Inner Ruler (qv under 'Ruler') is beyond perception and conception, 2.48f
transcendence of the (three) states
(see under states, the three)
(s/a Fourth, states)
general account, 3.164-196
the three states include all the empirically knowable, 3.191f; 6.318
the three states only taught to show that they do not exist, 3.107
three states are imagined in Self like snake (qv) in rope, 3.178ff
transformation, pariṇāma
(s/a Brahma Sūtras, modificatíon)
Bhartṛprapañca on, 4.82f
the Self transformed itself into the world, B.S. (qv) doctrine, 2.21
world as a transformation of sacrificial oblations, 5.42
transmigration
a beginningless, painful and terrible ordeal, 2.65, 196f; 5.36f
as totally unreal, 2.8f

transmigration cont.
earliest surviving mention of transmigration is in Śatapatha Brāhmaṇa, 6.31
the transmigrant emerges from the confusion of the qualities of the intellect with the Self, 3.25f
who is the one who transmigrates? 3.19
Troṭaka, 1.28, 48; 6.107
turīya see **Fourth, the**

U

Uddyotakara, 4.128; 5.296
universals
(s/a recognition)
fact of recognition implies universals and undermines Buddhist theory of momentariness, 4.322f
illustrated by image of lute, 1.200
particulars arise from universals, not vice versa, 1.207f
spoken syllables must be universals or we would not recognize them, 4.118, 125f
Unmanifest, the
(s/a name and form, unmanifest)
as related to the Cosmic Vital Energy (qv), 6.83n
Bhartṛprapañca on, 4.82f
cosmic principle corresponding to Prājña (qv), 3.167
highest principle in the realm of transmigration, 2.156ff; 5.10; 6.302
lower than the Absolute, 5.230
name and form in unmanifest state, 2.156f
Vedic Unmanifest not the Unmanifest of the Sāṅkhya system, 4.227f
unreal
all pairs of opposites unreal, 1.200ff
defined, 1.190
Upanishads, classical
(s/a Pūrva Mīmāṃsā, rituals, Veda)
date of, 1.15
from term 'upanisat' used to mean 'secret name', 1.154; 6.75n
main doctrines of, 1.4ff
no contradictions in their teaching, 5.256f

Upanishads, classical cont.
no liberation outside the Upanishadic tradition, 3.195f
term 'upanisat' as 'secret metaphysical knowledge', 6.270
their metaphysical teaching rejected by PM, 4.1
they do not contradict ritualistic teachings of Veda, 5.258
they teach 'yoga' but not the 'Yoga system' of Patañjali, 5.280f
Upavarṣa
attacked sphoṭa (qv), 4.118, 120f
may have held that soul was knowable through empirical means, 4.3
perhaps believed that the Lord abstained from interfering with karma, 2.45
perhaps wrote a connected commentary on P.M.S. and B.S., 4.2
upāya see **device**

V

Vācaspati Miśra
attempted synthesis of Ś and Maṇḍana, 1.48
champions a form of Prasaṃkhyāna Vāda, 5.365n
date uncertain, perhaps later than Prakāśātman, 1.59n
his theory of nescience criticized by Sac, 6.337n
on sampat (qv), 4.147n
earliest surviving author to attribute B.S. to Vyāsa, 6.329n
quotes Śatapatha Brāhmaṇa on ritual for self-purification, 5.71
wrote commentary on Sāṅkhya Kārikās, 4.193
Vaiśeṣikas
(s/a atom, categories, effect, ether, inherence, knowledge (empirical), non-existence, occult force (adṛṣta), pain, Sāṅkhyas, Sat Kārya Vāda, soul)
Advaitin can attack them from platform of Sat Kārya Vāda, 2.113, 115f
Asat Kārya Vāda, 4.235
Bhartṛprapañca imitates an aspect of their theory of the self, 4.97
defects in their theory of soul, 4.258-266
denied joy in liberation, 1.242
faulty theory of consciousness, 1.231
faulty theory of soul, 5.8
faulty theory of transmigration, 5.37

Vaiśeṣikas cont.
further criticism of their theory of soul, 5.125, 189n
had a living system in Ś's day (unlike Sāṅkhyas), 4.229
held the ether to be partless, 5.347n
make pleasure and pain qualities of the soul (not of the mind, as in Advaita), 3.94n
may have forced the Sāṅkhyas into pluralism, 4.198
more rationalist than the Sāṅkhyas, 1.18f
provided basis of PM's philosophical system, 4.2, 5
refutation of their categories and atoms, 4.236-258
refutation of their category of inherence, 4.259ff
refutation of their theories of non-existence and of Asat Kārya Vāda, 4.266-271
Ś's refutation of inherence (qv) refutes their whole system, 4.172
sketch and refutation of their atomic theory, 4.236-241
the form of their doctrine attacked by Ś was atheistic, 4.231
their faulty theory of knowledge, 5.233f
their faulty view that desires reside in the self, 5.283f
their theory of atoms untenable, 4.101
theistic exposition of their doctrine by Praśastapāda, 4.128
theories of contact and inherence, 4.233
they only paid lip-service to the Veda, 4.127
three forms of positive non-existence (qv), 4.234
treated soul as an object among objects, 4.232
wrong theory that consciousness is produced in the soul, 1.216f, 227ff
wrong to claim that mind is eternal and atomic, 3.32f
wrong view that ether is eternal, 4.271-274
wrong view that soul is subject to pain, 4.274-277
Vaishnavism
brings new spiritual techniques not found in Veda, 1.8f
Nimbārka gave Difference in Identity (qv) doctrine a Vaishnava twist, 4.81
not purely Vedic, hence attacked by B.S., 1.19
Ś a Vaishnava, 1.9-12
Ś identifies Lord with Vāsudeva, 5.309
synthesis of Vaishnavism and Upanishads in Ś, 1.9

Vaiśvānara
(s/a Viśva)
2.184; 3.166f, 169f, 172, 176, 181; 4.82; 5.335; 6.13
as object of worship, 4.15
relation to OM qv (and cp. 6.179), 3.189
Vallabhācārya, 1.1; 3.90n
value
(s/a Consciousness, Self)
Self as highest value, 1.92, 122, 239f
vāsanā see **impression**
Veda
(s/a attribution (false), creation-texts, deities, ego-sense, eka-vākyatā, eulogistic passages, Hiraṇyagarbha, inference, injunctions, meditation, merit, Pūrva Mīmāṃsā, reason, revelation, ritual, standpoints, Upanishads)
accepts ignorant person's sense of agency at its face value, 3.48
can communicate knowledge of Self, 5.220f
can communicate metaphysical knowledge even though it is itself unreal, 5.236ff
cannot contradict perception in latter's sphere, 5.243, 321
chief function of Veda is to convey knowledge of Self, 5.262f
condemns duality, 4.88, 93
contrast between Bhartṛprapañca's and Ś's defence of utility of Veda, 4.94ff
derided by Materialists, Buddhists, Jainas, 4.126f
divisions of Veda, 5.312ff
even fanciful meditations on the Absolute imply the affirmation of its existence, 5.264f
explains merit and demerit and gives all knowledge worth knowing, 5.15f
fact that Veda teaches ritual does not mean it teaches that action is real, 5.259
gives information to those who have desires, 5.260f
he who accepts Veda need not accept dictates of empirical knowledge on every point: rationalist must do so, 4.132
in dreamless sleep Veda becomes 'no-Veda', 5.241
is eternal, 5.247f

Veda cont.
is the final means of knowledge (qv under 'knowledge, means of'), 1.127
is useless after liberation, 1.109
its affirmations and injunctions depend on superimposition (qv), 1.96
its different parts cannot mutually conflict, 1.110f
its teaching about the Self purely negative, 1.130f, 133f; 5.238f
itself denies that action will bring liberation, 4.51
knowledge-section does not contradict ritual-section, 5.263
may indicate Self through ego, 6.111f, 127
not contradicted by inference, 5.213ff
not contradicted by perception, 3.86; 5.243, 252
OM in Veda, 6.167f
origin and development of Vedic texts, 1.2f
Prapañca Vilaya Vāda will not harmonize the injunctive and metaphysical texts, 4.106ff
recitations of Veda begin and end with OM, 6.172
ritualistic and metaphysical texts not mutually contradictory because of the two standpoints (qv) form in which teaching may be given, 6.229f
ritualistic portion of Veda does not contradict metaphysical portion, 5.251ff, 263
ritualistic texts purposeful and may lead to higher forms of activity, 5.253
ritualistic texts true at their level, 5.253
rule for reciting its hymns, 5.246f
Self can only be known through Veda, 5.195-239
some Vedic texts ignore hearer's nescience and give out the highest truth, e.g. cry of Vāmadeva, 6.230
statement and refutation of PM view that Veda is only concerned with action, 4.17ff; 5.267ff
Teacher's (qv) use and interpretation of Veda, 5.312-343
teaches Absolute by negation, 5.238f
test of the authority of a text is its fruitfulness, 5.250f
texts conveying metaphysical knowledge not subordinate to injunctive texts, 4.14f
the authoritative source for knowledge of the Self, 3.177

Veda cont.
there are many rituals given in the Veda because people's desires are many, 5.103, 260f
unless they can be established as fanciful, Vedic themes for meditation should be accepted as true, 5.265f
utility of the Veda for all but the rare enlightened souls, 1.78f
world arises from words of Veda (cp. under 'name', 'OM'), 5.248f
wrong view of Logicians that Veda can be contradicted by perception, 5.212f
Veda, private recitation of (svādhyāya), 5.99, 100, 139, 191n; chief religious duty of householder, 6.42
Vedanta, post-Śaṇkara
contrast with Ś's treatment of Prājña, 3.204f (note)
sketch of some general features, 1.46-50
system-building in post-Ś Advaita, 4.171f
verbal knowledge see **knowledge, verbal**
vicious circle
(s/a logical maxims)
claim that any secular philosophy derives from an omniscient founder rests on circular reasoning, 4.132f
not solved by an appeal to beginninglessness, 4.130f
Vidyāraṇya
his account of māyā, 1.38f
Vijñāna Vāda
(s/a Buddhism, mentalism)
if Ś refuted its subjective idealism, this not a proof that he thought that external objects existed, 4.173
Vimuktātman, 1.48, 6.108, 212n
Vindhyavāsī, 4.193
Virāṭ, 2.168, 179; 3.166f, 171;
Bhartṛprapañca on, 4.82
Viṣṇu
highest abode of Viṣṇu attained through knowledge, 5.17
highest abode of Viṣṇu is transcendent source of world, 5.10
highest state of Viṣṇu always present but hard to attain, 6.96
is to be sought by cutting down the tree of saṇsāra, 5.108
meditation on Śālagrāma as Viṣṇu, 6.26

Viṣṇu cont.
meditation on Viṣṇu in stone image, 6.3
Ś a Vaishnava, 1.9-12
Viṣṇu Purāṇa
a pre-Śaṅkara work proclaiming illusory character of world, 1.36f
Viśva (=Vaiśvānara qv), 2.87; 3.166, 182, 185
Vital Energy in the individual organism
(s/a sense-organs, sheaths, Vital Principle)
at death, 5.50f
its five subdivisions, 3.35f
support of the organs, 3.26f
Vital Principle, cosmic Prāṇa
(s/a deities, gods, Hiraṇyagarbha, Lord, Prājña, sense-organs, vital energy)
Gauḍapāda's view that all objects, beginning with the cosmic Vital Principle, are only co-ordinated individual imaginations, 2.245
is first manifestation of Māyā, 2.85
is first manifestation of the Unmanifest (qv), 2.88f
is imagined through nescience, 1.88, 2.161,
is source of the deities, 2.178ff
vivarta, 2.99f (note); 6.79n
Void, Nihilism of the, 1.140; 2.116f; 4,332ff
Vṛṣagaṇa, 4.194, 196, 198
Vyūhas, 4.128f, 136ff

W

waking
(s/a dream, sleep, states, Vaiśvānara, Viśva, waking-dream-sleep)
a kind of dream, 3.7
transient, so not true nature of Self, 1.211f
waking-dream-sleep (triad), 1.89, 211ff; 3.7; 6.318f
Witness
(s/a Buddhism, Consciousness, dream, reflection on)
as 'Knowledge' of 'Reality, Knowledge, Infinity', 1.182
Bhartṛprapañca's view of Witness, 4.82
doctrine of presence of a Witness explains empirical cognition (qv under 'cognition, empirical'), as Buddhist idealism cannot, 4.309f, 327f

Witness cont.
does not feel 'I am the Witness', 5.235
error of taking Witness as reflected in mind for true Witness, 1.165f; 6.161f
importance of doctrine of Witness to refute Buddhism, 6.130f
is the 'limit' (sīmān) beyond which negation (qv) cannot go, 6.113
not established through a means of knowledge (qv under 'knowledge, means of'), 6.145
of all cognitions is changeless, 3.54f
of waking, dream and sleep must be one, 2.85
only object of Witness's knowledge is the mind, 6.159
perceives pain but is not identified with it, 3.34
presence of self-luminous Witness most evident from dream, 3.126
the Absolute is the inmost luminous principle within us (the Witness), 1.232
the Lord enters the body as Witness, like a king entering his city to preside, 1.211
the seer (Witness) always sees, 1.224
whatever is seen anywhere is seen by the Witness, 1.164
word and its meaning
(s/a agreement and difference, figurative use of language, knowledge (verbal), Patañjali, Sphoṭa Vāda, universals)
ākṛti theory, 4.164n f
Note on Indian theories of meaning, 2.210nf
relationship between word and its meaning is eternal, 2.194f; 5.247f
statement and refutation of Sphoṭa Vāda, 4.117-126
work see **action**
world, non-conscious, 2.35f
World of Brahmā see **Brahma-loka**
world-period (kalpa), 2.54, 139, 164-177, 183f; 3.159; 5.240
worlds, the three, 5.188n; 6.79n

Y

Yājñavalkya, gave up ritual on attaining knowledge, 4.15
Yāska, his six 'states of becoming' do not pertain to the Self, 2.241, 3.188

yoga
(s/a yoga, adhyātma, etc.)
Ā.D.S. teaching of 'yogas' as disciplines, 6.100f
distinguished trom knowledge, 6.188n
karma-yoga and samādhi-yoga, 5.310
Patañjali's yama and niyama preliminary conditions for attaining higher world, 5.60
practice recommended by opponent, 3.69
teaching in Upanishads, 5.280
yoga, adhyātma
analysis of term 'adhyātma' (but see also Bh.G.Bh.VIII.3, not included in Source Book), 6.100
assembled texts on adhyātma yoga, 6.92-104
not the yoga of Patañjali, 6.93
Yoga school of Patañjali
(s/a Yoga Sūtra Bhāṣya Vivaraṇa)
claims that yogins have knowledge of past and future events through grace of Lord, 1.234
Gauḍapāda and Ś on stilling the mind through yoga-practice, 3.129
importance of Patañjali's yama and niyama for karma-yoga, 5.120, 187n
its goals not the same as those of adhyātma-yoga or Upanishads, 6.93
its methods and techniques non-Vedic, 1.19; 5.279f
its wrong theory of a Lord who is mere world-architect operating on external material, 4.127f, 131f
no reason to deny the supernormal powers spoken of by Yoga school, 5.289
prescribes renunciation of hearth and home, 5.282
Self-knowledge through freedom from kleśas, 6.99f
Ś classes nescience as one kleśa amongst others in the manner of Patañjali, 6.77n
unfounded claim that unsupported teaching of Yoga school must be supported by lost Vedic texts, 5.280f, 361n
why Yoga school is criticized (cp. 1.19, 5.279f), 5.281f
yoga-standpoint in Gitā
karma-yoga defined, 6.149f
method of meditation described, 6.149

yoga-standpoint in Gitā cont.
standpoint of individual, 4.68
yogin of Gītā performs action for purification, 5.86ff
Yoga Sūtra Bhāṣya Vivaraṇa, 1.11, 44; 2.266 (note); 6.215n
yogī, yogin
different discipline of middling yogins, 6.101f
enjoys exalted states, 1.234, 245; 2.46f; 5.241, 289
exalted visions of yogī not liberation, 4.58f
has abnormal perception, 2.113
may create many bodies for himself, 2.192
the highest are asparśa-yogins (qv under 'asparśa-yoga'), 6.101
yogins 'proper' of Gītā Chapter VI are solitary renunciates, 6.43

The Śaṅkara Source-Book

A Conspectus of the Contents of the Six Volumes

Volume I — Śaṅkara on the Absolute

I. SOURCES OF ŚAṄKARA'S DOCTRINE: HIS LIFE & WORKS

1. A Doctrine of Transcendence
2. Vedas: Saṃhitās, Brāhmaṇas, Upanishads
3. The Smṛti: Viṣṇu worship and Śiva worship
4. The Bhagavad Gītā
5. The Brahma-Sūtras and their Background: Bhartṛprapañca
6. The True Tradition: Gauḍapāda, Draviḍa, Brahmanandin, Sundara Pāṇḍya
7. Doctrine of Illusion before Śaṅkara: Māyā Vāda and Avidyā Vāda
8. Śaṅkara's Date, Life and Works
9. Śaṅkara's School

II. THE DOCTRINE OF NESCIENCE

1. The Nature and Results of Nescience
2. Nescience as Non-Comprehension and False Comprehension
3. The Self and the Not-Self: Non-Discrimination and Mutual Superimposition
4. The Standpoint of Nescience and the Standpoint of Knowledge

III. KNOWLEDGE OF THE ABSOLUTE

1. The Absolute is already known in a general way
2. The Absolute is not known as an object
3. The Path of Negation
4. Going beyond the Mind

IV. THE ABSOLUTE AS BEING, CONSCIOUSNESS AND BLISS

1. The Definition of the Absolute as 'Reality, Knowledge, Infinity'
2. The Absolute as the Self-Existent Principle
3. The Absolute as the Self-Luminous Principle
4. The Absolute as Bliss

Volume II — Śaṅkara on the Creation

V. THE ABSOLUTE AS CREATOR AND CONTROLLER

1. The Absolute as Creator and Controller of the World
2. The Absolute as the Lord
3. The Absolute as the Material and Efficient Cause of the World
4. The Absolute as Inner Ruler
5. The Absolute as the Lord of Māyā

VI. THE WORLD AND ITS PRESIDING DEITIES

1. Sat-kārya Vāda
2. Name and Form: Indeterminability
3. World-periods and Theory of the Elements
4. The Presiding Deities

VII. THE ACOSMIC VIEW

1. The Creation-texts as a Device to teach Non-Duality
2. Nothing can come into being
3. The Argument from Dream

Volume III — Śaṅkara on the Soul

VIII. THE SOUL AND ITS ORGANS AND BODIES

1. The Soul as the Self viewed under External Adjuncts
2. The Organs and Bodies of the Soul
3. The Light that illumines the Soul
4. The Soul and the Lord are not distinct

IX. THE 'STATES' OF THE SOUL AND THEIR TRANSCENDENCE

1. Dream
2. Dreamless Sleep
3. Turīya

CONTENTS OF THE ŚAṄKARA SOURCE BOOK

Volume IV — Śaṅkara on Rival Views

X. REFUTATION OF INADEQUATE BRAHMINICAL DOCTRINES

1. Refutation of Liberation through Action
2. Refutation of Liberation through Knowledge and Action Conjoined
3. Refutation of Bhedābheda Vāda
4. Refutation of the Pāśupatas and Pāñcarātras
5. Refutation of Sphoṭa Vāda

XI. REFUTATION OF NON-VEDIC WORLD-VIEWS

1. Dialectic (tarka): its Purpose and Rules
2. Refutation of Materialism
3. Refutation of the Sāṅkhyas
4. Refutation of the Vaiśeṣikas
5. Refutation of the Buddhist Schools
6. Refutation of the Jainas

Volume V — Śaṅkara on Discipleship

XII. ADOPTING THE PATH

1. The Wheel of Transmigration
2. The Injunction to Adopt the Path
3. Preliminary Qualifications for the Path
4. Spiritual Qualities to be cultivated on the Path

XIII. THE VEDA AND THE TEACHER

1. The Self can only be known through the Veda
2. The Veda, the Smṛti and Reason
3. The Approach to the Teacher
4. The Teacher and the Texts

Volume VI — Śaṅkara on Enlightenment

XIV. THE INDIRECT PATH

1. Meditation in the Context of the Vedic Ritual (upāsanā)
2. Realization of Identity with Hiraṇyagarbha
3. The Path of the Flame
4. Supernormal Powers on the Indirect Path

XV. THE DIRECT PATH

1. Adhyātma Yoga
2. Devotion (bhakti)
3. Communication of 'That Thou Art'
4. Meditation (dhyāna) and Repeated Affirmation (abhyāsa)
5. Meditation on OM

XVI. THE ENLIGHTENED MAN

1. Enlightenment is not a change of state

Shanti Sadan Publications

Original works on Adhyātma Yoga,
and its application in daily life

✦

by Hari Prasad Shastri

THE HEART OF THE EASTERN
MYSTICAL TEACHING

MEDITATION — ITS THEORY AND PRACTICE

SEARCH FOR A GURU

TEACHINGS FROM THE BHAGAVAD GITA

WISDOM FROM THE EAST

YOGA HANDBOOK

✦

by Marjorie Waterhouse

TRAINING THE MIND THROUGH YOGA

POWER BEHIND THE MIND

WHAT YOGA HAS TO OFFER

✦

also from Shanti Sadan

A SHORT COURSE OF MEDITATION

Translations of Sanskrit Classical Texts

✦

by Hari Prasad Shastri

ASHTAVAKRA GITA

AVADHUT GITA

DIRECT EXPERIENCE OF REALITY
Aparokshānubhūtī
with commentary

PANCHADASHI
A 14th Century Vedāntic Classic

THE RAMAYANA OF VALMIKI
in three volumes

TRIUMPH OF A HERO
Vīra Vijaya of Swami Mangalnāth

VERSES FROM THE UPANISHADS
with commentary

WORLD WITHIN THE MIND
Teachings from the Yoga Vāsishtha